D0787906

CEASELESS TURMOIL

Ceaseless Turmoil

DIARIES, 1988–1992

James Lees-Milne

Edited by Michael Bloch

JOHN MURRAY

First published in Great Britain in 2004 by John Murray (Publishers)
A division of Hodder Headline

The moral right of the author has been asserted in accordance
with the Copyright, Designs and Patents Act 1988.

1 3 5 7 9 10 8 6 4 2

A CIP catalogue record for this book is available from the British Library

ISBN 0-7195-6578 2

Typeset in 11.5/13pt Bembo by Servis Filmsetting Ltd, Manchester

Printed and bound by
Clays Ltd, St Ives plc

Hodder Headline policy is to use papers that are natural, renewable and recyclable
products and made from wood grown in sustainable forests. The logging and
manufacturing processes are expected to conform to the environmental regulations
of the country of origin.

John Murray (Publishers)
338 Euston Road
London NW1 3BH

To Patric Dickinson
Rouge Dragon Pursuivant, 1978–89

'I did not [as a child] favour any of the careers [my mother] planned for me. I was consistent in my longing to become Rouge Dragon Pursuivant and spend my days in comfortable surroundings manufacturing for myself a totally fictitious but noble ancestry deriving from some Knight of the Round Table.'

James Lees-Milne, *Another Self* (1970), Chapter II

Contents

Preface

James Lees-Milne used to say that one of the main spurs in life, espe-cially in old age, was curiosity; and during the five years covered by this, the eleventh volume of his diaries, he had much need of this resource. Just after it opens in 1988, in his eightieth year, he was found to be suffering from a malignant tumour on the right cheek. Several weeks of painful treatment followed ('Truly, I don't remember ever suffering such agony as I am now undergoing'). Although this proved effective, it took much out of him, and he was never quite the same again. In the past, he had been able to rely on the ministrations of Alvilde, his talented managing wife; but she was experiencing a decline more rapid than his own. Early in 1990 she underwent a haz-ardous heart operation; two years later, she narrowly survived an illness which deprived her of her characteristic alertness and left her a permanent invalid. In his early eighties, Jim found himself increasingly having to care for her as well as for himself, and to discharge domes-tic responsibilities which had formerly been hers.

Although these circumstances inevitably took their toll of his energy, he remained astonishingly active. Most weekdays he drove from Essex House on the Badminton estate, where he lived with his wife, to his library (formerly William Beckford's) at 19 Lansdown Crescent, Bath, where he put in a full working day as a busy writer. Despite failing eyesight, he continued to read voraciously: on 9 September 1991, he mentions having recently devoured the whole of *Paradise Lost*. He regularly visited London, staying at his club, Brooks's, and packing in a busy schedule of meetings with friends, exhibitions, and research for his books. He travelled much about the country, often driving long distances, paying visits and studying country house archi-tecture, his old love of which had revived in recent years. He still went for fairly long walks, and made sightseeing trips abroad. As well as keeping up with a large (if steadily contracting) circle of existing acquaintances, he showed a remarkable facility for making new friends.

What was the motor which drove him to do so much at a time when he was frequently exhausted or depressed and rarely felt well? For all his apparent vagueness, his mind remained sharp; and he possessed a strong self-discipline and will to carry on, reinforced by the feeling, not unusual in those of a basically melancholy disposition, that he dare not slow down for fear of stopping altogether. But the great stimulant in his life was curiosity. He drew constant inspiration from art, literature, human idiosyncrasy, gossip, even the television news. In a sense, it was his diary – or rather, the prospect of finding intriguing things to say in it – which kept him going. For these diaries are no perfunctory record; they capture the flavour of every meaningful experience in his life, and are comparable in their wit, candour and sharp observation to any of the preceding volumes.

Had he written nothing else during these years, it would have been an impressive achievement; but he also produced three considerable (if very different) books. The first (1990) was a novel, on which he had been working for almost a decade, about a handsome German count, a prisoner in England during the First World War, who seduces first an English schoolboy, then the boy's mother. He considered it a masterpiece, and felt frustrated that no one else seemed to do so, and that it was rejected by every mainstream publisher. (It was finally published by his great-nephew Nick Robinson.) The second (1991) was a biography, which had involved much research, of the statesman and art collector the 6th ('Bachelor') Duke of Devonshire (1790–1858). This was not a subject which filled him with much enthusiasm, and he had undertaken it at the behest of his old friend 'Debo' Devonshire, of whom he saw much during these years, at Chatsworth and elsewhere. The third (1992) was a volume of memoirs about his early years working for the National Trust, and his role in that institution's acquisition of some of its most splendid country houses. This book – elegiac, gently ironical, fascinatingly (and quirkily) informative – appeared to rave reviews: he researched and wrote it in a few months, and it came out in his eighty-fifth year.

In their eighties, many writers find that their days of glory are past and they are becoming forgotten. Jim's experience was quite the opposite: formerly considered a minor figure, he was now emerging as a grand old man of English letters and architectural conservation.

He had an ever-growing fan following. There was much demand for the reprinting of his works, notably the four volumes of his 1940s diaries. His eightieth birthday was celebrated with lavish encomiums in the *Daily Telegraph*, the *Spectator* and *Country Life*. This recognition was all the more pleasing to him for coming so late. It gave him particular satisfaction to find himself solicited by his Eton contemporary 'Jock' Murray: it was 'a thrill to be published at last by this Rolls-Royce of publishers' (10 May 1990). On the other hand, he had no hesitation in turning down a CBE, the National Art Collections Fund's 'Life Achievement Award', and the opportunity to be photographed by Lord Snowdon.

The editing of these diaries, which are so close to the present day, has presented certain problems; but it would destroy their whole character if one were to remove every waspish witticism about the living. Jim (who was as candid in writing about himself as about others) clearly felt much affection for most of his 'victims', citing with approval (27 February 1991) Hugh Massingberd's dictum: 'It is not one's friends' virtues but their foibles which endear them to one.' I have naturally preserved the (no doubt apt) references to myself as sluggish, lacking in social graces and full of odd habits. I am grateful to George Crawshay, Debo Devonshire, Patric Dickinson, Ian Dixon, Alexandra Erskine, Sue Fox, Selina Hastings, Bruce Hunter, John Kenworthy-Browne, Jonathan Kooperstein, Hugh Massingberd, R. B. McDowell, Tony Mitchell, the late Diana Mosley, Roland Philipps, Stuart Preston, Liz Robinson, Nick Robinson, Francis Russell, John Saumarez Smith, Tony Scotland, Moray Watson and Caroline Westmore for their various contributions.

Michael Bloch
mab@jamesleesmilne.com
January 2004

For information about James Lees-Milne's life and work, and Hugh Massingberd's play *Ancestral Voices* based on these diaries, visit the official James Lees-Milne website at www.jamesleesmilne.com

And from this chasm, with ceaseless turmoil seething,
As if this earth in fast thick pants were breathing,
A mighty fountain momently was forced . . .

Samuel Taylor Coleridge, *Kubla Khan*

1988

Saturday, 2nd January

Selina Hastings[*] called on her way to stay with Lady Harlech,[†] looking prettier than ever with her vernal complexion and wearing smart two-piece suit. Told us she had lunched at Chequers over Christmas. Mrs Thatcher[‡] on greeting her said, 'I know who you are perfectly well.' After luncheon she expressed a desire to have two minutes' talk with S. – which lasted not a second more, and was about the masseuse they share. Selina hoped to ask some questions, but was unable to get a word in edgeways. When the two minutes were up, the Prime Minister rose, smiled sweetly, and moved on to the next guest.

Sunday, 3rd January

My total, abysmal muffishness shames me. I used to think it did not matter that I could not mend a fuse, or even put a light bulb into a socket. Now I think it is despicable. How I have got through life I don't know. Such elementary tasks ought to be taught in schools like Eton. Perhaps they are today. Working class children learn them naturally at father's knee, almost imbibe them with mother's milk.

Tuesday, 5th January

To see my specialist Mr Young for result of my biopsy.[§] Hoped desperately it would be all right, but from head-shaking of my GP and dentist, feared the worst. Entered No. 20, The Circus. Shown into

---

[*] Lady Selina Hastings (b. 1945); dau. of 13th Earl of Huntingdon; writer and journalist.
[†] Pamela Colin (b. 1934); m. 1969 (as his 2nd wife) 5th Baron Harlech (d. 1985); writer on cookery.
[‡] Margaret Roberts (b. 1925); m. 1951 (as his 2nd wife) Denis Thatcher (later 1st Bt, d. 2003); MP (C) Finchley, 1959–92; Prime Minister 1979–90; cr. life peer, 1992.
[§] Of 'the swelling on the right side of my face' (*Beneath a Waning Moon*, 17 December 1987).

consulting room by girl in white coat, so bloody bright and cheery. Mr Young proffered a limp hand. I am always reluctant to shake hands with doctors because it means they must wash them immediately. Instead I grasped his finger-tips. He dropped his eyes and looked furtive, so I knew. 'Well,' he began. I interrupted with, 'I presume it is malignant?' 'Yes,' he said. If I hadn't asked him, would he have told me directly, or left it to Dr King? He said I would need treatment from a radiologist. I told him I would rather not, for the sooner I died the better, having had cancer once already. But he remonstrated gently, pointing out that, if I did nothing, the cheek would suppurate and I would be unable to wear my dentures. That decided me. A[lvilde] and I had a long discussion and decided that it would be absurd to make a mystery of it because my face would in due course reveal all. So I am telling any friend who is interested. But I don't want commiseration, or to discuss with strangers.

Wednesday, 6th January

I told M[ichael Bloch]* my news this morning. He was very upset and told me how much I mattered to him. I wanted to reciprocate and tell him what he knows already, but could not get the words out, so just hung up. When I managed to compose myself I rang him back, to his relief, as he feared he must have said something to displease. As if he could. I also rang up dear Clive Charlton† and told him the verdict. He was encouraging and cheering, telling me to keep my pecker up. Of course they all have to make light, even my darling A., who is so wise and caring.

Thursday, 7th January

I sit awaiting my appointment with the radiologist, like Patience on a Monument. Meanwhile I continue pegging away at the Bachelor Duke's‡ boring diaries, because otherwise I would go mad.

---

* Author and barrister (b. 1953); friend of J.L.-M. since 1979, at which time he was a Cambridge postgraduate student; had since lived in Paris, assisting the Duchess of Windsor's French lawyer, Maître Suzanne Blum (see notes to 24 June 1988); then writing a book on the ex-King's life in exile.
† The specialist who had dealt with J.L.-M's prostate cancer in 1984: see *Holy Dread*.
‡ William George Spencer Cavendish, 6th Duke of Devonshire (1790–1858), Whig statesman, collector, and patron of Sir Joseph Paxton, on whose biography J.L.-M., at the behest of his friend 'Debo' Devonshire, had been working for almost a year.

Saturday, 9th January

Selina comes to stay the night, always a welcome guest. We dine with the Loewensteins.* Selina very entertaining and sharp. A. calls her 'the acid drop'. I am pleased by a review of my little *Venetian Evenings*†
in *Books*, admittedly a slight mag, but any kind of recognition is pleasing.

Sunday, 10th January

Spent morning talking to Selina, who had been told about my impending treatment by Andrew [Devonshire].‡ Was very sane and sparing of compassion, while expressing interest in my symptoms and wanting to know how I felt when I awoke in the night. She told me she might be able to get me a fatal dose which a doctor once prescribed for her mother in Africa when she was frightened of being captured and tortured by natives. Said it was important not to take too little or frightful consequences would ensue, which did not reassure. But her offer may come in handy if my illness becomes terminal – though I can't decide whether it is sinful to take one's life or not.

Selina believes that Ros§ can still see to read a little. She notices that whenever Ros asks her to read out to her the pile of letters by her bed, they are always from fans, never the tax inspector or the telephone company.

John Cornforth¶ rang up to confirm what I suspected, that Anne Rosse** is quite dotty now. Communication by letter or telephone quite useless. Advises me to send an occasional post card and gave me the address of her housekeeper who can give news of her.

---

* Prince Rupert zu Loewenstein (b. 1930), financial adviser, of Biddestone Manor, Gloucestershire; m. 1957 Josephine Lowry-Corry.

† A book written in 1986 and recently published by Collins, in which J.L.-M. describes his favourite buildings in Venice.

‡ Andrew Cavendish, 11th Duke of Devonshire (1920–2004); m. 1941 Hon. Deborah ('Debo') Mitford (b. 1920).

§ Rosamond Lehmann (1901–90); novelist, interested in psychical research; m. 1st 1923 (diss. 1928) Hon. Walter Runciman (later 2nd Viscount Runciman of Doxford), 2nd 1928 (diss. 1944) Hon. Wogan Philipps (later 2nd Baron Milford). Her biography by Selina Hastings was published by Chatto in 2002.

¶ Architectural historian (1937–2004) on staff of *Country Life*.

**Anne Messel (1902–92); m. 1st Ronald Armstrong-Jones, 2nd 1935 Michael Parsons, 6th Earl of Rosse (he d. 1979); lived at Nymans, Sussex.

Tuesday, 12th January

A. accompanied me to Bath Clinic, where we were interviewed by Dr Rees, radiologist. Charming, clever and direct young man, absolutely frank. Told me I would have to undergo treatment on cheek daily in Bristol for four weeks. Would suffer loss of taste and much soreness but no loss of hair, etc. He took some preliminary tests. If these are satisfactory, I start treatment next week.

Wednesday, 13th January

Radio Four had a 'phone-in' about homosexuality. I don't know what annoys me more, the biblical abhorrence of pious Christians or the exhibitionism and proselytising of the Gay Brigade. There should of course be no prejudice, harassment or loss of rights – but equally no flaunting of sexual deviancy. It is nobody else's business what a person does in private, provided no violence or cruelty is involved. As for the Church, no candidate for ordination should be questioned about his inclinations, and no objection taken if he is living with a person of his own sex, provided all is done discreetly; but no promiscuity should be tolerated among the clergy, whether homo or hetero. Is this illogical of me?

Diana Mosley* and Pam Jackson† came at noon, and we all went to lunch at the House.‡ Much chat and laughter. Diana asked my advice about the publication of *her* diaries for the Thirties. I was all for it. They will attract fascinated attention, if some hostile reviews. The two sisters and Daphne [Fielding]§ are going together to South Africa for six weeks. There is bound to be trouble – already each of them takes one of the others aside to grumble about the third. Woman told me that she had been asked to talk to Moreton-in-Marsh Historical

---

* Hon. Diana Mitford (1910–2003), with whom J.L.-M., then a schoolfriend of her brother, had been in love aged eighteen; m. 1st 1928 Hon. Bryan Guinness (1905–92; later 2nd Baron Moyne), 2nd 1936 Sir Oswald Mosley, 6th Bt (1896–1980); lived in Orsay, France.
† Hon. Pamela ('Woman') Mitford, 2nd of Mitford sisters (1907–94); m. 1936 (as 2nd of his 6 wives) Professor Derek Jackson (d. 1982).
‡ Badminton House.
§ Hon. Daphne Vivian (1904–97); novelist, mother of Caroline, Duchess of Beaufort; m. 1st 1926 Henry Thynne, later 6th Marquess of Bath, 2nd 1953 Xan Fielding, war hero and writer.

Society about her memories of her grandfather Redesdale.* How old were you when he died, I asked? Seven, she replied.

Thursday, 14th January

Mr Rees telephones me to confirm that my treatment will begin next week. At night when depressed I imagine 'the thing' gnawing away at me, undermining me. I have finished the Bachelor Duke's diaries and rung up Debo to arrange their return. Her secretary told me she had just left to stay with Woman. I immediately drove the thirty miles to Woman's house to leave them there before Debo arrived.

Friday, 15th January

To London for the day, my last visit for weeks. Changed books at London Library. The Librarian, Matthews,† told me that the next volume of Dickens's letters contains many references to the Bachelor Duke. I was furious with my opticians, Dixley's, as the spectacles I ordered before Christmas were not yet ready. M. lunched at Brooks's. Said he barely noticed the swelling and detected no difference in me. But then he wouldn't, unless I moaned. I asked if he minded my giving my manuscript diaries up to 1979, the year we met, to Rota‡ to sell with the rest of my papers, M. to get the years from 1979 onwards to deal with as he sees fit. He thought this a good plan.

On the whole, I think that cancer has made me nicer and perhaps more spiritual, though no less selfish.

Alvilde's cousin James Armstrong came for the night, bringing pretty married daughter. Now fifty-eight and much aged.§ Works for the Australian Security Service, rather mysterious about precise job. He has become an Australian citizen, and wears the Order of Australia in his buttonhole like the Légion d'Honneur.

---

* Bertram Freeman-Mitford, (1837–1916); diplomatist, Japanese specialist and squire of Batsford House, Gloucestershire; cr. Baron Redesdale, 1902.
† Librarian of London Library, 1980–93, and noted indexer (b. 1927).
‡ Bertram Rota Ltd of Long Acre, dealers in rare books and manuscripts, who eventually (1991) sold J.L.-M's papers to the Beinecke Library at Yale.
§ J.L.-M. had last referred to him in his diary in 1953, at which time he was an 'eminently personable' naval lieutenant (*A Mingled Measure*).

Saturday, 16th January

Derry and Alexandra [Moore]* came for luncheon, I think to be kind to me. Very sweet of them; but although I have decided to make no mystery of my complaint, I find it a bore talking about it to all and sundry. D. rather haggard, the result of too much dashing about the world in Concorde.

Sunday, 17th January

We lunched with Billy Henderson† and Frank Tait,‡ both comfort figures. Frank has had exactly the same treatment as I am about to undergo, and was able to reassure me.

Wednesday, 20th January

Simon Blow's§ *Broken Blood* is a fascinating and brilliantly-written book, as I have written to tell him. Points a moral all right, though I wonder if he is the right person to point it, being motivated not a little by resentment. It is an excellent story about the decent, industrious Tennant family from Glasgow marrying into the decadent Wyndhams and going to pot in consequence. Pamela Wyndham¶ was a ghastly woman who ruined the lives of all her children. Only her son Christopher Glenconner** managed to escape her baleful influence.

Thursday, 21st January

Darling A. accompanied me to Bristol Hospital and waited while they made a sort of death-mask of me, needed for the treatment. Her

---

* Dermot, Viscount Moore (b. 1937); photographer, son and heir of 11th Earl of Drogheda; m. (2nd) Alexandra, dau. of Sir Nicholas Henderson, diplomatist.

† Painter (1903–93); sometime aide to Lord Linlithgow and Lord Wavell as Viceroys of India.

‡ Australian-born child psychiatrist (b. 1923).

§ Writer, former racing jockey (b. 1943); yr s. of Purcell Blow (er s. of Detmar Blow [1867–1939], architect and adviser to 2nd Duke of Westminster) and Diana Bethell (dau. of Hon. Claire Tennant). *Broken Blood* (Faber, 1987) was first of a series of works of family history and autobiography.

¶ Pamela Wyndham (1871–1928); dau. of Hon. Percy Wyndham of Clouds, Wiltshire; m. 1st Edward Tennant, 1st Baron Glenconner, 2nd Viscount Grey of Fallodon.

** Christopher Tennant (1899–1983); s. father as 2nd Baron Glenconner, 1920; m. 1st Pamela Paget, 2nd Elizabeth Powell.

devotion to me is beyond any recognition. She is efficient and fearless, takes up the telephone and gets straight to the fountain-head, refusing to be fobbed off by secretaries, whereas I am forever hesitant and fearful of being a nuisance or causing offence. After much thought, we decided that I should be a private patient, though the treatment would be the same were I 'on the Health'. But being private means I can ring up Dr Rees to discuss progress whenever I feel inclined; and he is very candid.

Friday, 22nd January

I go to London again, my treatment now due to start on Monday. To National Register of Archives in Chancery Lane,* to list the collections containing letters of the Bachelor Duke. Then to Dixley's, to return my new spectacles, through which I can see nothing. Lunched with Eardley [Knollys]† at No. 16 West Halkin Street. Both he and Fanny Partridge,‡ aged eighty-six and eighty-seven respectively, are under notice to quit their flats, and are uncertain what will happen to them. Then to Christie's for brief view of Camden Town [Group] exhibition.§ Have never seen so many indifferent paintings, to be sure.

We dined at the House, wondering how Caroline feels about the house on the edge of the park in which David is installing his mistress.¶ Yet in talking to David alone on a sofa afterwards I fell completely under his spell. He is worried about the future of Badminton; unless Harry or Eddy** produces a male heir, the dukedom will pass

---

* Maintained by Historical Manuscripts Commission (merged with Public Record Office in 2003 to form 'The National Archives').

† Painter (1902–1991), formerly on staff of N.T.; close friend of J.L.-M. since 1941.

‡ Frances Marshall (1900–2004); painter, critic and diarist, survivor of Bloomsbury Group; m. 1933 Ralph Partridge (d. 1960).

§ Group of artists led and inspired by Walter Sickert who exhibited at Carfax Gallery in 1911–12, including Duncan Grant, Augustus John, Henry Lamb, Wyndham Lewis and Lucien Pissarro.

¶ David Somerset, 11th Duke of Beaufort (b. 1928); art dealer; succeeded cousin to dukedom and to Badminton estate, 1984; m. 1st 1950 Lady Caroline Thynne (1928–1995), dau. of 6th Marquess of Bath, 2nd 2000 Miranda Morley (formerly the mistress referred to).

**Harry, Marquess of Worcester (b. 1952; m. 1987 Tracy Ward) and Lord Edward Somerset (b. 1958; m. 1982 Hon. Caroline Davidson), elder sons of 11th Duke of Beaufort. The 'male heir' appeared in January 1989 (see entries for 4 January and 6 March 1989).

to a distant cousin in Australia. Cannot decide whether to declare any of his works of art national heirlooms, for if he does so, future generations will be unable to sell. After much delay, Simon Verity* has written a grovelling letter and will come to put an inscription on the 'slab', as David calls it, of Master and Mary.†

Saturday, 23rd January

It is odd that, when I fall asleep over a book, I invariably dream, but the thread is never connected with the book I have been reading. My thoughts, I can almost see them, drift off the page in a wavy cord, but immediately acquire a different context. When given an anaesthetic, I have sometimes tried to continue my train of thought into the subconscious world, always without success. Always impossible to maintain the sequence.

Monday, 25th January

To Bristol for my first treatment. The death-mask fills with a delicious smell of the sandalwood with which I douche my face each morning. Dr Rees declared himself confident of destroying 'the thing' and hoped he might do so by the middle of next week; if he did, I would only need five more treatments to be on the safe side.

Saturday, 30th January

This morning I was visited in Badminton by Elizabeth Dixon, who wants to write a biography of John Fowler.‡ I told her that I thought Cornforth's book, written with John's assistance, was adequate. She worked for John towards the end of his life and found him bad-tempered, but he was then suffering from cancer of the throat. I said

---

* Memorial sculptor and letterer (b. 1945); commissioned, on J.L.-M's recommendation, to execute memorials to 10th Duke of Beaufort and his Duchess; m. 1970 Judith Mills.

† Henry Somerset, 10th Duke of Beaufort (1900–84); m. 1923 Lady Mary Cambridge (1897–1987), dau. of 1st Marquess of Cambridge (brother of Queen Mary, consort of King George V); leading figure of hunting world, known as 'Master' from the age of 8, when he was given his own pack of harriers.

‡ Interior decorator (1906–77), partner of Colefax & Fowler, who did much work in N.T. houses, and was the subject of an affectionate essay by J.L.-M. in *Fourteen Friends*.

no one was more fun in the old days – not that the old days were *that* much fun when they happened.

We lunched with the Loewensteins at Biddestone, who will be gone from there by the autumn. They told me that poor Miss,* J[osephine]'s mother, was burgled this week. A nice young man came to the door saying he was a plumber working on the adjoining house and asking if he could go upstairs to inspect some pipes. She in her eighties was instantly suspicious and told him to wait while she went to look herself. While she was gone, young man and accomplices somehow slipped in and made off with two Regency tables, a French commode, and various books and treasures.

Dining at the House I met the Raymond Carrs[†] and their son Matthew[‡] who is to marry Anne Somerset. Matthew attractive and very intelligent, with good manners. Said to be a first-rate painter. Lady Carr an intelligent but simple person who seems out of place in the Beaufort environment. Sir Raymond very clever too, of course. Used to be a great killer of upper class ladies and is that odd combination, don and fox-hunter.

Tuesday, 2nd February

Just before I left Bath for my treatment in Bristol, the telephone rang. It was Miss X., the frightful basement tenant we are trying to get rid of,[§] to say her bedroom had been flooded. I suggested she either contact my solicitors or call a plumber. Five minutes later the doorbell rang, and I was confronted with an unknown middle-aged woman. 'I am Miss X's mother,' she said. 'You must come down and do something about the water.' I declined. 'But this is my daughter's home and she is not well,' she continued. This raised my ire. 'Your daughter is a squatter in my house,' I retorted. 'It is not her flat at all. She is remaining there in flagrant breach of our agreement.' Woman then turned very nasty. 'She has every right to remain,' she hissed, 'as

---

* Hon. Mary Biddulph (1906–91); m. 1929–38 Montagu Lowry-Corry.

[†] Sir Raymond Carr (b. 1919; kt 1987); historian, specialising in Spanish history; Warden of St Antony's College, Oxford, 1968–87; m. 1950 Sara Strickland.

[‡] Matthew Carr, artist; m. 1988 Lady Anne Somerset (b. 1955), only dau. of 11th Duke of Beaufort.

[§] A saga which, to J.L.-M's increasing fury, had been going on since May 1987, as related in *Beneath a Waning Moon*.

you will find out when the case comes up.' I then told her that her
daughter had no sense of honour, adding, 'And she is a little bitch.'
That was a mistake. I rang Alvilde to tell her of the encounter, and
drove off to Bristol.

Saturday, 6th February

Billa [Harrod]* has come all the way from Norfolk to stay the
weekend, an act of true friendship before I depart to another sphere.
Overjoyed to see her, but after ten treatments my mouth is so sore I
can hardly speak, and eating is a torment. She told me an extraordinary tale about the two Hesketh brothers, Roger† and Peter.‡ (Peter
died two years ago, Roger last Christmas.) They adored each other,
but there was a shadow between them. An uncle who died in 1938
left many family treasures, Wrights of Derby, silver, etc., then valued
at £100,000 and now worth millions. As the elder brother, Roger
assumed they were left to him, and kept them all. Peter never raised
the matter during his lifetime, and Roger used them for his loving recreation of Meols Hall, which he rebuilt in the Palladian style and
made the chief interest of his later life. Now Peter's daughter is claiming her father's share of the treasures from Roger's widow and son.
What distresses Billa, who is devoted to Roger's memory (he having
been in love with her all his life), is that, in the course of this wrangle,
documents have come to light proving that Roger deliberately
cheated Peter of his share. An eerie country house saga.

Wednesday, 10th February

My thirteenth treatment at Bristol today. The usual machine being
serviced so they use an old one, a board to which I am tied like
Gulliver in Lilliput, forced to listen to rubbish on Radio One. I wondered how I would feel if I were trapped like this after an earthquake

---

* Wilhelmine Cresswell (b. 1911); Norfolk conservationist; widow of Sir Roy Harrod
(1900–79), Oxford economist and biographer of J.M. Keynes; friend of J.L.-M. since
1930s.
† Roger Fleetwood Fleetwood-Hesketh (1902–88) of Meols Hall nr Southport,
Lancashire; Mayor of Southport, 1950.
‡ Peter Fleetwood Fleetwood-Hesketh (1905–85) of The Manor House, Hale, Liverpool;
architect, writer, illustrator and sometime Hon. Representative of N.T.

or bombing, unable to budge or cry out. Would the droning radio be a comfort or irritant? I'm sure I would rather be killed outright than have to wait interminably for a possible rescue, unable to shift, stir or cry. My doctor is back from his skiing holiday and says 'the thing' has already diminished by two-thirds.

Wednesday, 17th February

Truly, I don't remember ever suffering such agony as I am now undergoing. Mercifully this may be my last week of treatment. Meanwhile we endure endless harassment from the bitch tenant, who has demanded we repair the damage caused by the recent flooding, which in the builder's view was caused by her letting either the bathwater or lavatory cistern overflow. Surely the responsibility for this sort of damage should be the tenant's? We thought up a wheeze, getting David Beaufort to instruct his agent Richard Wood to send us a notice to quit Essex House, leaving the Bath flat as our sole remaining residence. This I joyfully forwarded to our solicitor, who promptly telephoned Richard to ascertain whether his letter was a forgery.

Friday, 19th February

Had my last treatment this afternoon. Saw the doctor afterwards who is confident 'the thing' has been destroyed. Warns that I may suffer discomfort for another fortnight, but in fact the pain is already much reduced. A blessed relief.

Lady Walton has published a book on her husband Willie.[*] We met her at the Embassy in Rome.[†] A nice, clever, rather tiresome Argentinian woman. I never knew Walton, a chippy man who was snatched from Oldham by the Sitwells in the 1920s.[‡] His music is boring to me, like that of almost every composer born after 1900.

---

[*] Sir William Walton (1902–83); composer; m. 1949 Susana Gil.
[†] Where the L.-Ms had sometimes stayed during the ambassadorship (1983–87) of A.L.-M's cousin Thomas, 2nd Baron Bridges (b. 1927).
[‡] Walton was in fact studying at Oxford in 1920 when the Sitwells persuaded him to join them in London and set a miscellany of Edith's poetry to music in the extravaganza *Façade*. J.L.-M's own family had its roots in Oldham, where his father was born in 1880.

Saturday, 20th February

A. and I drove to Penselwood to see Audrey,* my first outing for a
month and one which depressed me to extremes. Audrey's cottage is
an absolute beast, so low-ceilinged that I could not stand upright in
the downstairs room. When not frozen by howling draughts, one is
blinded by smoke from the log fire. Surely something can be done for
this little old lady who lives in this hovel year in year out, never going
away? When away from her I love her deeply. When with her, am
exasperated beyond endurance. O vile beast me.

Saturday, 27th February

I never learn. I wrote a long letter to *The Times* expressing my horror
at the Pope's encyclical of last week enjoining the clergy to sell treasures from their churches for the benefit of the Third World.†
Particularly mentioned by him are gold and silver (so bang goes the
Pala d'Oro in St Mark's for a start), and paintings, i.e., altar-pieces by
Tintoretto, Tiepolo, anyone you care to mention. I am amazed that
no newspaper has criticised this proposed vandalism, and no museum
directors have written to protest in the press.

    I am better, but not perfectly well. Can eat without difficulty, but
taste little. Went to London on Wednesday, just to get out of my rut.
Quite enjoyed being in the London Library again, and entertaining
Eardley to lunch at Brooks's. Then to Lucian Freud‡ exhibition at the
beastly Hayward Gallery, not just a hideous building but very tiring
for the aged with its twisting stairs. Freud is of course a remarkable
painter. There is a hardness in the technique, a cruelty everywhere.
He must be the only artist whose self-portrait depicts his own life-size
penis and pubic hair in minute detail. To M., who gave me tea and
madeleines. Has almost finished his new Duke of Windsor book,
which he proposes to dedicate to me.§

---

* J.L.-M's sister (1905–90); m. 1st Hon. Matthew Arthur (later 2nd Baron Glenarthur),
2nd Cecil ('Tony') Stevens.
† J.L.-M. is presumably referring to the encyclical *Sollicitudo rei socialis* of 30 December
1987, a long and diffuse document offering priests 'guidelines' in social policy.
‡ Artist (b. 1922; CH 1983).
§ See entries for 24 June and 27 July 1988.

Sunday, 28th February

The Times having as usual ignored my letter about the Pope's encyclical, I sent a line to kind Hugh Massingberd* at the *Daily Telegraph*. He
asked me to dictate it down the telephone, and published it. Hugh
told me his uncle Peter Montgomery† had died. Peter was a gentle,
kind, humorous man, good-looking without being handsome, a
squire with a sense of duty. I had seen very little of him since the night
we spent together in the basement of the Piccadilly Hotel, both in
uniform, cowering from the bombs raining down on us.‡ The
bedroom we had been obliged to take when the raid started was
destroyed after we descended. We were nearly drowned in the flood
caused by smashed drains and tanks in the basement. In the morning,
after the all-clear, we wandered around Mayfair and St James's lament-
ing the damage done, wondering if the whole area would have to be
rebuilt. In the dawn, the skies were red with fires from the East End.
Peter's quirk was gerontophilia. He told me he used to sleep with a
great-uncle to whom he was devoted. I wonder if Hugh is aware of
this.

Nicholas Shakespeare,§ literary editor of the *Telegraph*, has, through
his friendship with Nick [Robinson],¶ asked me to write an article
on diaries – which sort I most like, which I think are failures, the
ingredients of a good diary, and so forth.** I said I would try, but my
confidence in being able to string two sentences together is low at
present.

---

* Hugh Montgomery-Massingberd (b. 1946); writer, journalist, publisher, genealogist,
and author (2002) of a play – *Ancestral Voices* – based on the diaries of J.L.-M.; then on
staff of *Daily Telegraph* (where as Obituaries Editor he created the modern, anecdotal style
of newspaper obituary).

† Captain Peter Montgomery of Blessingbourne, Co. Tyrone (1909–88); landowner and
musician; President of Arts Council for Northern Ireland, 1964–74.

‡ As depicted (though Montgomery insisted that the portrait of himself was fanciful) in
the last chapter of *Another Self* (1970).

§ Nicholas Shakespeare (b. 1957); successively literary editor of *The Times*, *Daily News* and
Telegraph (*Daily* and *Sunday*), 1985–91.

¶ J.L.-M's great-nephew (b. 1955), middle grandson of his sister Audrey; publisher, later
managing director of Constable & Robinson.

** See entry for 26 September 1988.

Thursday, 3rd March

To London for the day, to see Casey my oculist in Harley Street. He said my new eye (operated on last September) is working well, but the old (formerly good) one is now very bad. It too will have to be operated on, but he does not want to attempt this for at least six months, after what I have just undergone. I think henceforth I shall not wear specs except for reading. I drove back from the station without, and managed quite well.

Friday, 4th March

A dotty Beckford* enthusiast called on me in Bath without warning. I was displeased, but let him in. Rather a smelly youth. Wants to buy a plot of land in the Mendips and build his own tower. Has the money, being guitarist in a pop group. Claims to be haunted by presence of Beckford, which he 'felt' very strongly in my library. How Beckford attracts the loonies.

Tuesday, 22nd March

On the 8th, we flew to Morocco to stay at Hotel Tischka, Marrakech. Brand new hotel situated at very end of town, almost in desert. A decent building inside and out, modern but in Moroccan tradition. Food looked good, if only I could have tasted it. An English resident told us that at least four million tourists a year come to this town. It is pretty beastly too. Old Souk has scruffy little streets. New town well-planned by the French, with straight boulevards. The ancient monuments sparse and dull. With exception of our hotel, all modern buildings hideous. I did not enjoy our fortnight much. Blazing sun every day which A. loved, bathing in it beside the azure pool.

We were motored by taxi to La Roserie at Ouirgane, in foothills of Atlas Mountains. Nature made it a paradise, but man is turning it into a mess. We had a nice little chalet, by a small river diverted to rush through the grounds. Many birds and wild flowers. Unfortunately I

---

* William Beckford (1759–1844), writer, traveller, builder and collector. He had lived in Lansdown Crescent during his later years; and J.L.-M., who occupied his library at No. 19, had written a short but acclaimed biography of him, published by Michael Russell in 1976.

developed an attack of conjunctivitis. No village and no chemist, so we left early to return to Marrakech. Then A. contracted it.

I was struck forcibly by what the West is doing to the primitive world when, motoring back from Ouirgane to Marrakech, we passed through a small village in the plain which is a centre of the Berber race. It holds a market at certain dates to which Berbers come from far and wide, which happened to be taking place during our passage. These noble-looking people, on donkeys, on foot, the men clad in colourful jellabies, the women in long silk garments of every hue, plodded to the village and the rough-and-ready stalls piled with local produce and oddments. There were also eight charabancs out of which fat American ladies in tight white trousers and jangling with jewelry descended to mingle with the Berbers and get a sight of their primitive life, cameras clicking and whirring. The sort of thing that makes Wilfred Thesiger* reach for his revolver.

A. asked me what my idea of Purgatory was. I said a cocktail party in an overheated room. Hers was being obliged to watch animals being tortured.

Saturday, 26th March

Anne Somerset's wedding at Badminton, for which Margaret Anne Stuart[†] and Derek Hill[‡] stayed with us. They arrived for luncheon, to which we had also asked the Martin Charterises,[§] who turned up late owing to breakdown on motorway. I accompanied them all to church, but did not go to reception or ball. A. and I given 'family' seats, on balcony where Queen Mary[¶] used to sit. We had a fine view of the packed church, decorated like a floral hall. Air of spirituality non-existent. Smart guests dressed as for Ascot. Laura Marlborough[**]

---

* Explorer and travel writer (1910–2003; KBE 1995); Eton contemporary of J.L.-M.

† Margaret Anne Du Cane; interior decorator; m. 1979 as his 3rd wife David Stuart, 2nd Viscount Stuart of Findhorn.

‡ Landscape and portrait artist (1916–2000).

§ Lord Charteris of Amisfield (1913–99); Private Secretary to HM the Queen, 1972–77; Provost of Eton, 1978–91; m. 1944 Hon. Gay Margesson.

¶ Queen Mary had lived at Badminton during the Second World War (treating the house and estate as her own property and the Beauforts as her guests); she remained a legend in the locality.

** Laura Charteris (1915–1990); m. Jan. 1972 as her 4th husband 'Bert' Spencer-Churchill, 10th Duke of Marlborough (d. March 1972).

music. A proper biography will be written later on,[*] to include his affair with Benjamin Britten,[†] with whom he was madly in love for years, but who jilted him in favour of Peter Pears.[‡] He took it very badly, but it was probably just as well, for L. would have been crushed by Britten's superior genius. Interesting that both Britten and Lennox turned out to be naturally monogamous persons, rare with homos. Freda has all Britten's letters to Lennox, which must be fascinating. Britten also gave him many of his early scores, which Freda has had to lock away lest Lennox tear them up, as he has a mania for destroying papers the moment he is left alone.

Today we lunched with Jessica Douglas-Home[§] at The Mill, Quenington. She intrigues me vastly – mysterious, wheedling, attractive, gipsy, clever, earnest. I gave her a Chatsworth tray as an Easter present. A rare sunny day, and we ate on the grass at the front of the house. Uncomfortable, as picnics always are. She wanted to hear about my cancer, being hooked on the subject because of poor Charlie. She talked of her campaign to stop the wholesale destruction of old buildings and monuments in Romania. In Bucharest, they have wiped out not only the churches, but all palaces and houses which provide any reminder of the 'bourgeois' past. She is trying to get Unesco to intervene before the whole country suffers the same fate.

Gerda Barlow[¶] brought Peter Coats[**] to see us. He is the most self-centred man, who never stops telling stories aimed at his own glorification. Pathetically lonely, and will stay with anyone who will have him. Kept repeating that I was his oldest friend, older even than Billy Whitaker.[††] True perhaps in that we all attended prep school[‡‡]

---

[*] Now being written by Tony Scotland.

[†] Composer (1913–76; CH 1953, OM 1965, cr. life peer as Baron Britten, 1976); the affair lasted from summer 1936 to Christmas 1938.

[‡] Tenor and organist (1910–86; Kt 1978); partner of Benjamin Britten, with whom he lived at Aldeburgh and jointly created the Aldeburgh Festival.

[§] Jessica Gwynn; artist, stage designer, and author of a biography of her grandmother Violet Woodhouse (whom J.L.-M. visited at Nether Lypiatt Manor, Gloucs., during the war); m. 1966 Charles Douglas-Home (1937–85), editor of The Times, 1983–5.

[¶] Wife of Basil Barlow (1918–91) of Stancombe Court, Gloucestershire.

[**] Kinsman of J.L.-M. (1910–90); ADC to Lord Wavell as Viceroy of India; garden designer and horticultural writer.

[††] William Whitaker (1910–88) of Pylewell Park near Lymington, Hampshire; bachelor landowner.

[‡‡] Lockers Park, Hertfordshire.

together – but oh dear, not in endurance. I am sure he has never forgiven me for what I wrote about his beloved Chips* in my first diaries.
Peter looks like a ghost, with transparent skin and sunken eyes. Freda
is sure he has Aids, poor old thing.

Thursday, 7th April

I have always considered lawyers the enemies of the human race,
having seen during my days at the National Trust how their pedantic
follies lost us several splendid properties. This afternoon at two
o'clock, A. and I attended the hearing of our 'case' at Bath Guildhall
v. that beastly girl who refuses to leave our downstairs flat. We were
kept waiting an hour before finally being ushered into the presence of
Judge Davies. For the next two hours, our counsel and hers argued
some pettifogging point about whether the notice to quit served by
our solicitors should be held to expire on Lady Day or some other day.
All muttered in low voices so that we could hardly hear a word.
Reference made to nineteenth-century cases and famous lawyers of
the past; huge tomes containing relevant writings handed up to judge.
Neither we nor the bitch were called as witnesses. Finally we were dis-
missed for the day, another date being fixed to suit the convenience
of her, not us – though we are paying our costs while she (whose
mother is selling her house behind Lansdown Crescent for £750,000)
gets legal aid. The law is not just an ass – it is a fiend. A. and I return
to our car, fuming.

Saturday, 9th April

I can never remember a spring more glittering with wild flowers.
Primroses in abundance. Amelanchier almost out, a fortnight ahead of
time. Saw an unusual phenomenon in Vicarage Field, near the
Orangery. On an ancient and not very large chestnut tree, suspended
from a long twig (too slender to be called a branch), hangs a great wen
of encrusted, scoriated bark, the size of a football, covered with

---

* Sir Henry Channon (1897–1958), politician, socialite, diarist and intimate friend of
Peter Coats. In *Ancestral Voices*, J.L.-M. had recounted his involvement in a homosexual
intrigue, described him as 'a flibbertigibbet', and quoted a remark of Robert Byron that
he had 'put his adopted class before his adopted country' (Channon being American by
birth).

opening chestnut buds. Folly* and I very interested. Told A. I would like her to see it. Where, she asked. I said, close to the square stone on a slight mound where I would like my ashes to lie. Oh, she said, you would talk like that just on my return from France.

Thursday, 14th April

We dined alone with the Beauforts, the four of us waited on by Steven the butler and Bronwyn the parlour maid. On leaving the table, David said in apparent seriousness, 'I can never believe that anyone I invite really wants to come here.' 'What nonsense,' I replied, wondering who would refuse who had the opportunity. Can David, with his superb good looks, charm, rank (in the Victorian sense), and his marvellous house, famed far and wide, really mean it when he talks like this? A. asked David, rather rashly I thought, 'Who decides which trees on this estate should be cut down and where others should be replanted?' 'I do,' replied D., a trifle peevishly. 'I have planted twelve thousand trees since Master's death. Why, is anything wrong?' 'No, everything's wonderful.' The truth is that D. is not much of a conservationist, and unconcerned about hedgerows, brambles, elders and bird life.

Jane, our nice gardener girl, said to A. this morning, 'Isn't it wonderful hearing the birds singing so loudly?' Alas, A. and I now hear nothing at all. This is one of the sadnesses of age. No more dawn choruses. No more blackbirds' songs – there are many blackbirds about now. No more thrushes.

Friday, 15th April

Driving to Bath, I listened to Arthur Scargill† on *Desert Island Discs*. This man, whom I and thousands like me detest as a public fiend for his wicked iconoclasm and Marxist views, has a beautiful soft speaking voice. He spoke of his passionate beliefs, instancing how Tolpuddle martyrs, suffragettes, general strikers of 1926, etc. suffered defeats at the time in their efforts to promote freedoms which are now accepted. Similarly feels that World Socialism is bound to come (he

---

* J.L.-M's beloved whippet.
† President of National Union of Mineworkers since 1981, who had led its disastrous strike of 1984–5; former communist, and founder during 1990s of Socialist Labour Party (b. 1938).

may be right) in spite of present reverses. His choice of music included the Prisoners' Chorus from *Leonore* and the Slaves' Chorus from *Nabucco* – political choices, yet who would suppose such a barbarian would be familiar with Beethoven and Verdi? His choice of book *Huckleberry Finn*, and his luxury item, of all things, the *Mona Lisa*.

Saturday, 16th April

We drove to lunch with Loelia [Lindsay].* She was much aged physically, and very bent, but mentally more alert than when we last saw her. She still makes me laugh more than anyone I know – at moments I could scarcely get the words out for choking. Sad situation – depends on hired couples, none of whom are much good or stay more than a month. She is very immobile, and her little dog is dying. Poor dear. Even someone as social and desired as Loelia, who never missed a party and was a great dispenser of fun, is now, not exactly neglected, for she has some good friends, but inevitably left to her own devices.

Sunday, 17th April

Bamber Gascoigne† motored Midi‡ down to luncheon. She is slow in movement, but remarkably spry and alert. Bamber now a star. The bloom of his early youth has given way to a handsome middle-aged appearance. Full of projects, having at last got rid of *University Challenge*§ – which threatened to go on for ever, like *The Mousetrap*.¶ Is now doing a series on the arts. He darted from room to room looking at our pictures and objects, A. teasing him that he was mugging up for his programme. A bubbling extrovert, not overly sensitive, but charming and as good as gold. Told us that in summer he

---

* Hon. Loelia Ponsonby (1902–93), dau. of 1st Baron Sysonby; m. 1st (1930–47) 2nd Duke of Westminster ('Bendor'), 2nd 1969 Sir Martin Lindsay of Dowhill, 1st Bt (1905–81).

† Arthur Bamber Gascoigne (b. 1935); writer, broadcaster and publisher, son of 'Midi' Gascoigne; m. 1965 Christina Ditchburn.

‡ Hon. Mary O'Neill (1905–91); m. 1934 Frederick ('Derick') Gascoigne (d. 1974); friend of J.L.-M. since 1920s.

§ Long-running television quiz show featuring undergraduate teams, conceived and until recently presented by Bamber Gascoigne.

¶ Play by Agatha Christie, with record-breaking run (currently more than fifty years) in West End of London.

swims upstream from his Richmond terrace house to Ham House; works out how the tides are acting, then glides downstream in time for breakfast. Eager to meet the Loewensteins, who will be his neighbours at Petersham.

Wednesday, 20th April

Two quite successful days in London, staying at Brooks's. Left tube at Baker Street to look for house Bachelor bought his mistress – 22, Dorset Square. I found it (the numbers are unlikely to have been altered) on NW corner, opposite John Steegman's* flat where I used to go in the 1930s. A house which would never be occupied by a single household today. J.K.-B.† lunched at Brooks's, where we ran into what looked like whole staff of the N.T. Then to London Library, where found fascinating *Illustrated London News* article of 1844 about the Bachelor's party at Chiswick that June for the Emperor Nicholas. Then to see Rosamond [Lehmann], who was sitting up downstairs and answered the doorbell herself. Much thinner and beautiful, though pale and sad.

I then met Feeble‡ in Shaftesbury Avenue, where we dined before going to Apollo Theatre to see *Best of Friends*.§ Good seats in middle of stalls, but even so I could not see the faces on the stage. But heard every word of John Gielgud¶ playing Sir Sydney Cockerell.** Excellent and immensely enjoyable. As we left, Feeble was hailed by a couple. I tried discreetly to wait ahead, but she said to them, 'You know J.L.-M.', in that English way. Confronted by short clergyman in

---

* Art historian, poet, and author of a history of Cambridge (1899–1966).

† Expert on neo-classical sculpture, formerly on staff of N.T. and Christie's (b. 1931); close friend of J.L.-M. since 1958.

‡ Lady Elizabeth Cavendish (b. 1926); dau. of 10th Duke of Devonshire (and sister of Andrew, 11th Duke); Lady-in-Waiting to Princess Margaret; close friend of Sir John Betjeman during last thirty years of his life.

§ Play by Hugh Whitemore, about the friendship between Sir Sydney Cockerell (Sir John Gielgud), George Bernard Shaw (Ray McAnally), and Dame Laurentia McLachlan (Dame Wendy Hiller).

¶ Sir John Gielgud, actor (1904–2000), with whom J.L.-M., then an Oxford undergraduate, had a six-week affair in 1931 (as revealed in *Deep Romantic Chasm*).

** Director of Fitzwilliam Museum, Cambridge, 1907–38 (1867–1962); friend of the famous, becoming literary executor to William Morris, Wilfrid Scawen Blunt and Thomas Hardy.

parson's black suit, worn and shiny, with black dickie and dog collar, and dumpy, plain, clever-looking wife. It was the Archbishop of Canterbury.[*] Charming expression and unassuming manner, too much so. Shook hands. I didn't know how to address him – Your Grace? Sir? – so talked instead to Mrs Runcie, idiotically, of dogs and how they made it impossible for my wife and myself to be away at same time. As we emerged from theatre, Archbishop was surrounded by photographers and autograph hunters, whom he kindly obliged. His dickie had got detached from his collar and almost reached his ears. Archbishop Ramsey looked like an unmade bed; this one looks like a haystack that has been through a camel's eye.

Feeble is happy that Debo and Andrew are now so deeply devoted. Says that Debo has become the Prince of Wales's Egeria. On his return from the skiing tragedy in Switzerland,[†] he rushed straight to Chatsworth for comfort and advice. When I was there, D. indeed spoke to me of how wonderful she finds him, and how sad. Feeble thinks he is not kind to the Princess, whom he snubs in public. She is a poor little simple waif who only wants to have a jolly time.

Thursday, 21st April

Nick [Robinson] breakfasted at Brooks's, after which we both went to Leger Gallery to meet his brother Richard[‡] who is considering purchasing a Girtin[§] water-colour there. Richard had just been to the barber's and looked extremely spruce, youthful, lean and City-gentish. A contrast to Nick, who was scruffy, though in a dusty old suit for Brooks's benefit. Richard has changed jobs and is now a director of Rothschild's. Sounds all right to me.

To exhibition at Burlington House of Thyssen collection.[¶] Too

---

[*] Robert Runcie (1921–2000); 102nd Archbishop of Canterbury, 1980–91, known for his exuberant style, his ecumenism, and his ideological clashes with the Thatcher Government; cr. life peer, 1991; m. 1957 Rosalind ('Lindy') Turner.

[†] On 10 March 1988, while the Prince and his friends were skiing 'off-piste' near the resort of Klosters in Switzerland, they encountered an avalanche which killed one of the party, Major Hugh Lindsay, and severely injured another, 'Patti' Palmer-Tomkinson.

[‡] Youngest of the three Robinson brothers (b. 1957).

[§] Thomas Girtin (1775–1802); English artist, considered founder of modern water-colour painting.

[¶] Collection of paintings amassed by steel heir Baron Hans Heinrich Thyssen-Bornemisza, which eventually found a permanent home at the Villahermosa Palace, Madrid.

many masterpieces, most of them conventional but some marvellous – a Risen Christ, artist forgotten but with pathos of El Greco; early fifteenth-century portraits of young men; girl in a turban carrying bouquet, named 'Sense of Smell'. Then to lunch at Travellers' with Hugh Massingberd. How I like this sympathetic man. He wants to visit a house with me, and write about it in the *Telegraph*. We thought we might go to The Vyne in July and combine it with Highclere.* Then to tea at the Savile with M. and his friends Charles Orwin† and Philip Mansel.‡ P.M. a sympathetic, quiet, clever man, who has inherited a seat in Dorset but does not care for country life. From there to Paddington, and home.

Sunday, 24th April

A. and I drove to the Droghedas,§ another mission of mercy and extremely sad. We lunched. Joan did not eat with us, but upstairs. Garrett looking very ill and frail, white as a sheet and bent. He manages to potter round the garden with difficulty. Has a pacemaker to keep the heart ticking. After luncheon, Joan and nurse appeared at doorway. She too white as a ghost, staring ahead with bewildered expression. Yet still pretty. Paid no heed to A. who went to embrace her – though she did kiss me when Garrett ordered her to do so, muttering incomprehensible words. One murmurs back any nonsense, for she understands nothing. Garrett told us the nurses cost him £40,000 a year and he does not know how much longer he can find the money. But he may well die before her – I would give him a year at most. He is seventy-eight on Saturday. The two of them shuffled, he piloting her into the drawing room. A pitiable sight – so short a while ago they were the most glamorous couple in England. I must write my obituary of him for the *Independent* before it is too late.

---

* Two houses near Basingstoke, Hampshire: Highclere is the seat of the Earls of Carnarvon, The Vyne a property of the National Trust.
† Publisher (b. 1951) who had moved from London to Singapore in 1985.
‡ Historian (b. 1951), then writing a biography of the 18th-century soldier-statesman the Prince de Ligne; owner of Smedmore estate, Dorset, which had descended by inheritance since the 14th-century.
§ Garrett Moore, 11th Earl of Drogheda (1910–89); m. 1935 Joan Carr, pianist (d. 1989).

Wednesday, 27th April

Listening to a 'phone-in' on Radio Four as I drove to Bath this morning, I was surprised how many listeners were in favour of the House of Lords. The majority considered it the more responsible of the two Houses, more dignified, and the protector of the people against an autocratic Commons.* A strange reversal of affairs from 1911, when the Lords were considered enemies of the people. Only a few favoured the hereditary principle, no one pointed out that it was the sole way of getting young peers. No one suggested that the hereditary peers should elect a limited number from their ranks to sit in the upper chamber.

That silly ass Chloë† has chucked her job at Mlinaric's‡ decorating firm. The trouble with this child is that she has too high an opinion of herself. I keep telling A. that she must not worry herself over her grandchildren. She has done more than most grandparents do, and must now sit back and let them stew in their own juice. They are pushing thirty, after all. I was reminded of the death of my own Granny§ when I was twenty-seven, and the drive from Wickhamford [Manor] to Ribbesford [Hall]¶ with my father for the funeral. He was in too jubilant a mood. I too was fraught with horrid hopes that she might have left me some money, which I was in desperate need of at the time. I suppose all the young feel like this when their grandparents die. They do not miss them. Anyway, I did not benefit by one halfpenny from poor Granny's death.

Saturday, 30th April

Vicar** wonders why the Royal Family no longer stay at the House. I say it is surely because neither the Queen nor David was minded to

---

* Despite its large Conservative majority, the House of Lords had recently shown some liberal opposition to authoritarian legislation introduced by the Thatcher Government.

† J.L.-M's step-granddaughter Chloë Luke (b. 1959); eldest dau. of Hon. Clarissa Chaplin (b. 1934; only child of A.L.-M. by 1st marriage to 3rd Viscount Chaplin; m. 1957 Michael Luke).

‡ David Mlinaric, interior decorator (b. 1939).

§ Mary Emma Nesbitt (1853–1936); m. 1877 James Henry Lees-Milne (1847–1908).

¶ Tudor house and hunting estate near Bewdley, Worcestershire bought by J.L.-M's grandfather in 1904 and lived in by his widowed grandmother until the 1920s.

** Revd Thomas Gibson (b. 1923), Vicar of Badminton, 1974–93.

continue the tradition after old Master died. He thinks it is because the police protecting the Queen would bring their sniffer dogs, which might detect the drugs the young people take.

We lunched yesterday with the Loewensteins. Rupert frightfully pleased that his friend Bertie* has been made Grand Master of the Sovereign Order of Malta, the first time an Englishman has been elected since the thirteenth century. Says that he may not come to England, because as a sovereign it would be beneath his dignity to do so and not be invited to stay at Buckingham Palace.† I asked how many acres he owned. Josephine thought about two-and-a-half, next to the little house beside the Piranesi church in Rome.

Margaret Anne [Stuart], staying at the House, came today for a cup of tea. She told us that Rupert had fallen through the floor of a marquee where they were dancing last night, smashing a foot. He will be in plaster for months. Soon the telephone rang and Mick Jagger‡ asked if he might come round with girlfriend. I tried to escape upstairs, but was caught and made to return. They only stayed five minutes. Mick looking yellow and wizened, wearing a crumpled old tweed jacket over jeans, smelling of stale tobacco. We told him we had seen him on telly last night, when they showed an old pro-gramme of 1967§ in which he appeared with William Rees-Mogg,¶ a Catholic priest, an Anglican bishop and a stuffy politician. He groaned to remember this; but he came over as self-possessed, if foolish in his views, and very good-looking and attractive. Purpose of visit was to ask A. to ring up Christopher Selmes**

---

* His Most Eminent Highness Frà Andrew Willoughby Ninian Bertie (b. 1929); er s. of Lt.-Cdr J. W. Bertie, 3rd s. of 7th Earl of Abingdon and Lady Jean Crichton-Stuart, dau. of 4th Marquess of Bute; Prince and Grand Master of Sovereign Order of Malta from 1988.

† For more on the Order, see entry for 21 May 1988.

‡ Michael Philip ('Mick') Jagger (b. 1943; Kt 2003); singer and songwriter, co-founder of Rolling Stones, 1962; m. (2nd) 1990 Jerry Hall (b. 1956), his girlfriend of eleven years by whom he already had two children; Rupert Loewenstein was his manager.

§ The broadcast followed a famous *Times* leader by William Rees-Mogg published on 1 July 1967, entitled 'Who Breaks a Butterfly upon a Wheel?' and criticising a prison sen-tence passed on Jagger (later quashed on appeal) for possessing four amphetamine tablets.

¶ William Rees-Mogg (b. 1928); editor of *The Times*, 1967–81; chairman of Sidgwick & Jackson, 1985–88; cr. life peer as Baron Rees-Mogg, 1988.

** City entrepreneur (1946–88), who in 1975, aged twenty-eight, had been accused of fraudulent practices in a Department of Trade report.

at Lyegrove,* which he wants to view for a possible purchase.

Monday, 2nd May

Today, Bank Holiday, I motored to Chatsworth by the motorway, 185
miles; no problems because no lorries. Debo and Andrew alone.
Andrew tells me that his mother,† still alive, was given a photograph
of the Munshi‡ by Queen Victoria. I settle down to four days of work
at the Bachelor's papers in the old housekeeper's room.

Tuesday, 3rd May

Brian Masters§ arrives to stay, after lecturing at Middlesbrough. He
enjoys this and does it well, earning £100 per lecture, plus expenses.
Says the book he wants to be remembered by is his first, a biography
of Marie Corelli,¶ which sold few copies.

   In the evening, Debo takes me on a round of places connected with
the Bachelor – his grave in Edensor churchyard, close to Debo's three
little dead babies; Carlton Lees, remote farmhouse with cottages;
Monsal Dale; The Rookery, where he kept Eliza Warwick and which
my great-uncle Fred Lees rented for a time; the Russian cottage. We
also visited a Miss McLauchlan, nonagenarian daughter of former
Chief Keeper. She recently delighted Debo by telling her that her
father had lived in 'one of the Bachelor's birdcages', meaning love
nests for mistresses. Debo wanted her to repeat this for my benefit.

---

* House near Badminton formerly owned by J.L.-M's friend Diana, Countess of
Westmorland (d. 1983), which Selmes 'bought and sold at enormous profit to himself'
(17 September 1988).
† Lady Mary Gascoyne-Cecil (1895–1988), dau. of 4th Marquess of Salisbury; m. 1917
10th Duke of Devonshire (1895–1950).
‡ Designation conferred by Queen Victoria in 1889 on her Indian servant Abdul Karim,
whom she promoted to be her 'Indian Secretary' in 1894. He was adored by the Queen
but detested by her courtiers and her successor Edward VII, who sent him back to his
native Agra, where he died in 1909.
§ Writer (b. 1939) of prolific and varied output, who had achieved celebrity in 1985 with
his study of the mass murderer Denis Nilsen. He was then writing books about the zoo
owner John Aspinall, the princely family of Udaipur, the novelist E. F. Benson, and a disturbed adolescent named Gary.
¶ Best-selling novelist (1855–1924), specialising in 'occult romances'.

The dignified and rather deaf old lady was extremely evasive, though gave herself away by saying, 'You want me to talk of scandal to put it in a book.' D. and I got the giggles, in which the dear old thing joined heartily, though we could not make out whether she quite understood what it was about. I fancy she was rather shocked that Debo should raise such an embarrassing matter in front of a strange man.

Thursday, 5th May

The Ds away, I am quite alone at Chatsworth all day. Strange wandering in this immense empty house, sitting by myself in the vast dining room. But Henry the butler always about, ministering, and chatting between the courses.

Friday, 6th May

I left Chatsworth after smart luncheon party which included American Ambassadress, glamorous with liquid eyes and affable. 'I have enjoyed meeting you.' Does one believe it? Reached Badminton at six, first day of Horse Trials. Followed by Simon Blow, come to stay for two nights. We enjoyed having him, but now find that visitors tire us inordinately. Simon has got into much hot water over his book on the Tennants. The Glenconners are furious, and Emma's husband Toby* won't have the book in his house. He hasn't read it, of course. I agreed with Simon that Elizabeth Glenconner† probably put the others against. She is very disapproving and prim.

While we were having dinner, Margaret Anne, that harbinger of bad news, telephoned to announce that Billy Whitaker had died. She was staying with him last weekend, and when he got suddenly worse, tactfully left.

Saturday, 7th May

I lunched with the Hollands‡ at Sheepbridge Barn. Large party. Peter Coats was there, so I went up to him to say how sorry I was about

---

* Hon. Tobias Tennant, Oxford rowing blue and farmer (b. 1941); yr s. of 2nd Baron Glenconner; m. 1963 Lady Emma Cavendish, er dau. of 11th Duke of Devonshire.
† Elizabeth Powell; m. 1935 (as his 2nd wife) 2nd Baron Glenconner (he d. 1983).
‡ Sir Guy Holland, 3rd Bt (1918–1997); farmer and art dealer; m. 1945 Joan Street.

Billy. He had not heard the news, having been away from home, and was very upset. He said, 'How odd I should hear this from you, seeing we were both at school with Billy seventy years ago.' I sat on Joanie Holland's left, she having Lord Faringdon* on her right. We talked about Byron, about Venice, about art, in that absurd, earnest way which women love, as they keep a weather-eye on the parlour maid to make sure she serves the guests from the right, not the left.

Monday, 9th May

This morning Roy Strong[†] came to see me in Bath with BBC Radio Three to talk about the National Trust for a series to be called 'Pillars of Society'. Don't know that I was any good. Roy is charming, gentle and modest. Brought four copies of my diaries to sign; said my *Tudor Renaissance* [1951] first inspired his interest in Tudor art. I am bewildered at times when clever people tell me what I have done for the cause. He asked me if I thought that I had had insufficient recognition. Of course I deprecated that notion. I asked if he was relieved to be free of the V&A. He replied that he was, and that I was the first person to ask him such a question. It had been a nightmare constantly having to haggle with the Treasury over money, and having nearly every scheme and proposition thwarted for lack of funds.

Tuesday, 10th May

Selina [Hastings] stayed last night with us, on the way to see Lady Sibell Rowley[‡] in her Evelyn Waugh[§] quest. She said that Auberon Waugh[¶] held all the cards and played one biographer off against another. She thinks he hated his father and will do anything to

---

* Charles Henderson, 3rd Baron Faringdon (b. 1934), of Buscot Park, Oxfordshire and Barnsley Park, Gloucestershire; m. 1959 Sarah Eskdale.

[†] Sir Roy Strong (b. 1935; Kt 1982); Director, Victoria & Albert Museum, 1974–87; writer and broadcaster.

[‡] Lady Sibell Lygon (b. 1907), 2nd dau. of 7th Earl Beauchamp (on whose family Waugh based the Flytes in *Brideshead Revisited*); m. 1939 Richard Rowley (he d. 1952).

[§] Novelist (1903–66), whose biography (published 1994) was being written by Selina Hastings.

[¶] Evelyn Waugh's eldest son, the leading satirical journalist of his time (1939–2001); m. 1961 Lady Teresa Onslow, o. dau. of 6th Earl of Onslow.

discredit him. Selina praised my novel,* which she returned. Said I must not give it up. I said that since it had been turned down by at least half a dozen publishers I didn't see how I could send it to another. S. said that Anthony Blond† was starting up again as a publisher. Would I mind if she told him how much she liked it and urged him to take it? Would I?

Folly and I went this evening to Lower Wood to listen for nightingales. Not a soul in sight. I heard what I think may have been one of these elusive birds; but there was no final chug-chug-chug, and it may have been a blackbird. There is blinding melancholy in these deathly quiet late spring evenings, the sun sinking, nature deep green and gold.

Wednesday, 11th May

This evening Folly and I drove down to Swangrove. No nightingales ever heard up here. Little life; no more rabbits; few birds this beautiful evening. Lakes of bluebells, and primroses still. At the *rond-point* a covey of cowslips. I picked one, trying to catch that nostalgic gentle scent; but I couldn't. Sense of smell almost gone since my cancer treatment.

Monday, 16th May

The solicitor telephoned saying he could get no answer from the bitch's solicitor in reply to our letter offering her £1,000 to settle the case which is due to be heard next week. Thinks she is playing us like a fish, keeping us guessing until the last minute. I asked whether this would not annoy the judge, who might find a whole day of his time wasted if she accepted our offer at final moment. He did not seem to think so. 'You can do nothing,' he said. When I reported this to A. in the evening, she said we should send an ultimatum to the bitch's solicitor saying that unless she accepts our offer within forty-eight hours, the case is on. A. is far brighter than I am.

---

* The novel described in the Preface to this volume, finally published in 1990 as *The Fool of Love*.

† Flamboyant, bisexual Old Etonian publisher (b. 1928), who had admired the novel some years earlier (see *Beneath a Waning Moon*, 5 December 1985); formerly partner (with J.L.-M.'s friend Desmond Briggs) of Blond & Briggs, latterly of Muller, Blond & White.

Wednesday, 18th May

To London for the night. Left my gold pencil at Bentley's in New Bond Street to be mended, Freda Berkeley having recommended a young craftsman there, one Mark Evans, for the job. I was to have gone to a film with M., but he left a message at Brooks's to say he was suffering from a kidney stone and going in to hospital. I went to Marylebone Library to find out something about the Bachelor's mistress Eliza Warwick, but learnt nothing except that she did not keep the house in Dorset Square which he gave her after their break in 1837. Stayed night at Eardley's. Mattei* there, and a young man of great handsomeness from Parkin Gallery called Cassian de Vere Cole, putatively grandson of the famous Edwardian hoaxer but in reality of Augustus John by the infamous Mavis who shot Lord Vivian.† Clever, enthusiastic boy who causes havoc among the girls. E. not very well, and his flat getting rather squalid. He will be eighty-six in November.

Thursday, 19th May

By train to Brighton. Took taxi from station to Kemp Town. Looked carefully at 1 Lewes Crescent, double house which the Bachelor owned for many years. Exterior exactly as it was in his time. Saw old face glued to window beside front door, so I knocked. Cautiously an old lady opened the door. I said I was an octogenarian and fairly respectable. 'Same here,' said she. Sweet old thing, sort of superior landlady who has lived in this house for more than forty years. She let me in. So I saw the fine twisting staircase under glass dome (the dome itself destroyed by last October's gales when whole chimney-stack of neighbouring house fell through), and dining room with end alcoves. Also three plaster figures of, I think, vestal virgins, which she said had belonged to the Bachelor. Most satisfactory. Then I walked back to

---

* Mattei Radev (b. 1927); Bulgarian-born picture framer and gilder; friend of Eardley Knollys.
† Horace de Vere Cole (1881–1936); serial practical joker, who once successfully impersonated Ramsay Macdonald at a Labour Party meeting; m. 1931 Mavis Wright, also mistress of Augustus John (probably the true father of her son Tristan de Vere Cole), who was sentenced to six months' imprisonment in 1954 for maliciously wounding her then lover Anthony, 5th Baron Vivian (1906–1991; brother of Hon. Daphne Fielding, mother of Caroline, Duchess of Beaufort).

Brighton and continued to Brunswick Terrace, where I looked quickly at Eliza's house there. He kept his mistress at a distance. Then to local library where I drew a complete blank as to movements of Eliza after 1837. A mystery woman.

Saturday, 21st May

We dined with Sally Westminster.[*] She had staying Lady Cholmondeley,[†] suffering from *extinction de voix*, and Johnnie Faucigny-Lucinge[‡] who is in his mid eighties. They are on a Dendrologists' tour of Gloucestershire, worn out by their packed programme. Johnnie is a charming man, another Charles de Noailles,[§] the most civilised specimen of male humanity, which seems only attained by the French, and very few of them at that. He reminded me of a lovely walk we did from Roquebrune to Gorbio, talking the whole time. I had quite forgotten this, though I walked with so many friends on that beautiful footpath into the mountains from that horrid coast. Tonight he talked about the Knights of Malta, of which he is one – and an important one, having been the Order's ambassador to Brazil and Rome. He said that to be elected Master a candidate must serve seven years' apprenticeship and observe vows of chastity and poverty. Yet the poverty is mitigated by the comparative luxury provided by the Order, which is not poor. The Order owns no property and works of art; if these are bequeathed – which I imagine must be often, for a high percentage of members seem to be ancient queer bachelors – then they are sold for general funds. The obligatory number of quarterings varies according to the country, Austria being the most strict, as one might expect. Some members are elected on grounds of their extreme virtue, regardless of birth – though not many.

Sally very gentle and sweet. She spoke of her early life. When they were children, she and her sisters lived in a house which backed on to a railway line at Barnes. They got used to the noise of trains passing under their bedroom windows. But they suffered from rickets as a

---

[*] Sally Perry (1911–91); widow of Gerald Grosvenor, 4th Duke of Westminster.
[†] Lavinia Leslie; m. 1937 Earl of Rocksavage, later 6th Marquess of Cholmondeley.
[‡] Prince Jean-Louis de Faucigny-Lucinge (1904–92).
[§] Charles, Vicomte de Noailles (1891–1981); patron of arts, and arbiter of taste and manners; m. 1923 Marie-Laure Bischoffsheim (1902–70).

result of under-nourishment – not that they were poor, she added quickly, but they were neglected by their mother. This, she told us, is the cause of the extreme thinness of her legs.

Sunday, 22nd May

We had a luncheon party – the Guy Hollands, and Rory Young and wife.* We much liked the Youngs. Both craftsmen – she expert marbler and restorer of furniture, he a specialist in building construction, plasterer according to old-established fashion, no cement used by him. I took them into the church here. He was very informative about the marble used for the monuments, nearly all from Italy. The large Rysbrack sarcophagus must weigh a ton. How did they get it here? By sea from Leghorn to Bristol, then by wagon to Badminton? He knew at a glance how thick was the veneer of marble, how it was dowelled, how and where joined. Splendid young man. How I admire and feel small beside people, especially dedicated young people, who work with their hands and have knowledge, love and taste for their crafts.

Tuesday, 24th May

Today two BBC men came down and took me to lunch at the Lansdown Grove Hotel, to vet me for a film about architectural conservation and the National Trust. Nice they were. One Julian Henriques, dusky, gold earring, smiling, delightful. He is the producer. The other Patrick Wright, who will compère. I think I was all right, but I find these interviews a strain nowadays, keeping my end up, trying not to be slow and muddle-headed, trying to remember. They left at 2.45 and I hurried home to meet Simon Verity in the church at Badminton. He had gone, but to my inexpressible joy the 'Angels', as the Vicar will call them – Justice and Prudence, in fact – are up where they belong on the Grinling Gibbons[†] monument.[‡] They look splendid, and have transformed the monument, which is

---

* Rory Young (b. 1954); m. 1987 (diss. 1992) Jane Rickards.

† Wood carver (1648–1721).

‡ Since David Somerset's succession to the dukedom in 1984, J.L.-M. had been urging him to restore these figures, removed for some reason by his predecessor, to the 1st Duke's monument (see *Holy Dread*, 27 November 1984, and *Beneath a Waning Moon*, 2 June 1985).

more noble, less stiff, pointful. I always said to A. that I hoped to live to see them put back. Now I have.

Thursday, 26th May

David and Caroline dine with us alone. A. always provides a delicious dinner for these two, whom she dearly loves, as do I. After dinner I mentioned the reinstatement of the 'Angels'. They showed indifference, neither having even been to see them yet in their restored glory. C. said to me rather sharply, 'You were one of those who made such a fuss over their removal.' I have to be careful.

Friday, 27th May

On my return from Bath, I persuaded A. to come and look at Jus and Pru in the church. She was delighted and vastly impressed. We found the two Veritys working at them, Simon before our eyes assembling Jus's gold-tipped scales and sword. He disputed Pru's title; indeed, why should Prudence be gazing at herself in a glass, with a snake twisted around one arm? I can't get over the splendour of this monument. Simon said that surely there was no other parish church in England with a finer display of monuments. Both Veritys in working clothes, he wearing thick once-white sweater grey with dust, his hair covered with plaster. A splendid pair.

Then Folly and I walked in Vicarage Fields round the big house. Overjoyed to hear cuckoo singing its head off. On and on it went. I wept with pleasure. A marvellous, clear, brilliant evening light on the north front, all the pilasters, cornices and sharp angles shadowed by the slanting sun.

Sunday, 29th May

We lunched with the Griggs* at Tormarton. They are obliged to sell the house because Joanie [Altrincham] foolishly left it jointly to her

---

* John Grigg (1924–2001); writer, official biographer of Lloyd George; succeeded father as 2nd Baron Altrincham 1955, but disclaimed peerage, 1963; m. 1958 Patricia Campbell. His mother (Hon. Joan Dickson-Poynder; m. Sir Edward Grigg, cr. Baron Altrincham, 1945), a friend and neighbour of the L.-Ms at Tormarton House, had died the previous year (*Beneath a Waning Moon*, 14 August 1987).

two sons, and the other insists on selling. John is sentimental about the place and would like to buy or build a smaller house in the village. Iris Murdoch and John Bayley* lunching. I sat next to her. Very amiable she was, quiet, diffident and dowdy. He looks like a large tadpole turning into a frog, ugly and bald but jolly. Very forward in manner and anxious to please. They told me that nice things are said of me in Bevis Hillier's[†] first volume of John Betjeman's[‡] biography. She talked to me about the young's method of writing on computers, which she thinks must have an adverse affect on their style, as they no longer correct their own syntax but leave it to the machine. She writes all her books in longhand, then has them typed up in the old-fashioned way. Patsy's charming brother and wife staying from Northern Ireland. They railed against the Anglo-Irish Agreement,[§] saying it was infuriating that a foreign state should have a say in the government of their country. They live two miles from Clandeboye. I told him that Basil Dufferin[¶] had been my friend from private school days; that I knew Sheridan but little, but so much liked what I did know of him.

Monday, 30th May

Opened the *Daily Telegraph* at breakfast, and lo, an obituary of Sheridan Dufferin. This clouded my day. He was only forty-nine — and I was older than his father. Basil and I shared a dormitory with

---

* Dame Iris Murdoch (1919–99), Oxford philosophy don and novelist; m. 1956 John Bayley (b. 1925), Professor of English at Oxford.

† Writer, journalist and critic (b. 1940); Antiques Correspondent of *The Times*, 1970–84; the first volume of his life of Betjeman was about to be published by John Murray.

‡ Sir John Betjeman (1906–84); poet, broadcaster and writer on architecture; Poet Laureate, 1972–84.

§ Agreement signed by Margaret Thatcher and Irish premier Garret FitzGerald in November 1985, under which the Irish Government agreed that Northern Ireland should remain part of the United Kingdom so long as her people wished it, and the British Government agreed to allow the Irish Government a consultative role in the formulation of policy with regard to the Province.

¶ Basil Blackwood, 4th Marquess of Dufferin and Ava; politician and soldier, killed on active service in Burma, 1945; a contemporary of J.L.-M. at Lockers Park, Eton and Oxford. His son Sheridan, 5th and last Marquess (1938–88; m. 1964 Belinda 'Lindy' Guinness), lived at Clandeboye, Co. Down, which still flourishes under his widow.

Tom Mitford* in our last year at Lockers Park. Both Tom and Basil long gone – and now Basil's son. This is the end of the Dufferins – and of Clandeboye too, I suppose. Sheridan was a gentle, sweet-natured, art-loving man, attractive without being good-looking. I wish I had known him better. The *Daily Mail* has the headline 'Marquess dies of Aids'. The brutes.

Tuesday, 31st May

To London – travelling first class, though train empty. Joined A. at Leighton House [Kensington] for launching of last volume of Martin Gilbert's[†] Churchill biography, which I have no intention of reading. Wanted to see Leighton House. A beastly building if you except the Arab room downstairs with pool in middle. Lord Leighton[‡] was a hideously bad painter. Only his sketches are tolerable. Why on earth was he made a peer? The large room upstairs well suited to the rout we attended. By one o'clock it was crowded with stuffy, scruffy, dowdy people. John Grigg told me he was reviewing the volume, which was not good – a eulogy throughout, Gilbert allowing himself no comments or criticism. The Hayters[§] from Moscow talked of Nancy M.,[¶] saying that no one who had not met her could describe her brilliance and fun. We ate excellent snacks, but all the delicacies, smoked salmon, etc., wrapped in triple-decker sandwiches, whose contents spilt either on one's clothes or the floor.

I left A. and went to Queen's Gallery at Buckingham Palace. A marvellous exhibition of royal treasures, some of the finest furniture imaginable, English and French. What we owe to Frederick Prince of Wales, George III, and above all George IV. There was a Lawrence[**]

---

* Hon. Thomas Mitford (1909–45); only brother of Mitford sisters, whom J.L.-M. loved at Eton.

[†] Historian (b. 1936; kt 1995). The final volume of his official biography of Sir Winston Churchill, *Never Despair*, quoted J.L.-M's account of meeting the great man in the South of France in September 1957 (later included in *A Mingled Measure*).

[‡] Frederic Leighton; artist (1830–96); President of Royal Academy, 1878–96; elevated to the peerage the day before his death, the first artist to be so honoured.

[§] Sir William Hayter (1906–95); HM Ambassador to USSR, 1953–6; Warden of New College, Oxford, 1958–76; m. 1938 Iris Grey.

[¶] Hon. Nancy Mitford (1904–73), eldest of Mitford sisters, who lived in France after 1945; novelist and historian; m. 1933 Peter Rodd.

[**] Sir Thomas Lawrence (1769–1830); English artist.

of the Bachelor, rather skied so that I could not with my weak eyes see it in detail. Wearing fur cloak with brilliant crimson neckcloth.

Felt too exhausted to see Goya exhibition at National Gallery, so returned to Brooks's and lay on my bed for three hours before dinner. George Dix* and M. dined with me. They got on quite well, despite M's habit of remaining mum for the first half of the meal. George told his familiar story of how he and his mother met Hitler in Bavaria in 1935. M. intrigued, but left as soon as we had finished dining to work on his book. George said, what a clever man, and how interesting when he spoke.

Wednesday, 1st June

To Knole [Kent] with Julian Henriques and Patrick Wright. A sunny day but Arctic cold. Was distressed on entering park to see appalling tree devastation.† Camera crew arrived in van. P. Wright and I were made to walk from the screens passage into the Stone Court and walk down the colonnade, talking. This we did some four times, first attempts interrupted by aeroplanes flying over, etc. It is difficult to be natural on the fourth repetition. Then for two hours we continued our talk sitting on a bench in the park with our backs to the wicket entrance. The cold was intense, but because we had worn no great coats in the sheltered Stone Court, we could not wear them in the park. Can't remember much about what said, but it was all rather drivellish – I recalling my first visits to Knole in the mid 1930s as Eddy's‡ guest, and later interviews with his father Lord Sackville.§ Before we left, Lionel Sackville¶ called us into his part of the house to have a glance at Graham Sutherland's** portrait of Eddy hanging there.

---

* Friend of J.L.-M. since 1945, at which time he was a US naval officer.
† Following the great gale of October 1987.
‡ Hon. Edward Sackville-West (1901–65), writer and music critic; s. father as 5th Baron Sackville, 1962.
§ Major-General Sir Charles Sackville-West (1870–1962); s. brother as 4th Baron Sackville, 1928.
¶ Lionel Sackville (1913–2004); s. cousin as 6th Baron Sackville, 1965; m. 1st Jacobine Hichens, 2nd Arlie de Guingand, 3rd Jean Imbert-Terry.
** Artist (1903–80).

Wednesday, 8th June

I lunched in London with N.T. publicity man Warren Davis[*] to meet
Patrick Garland,[†] who told me that Paul Eddington,[‡] the actor in *Yes,
Minister*, proposed to do a one-man show based on my diaries. P.E.
regards the project as a sort of rest cure, his doctor having warned him
against overstraining his heart. P.G. will write the script and suggests
a trial at Aldeburgh, Bath or some N.T. country house. He thinks it
may take off and get to the West End. That would certainly be very
gratifying for me.

I knew I would like Patrick Garland because I remember how wonderfully he looked after John Betjeman during the Laureate's later
broadcasts. Indeed he is surprisingly like a member of John's old circle,
though not yet fifty. Full of witticisms and anecdotes at everyone's
expense. He said that his father knew John when they were children,
both P.G's grandmother and John's mother having come from
Australia, which I never knew. P.G's father remembers how worried
John's mother was when John got into what she regarded as a fast and
immoral set at Oxford. But Garland Senior reassured her that the
Warden of Wadham was protecting him. This of course was Maurice
Bowra.[§] Little did she know. Garland Senior remembers how John as
a small boy at preparatory school noticed and criticised buildings. John
taught him to look upwards when walking the streets. The two boys
were sent by their respective parents to Paris and told to visit a brothel.
John told P.G. that he hated the experience, while Garland *père*
enjoyed himself. P.G. did not know Bevis Hillier's volume about to
come out. Hillier had not been in touch with him.

P.G. said Paul Eddington is a very serious actor who makes a prodigious effort to identify himself with the characters he interprets on
stage. P.E. is going to Australia this autumn, but might be ready next
spring or summer for this task. All rather exciting. It staggers me how

---

[*] On staff of N.T., 1967–2002 (b. 1937); cousin of J.L.-M's late friend the architectural
historian Terence Davis (1924–83), author of *The Gothick Taste*. The idea of a one-man
show based on J.L.-M's diaries arose out of a suggestion by Davis that he give a public
reading from them at an N.T. house; J.L.-M. was unwilling, but suggested that an actor
be found to do the reading.

[†] Writer, broadcaster and theatre director (b. 1935).

[‡] Actor (1927–95), famous for his portrayal of the vacuous politician James Hacker in the
immensely popular 1980s television series *Yes, Minister* and *Yes, Prime Minister*.

[§] Sir Maurice Bowra (1898–1971); Warden of Wadham College, Oxford, 1938–70.

intellectual folk believe my embarrassing and mediocre diaries to have substance. P.G. spoke of them almost with reverence.

Thursday, 9th June

I listen to myself on Radio Three. I was on for about two minutes – whereas I remember having an interesting conversation with Roy Strong of about three-quarters of an hour. I shall not agree to these broadcasts in future because it is a waste of time, and disjointed snippets taken at random do nothing to enhance one's reputation.

Friday, 10th June

We dined with Caroline tonight, who said she needed help with entertaining Grace Dudley* in David's absence. On arrival we found some twenty people, including children and spouses. I sat next to Lady Christopher Thynne,† a tough and temperamental woman whom I don't like. Don't much care for her husband either, with his aggressive drivel. What a lot they all are, redolent of the worst aspects of the Edwardian age. A crowd of fatuous, arrogant drones, waited on by a regiment of servants. It is so archaic as to be barely true. I only cared for Caroline tonight, who has the sweetness of a wild deer.

Saturday, 11th June

I fetched Misha‡ from Chippenham station to stay the night. We had the Humphrey Stones§ and Mary Keen¶ to luncheon. No greater constrast to last night's dinner party could be conjured up. Mary such a dear and beautiful woman – M. adored her sparkling grey-blue eyes, grey hair, simplicity, naturalness and knowledge. Humphrey and Solveig are perfection, dedicated to arts and crafts, the quiet life, the

---

* Grace Kolin (born Dubrovnik, Yugoslavia); m. 1st Prince Stanislas Radziwill, 2nd 1961 (as his 3rd wife) 3rd Earl of Dudley (1894–1969).
† Antonia Palmer; m. 1968 Lord Christopher Thynne (b. 1934), brother of Duchess of Beaufort.
‡ Michael Bloch.
§ Humphrey Stone (b. 1942); typographical designer; m. 1968 Solveig Atcheson.
¶ Lady Mary Curzon (b. 1940), dau. of 6th Earl Howe; garden writer; m. 1962 Charles Keen (b. 1936), director of Barclay's Bank.

country. It was Humphrey's birthday and A. produced a chocolate cake with little candles which when you blow them out relight themselves and set fire to the sideboard. I gave him a copy of *Venetian Evenings*, by which he seemed pleased. M. is so strange. Sits speechless at meals until roused. Worked at proofs all afternoon after guests gone, apart from joining me on a short walk with Folly in Vicarage Fields. 'Why come to the country?' asks A. No domestic graces. Yet I am devoted.

Sunday, 12th June

The Veritys lunched, both adorable. She like a Burne-Jones drawing, he wearing a purple shirt, navy blue jersey, shabby corduroys. Delightful as ever, another proper working-with-hands man. Is deeply involved in making grottoes, which are now the rage, but a waste of time as they are necessarily ephemeral. Glorious day, sitting on the terrace. At 4.45 A. takes M. to the station, M. dawdling and A. getting very bossy and impatient. Poor M., his mind filled with his Duke of Windsor book. At 5 I set out for Chatsworth, getting there at 9.30. I find these long journeys a strain, but to cease to make them would be to surrender my independence.

Monday, 20th June

I spent the inside of a week at Chatsworth, working every day from early morning until 5.30. The kindness, the comfort and luxury, the help from all concerned overwhelming. By the time I left I felt I had got through the Chatsworth papers, in so far as I was going to – for there are limits, and time is running out for me.

Andrew went off almost every day on some dutiful excursion, to open the wing of a university or be filmed for Dutch television. The Devonshires had been warned by the police that burglars planned to raid Chatsworth, their main objectives the gold pilgrim bottles and the jewel-encrusted bird; so such items hidden away. Philip Jebb* came for one night. He is building a restaurant by the stables and had a meeting with the English Heritage man and Derbyshire planning man, both regarded with much dislike by the Ds. One evening we

* Architect (1927–95).

motored onto the moor to hear larks. Debo saw them and both Ds heard them; I neither saw nor heard, though straining eyes and ears. Nevertheless I am pleased that larks still exist on these remote wilds.

In one of the safes, I was fascinated to see a bound book entitled 'Georgiana Duchess of Devonshire's Letters to George IV', for I knew that George V had commanded Regy Esher* to burn these, one day when that illiterate monarch was visiting Esher in the Round Tower. Esher records the incident in his diary without further comment. On handling the said volume, I saw a note that Andrew had bought it in the 1950s from Oliver Esher.† So Regy evidently disobeyed his sovereign and went off with the letters. A good thing too. I was also shown an enormous uncut emerald the size of a billiard ball which was presented to the Bachelor by Dom Pedro of Brazil.‡

Wednesday, 22nd June

Gary Conklin,§ American who came with daughter to film me in Bath a year ago, telephoned from Eton at 2 p.m. to ask if they might come forthwith to film again and ask some more questions. I had just finished reading Lady Granville's letters, so said they might. They kept me until six, asking me to elaborate on some tales I told them last year – but I wonder how they will get over the fact that I was presumably wearing different clothes today, and must look older.¶ This film seems to be along the same lines as Henriques' – social and literary life before, during and after the last war. A mania for this period. Conklin had just come from interviewing Leslie Rowse** and Peter

---

* Reginald Brett, 2nd Viscount Esher (1852–1930), the *éminence grise* whose biography by J.L.-M., *The Enigmatic Edwardian*, had been published by Sidgwick & Jackson in 1986.
† Oliver Brett, 3rd Viscount Esher (1881–1963), who as Chairman of the Country Houses (later Historic Buildings) Committee had been J.L.-M's boss at the National Trust.
‡ Eldest son (1798–1834) of King John VI of Portugal; supported Brazilian independence and reigned as Emperor Pedro I of Brazil from 1822; succeeded to Portuguese throne in 1826 but abdicated in favour of his daughter.
§ American film-maker based in Pasadena, California (b. 1932). His *A Question of Class: English Literary Life between 1918 and 1945* was released in 1992.
¶ J.L.-M. was indeed changed from a year earlier (as can be seen from clips of Conklin's film on the James Lees-Milne website – www.jamesleesmilne.com).
** A. L. Rowse (1903–97); historian and Fellow of All Souls.

Quennell,* but was turned away from Eton when he arrived there
without warning.

Friday, 24th June

To London for the day. Trains both there and back late owing to
engine failure. Worked in London Library. Eardley lunched with me
at Brooks's, wearing a pretty summer blue suit and looking well and
extraordinarily young. Then to Onslow Square to talk to Virginia
Surtees† about Hart and Harriet Granville whose letters she is
editing.‡ Lovely flat full of Pre-Raphaelite paintings. Admired a pretty
parkscape which she said was of Mainsforth, seat of her Surtees ancestors. We discussed Siward Surtees who was a cousin at Redworth. She
knew all about Joanie and Isabel. Told me that when my cousin
Muriel divorced Siward it caused a scandal, she having hired detec-
tives to trace him to a brothel.§ Muriel was known as the Ayrshire
heiress, yet had little money that I knew of. Virginia splendid for her
age; tall and slim, her minute waist girdled with a wide black belt of
patent leather; only slightly affected; very sympathetic and easy to talk
to. We went together to the Royal Society of Literature for Nigel
Nicolson's¶ lecture on 'Diarists, Letter Writers and Telephonists'.
Excellent it was too. Roy Jenkins** in the chair. Nigel speaks as he
writes, in impeccable prose. Only he lisps a bit owing to false teeth. I

---

* Sir Peter Quennell (1905–94); writer, editor and journalist.
† Virginia Bell (b. 1917); adopted mother's name of Surtees; writer on the Pre-
Raphaelites and other subjects.
† Virginia Surtees (ed.), *A Second Self, The Letters of Harriet Granville 1810–1845*, Michael
Russell, 1990.
§ Muriel Thomson, a first cousin of J.L.-M's mother, m. 1898 (diss. 1928) Major Henry
Siward Surtees of Redworth, Co. Durham. J.L.-M. was well acquainted with their two
daughters: he had an adolescent sexual encounter (described in *Another Self*) with the elder,
Joan (1899–1939); and he was still in touch with the younger, Isabel (b. 1906; m. 1931 Sir
Joseph Napier, 4th Bt [d. 1986]) – see entries for 14 January 1992 and 20 October 1992.
¶ Soldier, politician and writer (b. 1917), yr son of Harold Nicolson and Vita Sackville-
West, who had donated Sissinghurst Castle, Kent, to N.T. in 1968, and invited J.L.-M.
to write his father's biography in 1976. He had edited the letters of his mother's some-
time love Virginia Woolf in six volumes.
** Roy Harris Jenkins (1920–2003); Labour politician and cabinet minister; President of
European Commission, 1977–81; Leader of Social Democrat Party, 1981–83; cr. life peer
as Baron Jenkins of Hillhead, 1987; m. 1945 Jennifer Morris (b. 1921; DBE 1985;
Chairman of N.T., 1986–90).

sat in front row with Elizabeth Longford.* She whispered to me, 'Do you keep a diary?' 'Sometimes,' I replied. I asked her if she came to this house in the Hamiltons' day. 'Duke of ?' she asked. 'No, General,' I replied.†

M's Duke of Windsor book‡ is being serialised in the *Daily Mail*. The newspaper has typically confined itself to publishing some sensational letters of the Duke which only come at the end of the book, which is otherwise sober and serious. Ali Forbes,§ whom I ran into in St James's Square, told me that he knew for a fact that the Windsors had not wanted these letters published. But he is wrong, for M. has shown me a copy of the Duchess's letter to Maître Blum¶ authorising her to publish them. Ali was extremely offensive, referring to 'Bloch whom you love', and saying that it had been 'a good wheeze' of me and Alvilde to get married.

Saturday, 2nd July

On Thursday Tony Mitchell** motored me to Kedleston [Derbyshire] to join the N.T. Arts Panel. A delicious day. Lovely to be with the Trust chaps, all so charming and clever. A most scholarly report had been prepared by Professor Leslie Harris of Derby, who knows everything about Kedleston; gives history of every room's redecoration, when and how. It bears out my theory that even the greatest country houses, built all of a piece at one period of history, can never be kept as first decorated. Harris shows that Kedleston was repainted internally

---

* Elizabeth Harman (1906–2002); writer; m. 1931 Hon. Frank Pakenham (later 7th Earl of Longford); romantic friend of J.L.-M. at Oxford (*c.* 1930), where she was known as 'the aesthetes' moll'.

† 1 Hyde Park Gardens, which then housed the Royal Society of Literature, had formerly been the residence of General Sir Ian Hamilton (1853–1947), married to J.L.-M's 'Great-Aunt Jean' (*née* Muir, 1861–1941).

‡ *The Secret File of the Duke of Windsor* (Bantam Press).

§ Alastair Forbes (b. 1918); American-born and English-educated journalist resident in Switzerland, famous for his social knowledge and his long and eccentric book reviews.

¶ Maître Suzanne Blum (1898–1994), the fiercely devoted Paris lawyer of the Duke and Duchess of Windsor from the late 1940s until their deaths, subsequently their principal executor, for whom Michael Bloch had been working since 1979; m. (2nd) 1967 General Georges Spillmann (d. 1980).

** Anthony Mitchell (b. 1931); N.T. Historic Buildings Representative 1965–96 (for Wessex Region, 1981–96); m. 1972 Brigitte de Soye.

at least once every thirty years, different colours each time. Martin
Drury* warned me that Patrick Wright who interviewed me at Knole
is a Marxist of the most mischievous sort. Martin knew that I had
taken him to see Lionel Sackville, who had complained about having
to admit the public one day a week into his wing – a statement which
could be used to make trouble.

Greatly enjoyed this visit which somehow rejuvenated me, renew-
ing my interest in architectural problems and invigorating my spirit.
Nevertheless I have today written to Dudley Dodd† tendering my resignation from the Arts Panel. I am sure I am right. One must go when
old. Besides, dear old Brinsley Ford‡ has resigned. This severs my connection of fifty-two years with the National Trust. *Eheu*!

Wednesday, 6th July

To London. First to Chesterfield Street§ to see the two pictures of
the Bachelor in Andrew's bathroom. One a debonair likeness of the
Duke in his droshky; the other of him in his Lord Chamberlain's
robes, holding an orb. Ariane Goodman¶ lunched with me at
Franco's in Jermyn Street. She is sweetness itself, so sympathetic,
gentle and adorable. Could marry her without a second thought. I
must turn to Jock Murray** for the Bachelor now, just to be with
her again. Then to British Museum Reading Room, where I waited
hours just for one volume of the Berry Papers to reach my place,
only to find that I had already seen all the letters of the Bachelor
therein.

---

* Historic Buildings Secretary (1981–95), subsequently Director-General, of N.T. (b.
1938).
† Deputy Historic Buildings Secretary of N.T., 1981–2000 (b. 1947).
‡ Sir Brinsley Ford (1908–99); sometime Trustee of National Gallery, Chairman of
National Art Collections Fund, and Hon. Adviser on Paintings to N.T.; Eton contem-
porary of J.L.-M.
§ The Devonshires' house in Mayfair.
¶ Ariane Goodman (b. 1955); publisher's editor, who (then at Collins) had worked with
J.L.-M. on his *Venetian Evenings*; now employed by John Murray; m. 1984 Andrew
Bankes.
** John Murray VI (1909–93), head of publishing firm; Eton contemporary and (from
1990) publisher of J.L.-M.

Friday, 8th July

What fools the Americans are to bomb that Persian plane, killing 290 passengers. How awful our oil rig exploding in the North Sea, killing 120 men. How dreadful England selling £6 billion of fighter planes to the Arabs. How deplorable the bloody President of Romania destroying whole villages inhabited by the Hungarian minority in Transylvania. How ghastly the world. There can be no hope of lasting peace. I give the planet until the end of the century – then *pouf*! Won't be there to witness, of course. Most troubles caused by over-population. Announcement yesterday that 15 per cent of the world's bird species have been eliminated already.

Archbishop Lefebvre* has been excommunicated. Will this con-demnation to eternal flames worry so intellectual and virtuous a man as him? He has all my sympathy, because it is the Church which has let him and his followers down, not the other way round. I would like to go to Ecouen where he lives and attend a proper Mass once again. He is brave to start a schism, for most schisms ultimately come to nothing – schismatics get bored after a generation or two, and conform. This does not mean that they are not right to schismatise in the first place.

Friday, 15th July

Derek [Hill] telephoned at breakfast to say he had seen Bruce Chatwin† yesterday, whose appearance is quite horrifying. Cannot stand and is wheeled in a chair. Is becoming a member of the Greek Orthodox Church next week, and has got the monasteries at Mount Athos to pray for him. I am amazed that he has succeeded in being accepted by that Church. I tried once and was rebuffed.

Saturday, 16th July

Met Hugh Massingberd at Chippenham by an early train and took him to Badminton to meet A. Both A. and I were shocked by his fat

---

* Marcel Lefebvre (1905–91); sometime Archbishop of Dakar; defied papal authority by founding Society of St Pius X to champion traditional practices including the Latin mass.
† Travel writer and novelist, suffering from Aids (1940–89).

and puffy appearance. But what an amiable man and good companion. Splendid old-fashioned manners. We spent a delightful day
together. Motored first to Dyrham [Park, Gloucestershire], where
Tony [Mitchell] conducted us round, informative and intelligent. A
nice young female photographer arrived from London and took pictures of me in soppy attitudes, beside a peacock, against a piano, next
to Neptune on the hill. We lunched at the Crown, where Hugh spoke
intimately. Told me he had got into trouble at his prep school when
the headmaster caught him kissing a boy whom he liked. Young H.
hadn't a clue why it was wrong to do so. His father, still alive and
younger than me, knows nothing to this day. Father a puritan of
deepest dye, appalled by recent disclosures of his late brother Peter's
relations with Anthony Blunt.* Hugh says the result of his childhood
experiences is that he is deeply shy and awkward in company. This I
witnessed today. It may also explain the subversive element in his
writing.

We continued to Flaxley Abbey.† Mr Watkins now eighty-eight,
dry and intensely boring, but welcoming. Min the old companion
scurrying for the tea trolley. The house is now a macabre shrine to
Oliver Messel.‡ Nothing since his time altered, but time has wrought
decay. No windows opened since Oliver's day. Smell of stuffiness. H.
to be polite offered to buy a guide book he saw lying about. It cost
him £12, I hope refunded by *Telegraph*. To his dismay, H. found that
it only gave history of the house up to the Reformation. Written by
Mr W., who insisted on autographing it.§ Hugh fascinated by whole
set-up, Oliver hovering overhead in every room. There is no house
and no family in England that Hugh does not know about, if not
know.

---

* Art historian (1907–83; Surveyor of the Royal Pictures, 1945–72), officially disgraced
in 1979 when it was revealed that he was a former Soviet agent.
† For the unusual 20th-century history of this mediaeval property in Gloucestershire's
Forest of Dean, see entry for 6 November 1988.
‡ Theatrical producer, designer and artist (1904–78); brother of Anne, Countess of
Rosse.
§ Hugh Massingberd writes of this episode in his memoir *Daydream Believer: Confessions
of a Hero-Worshipper* (2001): '. . . the owner, a ponderous retired businessman, manoeuv-
red me into forking out some vast sum for an immensely dreary tome he had produced
on the exhaustive history of the old Abbey going back to its Cistercian foundation in the
twelfth century. "You fell right into the crasher's trap, didn't you?" chortled the impish
Jim as I beggared myself.'

Saturday, 23rd July

I spent a week in Yorkshire, working at archives in Castle Howard [near York] and staying at Worsley Arms. Returned yesterday evening to find George Dix and Feeble Cavendish staying weekend. Was so tired I could hardly speak. Mercifully George had just arrived from America so was dog tired too, and we all went to bed at 9.30.

Feeble says she has not read John's biography by Bevis Hillier and won't do so, but is offended by the reviewers referring to his once having slept with Auden.* She said that, when the story first appeared in Auden's biog., John's solicitor asked him if he could swear on oath that it was untrue. John said he was rather tickled by the idea, but it was not true. So poor Jock [Murray] will have an angry letter.

Sunday, 24th July

We dined with Nick [Robinson] and Alice in their cottage to meet his landlord and friend Rupert Legge,† an agreeable young man with an amiable smile. Everyone was charming, yet I did not feel at ease. Could not hear what was said to me through the shouting and laughing. But after dinner talked to Rupert L. about his great-uncle Ronnie Cartland.‡ Tried to explain that, though earnest and patriotic, Ronnie was no prude. Rupert L. amazed me by saying that his grandmother, Barbara Cartland,§ writes about twenty books a year. She began this hectic career when she was seventy. She dictates each novel to one of her four secretaries, and never looks at the manuscript, which is provided with punctuation by a retired schoolmaster in her employ. Each novel sells about a million copies and is translated into every known language except Chinese. She only works in the morning. In the afternoon she does charitable work, sees friends and family; and she travels abroad four times a year, gathering plots.

---

* W.H. Auden (1907–73); poet.
† Hon. Rupert Legge (b. 1951) of Hamswell House nr Bath; yr s. of 9th Earl of Dartmouth; barrister and writer.
‡ A Conservative MP for Birmingham 1935–40 (1907–40); killed in action.
§ Authoress of more than 500 novels (1901–2000), whose daughter Raine (m. 1948–76 Gerald Legge, 9th Earl of Dartmouth) was Rupert Legge's mother.

Wednesday, 27th July

M. is having much publicity over his book. Today's *Times* has a long article about him, entitled 'Bounder or Biographer?' A rather nice photograph of him lying on his sofa like an oriental odalisque. When asked by the interviewer whether it was right to publish a letter in which the Duke of Windsor describes his female relations as 'a bunch of seedy, worn-out hags', M. suggested that this showed a poetic touch. I deprecate this remark and have warned M. that he makes a great mistake in mocking the Royal Family. It will always tell against him – *vide* John Grigg.* M. seems insensitive to the fact that the spectacle of himself and Maître Blum, with their Jewish backgrounds, attacking the Royal Family will make a disagreeable impression on some people. He asks if I have been embarrassed by his dedication of his book to me. Nothing can hurt me now, but much can hurt him. I feel protective of him and jealous of his reputation.

Sunday, 31st July

Oenone† for the weekend bringing lover, one Guy Lubbock,‡ a gent for a nice change, very easy, charming and good-looking. Knows lots of our friends' children and speaks our language. They slept together in one room, in one bed. How lucky they are, for we could never have done this in our grandparents' houses. We asked the Henry Robinsons§ for dinner to meet them. A successful evening. Susy told me that their son Alexander, after attending his sister's christening, was taken to see his grandparents' grave in the churchyard. 'Dig them up!' he said.

---

* In 1957 Grigg, then 2nd Baron Altrincham, provoked reactions which today seem astonishing when he published an article in the *National Review* (which he owned and edited) mildly criticising the monarchy for being out of touch. He was assaulted in the street, excluded from the radio programme *Any Questions*, and found a promising career as a Conservative politician in ruins.
† A.L.-M's granddaughter Oenone Luke (b. 1960), yr dau. of Hon. Clarissa Luke; m. 1992 Richard Gladstone.
‡ Old Etonian charmer (b. 1957).
§ Henry Robinson (b. 1953), of Moorwood House near Cirencester; J.L.-M's great-nephew, elder brother of Nicholas and Richard; farmer; m. 1984 Susan Faulkner.

Monday, 1st August

We watch the television news. Thousands of seals seen dying, gasping on the shores of the north-east coast, because of sea pollution, sewage, etc. What a filthy world. Article in today's *Times*, by the scientist who discovered the hole in the ozone layer over the poles, says that by the end of the century the human race will also be gasping for breath and dying. Damned good thing too.

Thursday, 4th August

A. and I and Folly set forth by road to stay three nights with Billa [Harrod] at Holt [in Norfolk]. Perfect old-fashioned weather for a change. Immensely enjoyed visit. Object to get away from [eightieth birthday] celebrations and sticky little gifts from greats, great-greats and steps, with their kind intentions. Even so, before departure this morning receive present from Peggy* with two fat embraces, and a case for my watch from Oenone's nice friend Guy Lubbock.

Friday, 5th August

We lunch with Sybil Cholmondeley† at Houghton [Hall, Norfolk], not open to public today. She is rising ninety-four and frail, yet robust mentally, full of anecdotes and fun. Took us round the house after, through all the state rooms. Lavinia Cholmondeley staying with her son David Rocksavage,‡ charming and sensitive young man, immensely handsome. Told me that he hates shooting, and the neighbours think him wet in consequence. The Houghton shoot adjoining Sandringham will be an embarrassment to him, for he is to inherit Houghton from his grandmother. (His parents live at Cholmondeley [Castle, Cheshire].) Billa told us he was queer, on account of which he spent some years living in Paris. (Surely that can't have been the reason? Tax, more likely.) I hope nevertheless that he eventually marries and produces an heir. Before departure we visited the harness

---

* Peggy Bird, the Lees-Milnes' daily help.
† Sybil Sassoon (1894–1989); m. 1913 5th Marquess of Cholmondeley (d. 1968); châtelaine of Houghton Hall, Norfolk.
‡ Earl of Rocksavage (b. 1960), o.s. and heir of 6th Marquess of Cholmondeley (whom he succeeded as 7th Marquess and Joint Hereditary Lord Great Chamberlain of England, 1990).

room, beautiful bridles with silver crests on eye blinkers, all polished and shining. A cousin of Billa's came to dinner, Robert ffolkes,* baronet. Middle-aged and unmarried. The aristocracy seems doomed to extinction. I like the double ffs, deriving from George IV's reign and Sir Walter Scott, I suppose.

Saturday, 6th August

I am eighty. Have been so since 1.30 this morning. A beautiful day dawns, misty sunlight. Folly and I join A., who hugs me and gives me *Who's Who* for 1988, a smart cotton pullover, and Bevis Hillier's *Young Betjeman*. We buy the *Daily Telegraph* in Holt. On front page of literary section an article about me by sweet Hugh Massingberd, which gives me enormous pleasure. Too eulogistic, but most welcome. We visit the Lasts'† curious garden at Corpusty, greatly expanded and now something splendid. A mill house on the noisy village street. Then we visit Felbrigg [Hall, near Cromer] and lunch there very well. Kind ladies in the house come up and ask to shake my hand. I feel like John Betj. In the evening, Billa motors us to Burnham Market for a concert in church organised by Margaret Douglas-Home.‡ Violin and piano. In the interval we talk to Sylvia Combe§ who reminds me that I stayed with her on my fiftieth birthday. She says I was in tears on that occasion.

Sunday, 7th August

We lunch with Priscilla Bacon¶ in her dower house at Raveningham. She has Joshua Rowley** and the Graftons†† to meet

---

* Sir Robert ffolkes, 7th Bt (b. 1943).

† Two brothers, one of them a poet, whose garden, 'profuse in plants and flowing with water', and featuring 'grottos, follies and busts', the L.-Ms had first visited in August 1980.

‡ Lady Margaret Spencer (1906–96), yr dau. of 6th Earl Spencer; m. 1931 (diss. 1947) Hon. Henry Douglas-Home (1907–80), yr s. of 13th Earl of Home.

§ Lady Sylvia Coke (b. 1909), dau. of 4th Earl of Leicester; m. 1932 Simon Combe (d. 1965); she lived at Burnham Thorpe near King's Lynn.

¶ Priscilla Ponsonby (b. 1913); m. 1936 Sir Edmund ('Mindy') Bacon, 14th Bt (he d. 1982).

** Sir Joshua Rowley, 7th Bt, of Tendring Hall, Suffolk (1920–97); Deputy Secretary of N.T., 1952–5.

†† Hugh FitzRoy, 11th Duke of Grafton (b. 1919); Chairman of Society for Protection of Ancient Buildings; m. 1946 Fortune Smith, Mistress of the Robes to HM The Queen from 1967. In the 1950s, as Earl of Euston, he had been N.T. Historic Buildings Representative for East of England.

us. Both Joshua and Hugh enormous in girth and ill-looking. Fortune whispering confidences into an ear which can no longer take them in. Graftons gave me a book, which was kind. The big house a disappointment, largish Georgian much altered by Mindy's father in 1920s. But excellent pictures — two self-portraits by Sir Nathaniel Bacon, and a little Gainsborough of the baronet's dog (a try-out before he was allowed to paint the family). Boring garden. We drove from there to the Menagerie at Horton [Northamptonshire] to stay night with Gervase [Jackson-Stops].* The perfect gem, beautifully decorated, amazingly restored, lovely big room with plasterwork. I think of poor Robert Byron.† How pleased he would be to see it now. Filled with good things and overflowing with books on shelves and floor.

Tuesday, 9th August

On return to Badminton last night found an avalanche of cards and letters congratulating me on being so disgustingly old. Also another article about me by John Martin Robinson‡ in *Spectator*, excellent and less embarrassing than Hugh's eulogy. Photograph of me in *Telegraph* has aroused favourable comment. Aristocratic, says M.; sexy, writes Myles Hildyard.§

Saturday, 13th August

John Cornforth stays a night. He lacks wit and humour, but has a slight streak of malice which is new since I last saw him. We spend an excellent evening with the Mitchells at Dyrham.

---

* Architectural historian and adviser to N.T. (1947–95).
† Travel writer, Byzantinist, architectural conservationist and aesthete (1905–41); his biography by James Knox (see entry for 24 April 1990) was published by John Murray in 2003.
‡ Librarian to Duke of Norfolk, and writer and consultant on architectural and genea-logical subjects; Fitzalan Pursuivant of Arms (later Maltravers Herald of Arms) Extraordinary, and Vice-Chairman of Georgian Group (b. 1948).
§ Squire of Flintham Hall, Nottinghamshire (b. 1914); war hero, local historian, and sometime Honorary Representative of N.T.

Tuesday, 16th August

I take A. to Heathrow, she flying with Clarissa[*] to Tangier. I feel deeply unhappy when I hug her at Terminal 2. Yet on driving away I have an unaccountable feeling of release, a sense of relief that I can now, not indulge in wickedness any longer, but lie back and collect my thoughts.

Thursday, 18th August

I go to London for the day to see M., who lunches with me at the Cavalry Club. We agree it is well-ordered, opulent, stuffy and conventional. M. met me in the hall having looked for me in the morning room, where he heard one old man with bristling moustache saying to another, 'He wrote the funniest book called *Ancestral Voices*'. Spent afternoon in London Library. Caught six o'clock train and was back in time to dine with Sally [Westminster]. She had Lady Rose staying, divorced wife of Sir Francis,[†] clever and formidable bluestocking who lives in Corsica. Also Tony Bowlby,[‡] who impressed me by saying he read the science column in *The Times* every day. Says he is perplexed, as Einstein was, that light travels both in waves and particles. Also believes that the Muslim religion is wholly irreconcilable to the modern way of living – in which case the million or so of the brutes now living in this tiny island will not be much help to us in the long run.

Friday, 19th August

Freddy Ashton[§] has died aged eighty-three. A wonderful artist, with his humour and sense of what was aesthetically right. I recall the enjoyable day A. and I spent at his Suffolk house when he dictated his article to her for *The Englishman's Garden*. How funny he was. We still have the tape. My memories of him go back to the early 1930s when

---

[*] Hon. Clarissa Chaplin (b. 1934); only child of A.L.-M. by her 1st marriage to 3rd Viscount Chaplin; m. 1957 Michael Luke.

[†] Sir Francis Rose, 4th Bt, artist (1909–79); m. 1st 1943 Dorothy Carrington, writer, 2nd 1967 Beryl Davis.

[‡] Sir Anthony Bowlby, 2nd Bt (1906–93); m. 1930 Dora Allen; former neighbours of L.-Ms at The Old Rectory, Ozleworth, Wotton-under-Edge.

[§] Sir Frederick Ashton (1904–88); choreographer; Director of Royal Ballet until 1970.

he was deeply in love with Desmond [Parsons].* I was frantically jealous, and told him so years later. He said he had been just as jealous of me. Whenever we met, which was alas seldom and usually on formal occasions, he would take me aside to whisper a word of remembrance of Desmond. It became a link between us which others knew nothing about. A whisper in the Royal Box at Covent Garden, at a memorial service, behind the asparagus bed in Suffolk. I don't as a rule care for jokes in art – *vide* Falstaff, Laughing Cavalier, *Così fan tutte*, etc. – but in *Cinderella* Freddy created a miracle of art and funniness combined.

Saturday, 20th August

J.K.-B. staying, very affectionate and loaded with presents of food and wine. Yet even the modest amount of housekeeping which his visit involves is a strain. What with Folly's demands, the slowly diminishing pile of birthday letters, this that and the other, I can't settle to read or think.

Sent J. to lunch with the Mitchells while I lunch with the Michaels of Kent† at Nether Lypiatt [Manor, Gloucestershire]. Sign visitors' book in hall and see Caroline's name above mine. We would have come together had we known. A long wait till nearly two before we eat. Two couples, one called Sherwood I think, he the owner of the Orient Express and Cipriani's in Venice, a great beefy man with a bland smile; she, Shirley, dressed in Reckitt's Blue,‡ with black hair and intelligent face, who tells me she was a scientist 'before we became so rich'. I am put on the right of the Princess, who is very friendly. Takes me by the hand and leads me to the seat. I like her exuberance, intelligence, sharpness, quickness. She gets me to sign four copies of my little Cotswold book,§ which she then hands out to the other guests. She talks too much, perhaps. I watch her. Still a handsome

---

* Hon. Desmond Parsons (1910–37), brother of 6th Earl of Rosse; romantic friend of J.L.-M. at Eton.

† HRH Prince Michael of Kent (b. 1942), yr s. of HRH Prince George, Duke of Kent, 4th son of King George V; m. 1978 (as her 2nd husband) Baroness Marie-Christine von Reibnitz (b. 1945).

‡ Bright blue clothes-washing substance popular during first half of 20th century, manufactured by Reckitt & Sons Ltd of Hull.

§ *Some Cotswold Country Houses* (Dovecote Press, 1987).

woman, in a simple, pretty blue and white frock with a minimum of jewelry. He at far end of long table wearing check shirt open at sunburned neck with gold chain and cross suspended, a blazer with bright gold buttons, blue trousers and black shoes.

Marie-Christine says to me that the Prince is reading a book dedicated to me. 'He is deeply shocked', she begins, and I fear the worst, 'by . . . the dreadful way they treated the Duke of Windsor. He used to see the Duke in Paris and was very fond of him, not so much of her.' The Princess told me to talk to the Prince about the book after luncheon, which I did. He remarked how well-balanced and clearly written it was. That showed some intelligence. He is a dear little man and no longer shy with me, makes little jokes and is rather simpatico. Was charitable about Nicholas Ridley's* dilemma in having to build more houses in the Cotswolds, though is dismayed by the new village recently built to the east of the house. Even this remote, secluded place is now surrounded. She aired her grievances against the Family. Said that because she and her husband received nothing from either the Queen or the Civil List, they could do more or less as they pleased, but in consequence came in for much criticism. That the Queen was enormously rich but did not have much to spend her money on, the upkeep of her palaces and children all paid for by the state. That the real demons were the Household, who ruled the roost. That she hated the press, who never gave her credit for the good things she did – 'though occasionally', she added a trifle archly, 'I do something naughty'.

Did not get away until five. Alone with her would have been more fun. She calls me James – which I like, just as I like being kissed on both cheeks. And I enjoy hearing indiscretions. She said that, before she married, the Queen told her that unless she joined the Anglican Church her children would be cut out of the succession. She replied that, though a bad Catholic, nothing would induce her to renounce her faith, unless Michael asked her to do so. He of course deferred to her. I don't know what the status of the children now is.[†]

---

* Conservative politician (1929–93), then Secretary of State for the Environment, who was later forced to resign from the Government (see entry for 14 July 1990).
[†] Unlike their father, they remain in line of succession to the throne.

Friday, 26th August

The bitch tenant has finally vacated the flat, but D–Day has come and gone without any word from her about our settlement offer of £1,000. Today I fetched A. from Heathrow. Thank God she is back, and rested, having had wonderful weather, whereas here it rained almost every day. I have settled that Eardley and I are to go to Switzerland for eight days. Very tiring, ringing up hotels and visiting Thomas Cook. I have at last finished answering letters of congratulation for being eighty. I would guess I received about that number. One lady writes, 'I have been re-reading *Midway on the Waves* and have "felt" your father close at hand.[*] He wants me to let you know how happy he is that you have drifted back to the Church of England.' Now would my dear parent have minded that much? True, he was cross when I went Papist [in 1934].

Sunday, 28th August

By long invitation, three old ladies came to lunch with us. A. very bored by them, but Alice Fairfax-Lucy[†] and Constantia Arnold[‡] are very old friends of mine of whom I am fond. A. finds Alice affected. So she is, but this makes her no less loved by me. She was once pretty and winning; now her face has slipped and collapsed, pudding-wise. She wore dark glasses throughout the meal. Constantia was never a beauty, but always full of fun and shrewdness. The other lady, who acted as Alice's chauffeur, was Mrs Gwynne-Jones who did the charming water-colour of Beckford's library.[§] I found her a little withdrawn and stiff, doubtless shy. Nice woman and good artist. She knew old 'Mrs Betty' [Montgomery][¶] at

---

[*] The fourth and latest volume of J.L.-M's diaries, published by Faber & Faber in 1985 and covering the years 1948 and 1949, described the death of his father George Lees-Milne (1880–1949).

[†] Hon. Alice Buchan (1908–93), dau. of 1st Baron Tweedsmuir (the novelist John Buchan); m. 1933 Brian Cameron-Ramsay-Fairfax-Lucy, later 5th Bt, of Charlecote Park, Warwickshire (1898–1974).

[‡] Constantia Fenwick; m. 1936 Ralph Arnold of Cosham, Kent.

[§] Presented to J.L.-M. at a party at Fenton House, Hampstead to mark his retirement from the N.T. Properties Committee, 13 December 1983 (see *Holy Dread*).

[¶] Alberta ('Betty'), dau. of Queen Victoria's private secretary Sir Henry Ponsonby; m. William Montgomery. J.L.-M. (as related in *Ancestral Voices*) had befriended her when she was a widow in her eighties, and enjoyed her sharp, eccentric views.

Windsor during the war, and was funny recalling her hates against Queen Victoria.

Saturday, 3rd September

Arrived home last night, worn out after driving in the rain from Castle Howard. My state of near-collapse not mitigated by the discovery that one of the 'greats' was staying. It took me until this afternoon to recover from the strain of this long journey, reading signs and following the road. Spent two days at Castle Howard during this second visit, hardly worthwhile as the Bachelor's letters I saw there of little interest. Paid £20 for the privilege, and £100 for two nights in the Worsley Arms. Fighting my way to the cafeteria through the Castle's vaulted basement, I pondered on the tricks of time. There I was aged eighty, old and venerable, struggling to get a bun and nescafé, eating cheek-by-jowl with 'bedints'* off a flooded plastic tray. Whereas thirty years ago I stayed in the state bedroom and dined with George and Cecilia† in the state dining room. Such contrasts are the spice of life.

Monday, 5th September

I drove to Wickhamford today, A. unable to come because she was returning the great-grandchild to London, thank God. Anyway she would not have understood my pious pilgrimage, for Wickhamford means nothing to her. I would have liked to have my sister Audrey with me, but even she would not have appreciated the Holy Communion which the very nice Vicar of Badsey gave me at eleven o'clock, eighty years to the hour since my christening in 1908. Sat in the chancel; I would have liked to be in our old pew in the nave, but that would have been inconvenient for the Vicar. So I perched on one of those two tall oak Puginesque chairs facing the Sandys monuments. A wonderful experience taking the Sacrament in the same beloved church where I first did so eighty years ago. The church is beautifully kept, the brass hinges to the pew doors brightly polished. I regret the

---

* 'Bedint' was a word from the private language of Harold Nicolson and Vita Sackville-West, meaning 'common'.
† George Howard of Castle Howard, York (1920–84); sometime N.T. Honorary Representative for Yorkshire; Chairman of BBC, 1980–3; cr. life peer as Baron Howard of Henderskelfe, 1983; m. Lady Cecilia FitzRoy (d. 1974), dau. of 8th Duke of Grafton.

strip lighting my father put in just before his death, to replace the old hanging oil lamps. I talked to the Vicar afterwards. The people in the Manor, whom he likes, do not attend, but are generous in a crisis. I gave him £100 towards the upkeep and shall haunt him ever after if the PCC spends it on converting the heathen.

When the Vicar left I took Folly for a short walk across the funny old bridge, with its narrow 'V' stile at either end, across the brook into Badsey field, full of thistles and nettles and unkempt. Looked into the Manor garden through the trees. Then walked a little way up the lane past the Donkey Patch. There were apples tumbling off a few orchard trees close to the large sycamore. Apart from the field, and the clumps of trees which give a park-like effect, the country around is very bare and built upon. Then I returned to the churchyard and read the head-stones with their familiar village names – Taylor, Mason, Colley. One to Mrs Hartwell, whom I have written about in *Another Self*,* and who lived in the row of red-brick cottages on the site of that horrid fake my father built, Hodys. Her husband died the year I was born; she lived from 1852 to 1935.

I re-entered the church. The old stone-flagged floor with ventilator flue now covered with a genteel grey carpet. Deep red carpet in chancel, not quite the thing. Tombs in splendid condition and the thumbs of Sir Samuel Sandys, which my father seized from an American woman visitor who broke them off as a souvenir, are still in place, showing the marks of the breaks. The funny neo-Gothick font, which Papa and I fetched from Ombersley (where old Lord Sandys gave me a box of cigars for some favour now forgotten), still in the chancel. How low the ceiling where Mrs Hartwell got tangled up with the bell-rope, just above the oak cupboard where the Vicar keeps his copes. The panelling came from Ribbesford and is early sixteenth-century, rather rare, associated with the Acton family who owned Ribbesford in Henry VII's reign. I doubt whether anyone in the village now knows what it is or by whom it was given. I inherited it from Uncle Milne† and brought it from Scotland.

Perhaps foolishly, I decided not to call at the Manor to ask to walk in the garden. I think the present owners are the people who asked

---

* She appears in the book as a benevolent but bizarre widow who was the mainstay of the village church, and once while bell-ringing got carried into the air and ducked in the font.

† Alec Milne Lees-Milne (1878–1931) – see entry for 30 December 1992.

me to come over and talk of the past and I refused, saying it was too painful. Instead I drove round to the field where asparagus was grown in the Great War, now full of sheep, and walked down to the brook which separates the field from the garden. Splendid view of the house all spread out. Instead of being black and white it is now black and yellowish, which I don't much like. Church visible on extreme right, pine trees planted by Papa now higher than the church tower. Much activity – someone up a ladder attending to the window of Mama's bedroom, woman pushing a wheelbarrow into the yard. Two dogs noticing me started to bark, people stared at me, suspecting me no doubt of evil intent, and I turned and walked slowly back to the car.

Saturday, 10th September

A. and I motor to Bolton Abbey [Yorkshire], where we stay three nights. A shooting party packing up as we arrived. Amongst them the Becketts, Martyn so charming and son Richard enchanting, with the humour, the gaiety, and something of the looks of his grandfather Oliver Esher.* Indeed, he thanked me for having recorded so much about Oliver in my early diaries. The Hall is an overgrown shooting lodge, with numerous rooms leading off one another down a long passage. Gatehouse room on ground floor interesting enough with groined ceiling. Paintings of classical empresses once filled the panels. The only cosy room is the drawing room with painted ceiling by Crace. Wine-coloured wall hangings, much dilapidated, and deep wine curtains, brought from Londesborough. All very redolent of the Bachelor Duke.

The shooters having left, we were alone with Andrew and Debo, very cosy. Were taken to lunch with Lord and Lady Halifax† at Garrowby, totally rebuilt by Francis Johnson‡ of pale pink brick. A Georgian pastiche outside; more original inside, and wholly pleasing. He a jolly man with red-veined face, said to be irascible and difficult. She a near-beauty, previously married. They have a chapel in the house, where they still worship every morning. Some fine pictures, a so-called Holbein of a young man, a Claude, many sporting pictures

---

* Sir Martyn Beckett, 2nd Bt (1918–2001); architect; m. 1941 Priscilla, dau. of 3rd Viscount Esher.
† Charles 'Ernie' Wood, 3rd Earl of Halifax (b. 1944); m. 1976 Camilla Younger, formerly m. to Richard Parker Bowles.
‡ Yorkshire architect (1911–95).

inherited by his mother from The Durdans. Beautiful park on slopes
of Garrowby Hill overlooking Vale of York, the Minster a distant spot
on the horizon, but not improved by new water gardens and artificial
lakes and pools of which Repton* would not have approved.

Monday, 12th September

While the others go to a horticultural show, I remain and make notes
of Bolton and walk to the Strid. The Wharfe very splendid here –
praised by Wordsworth and Ruskin and immortalised by every landscape water-colourist.

Yesterday evening Andrew gave me before dinner a small plaster
bust of the Bachelor Duke – most kind and much appreciated by me.
He is very blind now and cannot read books. Can just manage news-
papers because the columns of print are so narrow, and can see the
television sideways, so to speak. Debo says he has never once complained of his blindness. Sits out of doors when the sun shines, gazing
into space and thinking. Lying full-length on the sofa, he called out
to Tommy, the young butler, 'I am going to London tomorrow and
want you to give me some money.' 'Yes, Your Grace,' replied Tommy
in a matter-of-fact way.

During this visit we met the Hartingtons,† whom we scarcely knew
before. She has become very pretty, full of self-confidence and charm.
He also has charm. We were taken to Beamsley Hall, their house a mile
or two away, with fine garden and full of good things – Picasso drawings, Matisses inherited by her from her mother. An air of fantasy about
the house, with its modern drawings and Vandyke portraits and enormous frameless paintings of tulip-heads by the McEwen boy. A decent,
intelligent, public-spirited couple who live here all the year round.

Tuesday, 13th September

We leave at ten o'clock. Debo says to Decca,‡ 'You have no idea how
tireless the old octogenarian is. After motoring all the way to

---

* Humphry Repton (1752–1818); landscape gardener.
† Peregrine Cavendish, Marquess of Hartington (b. 1944), o.s. of 11th Duke of
Devonshire (whom he succeeded as 12th Duke, 2004); m. 1967 Amanda Heywood-
Lonsdale.
‡ Hon. Jessica Mitford (1917–96); m. 1st 1936 Esmond Romilly (1918–41), 2nd 1943
Robert Treuhaft (1912–2001); satirical writer living in USA, the 'communist' Mitford sister.

Garrowby and back, he then walked to the Strid.' 'O lucky Jim, how I envy him',* Decca sings down the telephone.

Saturday, 17th September

Eliza Wansbrough† was motored over to tea by her new neighbour John Cambridge,‡ former Ambassador to Morocco. He is very good to Eliza, and having come to live in her village has taken her in hand. Distinguished-looking and highly civilised man. I deduced he was queer, not from his mannerisms, but a slightly finical mind, a certain over-fastidiousness, and the fact that he knows Christopher Selmes who bought and sold Lyegrove at enormous profit to himself. Poor Eliza now hears hardly anything one says, and the effort of getting through to her is exhausting.

We dined with the Loewensteins at Biddestone for the last time. As we were thirteen, twelve sat down at the dining table and a small side-table was provided for Rupert. A sad moment. Rupert embraced me with a hug. How we shall miss them. We have so few real friends left here. Lord Warwick§ staying. Has splendid manners and is out to please, but leads an empty life in Paris, having shed all his responsibilities, including Warwick Castle and his Canalettos.

Sunday, 18th September

Mary Downer¶ came from staying the weekend with the Carringtons.** She told them the Yorks†† were coming to Australia.

---

* Lines of a traditional song which, in an arrangement by John Addison, was used in the Boulting Brothers' film (1957) based on Kingsley Amis's novel *Lucky Jim*.

† Elizabeth Lewis (1897–1995); dau. of Sir George Lewis, 2nd Bt (and granddau. of Sir George Lewis, 1st Bt, famous late Victorian solicitor); m. 1928–38 George Wansbrough.

‡ Diplomatist (b. 1928); HM Ambassador to Morocco, 1982–4.

§ David Greville, 8th Earl of Warwick (1934–96); m. 1956–67 Sarah Beatty.

¶ Widow of Sir Alexander Downer (1910–81), Australian politician and High Commissioner in London, 1964–72.

** Peter Carington, 6th Baron Carrington (b. 1919); Conservative politician; High Commissioner to Australia, 1956–59; Foreign Secretary, 1979–82, resigning over Argentine invasion of Falklands; Secretary-General of NATO, 1984–8; KG 1985; m. 1942 Iona McClean.

†† HRH Prince Andrew (b. 1960, cr. Duke of York 1986); m. 1986–96 Sarah Ferguson (b. 1959).

'Don't have anything to do with them, they are *dreadful*,' said Lord C. Gerald Harford* endorsed this sentiment, having been present at a dinner party at which the Duchess stopped the conversation with a story which was puerile, filthy and vulgar. The Loewensteins came for a drink before luncheon, wishing to meet Mary, as they are going to Adelaide in the trail of Mick Jagger. Mary the sweetest of women, with her fascinating Australian drawl.

Tomorrow A. is going to the King of Jordan's new house in Surrey to advise on the garden, which she is sure will be hideous and full of rhododendrons.

Monday, 19th September

Desmond Briggs† spoke to me of Japan, having just visited that country where he has publishing interests. He was amazed that his host did not lock the front door before retiring for the night. Apparently nobody steals. Social life there is very different to ours. Workers' loyalty to their firms is absolute. There is no distinction between managers and workers, who eat together. After working hours, the men gather at the equivalent of the nearest pub to discuss their work. There are no trade unions, for there is no need for workers to be protected from their employers. Very few women work, and wives are seldom seen. They appear from the kitchen bearing food, and bear and rear children, but otherwise their lives are restricted and dreary.

J.L.-M. sets out on a walking holiday with Eardley Knollys at Adelboden in the Bernese Oberland.

Tuesday, 20th September

A. drives me to Chippenham and insists upon finding a porter to take my heavy bag across the line. We part fondly. M. meets me on the platform at Paddington with a trolley, then wheels suitcase to café where we eat eggs and bacon. It is 7.15 p.m. Tomorrow is the Jewish

---

* Then squire of Little Sodbury Manor, Gloucestershire (b. 1948); m. 1985 Camilla, dau. of Alistair Horne.
† Publisher (1931–2002); novelist (as Rosamond Fitzroy); a JP for Wiltshire. He and his partner Ian Dixon were solicitous friends to both L.-Ms.

Day of Atonement and M. says he should already be fasting and con-
templating his sins. I tell him that I do not want to be responsible for
his shirking his religious duties. I stay night with Eardley.

Wednesday, 21st September

Eardley and I meet with great kindness over our heavy luggage, at
Victoria, Gatwick, Bern and Frutigen. Compassion for the aged most
manifest. Swiss landscape very green. Quite hot after London. Trees
abound, too many pines. Buses so smart and clean they must be
washed twice a day.

   Adelboden at first sight disappointing. Lowering clouds, grey sky.
Houses going up all around. Our hotel an overgrown modern chalet.
We have nice adjacent double rooms, each with bathroom and
balcony. Dare not ask the price. Good dinner in restaurant. Sitting in
lounge afterwards, we are approached by smiling, red-haired proprietress with enormous fat husband, just returned from South of France
where they have gone for sun. A bad augury for this place. Madame
says to me, 'I have just read article about you in the *Spectacle*', rather
surprising from a Swiss hotel proprietress.

Thursday, 22nd September

Wake up to brilliant sunshine. From my balcony I see wonderful
mountain panorama – green meadows sloping steeply first to pine
forests, then to rigid brown cliffs of fearsome height (of the sort from
which dear Robin Fedden* would have dangled on ropes), then to
snow-patched tops. Immediately below the hotel are new buildings,
all with grim grey-black roofs of manufactured tiles. In fact
Adelboden is spreading before our eyes. Next door a vast crane and
bulldozers are preparing for a new hotel. Beyond that another hotel
is finishing. Yet everything is 'in keeping', as they say – all traditional
chalets, some very pretty.

   We arrange terms with kind and helpful proprietress Frau
Sternimann – demi-pension, dinner in, luncheon out. Lavish buffet
breakfast. At midday, we walk to west of town, a gentle walk through

---

* J.L.-M's successor (1951–68) as Historic Buildings Secretary of N.T. (1909–77); writer
and mountaineer; m. 1942 Renée Catzeflis.

pastures, and eat at a small restaurant – just a lager and a meringue for me. Delicious day. I wear my blue linen hat to keep boiling sun off bald head. Feel tired but relaxed on return. In evening I finish article for *Spectator* on our experience with the bitch – though the full drama may not yet be over.

Friday, 23rd September

Disturbed in night by violent peals of thunder rolling around mountains. Wake to dismal sight of thick black fog. Soon sun starts filtering through, and by noon it is another lovely day. Begin reading John Gaze's* history of National Trust for review.† This afternoon we walk to east of town. Sweet-smelling cows, all with bells, some heavy and deep-toned, others small and tinkling. Cows palest honey and clean, like everything here. Walking back we descend steep path of steps cut in the turf. Eardley goes ahead, calling out, 'Take care!' Too late – I twist right foot and fall. Hobble home, foot very swollen. E. makes light and insinuates that I am putting it on. So I show him swelling, from which he averts his eyes.

Saturday, 24th September

Though ankle hardly hurting at all, I do not go for a walk. Lovely day, sitting on balcony with hat on, reading John Gaze's good but overlong book.

Sunday, 25th September

Cannot decide which church to go to. Decide against R.C, for Mass irritates me these days to screaming point. Go to what Frau Sternimann calls the Protestant Church at 10.15. Climb to gallery to have view of proceedings. Whole building packed with old, middle-aged and young. Old church, well restored and refurbished, plain whitewashed walls, timber ceiling, gallery supported by heavy wooden trusses. An air of jollity, congregation chatting as they might before a political meeting. The Minister, clad in black with white

---

* Chief Agent of N.T. 1976–82 (1922–87).
† *Figures in a Landscape* (1988).

cravat, standing facing congregation on altar steps, says something which causes a ripple of laughter and smiles. Several dreary hymns. At given moment, my neighbour shakes my hand warmly and beams. I beam back. Some people object to this new habit. I think it is a good idea. Shows good will to all men. We stand during prayers, sit during oration. Service over in an hour. No atmosphere of mystery or even of sanctity, but feeling of bonhomie.

In afternoon, E. and I go for another ramble on the flat, lunching at an inn. We continue eastwards until we reach a secluded glade. Tiring, but foot no worse. I speak to A. on telephone. She says the Queen of Jordan* a perfectly charming young woman, and she has taken on the job of doing her Surrey garden.

Monday, 26th September

Am writing review of Gaze book when E. calls out to ask if I am ready to go on an expedition. It is such a perfect day I cannot refuse. We catch minibus to foot of funicular which ascends Engstilalp, mountain to south of Adelboden. A precipitous ascent, cabin stuffed with passengers like sardines. Awful visions of being stranded owing to electricity failure, or of slender wires snapping, plunging us to our deaths. I dare not look out of window. We arrive in a sort of crater. Marvellously invigorating air. Directions for long walks, but these involve climbing which neither of us are up to, and there are too many tourists. We soon descend. On our return, I buy Saturday's *Daily Telegraph* which contains my article on Diaries. Not too bad. As I write at 6.15, the sun is just touching the ginger rock and snow-covered ridges of the mountains in front of me.

The proprietress has made me write in her cherished guest book. All contributions trite and jejune, including my own which compares ourselves to rather aged skylarks singing in happiness. The reference to age has enraged E., as I knew it would. He is very touchy on the point.

---

* Queen Noor (b. 1951 in USA as Lisa Najeeb Hallaby); m. 1978 (as his 4th and last wife) King Hussein of Jordan (1935–99).

Tuesday, 27th September

E. complains bitterly to me that his long friendship with Dadie Rylands* is over. Dadie never answers his invitations to stay at The Slade† or asks to see E., who is deeply hurt. But I wonder if the reason may not be E's crustiness and loss of sociability. All the old jokes and giggles have gone. Instead he is inclined to be dictatorial, contemptuous of others, often snubbing. Contradicts me flat and dismisses my opinions. His counter-snobbism is irritating – he despises any friend of mine who has a title. Expects me to be as absorbed as he is in his Mattei, and his new obsession, the handsome youth called Cassian whom I once met. Having borrowed my copy of the *Telegraph*, he does not so much as refer to my article therein. So like him. The relationship between very old friends is nearly always sad. They grow tired of and bored with each other. Yet for old times' sake they maintain an uneasy affection and loyalty. Does he find me as irritating as I find him? He must.

I am impressed by the way the Swiss shopkeepers, in closing between midday and two o'clock, shut the doors of their shops but leave their goods on the pavement. Apparently no one steals, and since there are no dogs to lift their legs against them, they remain untouched and unharmed. No dogs; no birds, apart from an occasional little chaffinch or bullfinch hopping about the front door of the hotel; but no burglars.

Wednesday 28th September

My foot is little better, and causes me to limp. Has entirely spoilt my walking progress – and Eardley's fun, the principal object of this jaunt having been to regain our walking powers. Weather clouding over today and the beautiful pearly full moon invisible tonight. I have followed it nightly through my little binoculars, every contour visible. Sky very clear here, as it rarely is at home.

J.L.-M. returns to England.

---

* George Rylands (1902–99); Shakespearean scholar and Fellow of King's College, Cambridge.
† Eardley Knollys's house near Petersfield, Hampshire.

Saturday, 1st October

The Swiss are incorrigibly whimsy. They love Mickey Mouse and Donald Duck art. All their postcards are jokey. They even inscribe the equivalent of servants' hall jokes on their buildings, and drawings too. Swiss women are middle-aged, prim, respectable and wear buns. Yet there are no burglars, and no blacks. There is that much to be said for them.

Monday, 3rd October

Sachie [Sitwell]* has died at ninety-one. My appreciation of him published in today's *Independent*, under a very full and good obituary by Jamie Fergusson.† Francis Sitwell‡ telephoned to ask if I could come to the funeral at Weston on Saturday and lunch with them after. I said I would consult A. on telephone, she being at La Fourchette.§ She said it would be absurd to go, as I saw so little of him. But I saw a good deal of him before we were married. Yet she may be right, for it is a long way to motor and I feel dreadfully tired. Sachie was always afraid of death, though a confirmed atheist.

Saturday, 8th October

Sally [Westminster] most kindly motored me to Sachie's funeral. Took place in the little village of Moreton Lois [Northamptonshire], a mile from Weston. Pretty church with mural tablets which I could not read from where we sat. We had reserved seats in the front. Church packed with friends from London, and locals. Peter Quennell gave a short, too short address about his old friendship with Sachie, describing him as the greatest genius of the three Sitwells. Peter had cut his forehead, across which he wore an old bandage, exuding blood. He looked extremely

---

* Sir Sacheverell Sitwell, 6th Bt (1897–1988); poet and writer; m. 1925 Georgia Doble (d. 1980).

† Founding obituaries editor of *Independent*, whose father was a second cousin of J.L.-M. (b. 1953).

‡ Yr s. (1935–2004; m. 1966 Susanna Cross) of Sir Sacheverell, who inherited the property at Weston (his elder brother Reresby [b. 1927; m. 1952 Penelope Forbes], heir to the baronetcy, having inherited Renishaw, Derbyshire from his bachelor uncle Sir Osbert, 5th Bt [d. 1969]).

§ Mick Jagger's French property where she was designing the garden.

old and emaciated, wife supporting him up altar steps. Moira Shearer
and Ludovic Kennedy* recited four of Sachie's poems. Sally found them
childish, but I was moved by them. We returned to Weston where
Francis and wife had laid on excellent stand-up luncheon for almost
whole congregation. Gertrude [the housekeeper] there looking surprisingly young. Grasped my hand with tears and told me of Sachie's
peaceful end in his sleep. 'To think that I have looked after this wonderful genius for sixty years.' I too was on the verge of tears, though I
think few others were, because of Sachie's great age and readiness to
die. Reresby a great bore, telling long-winded stories with a hint of
loucheness. Before leaving, seeing Reresby at the door of Sachie's little
writing room, I asked whether I might have a look at it for the last time.
He let me and Sally in, saying, 'This may be my last time too. My
brother and I are not friends.' 'In which case,' I replied, 'this is the
moment to become friends again.' Baba Metcalfe† embraced me and
said she would be coming down to Bath to see her mother's dresses and
would like to lunch with me. Sally a surprisingly good companion, her
sweetness outweighing her silliness.

Sunday, 16th October

We motor to Wilton [near Salisbury, Wiltshire] for David Herbert's‡
eightieth birthday. As we drive, the mist rises and a beautiful autum-
nal day emerges. David greeting friends with embraces and darlings.
Our host Lord Pembroke,§ tall, slim, handsome man with aquiline features, advances to meet us, saying 'I am Henry'. Some forty of us sit
at separate tables in the library. I am seated next to Candida Lycett
Green¶ and Moyra Lubbock, charming mother of Oenone's nice

---

* Ludovic Kennedy (b. 1919; Kt 1994); broadcaster, politician and humanitarian cam-
paigner; m. 1950 Moira Shearer, ballerina and actress.
† Lady Alexandra Curzon (1904–95), dau. of Marquess Curzon of Kedleston; m. 1925
Major E. D. 'Fruity' Metcalfe.
‡ Hon. David Herbert (1908–95), yr s. of 15th Earl of Pembroke; Eton contemporary of
J.L.-M.; resident in Tangier.
§ Henry Herbert, 17th Earl of Pembroke, film director (1939–2003); nephew of David
Herbert.
¶ Candida (b. 1942), o. dau. of Sir John Betjeman and Hon. Penelope *née* Chetwode; m.
1963 Rupert Lycett Green, founder of Blades, fashionable tailors; writer on architec-
tural and horticultural subjects and editor of her father's letters.

friend Guy. (A. sits next to the father, equally charming.)* She too is longing for the pair of them to marry, but agrees there is nothing one can do to bring it about.

Candida told me that her birthday present to David was a Victorian book of illuminations which I had once given her father, and inscribed. Strange that only two days ago I was wondering what had become of that book, which I hadn't thought about for twenty years. She also said how much she resented 'the little man's criticisms of my dad' – i.e., Bevis Hillier's very occasional unfavourable remarks about John Betjeman. As an example, she mentioned his emphasis on her Chetwode grandparents'† disapproval of the marriage. Yet John himself deliberately emphasised Lady Chetwode's objections because he found them funny, always hooting with laughter at her 'middle class Dutchman' jibe. And to be fair, Lady C. did object a good deal – as she had also done with her daughter's previous suitor, dear Johnnie Churchill,‡ whom she described as 'a parlour trick man'.

David made a nice little speech of thanks to us for coming, and to his nephew Henry for giving the luncheon. We were all nearly in tears, as was he. It is always moving to see how one's contemporaries are held in affection by the younger generation.

Friday 28th October

Gervase [Jackson-Stops] stayed the night with us. He is a dear little good egg, so full of life and enthusiasm. He made us do what we have never yet done – motor into the park after dinner to look at the House illuminated by the anti-burglar searchlights. A hazy moon to the east, just on the wane; stags roaring in the background. He and I then sat up watching the Prince of Wales talking about modern architecture. I agreed with every word, as did Gervase. He spoke well and confidently, never tripping up. Very outspoken on how during the Sixties the landscape was blighted by tower blocks etc. The next morning the

---

* Lieut.-Commander Roger Lubbock (b. 1922); m. 1955 Moyra Fraser, actress (formerly married to Douglas Sutherland, author of *The English Gentleman*).
† Field Marshal Lord Chetwode (1869–1950); Commander-in-Chief of the Army in India, 1930–5; m. 1899 Hester Stapleton-Cotton. Their dau. Hon. Penelope (1910–86) m. John Betjeman, 1933.
‡ J. G. Spencer-Churchill (1909–92), nephew of Sir Winston; artist; friend of J.L.-M. since they had crammed for Oxford together in the 1920s.

papers already full of headlines nagging at the poor Prince; but the majority of his audience will be behind him. The modernist architects build for themselves without considering either the public at large or the wretched victims obliged to live in their terrible cages of torture.

Sunday, 30th October

We lunched with Candida and Rupert [Lycett Green] in their new house near Oare [Wiltshire]. A plain, nondescript little farmhouse, nothing to speak of after Blacklands. But a good setting at the foot of lovely downs. The Henry Keswicks* present, who own Oare [House]. She, charming and beautiful, is the daughter of Lord Lovat and hence a great-niece of Diana Westmorland,† of whom we spoke. He a tall, shapeless, jolly man. Candida's two boys so noisy, letting off fireworks on the kitchen table, that we could hardly hear what was said. Saw John [Betjeman]'s library stacked in a small, congested room. Candida loves these books and wants to build a wing to house them. Is also devoted to her mother's memory and is planting a strange garden of mauve and yellow, Penelope's favourite colours.

In the evening, we watched Patrick Wright's television film in which I feature, called 'Brideshead and the Tower Blocks'. I saw with horror a very frail-looking old man, with scrawny neck and puff of white hair at rear of head, advancing into the Stone Court at Knole beside tall, upright P.W. This was a shock, for although I often feel ghastly and tired, I still think of myself as a middle-aged man. One catches up slowly with the stark facts only too apparent to others. As I sat in front of the wicket, in a bitter wind but wearing only a summer suit, the cold gave me a pinched look. My voice seemed deeper than usual, and my utterance was slow. I fancy I looked just as dear Lord Sackville looked when I visited him in his eighties – rather dandified, neat, red-faced, meticulous and slow. P.W. introduced a political note by contrasting Knole with St John's Institute, Hackney, the one aristocratic and lavishly maintained, the other plebeian and neglected.

---

* Henry Keswick, merchant banker (b. 1938); owner of *Spectator*, 1975–81; m. 1985 (as her 2nd husband) Annabel Thérèse ('Tessa'), dau. of 17th Lord Lovat.
† Diana Lister (1893–1983), dau. of 4th Baron Ribblesdale; m. (3rd) 14th Earl of Westmorland (d. 1948); regarded by J.L.-M. as 'far and away my closest friend down here' (4 December 1983).

All Saints' Day, Tuesday, 1st November

To Eton for the night, to stay with the Charterises. I found driving in the failing light a strain, and needed a stiff whisky on arrival. How nostalgic Eton in November, mists rising through setting sun. Martin Charteris in bed with pneumonia, so Gay received us. A dinner for thirty, given jointly by Provost and Headmaster. We knew none of the guests, most of them clever academics. Bit of a strain keeping up. Headmaster Anderson and wife* both delightful. She teaches English. Vice-Provost an economist. We ate in College hall, more restored than I remember; after pudding we saw the kitchen, fifteenth-century and likewise over-restored, claimed to be the oldest still in use; then through the glorious library to the Election Room where we had dessert at a long table with silver candles and tankards, having brought our napkins. At dinner I sat beside Mrs Anderson, who reminded me of K. Kennet,† with her grey hair close-cropped like a boy, and her enthusiasms. She told me that Eton was flourishing, having gone through a bad patch under Chenevix-Trench‡ when it sank to a low level of dissipation. The boys now eager and happy. Buildings too in apple pie order (we looked out of our window in the morning to see roofs and walls restored). Lupton's Tower clock striking the quarters, on the hour the highest note, brought back melancholy memories.

Several masters expressed their liking for *Another Self*. Indeed I get tired of this book being praised, just as Harold grew to regret *Some People*.§ Mrs Anderson quizzed me about several of the stories, but I would not be put upon. She has read it to her class of boys who,

---

* Eric Anderson (b. 1936); Headmaster of Eton, 1980–94 (Provost from 2000); m. 1960 Poppy Mason.

† Kathleen Bruce (1878–1947); sculptor; m. 1st 1908 Captain Robert Scott 'of the Antarctic' (d. 1912), 2nd Edward Hilton Young (1879–1960), Liberal politician, cr. Baron Kennet, 1935.

‡ Anthony Chenevix-Trench (1919–79); Headmaster of Eton, 1964–70, notorious for his readiness to administer corporal punishment. He was also over-fond of alcohol, and went on to become Headmaster of Fettes, where his charges included the future prime minister Tony Blair.

§ J.L.-M. had to some extent modelled his *Another Self* (1970) on Harold Nicolson's *Some People* (1927): both works are autobiographical novels written in the first person, describing how their authors were 'tested' by being faced, at various moments of their youth, by hilarious embarrassing situations.

instead of being amused like the adults, were appalled by the predicaments I got into.

Sunday, 6th November

We dined with the Thomas Messels[*] at Wotton-under-Edge.[†] Large party, including Sally [Westminster] and the Snowdons.[‡] Sat next to Lucy Snowdon, who is charming and clever. Looks plain at a distance and handsome close to, unusual. Talked to her and Tony afterwards about Anne Rosse, now a great trial. Lucy fags for her ceaselessly which Anne takes for granted. I gather half the trouble is the bottle, poor thing. Tony extremely friendly with me as always, embracing me on both cheeks. Said he missed his Uncle Oliver [Messel] more than anyone. We agreed the story of Flaxley Abbey would make a splendid film. Mr Watkins, as a poor boy living in the neighbourhood, looks wistfully across park at large house. Eventually buys it from Crawley-Boevey family. Mrs Watkins goes to a play designed by Oliver Messel. Writes to him. Oliver's mother dies and he is miserable. Regards Mrs W. as a substitute. She falls head-over-heels in love with O. At first Mr W. resents it, but seeing no harm can possibly result, acquiesces and himself falls for O. Oliver sells much of his inherited furniture to the Ws, and arranges it in the house. The Ws will not touch an item in the house unless it is arranged by O., unarranged rooms remaining under dust-sheets. O. dies. Mrs W. dies. Mr W. still living there with Min . . . When we left, Tony said he would like to photograph me, and was quite pressing. A. said I should agree, it is such a compliment. But I don't want to be photographed.

Thursday, 10th November

Dining with us, David [Beaufort] spoke about Lucian Freud, with whom he lunches once a week. Freud brings his mistress of the

---

[*] Thomas Messel (b. 1951); designer and furniture maker; m. 1981 Penelope Barratt.

[†] Nearest village to Alderley Grange, where the L.-Ms had lived from 1961 to 1974.

[‡] Antony Armstrong-Jones (b. 1930); son of J.L.-M's friend Anne, Countess of Rosse (aunt of Thomas Messel) by her 1st marriage, and nephew of Oliver Messel; photographer; m. 1st 1960 HRH Princess Margaret, 2nd 1978 Lucy Davies; cr. Earl of Snowdon, 1961.

moment, currently the wife of Y., who is expected to remain silent. Freud himself sometimes goes into a brown study and does not talk, strange for D. who was brought up, as we all were, not to allow silences. Freud is totally dedicated to his painting, at which he works all day long, and with which he is never satisfied. He hates praise of his work by reviewers who fail to see its failings. He longs to produce one flawless masterpiece. Is obsessed with sex and often has to have it on the spur of the moment – while walking round a garden, in the bath, between courses. Apparently he has no trouble getting women to oblige him in these unromantic urges. I asked, rather absurdly, whether he was a nice character. D. said yes, he is fundamentally generous and kind. I would not have guessed so.

Saturday, 12th November

We lunched with the Griggs at Tormarton, taking Oenone and Guy Lubbock who are staying with us. O. holds her own and is very *sortable*, in spite of her ignorance of everything except her own work. I sat next to Mrs Alexander, wife of cosy professor sitting at other end of table, and authoress of that enchanting book *Estonian Childhood* which so moved me.* She often returns to Soviet Estonia and says there is no danger now, though her maiden name still induces suspicions and she is followed everywhere. Has no relations left there, and few friends. I asked if the Soviets spoke the same Russian as she and her sort. No, she said, they spoke it 'too sweetly' – less clipped, with sing-song inflections.

Monday, 14th November

Towards the end of his sad, degraded life, Bonnie Prince Charlie wrote to his brother the Cardinal[†] that he was 'bothered in the head'. This is my experience now – nightmares day and night, awake or

---

* Tania Alexander, translator and expert on Chekhov; her memoirs, published by Jonathan Cape in 1987 as *A Little of All of These*, were reissued in paperback as *An Estonian Childhood*.

[†] Princes Charles Edward Stuart, 'the Young Pretender' (1720–88) and Henry Stuart, Cardinal Duke of York (1725–1807); sons of Prince James Stuart, 'the Old Pretender' (1688–1766), who in the Jacobite canon were his successors to the throne as Charles III and Henry IX.

asleep, or rather half-asleep which I am most of the night. Not a head-ache exactly, no violent pain, just a bother in the head, like the grinding of a coffee machine. Days when I am completely free of these 'bothers' are rare. I then feel wonderfully well and begin to suppose I am as good as I was.

Tuesday, 15th November

Paul Hyslop* is dead. Jamie Fergusson telephoned, asking if I would write a piece for the *Independent*. I said I would rather not. I was not deeply fond of that poor old crosspatch, and don't want to look like a vulture descending on every corpse that falls. Paul was an appendage of Bloomsbury. When I first knew him in the 1930s, he and Raymond Mortimer† lived in Gordon Place in a flat decorated by John Banting,‡ charming and attractive in the Duncan Grant§ manner. Thence they moved to Islington, where they inhabited the most desirable old house with a vast garden. Paul was a good-taste, conventional architect, who built Fairlawne [Kent] for Victor Cazalet¶ and transformed Buscot [House, Oxfordshire] for Gavin Faringdon.** He did much work for the National Trust, to which he was introduced by Eardley and me – kiosks at Stourhead, a staircase at Knole. But he was cantankerous and annoyed the agents. Very good-looking in his youth, he became a pipe-sucking, quizzical, grunting creature. Latterly he annoyed me by writing to me about my books before they came out, having winkled proofs out of booksellers. He had a twinkle in his eye, but more mischief than bonhomie.

Peter Quennell telephoned this morning, to cancel our luncheon. Voice unrecognisable, like an old-fashioned gramophone record running down. Has had an operation and awaits results. Poor old Peter.

---

* Architect in the classical tradition (1900–88).
† Literary reviewer (1895–1980); close friend of Paul Hyslop.
‡ Artist and stage designer (1902–72).
§ Artist associated with Camden Town Group and Bloomsbury Group (1885–1978).
¶ Conservative MP (1896–1943); wartime liaison officer between British Government and Polish leader General Sikorski, with whom he died in an air crash.
** Gavin Henderson, 2nd Baron Faringdon (1902–77).

Monday, 21st November

We lunched with Woman [Pamela Jackson] at Caudle Green. Jamie Neidpath brought his father Lord Wemyss,* widower, who is staying with him at Stanway. Very old, though younger than I – arrived at Lockers Park just as I was leaving. He told me how his grandmother came down to the school to announce the marriage of his mother, Lady Elcho, to Guy Benson.† She said, 'I have something important to tell you. You mustn't mind. Letty is going to marry Guy.' He didn't mind one bit, and wondered why he should have been expected to. Woman gave us wonderful luncheon of mutton and apple crumble. She talked of Nancy's beastliness to her as a child, and gave a hilarious account of her good work during General Strike in opening a tea place on the London road by Asthall [Hall, Oxfordshire]. I laughed till I cried – the exaggerated Mitford voice, so natural to her. Jamie said my life of Regy Esher was the best biography ever written, which is flattering exaggeration coming from a highly intelligent and well-informed young man. He is a charmer.

Wednesday, 23rd November

Listened last night to Mozart's Symphony No. 40 in G minor (K.550). The announcer explained beforehand that it was written when Mozart was in dire financial straits and misery. I think I understood a little of what was in his mind when he was composing this beautiful and haunting piece. There is a recurrent little downward-drooping phrase of harrowing unhappiness. The symphony culminates in a movement of infinite poignancy, suggesting his rage and indignation with the world for treating him with such disdain and neglect.

Sunday, 27th November

This morning my article in the *Telegraph* about Nicholas Ridley's frightful speech saying the old families should clear out of their houses if they cannot afford to keep them up to make way for the *nouveaux*

---

* Francis Charteris, 12th Earl of Wemyss and 8th Earl of March (b. 1912); his er s. and heir James, Lord Neidpath (b. 1948) of Stanway, Gloucestershire.
† Lady Violet Manners (1888–1971), 2nd dau. of 8th Duke of Rutland; m. 1st 1911 Lord Elcho, er s. of 11th Earl of Wemyss (killed in action, 1916), 2nd 1921 Guy Benson, merchant banker (1888–1975).

riches, and about the Mappa Mundi. Printed exactly as I sent it in for a change. A. thinks I went too far in saying that the Dean and Chapter of Hereford should be boiled in oil.*

Tuesday, 29th November

I began Chapter 1 of the Bachelor this morning, writing a page and a half. At this rate it will take me ten years to finish. Had to leave Bath at 3.45 as it was becoming dark and foggy. These short days retard me greatly.

Thursday, 8th December

As a sort of echo of times past, a wave of pleasure passes over me when A. goes off to London for the night. I am now free to take my own time, do silly fuss-pot things, get on with letter-writing without being called on to do things I don't want to do. But when she has been away for twenty-four hours, I long to have her back, and begin to worry about her. Folly and I are quite happy; I sleep with her cosily in A's bed, relishing her little grunts in the night, and the way she rests her muzzle on my feet.

I am pleased to hear from Warren Davis that my diaries are now being put into dramatic shape for the actor Eddington, and that I shall be sent the draft within weeks. Pleased too to hear from Charles Moore,[†] editor of the *Spectator*, that my piece about the bitch is 'running', as he puts it, in the Christmas number. He also asked if I would write an obituary for them of the Queen Mother. I told him I would find this difficult, as I did not know her. I did not say that I had never cared for her personality. When he rang off I sensed he was disappointed with me.

Friday, 9th December

Yesterday before leaving Bath at 4.30 I rang up Audrey, about whom I have been worried lately. Was surprised to receive no answer, for I

---

* The Mappa Mundi, compiled *circa* 1290, was 'saved' for Hereford Cathedral and became the centrepiece of a museum opened there in 1996.
† Editor of *Spectator*, 1984–90, *Sunday Telegraph*, 1992–5, *Daily Telegraph* 1995–2003 (b. 1956).

could not suppose she was in her garden at that hour. This morning Dale* telephoned to say Audrey had had a stroke while cutting up meat for her cat. Managed to crawl to telephone and ring up Dale. She and James sent for doctor and whipped her off to Yeovil Hospital. She cannot speak, not a good prospect for her eighty-three years. Poor darling. Waves of sadness and remorse assail me.

Sunday, 11th December

We lunch at Midford Castle. Such good friends, the Briggses.† Two of their children there, Emily clever and bright, with two-week-old baby, and eldest son Barnaby, handsome, friendly and intelligent. He had just been to Siam where he stayed with a holy man in a monastery, discussing their common interest in forestry. What could be more splendid, yet this charming boy can't find a job.

The *Guardian* has asked me to write a piece about Mrs James de Rothschild‡ and the Waddesdon collection, she having died at ninety-three. I got out of it by suggesting Bobby Gore,§ who knew her better than I. An impressive woman, very authoritarian. I shall never forget how she humiliated me years ago at Waddeson when the Director of the Louvre conducted a party of art historians round the house and I was made to translate his rapid and technical French. I suffered agonies of shyness and confusion, disliking the Louvre man as much as I did her.

Tuesday, 13th December

To London for the night, my first visit for two months. Having written to Emily announcing my calling at two o'clock, I sallied forth

---

* Audrey's daughter by her 2nd marriage, Dale Stevens (b. 1944); m. 1964 James Sutton (b. 1940), mechanical engineer, yr s. of Sir Robert Sutton, 8th Bt.
† Michael Briggs, businessman and aesthete, later Chairman of Bath Preservation Trust, of Midford Castle near Bath; m. 1953 Isobel Colegate, novelist.
‡ The neo-renaissance Waddesdon Manor and its gardens were created in the 1870s by Baron Ferdinand de Rothschild. On his death in 1922 Waddesdon passed to his cousin James ('Jimmy') de Rothschild, who filled it with 18th-century French furniture and works of art inherited from his father Baron Edmond. On James's death in 1957, it was bequeathed with its collection to the N.T., his widow 'Dolly' (Dorothy, *née* Pinto) continuing to live on the estate until her own death in 1988.
§ Francis St John Gore (b. 1921); adviser on pictures to N.T., 1956–86; Historic Buildings Secretary, 1973–81.

from Brooks's, bearing bottle of sherry and cheque.[*] On arrival at Sutton Estate, went to office to check that E. and Dolly had not moved flat since my last visit. Man told me Emily was dead, had leg amputated three months ago and died after operation. Greatly shocked. Wondered why Dolly never told us. No answer when I rapped on Dolly's door. Neighbour said she had gone to day centre – perhaps to escape seeing me, for the emotion. Left bottle and cheque, and went on to Devonshires' solicitors in Buckingham Palace Gate to see Bachelor Duke's will.

Walking from there to Eardley's, I enjoyed looking through the windows I passed, at the witching hour before people draw curtains. Thought how fascinating London is. Read blue plaque to Wilfrid Scawen Blunt,[†] who lived in Buckingham Palace Gate until 1909. Passed by St Peter's, Eaton Square. Church totally gutted by fire.[‡] Somehow a fine sight. It was always rather gloomy within. I recall attending beloved Angus Menzies'[§] memorial service there. The shell is fine Grecian. In Belgrave Square, was amazed by plaque on a stalk inside the garden, inscribed 'In Homage to Leonardo the Vitruvian Man', put up by Mr and Mrs Habfart of Birmingham, Massachusetts. How extraordinary Americans can be.

E. looking younger than for many a year. We gossiped for an hour. He actually sent his love to A. Rushed away to Oxford & Cambridge Club for supper with M. Bluemantle Pursuivant[¶] talking to him by fireside, nice chubby man whose brother has been held hostage in Lebanon for three years. M. and I went to Comedy Theatre to see Alec Guinness[**] in *A Walk in the Woods*.[††] A treat, A.G. so brilliant and sardonic. We drank lime juice afterwards at Brooks's.

---

[*] 'Miss Emily' had been housekeeper at Geoffrey Houghton-Brown's house in Thurloe Square, South Kensington, in which J.L.-M. had kept a flat from 1946 to 1961; since then, he had made an annual pre-Christmas visit to her and her sister Dolly.

[†] Poet, travel writer and diarist (1840–1922); grandson-in-law of his hero Lord Byron.

[‡] The fire of 1987 destroyed the Victorian interior while leaving the Georgian shell intact.

[§] Bachelor cousin of A.L.-M. (1910–73).

[¶] Terence McCarthy (1954–2003); Bluemantle Pursuivant 1983–91; elder brother of John McCarthy (b. 1956), hostage in Beirut 1986–91.

[**] English stage and screen actor (1914–2000, Kt 1959) who, as revealed in his memoir *Positively Final Appearances* (1999), was a fan of J.L.-M's diaries.

[††] Play about the Cold War, by Lee Blessing.

Sunday, 18th December

A. and I motored to Yeovil to see Audrey in hospital there. A dark,
foggy morning. Found it difficult to read signposts. Reached hideous
hospital at 12.30. Few nurses about. Saw little Audrey sitting in a ward
of eight trying to eat an ice cream with her left hand. Think she recognised us. She looks dreadfully ill, the right side of her poor face still
blotched with marks of the fall she had. She cannot speak and was
pitiful yet contented-seeming. Occasionally smiled and even laughed
a little. Don't know that she understood what we said. We gave her
presents which meant nothing to her, I a scented head pillow, A. a
beautiful white shawl which she put around her. All the while the
other seven lay silent as corpses, while the television blared nonsense
like a snowstorm. O the poignancy of it all.

Friday, 23rd December

Coote Lygon* motored us to Chatsworth for Christmas. Staying were
Woman, Kitty Nairne† and us.

Saturday, 24th December

Henry [the butler] announced at breakfast that His Grace had left for
London, his mother taken very ill. In fact the Dowager Duchess died
before he arrived. He was back by 5.30 in cheerful mood, saying it
was a relief as for ten years she had been a cabbage, knowing no one.
But Debo says he loved her dearly.

Sunday, 25th December

We all came down to breakfast this morning, bringing presents.
Debo had made a rule that nothing be given costing more than £5.
Of course we all cheated, Andrew heavily by giving us a basket
of good wine. He is also making me an honorary member of

---

* Lady Dorothy Lygon (1912–2002), yst dau. of 7th Earl Beauchamp; m. 1985 (as his 2nd
wife) Robert Heber-Percy (1912–87) of Faringdon House, Oxfordshire.
† Lady Katherine Petty-Fitzmaurice (1912–95), dau. of 6th Marquess of Lansdowne; m.
1933 Hon. Edward Bigham, later 3rd Viscount Mersey (d. 1979); succeeded brother to
Lordship of Nairne, 1944.

Pratt's,* most flattering, though I doubt if I shall go as I am not convivial with hearty males. I gave him a presentation copy of my *Images of Bath*,† beautifully bound for the library. A. gave me a corduroy coat, a black Derry jacket for the evenings, and a pair of slippers. I gave her a matching necklace and earrings from the Gazebo, Cirencester, and a few other trashy things. We all went to church. Too much eating, too little exercise, too much dozing and too little reading.

Monday, 26th December

I went round the house by myself, looking at things for the book. Also walked with Folly around the pleasure grounds.

Tuesday, 27th December

In the morning Debo motored us to Hartington, pretty little Peak village some way from Chatsworth from which the courtesy title taken. After tea, Mr Root, ex-agent, showed me Wyatville's‡ drawings for his improvements and extensions to the house.

Poor old Philip Magnus§ is dead. He was always friendly, and encouraging about my writing. Pedantic, an old fogey, too correct and prim. Once told me that he adored the company of Jamesey Pope-Hennessy,¶ but took care never to be alone in a room with him. Jamesey much amused when I repeated to him.

---

* Gentleman's club off St James's Street, owned by 11th Duke of Devonshire; when once asked if he belonged to it, he replied, 'it belongs to me'.
† Published by Bamber Gascoigne in 1982.
‡ Sir Jeffry Wyatt (1766–1840); architect, known for his remodelling of Windsor Castle under George IV; changed name to Wyatville to distinguish himself from uncle James Wyatt (1746–1813).
§ Sir Philip Magnus-Allcroft, 2nd Bt (1906–88); historian; m. 1943 Jewel Allcroft of Stokesay Court, Shropshire; formally assumed name of Allcroft in addition to that of Magnus, 1951.
¶ Writer (1916–74) with whom J.L.-M. was romantically involved in 1940s, who in January 1974 was done to death by ruffians he had invited into his flat in Ladbroke Grove.

1989

Selina [Hastings] staying the weekend, always a lovely guest. On New Year's Eve we took her to dine with Desmond [Briggs] and Ian [Dixon]. They gave us grouse, marvellously cooked. On Sunday morning the House came before luncheon, making such a noise that even Selina said she could hardly hear a word. David told her that the Prince of Wales had asked him whether he thought £40,000 a lot to spend on a dining table. David replied that it depended on the table. Anyway, he added, surely your mother has a few spare ones. 'My mother', he replied, 'would never dream of giving any of us a stick of furniture.' Then the John Griggs came for luncheon. He has been commissioned to write the last volume of the history of *The Times*.

I have had a Christmas card from Patrick Garland mentioning that the dramatisation of my diaries is going ahead, the first performance booked for August under the title *James at War*.* I hope it will not be on the weekend of the 13th when we celebrate A's eightieth birthday here. I am also slightly sensitive about the title, as some reviewers of the diaries criticised my 'war', unaware that I had served in the army, admittedly for a short period before that bomb in Hyde Park Square.†

Wednesday, 4th January

Caroline asked me to enquire of my new friend Rouge Dragon‡ (whom I have yet to meet) by what title they should call Harry

---

* The play was not finally produced, owing to Paul Eddington's declining health. Hugh Massingberd's dramatisation, *Ancestral Voices*, starring Moray Watson, opened at the Jermyn Street Theatre in November 2002 and at the time of writing (January 2004) is still going strong as a touring production.

† J.L.-M. spent a few months in an Irish Guards training battalion before being caught in a London bomb blast in October 1940. This triggered off a nervous disorder eventually diagnosed as Jacksonian epilepsy. After a year's convalescence, he was discharged from the army and allowed to return to his old job at the N.T.

‡ Patric Dickinson (b. 1950); Rouge Dragon Pursuivant, 1978–89; Richmond Herald of Arms from 1989. He had been put in touch with J.L.-M. by Freda Berkeley.

[Worcester]'s child if he is born a boy later this month. He has sent me a long reply dismissing my suggestion of Earl of Glamorgan on the grounds that the grant of this title was never confirmed by Charles I, who seems to have changed his mind after promising it to the then Marquess of Worcester. For reasons hard for a layman to understand, he suggests instead Earl of Somerset, even though this is not a title enjoyed by David. He sent me reams of fascinating papers on the subject, which I have dropped at the House and are now being studied.

Saturday, 7th January

John Julius [Norwich] and Mollie* lunched. They have bought a dere-lict mill house near Castle Combe, at the head of a pretty valley. He is full of enthusiasms, a great worker, successful television showman, but not a man of sensibility like K. Clark.† A good writer but no scholar. Has a quick eye for the humorous, yet lacks a sense of humour. Too pleased with himself to be lovable; mulled wine in a cold decanter. Mollie, his adoring slave, is an attractive, clever woman. We talked of Mrs Thatcher. J.J. told how, soon after she became Prime Minister, he as chairman of some opera thing had to take her to *Tosca*. To his amazement, she knew everything about the history of past per-formances, when and where and who sang in them. When the per-formance was over, he asked whether she had not thought it a splendid one. 'Yes,' she replied, 'but her *fichu* should not have been scarlet but cerise.' That tells much about her. He said it was quite possible that Mrs T's grandmother, a housemaid at Belton, was seduced by Harry Cust,‡ who was the real father of Diana [Cooper],§ and notorious for

---

* John Julius Cooper, 2nd Viscount Norwich (b. 1929); writer, broadcaster, and Chairman of Venice in Peril Fund; m. 1st 1952–85 Anne Clifford, 2nd 1989 Hon. Mary ('Mollie') Philipps (*née* Makins, dau. of 1st Baron Sherfield and formerly wife of Hon. Hugo Philipps, later 3rd Baron Milford).

† Kenneth Clark (1903–83); art historian, Surveyor of the King's Pictures, 1934–44; cr. life peer as Baron Clark, 1969.

‡ Henry John Cockayne Cust (1861–1917); editor, *Pall Mall Gazette*, 1892–6; MP (C) Grantham, 1895–1900; heir presumptive to cousin 4th Baron Brownlow (1844–1921) of Belton, Lincolnshire.

§ Lady Diana Cooper (1892–1986), Lord Norwich's mother; ostensibly dau. of 8th Duke of Rutland, though she supposed her father to have been Harry Cust (a supposition now acknowledged by *Burke's Peerage*); m. 1919 Alfred Duff Cooper (1890–1954), cr. Viscount Norwich, 1953, diplomatist, politician and writer.

his attentions towards girls in service. Diana always referred to Mrs T. as her niece.

When they had left, I took Folly for a walk, meaning to do the Cherry Orchard circuit. A beautiful day. When we reached Allen Grove Farm I fell for some reason, full length. Lay for a minute trying to decide whether I was hurt. Folly unconcerned. I had just grazed my knee, but was covered in cow-dung so decided to turn back. The sun was setting, a great golden ball. As I looked at the Orangery, the eight windows blazed like orange fire, so vividly that I almost felt arsonists had been at work.

We dined at the House. I sat between Caroline and Tracy [Worcester], latter due to give birth within seven days. She wore the tightest garment possible, hideous if not indecent.

Sunday, 8th January

We went to Wincanton to see Audrey in a sort of cottage hospital for geriatrics. She now has a room to herself, which she does not like as there is no life going on. Has no radio or television. I came away depressed, although she seems better, and has recovered her speech. But I doubt her ever recovering to lead a normal life. Yet I am impressed, for in her distress she has developed a sort of authority. After we had been with her for half an hour, she made it plain that she had had enough and wanted us to go.

Monday, 16th January

Listened on Radio Three last night to French cabaret songs from the 1940s, such as *La vie en rose* sung by Edith Piaf.* So melodic and haunting, and absolutely French. No other race could have produced them. Wonderful songs, passionate and sentimental, yet with more than a touch of French cynicism and superiority. Cruel as well as sexy, for the French are that. If French is not the most beautiful language in the world, it is the most mysterious and magical. There is an affinity with the Scots tongue; I think Glaswegian approaches it in a bastard sort of way.

---

* Paris chanteuse (1915–63).

Wednesday, 18th January

To London for the night. Changed books at London Library. At Brooks's, Andrew Devonshire was sitting enthroned in the hall, holding forth. Pointing to the gouache of Charles James Fox* over the fireplace, he told his audience that members should regard it not as a portrait but an icon, for it was the very spirit of Brooks's. Joined dear old Geoffrey Houghton Brown† in Thurloe Square, he looking frail but distinguished. He took me to the Venezia, his nightly dining room, where we had difficulty hearing each other. He told me that, during the war, he bought a ring which had belonged to Pope Paul II, builder of Palazzo Venezia in fifteenth century, for £20. Christie's have just sold it for £42,000. I accompanied G. to his door, he going feebly though looking the picture of Edwardian benignity with his topcoat, trilby hat and stick. I thought I would walk back to Brooks's in spite of the cold, but jumped into a taxi on reaching Knightsbridge. London now empty of pedestrians, rather frightening, and I didn't fancy that underground passage at Hyde Park Corner.

Thursday, 19th January

To Somerset House to search for the will of the Bachelor's mistress Eliza Warwick. To my surprise there were numerous Eliza and Elizabeth Warwicks. I looked up four, but don't think any of them was my lady. A beautiful sunny winter's morning, mist rising from river. Wandered to Law Courts to admire Gothic hall, then crossed to Temple. How lovely those ranges of seventeenth-century chambers, so well restored since war. Had nostalgic feelings at 4 King's Bench Walk. Harold [Nicolson]'s‡ old rooms no longer seem to be residential, glass door at entrance. Felt inspired to write a book of reminiscences mingled with philosophising, based on places which have

---

* Whig statesman (1749–1806), known for his impassioned oratory and colourful private life.

† Dilettante and painter (1903–93), who had been J.L.-M.'s South Kensington landlord from 1946 to 1961.

‡ Hon. Sir Harold Nicolson (1886–1968), yr s. of 1st Baron Carnock; diplomatist, writer, politician, broadcaster, gardener and restorer of Sissinghurst Castle, Kent; m. 1913 Hon. Victoria ('Vita') Sackville West (1892–1962); intimate friend, from 1934 until his death, of J.L.-M., who often stayed at his chambers in King's Bench Walk, Inner Temple, between 1935 and 1939, and who wrote his biography in two volumes (1980–81).

coloured my life – Ribbesford (done in a sense),[*] Eton, Magdalen, Park Lane,[†] Portman Square,[‡] K.B.W., Buckingham Palace Gardens,[§] and so on. Curiously enough M., when I called on him for tea, suggested something similar. He also reminded me that we met ten years ago next month.

Rouge Dragon lunched at Brooks's. I liked him. Very intelligent, well-informed and correct; in looks a handsome Sebastian Walker,[¶] which does not mean handsome. Talked non-stop. I found him difficult to hear, and had to guess much. To Heywood Hill, where Joan Haslip[**] praised my Esher; then to Sotheby's exhibition of pictures from Monet to Freud. Too fast – yet how else can one?

Bruce Chatwin is dead. A grievous loss to literature, the papers say. For one so comparatively young and recently acknowledged the obituaries are amazingly long and eulogistic. You would suppose Lord Byron had died. Does he deserve it? I think of Bruce with fascination and a certain repulsion. He had a very original mind, and was one of the most physically attractive mortals. I used to tell him that he looked like a fallen angel. He, Charles Tomlinson[††] and I were a sort of trio, all living within a mile of each other, yet not on letting-down-hair terms, quite. I was stimulated by him when we went for long, rapid-striding walks around Alderley. Once we walked from Badminton to his house at Ozleworth, down Worcester Drive, past Oldfield, till we crossed the Bath–Stroud road by Tresham, he never halting in stride or talk. But I was irritated by his false cackle. He was a great self-pusher and publicity seeker, and a terrible show-off. I recall one evening when Bruce and I dined alone at Alderley. He and I sat before the fire, drinking and talking late into the night. I wondered whether to ask him to stay the night, and decided not. Just as well, perhaps. He was very beguiling, stretched on the rug in a cock-teasing attitude. He

---

[*] Ribbesford (once spelled Wribbesford), J.L.-M's grandmother's house near Bewdley, was the model for 'Wribbenhall', the setting for J.L.-M's first novel, *Heretics in Love* (1973).
[†] Off which J.L.-M. lodged in Norfolk Street during the early 1930s.
[‡] Where the proconsul and politician George, 1st Baron Lloyd (1879–1941), for whom J.L.-M. worked as private secretary from 1931 to 1935, had his London house and office.
[§] Site of the N.T's pre-war headquarters.
[¶] Children's publisher (1942–91).
[**] English writer living in Florence (1912–94).
[††] 'Wordsworthian poet . . . living a secluded life of asceticism and abstemiousness' (*Beneath a Waning Moon*, 8 February 1986) (b. 1927).

was, with all his intense vanity, discreet. Yet on this occasion he admitted that he would never decline to sleep with any male or female if pressed, but only once. Nonce with me.

Sunday, 22nd January

A beautiful television documentary about Paddy Leigh Fermor,[*] whom the presenter referred to as Fer-*mor*. He never faltered, even when quoting from Hamlet or Horace. Says his memory is visual – a thing once seen never forgotten by him. His chief interest in life has been the history of the ancient world. He blesses the day he was taught Latin. Is still handsome in a square-faced way, though getting pot-bellied; has all his hair. I see that many little houses are going up in beautiful Mani, which was totally unspoilt when he went to live there.

Tuesday, 24th January

Watched programme about Emperor Hirohito.[†] It appears he was a fiend who condoned savage treatment of prisoners of war and positively organised the Pearl Harbor raid. When in 1945 he finally announced to his people that Japan was defeated, they heard his voice for the first time. And they did not understand a word, as he spoke the archaic language of the court.

Thursday, 26th January

Listened to wireless documentary about Yeats.[‡] A whimsy old bore, and a crosspatch. Hated music. I agree with his view that words set to music are destroyed by the music – the battle between poetry and melody is always lost by the former. Otherwise a very disagreeable man, and pretentious.

---

[*] English writer living in Greece (b. 1915; Kt 2004); m. 1968 (as her 2nd husband) Hon. Joan Eyres-Monsell, photographer (1912–2003).
[†] 124th Emperor of Japan, who succeeded to the throne in 1926 after five years as Regent (1901–89).
[‡] William Butler Yeats (1865–1939); Irish poet.

Saturday, 4th February

The Vicar claims that he had an ancestress who was buried alive around 1800. A robber prised open the lid of her coffin and cut off a finger which wore a valuable ring, to be greeted with a groan. Robber fled; ancestress then rose and walked home. Vicar says story is told on her tomb in some Yorkshire village church. Her statue is shown with cut-off finger, for she lived many years after the event.

Wednesday, 8th February

To London yesterday for night. Went to Sion College, Blackheath, Victorian Gothic theological library, in vain search for information about Revd Mr Beamish, fashionable evangelical clergyman who was a great influence on Bachelor Duke. J.K.-B. dined and talked of neo-classical sculpture. He finds it hard to understand the philosophy which guided Canova[*] and the like. Whereas Michelangelo, or even Henry Moore,[†] found inspiration in the marble or stone – one thinks of Michelangelo's unfinished figures emerging as it were from the marble – the nineteenth-century sculptors had no seeming affinity with their material. Their works were of divinities, even when supposed to represent humans such as Pauline Borghese.[‡] I used not to admire them, but have come to appreciate the *Endymion* at Chatsworth.[§]

This morning Nick breakfasted, looking pale but distinguished. I can talk to him openly now about my Will and my wishes. Spent morning at Public Record Office, Chancery Lane – shades of dear Noel Blakiston[¶] – looking through lists of will-makers between 1837 and 1858 in vain hope of finding elusive Eliza Warwick. Then lunched at Garrick with Mark Amory[**] who is writing biography of Gerald Berners.[††] A nice, smiling man, tall, sallow, balding. He spoke very

---

[*] Antonio Canova (1757–1822); Italian sculptor.

[†] English sculptor (1898–1986).

[‡] Napoleon's sister (1780–1825), a famous beauty who sat for a number of Venus-like sculptures by Canova, now in the Galleria Borghese, Rome.

[§] Commissioned from Canova by the Bachelor Duke in 1819 for £1,500.

[¶] Sometime Assistant Keeper of Public Records (1905–84); m. 1929 Georgiana Russell (1903–95).

[**] Writer and journalist (b. 1941); literary editor of *Spectator*.

[††] Gerald Tyrwhitt-Wilson, 14th Baron Berners (1883–1950), of Faringdon House, Oxfordshire; composer, writer and aesthete, whose biography by Amory, *The Last Eccentric*, appeared in 1998.

fast like a Cecil, and I had difficulty keeping up. I warned him that I did not know Gerald intimately. He asked what I thought about the relationship with the Mad Boy.* Well, I said, of course Gerald must have been in love with him from the start, and possibly throughout; but he must have reconciled himself to no return, and kept the love of a paternal sort. Amory suggested my writing a book of memoirs of friends.† I said I might, if spared by the Bachelor.

By taxi to Clareville Grove. Found a great change in poor Rosamond [Lehmann]. Much thinner, hair short and straight. Her lower teeth were out, in fact on table beside her, which gave her a parrot-like appearance. Her son Hugo‡ there when I arrived, going through her letters and paying her bills. She seemed rather wandery while he remained, but became lucid when he left. She is very pitiable. Never gets out of bed. Cannot read one word of anything. Time means nothing to her. She kept remarking on my thinness. Are you sure you can be well, she asked? I asked her if I looked skeletal, as Audrey had remarked. Yes, she said, your head is like a skull.

Taking taxis everywhere, I spent well over £100 on this jaunt, which was not an unalloyed success or pleasure.

Sunday, 19th February

This evening watched Simon Rattle§ conducting excerpts from Berlioz,¶ and speaking about the composer in between. The enthusiasm and finesse of this young man, with his mane of bushy hair enclosing sensitive oval face, is astonishing. Eyes that speak volumes. His beauty arresting. Intense love of Berlioz, whom he considers precursor of modern composers like Stravinsky.** Fascinating to watch close-ups of his conducting and see his expressions of fervour, of almost mystical involvement in the music. Had never witnessed such a thing before, and never could in real life. This is what television has

---

* The handsome but unstable Robert Heber-Percy (1912–87), Berners' great love.
† It was published by John Murray in 1996 as *Fourteen Friends*.
‡ Hon. H.J.L. Philipps (1929–99); only son of Rosamond Lehmann and Wogan Philipps, 2nd Baron Milford (whom he succeeded as 3rd Baron, 1993); m. 1st 1951 Margaret Heathcote, 2nd 1959–84 Hon. Mary Makins (who m. 2nd Viscount Norwich, 1989), 3rd 1989 Mrs Felicity Leach.
§ Conductor (b. 1955).
¶ Hector Berlioz (1803–69); French composer.
** Igor Stravinsky (1882–1971); Russian composer.

done for us. I looked him up in *Who's Who*, and saw he was thirty-four. He looked twenty to me.

Saturday, 25th February

Richard Robinson motored me to see Audrey in his grand Mercedes full of gadgets. Loudspeaker system playing Haydn; telephone on which he rang up his wife telling her not to put on the vegetables for another half-hour. A. is put off by this tycoon yuppie boy and thinks he wants shaking. But he is a sweet, gentle character, clever and sensitive. Poor Audrey gets very muddled in speaking, switching from one subject to another. At one moment she was talking about her sad situation when Matthew [Arthur] left her in the 1930s; this turned into a dog she had had getting run over by a bus. Richard touchingly gentle and sweet with her. I was surprised that he had never heard of Stourhead [Wiltshire], for he is interested in architecture. Is also chairman of the Knightsbridge Environmental Committee and has been asked to stand for Westminster Council.

Sunday, 26th February

We lunched with the Johnstons,* I sitting between Susanna and a nice young woman called Judith Swire,† sister of Lord Northampton.‡ Told me she had made an inventory of Harold [Nicolson]'s books at Sissinghurst for Nigel. Grew to love Harold from the annotations in his books. Found a letter from Gerald Berners in a book given to Harold around 1935 in which he recounts visit to Hitler, assuring Harold that Hitler a man of utmost charm and sincerity, with honest blue eyes. Lady J. feels she can't return to her old home, Compton Wynyates [Warwickshire], which has been spoilt by her brother's wives, of whom there have so far been four. He has sold much, including the finest collection of Etruscan pots in England. How rotten so many of the eldest sons of the aristocracy are.

---

* Nicholas Johnston (b. 1929), architect; m. 1956 Susanna Chancellor.

† Lady Judith Compton (b. 1943), dau. of 6th Marquess of Northampton; m. 1970 Sir Adrian Swire, Chairman of John Swire & Sons Ltd, 1987–97.

‡ Spencer Compton, 7th Marquess of Northampton (b. 1946); m. 1st 1967 Henriette Bentinck, 2nd 1974 Annette Smallwood, 3rd 1977 Hon. Mrs Rosemary Dawson-Damer, 4th 1985 Hon. Mrs Michael Pearson, 5th 1990 Pamela Kypnos.

Monday, 6th March

Caroline dined with us last night. She told us that, after many hesitations and contradictions, Glamorgan has finally been accepted by the College of Arms as the grandson's title. I may have been responsible for this, and feel absurdly pleased. She was extremely funny recounting her experiences in the Himalayas, but she is difficult to capture on paper – it is the way she tells rather than the tale. Described how after an arduous climb, clinging onto tufts of grass, etc., they reached perimeter of a walled city. The proper entrance was the other side of the hill; they had come the attackers' way. When they asked their guide where their entrance was, he pointed to a hole in the ground. Through this they had to slither for nine feet, like snakes going through a drain. C. torn to ribbons, yet was so exhausted after the trek that it was something of a relief to be lying down, even on her face.

I am amazed by the rich. Caroline wanted to visit Botswana. When the bill for the expedition came, she read it as £9,000. She thought this rather a lot, but David said after all, they had but one life, etc. It then transpired that the 9,000 were not £ but whatever the local currency is, equivalent of £1,000.

Wednesday, 8th March

Listened to wireless programme about A's gardening friend Hilda Murrell, murdered mysteriously five years ago.[*] Letters read out with beautiful descriptions of plants and the Shropshire countryside. Young commentators holding her up as a latter-day saint because of her dedication to Green and anti-nuclear causes, even suggesting she may have been killed by nuclear pros. I asked A. how she first came across her. She said it was at Sissinghurst, with Vita [Sackville-West].[†] A lesbian, I imagine. I wonder whether that had anything to do with her appalling end.

---

[*] See *Holy Dread*, 30 March 1984.
[†] Hon. Victoria Sackville-West (1892–1962); writer, poet and gardener; m. 1913 Hon. (later Sir) Harold Nicolson (1886–1968); conducted affair with A.L.-M., 1954–57.

Tuesday, 14th March

To London for night. Terrible day of horizontal rain. Papa's umbrella blew inside out, and I had to leave it at Briggs to be repaired. Dined with M. at Oxford and Cambridge Club to meet Philip Mansel and M's new friend the Vicar of Z. Greatly liked Mansel, quiet, smiling, clever man, very liberal and anti-God. Vicar very queer, which I don't quite approve of in vicars, but bright, curious and well-read. At one point he rose in his seat to defend the Church against Mansel's diatribes; I think he got the worse of the exchange, but give him full marks for gallantry. I found it hard to hear what any of them said, and hope they did not find me dense and dull. Returned to Brooks's where talked until midnight with John Jolliffe,* he not drinking his first whisky. Said how devoted he was to his aunt Helen Asquith,† the most virtuous and understanding lady. I was in awe of her at Oxford.

Wednesday, 15th March

Dear Nick came to breakfast at Brooks's, looking well and handsome. He is so sympathetic, almost my dearest friend. Then to change books at London Library, and to National Gallery. Looked first at Anrep's‡ splendid mosaics, including Eddy [Sackville-West] at piano with lid open. Then at Impressionists, wondering whether their pervasive blue was inspired by the blue overalls worn by all French *ouvriers*. Then at Keats's Claude, *The Magic Castle*, dreamlike and wonderful.

To Philip Magnus's memorial service at St James's, Piccadilly. Very few people there, which reassures me that I am right to tell my executors I do not want one.§ Two nephews were ushers, the new baronet and a Sebag-Montefiore, both ugly but charming. They directed me to a good pew, and thanked me for coming – nice of them, though I

---

* Hon. John Jolliffe (b. 1935), yr s. of 4th Baron Hylton and Lady Perdita Asquith; writer.

† Lady Helen Asquith (b. 1908); eldest dau. of Raymond Asquith (killed in action, 1916; er s. of H.H. Asquith, Prime Minister 1908–16, cr. Earl of Oxford & Asquith, 1925) and Katharine *née* Horner.

‡ Boris Anrep, Russian mosaicist (1883–1969).

§ He nevertheless got one, organised by the N.T. at the Grosvenor Chapel (and well-attended).

came for P's sake and not theirs. Lord Boyd-Carpenter[*] gave an uninspiring address, remembering his first meeting with Philip towards the end of the war when P. was a major in Rome, and arranged for B.-C. to have audiences with both the Pope and the King of Italy. I somehow don't envisage that rather stuffy, over-correct, sub-fusc figure as a scintillating socialite. Kenneth Rose[†] sitting at far end of my bench. When service over I approached to ask if he would lunch with me at Brooks's to meet obituaries editor of *Independent*. He declined too abruptly, his beady eyes swivelling around looking for prey. Suddenly he pushed past me, saying 'I must have a word with Baba'.[‡] I gave way and followed. Lady Baba turned to me and kissed me on both cheeks. I fancy Kenneth looked *chétif*.

Jamie Fergusson lunched at Brooks's, and later accompanied me to Dickens's house in Doughty Street, which I wished to see in order to decide whether to leave them my lock of Dickens's hair. Decided against, for this museum is very depressing with its linoleum and glass cases with dust lying upon manuscripts.

Friday, 17th March

We dined alone with David, sitting cosily at a table in the library before a roaring fire. Much as I like him and enjoy his company, I don't love him or ever feel intimate. Yet he is the kindest man alive (perhaps also the cruellest). When A. mentioned I might have to quit my library, he at once offered to find a room for me in the House. After dinner he took us round the west wing, to a room over the *porte-cochère* in a passage hung with washed linen. I did not fancy this. Then to the upstairs of north wing. Didn't fancy the larger room here either, and wondered if I could bear to be parted from Bath. During dinner, he said he would be quite unable to live here were he not earning a great income from his gallery,[§] and wondered whether the Worcesters, when the time came, would either want to live in the House or be able to afford to. We said that in any case they would be spared the capital outlay he had so lavishly provided.

---

[*] John Boyd-Carpenter (1908–98); Conservative politician, who had been President of Oxford Union when J.L.-M. was an undergraduate; cr. life peer 1972.
[†] Historian and journalist (b. 1924); 'Albany' of *Sunday Telegraph*.
[‡] Lady Alexandra Metcalfe.
[§] Marlborough Gallery in Albemarle Street, founded in 1946.

Saturday, 18th March

We had a nice luncheon party of Rosalind Morrison,* the Eeleses†
and Anthony Hobson.‡ Adrian Eeles a quiet, unassuming, intelligent
man. I asked him if the ghost of Bruce Chatwin was haunting their
house in Ozleworth. He did not like Bruce, considered him a fraud,
does not even think him a good writer. People stroll to their door
asking if this was the house B.C. lived in. Anthony very quick, and
smart with repartee. When I asked him to autograph his book *Libraries
of the World*, he said he had already done so. I looked, and he had. Felt
an ass. Ros fading in looks, alas.

Sunday, 19th March

We lunched at Widcombe Manor with the Warrenders.§ Rupert and
Josephine [Loewenstein] staying. Rupert talked about Jonathan
Guinness's book,¶ which has upset Diana [Mosley]. R. says it is a horrible book, but shows genius. J.G. has put himself into the mind of
his concubine and described her somewhat squalid experiences vicariously. Lord and Lady John Manners** also lunching. He is offhand,
with that patrician disdain and self-assurance which maddens the
middle classes. Asked me if I had influence with the National Trust to
the extent of persuading them to hand back country houses to two
friends of his. I endeavoured to explain the nature of inalienability,
and asked if Francis Dashwood†† was one of the friends. He admitted
this. So I told him that had not Johnnie Dashwood made West

---

* Rosalind Lygon (b. 1946), granddau. of 7th Earl Beauchamp; m. (2nd) 1984 (diss. 1999) Hon.
Charles Morrison (b. 1932; Kt 1988), yr s. of 1st Baron Margadale, MP (C) Devizes, 1964–92.
† Adrian Eeles; dealer in prints.
‡ Bibliographical historian (b. 1921); m. 1959 Tanya Vinogradoff.
§ Hon. Robin Warrender (b. 1927), yr s. of 1st Baron Bruntisfield; m. 1951 Gillian
Rossiter; underwriting member of Lloyds.
¶ Hon. Jonathan Guinness (b. 1930); er s. of 2nd Baron Moyne (whom he succeeded as
3rd Baron, 1992) and Hon. Diana Mitford; m. 1st Ingrid Wyndham, 2nd Mrs Suzanne
Phillips. His book *Shoe: The Odyssey of a Sixties Survivor* (Hutchinson, 1989), contained
an account of his extra-marital affair with the 'hippy' Shoe Taylor (1944–2003) by whom
he had had three children.
** Lord John Manners (b. 1922), yr s. of 9th Duke of Rutland; m. 1957 Mary Moore.
†† Sir Francis Dashwood, 11th Bt (1925–2000); tenant and restorer of West Wycombe
Park, Buckinghamshire, which his father, Sir John Dashwood, 10th Bt (1896–1966; m.
1922 Helen Eaton [d. 1989]) had donated to the N.T. in 1943.

Wycombe [Park, Buckinghamshire] over to the Trust, Francis would certainly not be living there today, as Johnnie would have flogged house, contents and park – he had already sold much of the estate right up to the village. Lord Bad Manners said that his father, late Duke of Rutland,* and Eddy Devonshire† never got on, though close neighbours at Haddon and Chatsworth. It was that Whig versus Tory prejudice which persists to this day. The Whigs had a great sense of money and power, but never unbent towards the common man, whereas the Tories had the common touch. He complained that dukes were becoming extinct. I mentioned that several royal dukes had been created this century whose lines were continuing. Oh pooh, he said, they're not real ones.

Hugh Grafton is giving a party at the National Portrait Gallery to celebrate his seventieth birthday. We are invited, and can't go. After much soul-searching, I have sent him my miniature of James III.‡ If he likes it, it will join the finest collection of family portraits in private hands in England. The problem with giving an object one values to the rich is that they accept it as a matter of course and barely acknowledge the gift, let alone sacrifice made by non-rich friend.

Wednesday, 22nd March

We motored to Osterley [Middlesex] and back, two hundred miles, for luncheon given to Graham Thomas, N.T. garden adviser, on his eightieth birthday. Several old N.T. friends. Lunched in breakfast room at separate tables, buffet style. Went round the house with Martin Drury afterwards. He feels as I do about the horrible redecorations of library and upstairs bedrooms by the V&A. Incredible to us that these academic pedants have such bad taste. But Martin tells me the V&A are handing both Osterley and Ham over to the Trust with endowment of £10 million – which is little enough, but will enable N.T. to scrap what the museum have done. They have certainly made a museum of this house, a country house no longer.

---

* John Henry Montagu Manners, 9th Duke of Rutland (1886–1940).
† Edward William Spencer Cavendish, 10th Duke of Devonshire (1895–1950).
‡ Prince James Francis Edward Stuart (1688–1766), known to Jacobites as the Chevalier of St George and to Hanoverians as the Old Pretender; o.c. of King James II and Mary of Modena; claimed to be King James III of England and VIII of Scotland on father's death in 1701; attempted unsuccessfully to regain throne, 1708 and 1715–6. J.L.-M. had told his story in *The Last Stuarts* (1983).

Saturday, 1st April

Staying with Eardley alone at The Slade. I used to think it rather a horrid little redbrick Edwardian box. True, it has no architecture outside; but inside it is almost ideal for a single person, or in the case of E. and Mattei, two who are seldom here together. Of course made charming by E's paintings and Regency furniture. There is a distinct period and sub-Bloomsbury feel. Reminds me of Raymond [Mortimer]'s and Paul [Hyslop]'s house in London, very art-Twentyish, a taste I find sympathetic. Every reference and art book to hand. Cosy deep sofas. Then the situation almost ideal, unspoilt landscape, fields with cows sloping across a small valley to woods. E. in benign mood, and wonderful for his age. He is utterly independent, drives, cooks, does housework, paints as though twenty years younger than eighty-six. Only a little deaf. Most reprehensible of me to be irritated by deafness in another. I suppose it is because we talk incessantly. E. walked off after breakfast and worked. I read and wrote letters and walked. Gorgeous weather, like May. Bluebells on verges.

Thursday, 6th April

A. went to Spain today on dendrological tour. I anxiously listened to the news lest her aeroplane had crashed. Alex Moulton[*] dined, dinner all prepared by A., places laid, dishes with this and that, written directions. Oh, the coffee cups. I was rather apprehensive about encountering Alex, since I behaved rather ill in declining to go on our annual jaunt in his precious Rolls last year. This evening he diplomatically made no mention of further tours. Very didactic as usual, which amuses me. Expressed horror at encrusted state of Aga stove, explaining that thereby not only would heat be lost but the rate of increase of fuel, calories, calefactories, etc., etc. We discussed the lack of morals in public and business life. Alex said that all the city malefactors, Saunders,[†] Rowland,[‡]

---

[*] Dr Alexander Moulton of The Hall, Bradford-on-Avon, Wiltshire (b. 1920); engineer and inventor; friend of J.L.-M. since 1943.

[†] Ernest Saunders (b. 1935); Chief Executive of Guinness plc, 1981–6, who was convicted with others in 1990 of organising an illegal share support operation in connection with Guinness's attempt to take over the Distillers Company.

[‡] Rowland T. ('Tiny') Rowland (1917–98); born Roland T. Fuhrop in India; tycoon who made a fortune in Africa, and was said by Edward Heath to represent 'the unacceptable face of capitalism'.

etc., were Jews, whose misdeeds arose from their ingrained protective instinct as a hungry, homeless minority. I remonstrated with him over this, but he was quite unrepentant, though not at all anti-Semitic.

Tuesday, 18th April

Got back last night from Ireland, where I swore never to go again, and had not been for twenty years at least.* Stayed at Lismore Castle [Co. Waterford] with the Devonshires. Travelled there Thursday; came back Monday. A stupendous pile and the most picturesque site imaginable. Sheer above the Blackwater River, with a thin slip between castle and water of pouffy trees and yews, like cushions onto which one is almost tempted to jump, expecting to be bounced back. To left and right, east and west stretches the river, wide and fast-flowing, its long line broken only by tributaries. My bedroom in Flag Tower facing north overlooking the water meadow, tops of Knockmealdown Mountains in distance. Vast castle round central courtyard. Agent lives on one floor of east wing; family and staff in north wing; offices in part of south wing; the rest empty. A wonderful place, but melancholy, like everything Irish. One merely has to live in this strange, remote, isolated world to become eccentric, casual and forthright.

I got there to find Debo, Kitty Mersey and latter's charming daughter-in-law Anthea Bigham.† Andrew joined us on the Saturday. This is the Devonshires' annual visit, and he will have spent two nights, she a week. Neither of them may step outside the house, not even into the garden, without two policemen, guns at the ready, following at a discreet distance. I think the embarrassment of this and the trouble it gives explains why they come so seldom. Enjoyable visit and profitable Bachelor-wise. Hideous Pugin‡ furniture which inspires amazement if not admiration. 'Do you feel His presence here?' asks Andrew.

I consider Debo the most remarkable woman I know. Because she is a Duchess? Largely yes, because this status has brought out her astonishing Mitford qualities. I feel that, in any crisis, she would come out top, organise, keep her head, show her innate courage and self-

---

* He had visited Donegal in August 1971 to stay with Derek Hill (*A Mingled Measure*) and Northern Ireland in August 1977 to stay with Mairi Bury (*Through Wood and Dale*).
† Anthea Seymour; m. 1965 Hon. David Bigham (b. 1938), yr s. of 3rd Viscount Mersey and Katherine, Lady Nairne (see notes to 23 December 1988).
‡ A. W. N. Pugin (1812–52); architect and designer with a passion for the Gothic.

assurance. As it is, her charm, her 'unbending' (for she does have to unbend from her Olympian height), and her dignity never fail to captivate.

Monday, 24th April

More ducal society. A. being at La Fourchette, Caroline and David ask me to dine. She interrupts too much, while he sits with a suppressed martyr's smile on his thin lips. He had come from Waddesdon, where Jacob Rothschild* has inherited Mrs R's ugly house full of good things. David advised him to take a flat in the Manor, which he considers hideous. I admire the quality of the stonework very much indeed.

Today I went to tea with poor Eliza Wansbrough. She has become tiny, leaning on a gnarled stick like an ancient witch. Discovered only yesterday that all her jewelry missing, every single item, all taken from the box in her bedroom. She does not know when this happened. Clearly someone walked into the house while she was sitting alone in her little room downstairs. Rather hard on an old woman of ninety-four.

Thursday, 4th May

To London. Took cab to Apsley House. So full of interest and redolent of Iron Duke. Pleased to see, well-displayed off entrance hall, splendiferous full-length portrait of Gerry,† who did so much. How right 1st Duke was to choose yellow silk for walls of Waterloo Room. The red put in place by 2nd is not good.‡ Lamentable Ministry of Works taste in carpets. Lunched at Boodle's with Derek Hill, his sweet self. He touchingly admitted that some of his portraits had been failures recently. Advised me to go to three exhibitions – Corot,§

---

* Hon. N.C.J. Rothschild (b. 1936); er s. of 3rd Baron Rothschild (whom he succeeded, 1990) and Barbara Hutchinson (see entry for 15 September 1989); m. 1961 Serena Dunn.
† Lord Gerald Wellesley (1885–1972); succeeded nephew 1943 as 7th Duke of Wellington; architect and architectural conservationist; m. 1914 Dorothy Ashton.
‡ Arthur Wellesley, 1st Duke of Wellington (1769–1852), of whom *Debrett's Peerage* writes: 'the brilliant services of "the Great Duke" are unrivalled in history, but too varied to be particularised in this volume'; his eldest son Arthur Richard, 2nd Duke (1807–84), sometime Master of the Horse and Lord Lieutenant of Middlesex.
§ Jean-Baptiste-Camille Corot (1796–1875); French artist.

Degas* and Emily Patrick.† I went to all three. Saw a Corot the same size as mine and not unlike, on sale for 375,000 dollars, no less.

Sunday, 7th May

Such weather as I don't recollect even in sunniest Mays. Five days of cloudless skies. I fear greenhouse effect. Walk with Folly through Vicarage Wood and hear cuckoo in distance. We have the Horse Trials, crowds and noise. Freda [Berkeley] staying weekend; adores Trials, though more interested in shopping than horses. On Sunday morning a snob lot from the House calls for drinks. The Ashcombes,‡ he shy, she friendly; the Vesteys,§ he very nice, she charming.

Friday, 19th May

We dine with David Beaufort alone, sitting afterwards in the little drawing room with windows open, view of long avenue eastwards in twilight, smell of hay and wisteria, deep blue haze and total stillness. D. tells us he is buying, as intermediary for Getty Museum, a very important picture which has lain undiscovered since 1815, an Ingres¶ of Caroline Murat.** He has to make certain that it has not been stolen, nor smuggled to Belgium where seller lives. D. arranged for greatest living expert on Ingres to see it in Zurich yesterday. He thinks nothing of flying across Europe and back in one day.

Sunday, 21st May

We lunched at Lasborough Manor [near Tetbury, Gloucestershire] with Jonathan Scott and wife,†† unknown to us but friends of Mary Keen. They have bought back the house which previously belonged

---

* Edgar Degas (1834–1917); French artist.

† English artist (b. 1959).

‡ Henry Cubitt, 4th Baron Ashcombe (b. 1924); m. (3rd) 1979 Mrs Elizabeth Dent-Brocklehurst of Sudeley Castle, Gloucestershire.

§ Samuel Vestey, 3rd Baron Vestey (b. 1941); m. (2nd) 1981 Celia Knight.

¶ Jean-Auguste-Dominique Ingres (1780–1867); French artist.

** Napoleon's sister (1782–1839); m. Joachim Murat (1767–1815), King of Naples, 1808–14.

†† Ian Jonathan Scott (b. 1940); Director of Barclay's Bank, 1980–92; Chairman of Reviewing Committee on Export of Works of Art, 1985–95; m. 1965 Annabella Loudon.

to his grandmother. I remember it as a romantic, down-at-heel Cotswold manor. Now absurdly over-restored with yuppie-style Versailles garden laid out in the valley. Long drawing room upstairs with swagger Tudor fireplace, so high that it thrusts itself through ceiling. He is a tight-lipped, clever merchant banker, chairman of Export of Works of Art Committee to which I once briefly belonged. Said to me after luncheon, 'I have long meant to tell you that your book on Italian Baroque [1959] inspired me to become addicted to that style.' I fear he has been taken in, for in those days there were few books of that sort.

Monday, 29th May

Nick motored me to Penselwood. Audrey sitting in the octagonal hut. Little better, but can talk. There is no one else who can share my childhood memories. We talked of Ribbesford. She said I had written a 'mischievous' novel featuring Wall the butler, which is high marks for her to have made the connection.* In telling a story of how she stole silver buttons from the footmen's liveries she laughed so much she almost choked. It affected me likewise. Nick looking at us as though we were lunatics.

Thursday, 1st June

Was telephoned in Bath this morning by youngish academic at Lincoln College, Oxford called Edward Chaney† who had written to me about his biography of Inigo Jones.‡ I warned him I knew little now. He nevertheless begged to meet me, and see Beckford's library. I dare say that were it not for Beckford I would meet no one new. He came for tea. Tall and bearded with the bluest eyes, like the Son of God. Refreshingly right-wing in his views. Told me he had lunched

---

* See notes to entry for 19 January 1989.
† Art historian (b. 1951), expert on 'the Grand Tour'; lived in Florence, 1978–85; Fellow in Architectural History at Lincoln College, Oxford, 1985–90, subsequently Professor of Fine and Decorative Arts at Southampton Institute; was in 2003 preparing an edition of Inigo Jones's *Roman Sketchbook* for Roxburghe Club.
‡ Architect (1573–1652) who introduced Palladian style to England; Surveyor of the King's Works, 1615–35; J.L.-M. had written a book about him, published by Batsford in 1953.

last week in Florence with Harold Acton[*] and John Pope-Hennessy,[†] the latter frailer than the former and no longer fierce. Chaney was very flattering, praising my article in *Modern Painters*, treating me with a deference I don't deserve. A delightful man.

Saturday, 3rd June

Why I continue with this diary God knows. Pedestrian and costive, like my life now. M. will doubtless destroy. Yet there is Mr Rota,[‡] hovering. This courteous man writes me sensitive letters explaining why no antiquarian bookseller would buy my library in my lifetime and let me hold on to it until death.

The Mappa Mundi situation looks bad. I was thinking of buying a £1,000 share, but see today that the scheme is falling through. Far more important than the Rose Theatre,[§] which is a sorry hullaballoo over a few stones which Shakespeare can never have seen or trod. Yet on listening to Peggy Ashcroft[¶] and James Fox[**] I was nearly convinced. There followed Athene Seyler[††] on her hundredth birthday. This wonderful old Trojan recited faultlessly the long passage of Shakespeare which she had spouted at her first audition more than eighty years ago. She also sang an 1890s music hall air. Truly splendid.

I lunched with the Henrys [Robinson] at Moorwood. She is about to have her third child; he, like most young fathers, is dismayed by the prospect, and slightly bored with the two already there. On my return home, a sudden inspiration made me divert to Coates to glance at my Bailey grandfather's grave.[‡‡] My hunch was right – he, born before

---

[*] Sir Harold Acton (1904–94); writer and aesthete; owner of Villa La Pietra, Florence.

[†] Sir John Pope-Hennessy (1913–94); art historian and museum director, then living in retirement in Florence; elder brother of J.L.-M's late friend 'Jamesey' P.-H.

[‡] Anthony Rota (b. 1932), Managing Director of Bertram Rota Ltd, who were seeking a buyer for J.L.-M's papers.

[§] The site of the theatre, built by Philip Henslowe in 1586, had been discovered during excavation work earlier that year, but promptly covered up again for conservation reasons. It was opened to the public in 1999.

[¶] English actress (1907–91; DBE 1956).

[**] English actor (b. 1939).

[††] English actress (1889–1990), known for her comic roles in plays and films.

[‡‡] J.L.-M's grandfather Henry Bailey (1822–89), 5th and youngest son of iron and railway tycoon Sir Joseph Bailey, 1st Bt; m. (2nd) 1881 Christina Thomson (1849–96); devoted his life to hunting and shooting at Coates, his estate near Cirencester.

Shelley's death, died just after Athene Seyler was born. What a connection for my great-nephew's offspring if they live to be a hundred.

Thursday, 8th June

John K.-B. lunched with me in London. Affectionate as always, but
he notices that I am becoming vague and inattentive. Keeps saying
things like, 'You aren't losing your balance, Jim?' with an apprehensive look. He told me two dreadful things. First, Lord Tavistock[*] is
selling Canova's *Three Graces*, for which he has been offered £7
million by Getty Museum. John has testified to Export of Works of
Art Committee on importance of this group, for which the Woburn
sculpture gallery was more or less built. He says this is but one example
of country house owners rushing to sell their treasures to America, a
phenomenon he attributes to the Washington exhibition of four years
ago.[†] Secondly, he says the National Trust want to build a hotel on the
land they own at Stonehenge. I find this hard to credit.

Sunday, 18th June

We are living through a heatwave, which sends me into a nostalgic
dreamland. Delicious it is here. The garden still green and a bower of
flowers and foliage, like a pre-Raphaelite canvas. Yesterday we
lunched with the Hollands. Joanie always sweet to me and makes me
sit beside her, demoting many a high-ranking guest on my account.
On my other side Fleur Cowles,[‡] a silly lady I thought with her dark
spectacles, talking about herself in Thirty-ish whimsy manner. Must
be extremely rich to have house in London, house in Sussex, castle in
Spain, crossing to America twice a year by Concorde, which she says
travels faster than a bullet from a rifle. Thinks that within five years
we shall be 'fired' to America in a windowless rocket and the journey
will take a mere thirty minutes. What is the point?

---

[*] Henry Russell, Earl of Tavistock (1940–2003); er s. of 13th Duke of Bedford (from
whom he received Woburn Abbey in 1970s, and whom he briefly succeeded, 2002).
[†] The exhibition *Treasure Houses of Britain: Five Hundred Years of Private Patronage and Art
Collecting* had taken place at the National Gallery in Washington from November 1985 to
March 1986, its opening attended by J.L.-M. on his only visit to America (see *Beneath a
Waning Moon*).
[‡] American writer and artist; m. (2nd) Tom Montague Meyer.

I listened to Isaiah Berlin's* talk about how classical thought was overtaken by the romantic in philosophy. What a mind! Faultless delivery, but a rapidity of thought which is marvellous. Witty too. It sounded as if he was speaking *extempore* rather than reading from a script. A. says I should write to him. But I can't write just to tell him how clever I think he is.

Monday, 19th June

Last night A. and I drove through the park after dinner. The full moon an enormous mauve ball blazing through the tree tops. All the deer assembled before the house, as they are wont to be at dusk. In the north-west, a sunset of Turneresque splendour. It lit the House with an unearthly light, sometimes silver, sometimes orange.

Brigid Salmond† lunched. Her brother, who is general factotum at Dodington,‡ eats in the house with the Kents, new owners, very nice and unsnobbish, he a property developer. When Brigid was there for luncheon, she asked out of curiosity to go to the loo. Went through their bedroom, and saw embroidered on the bed cover, 'Better to be *nouveau riche* than not *riche* at all'.

Saturday, 24th June

I finished the Bachelor yesterday – that is, got down his tale from birth to death. Am as amazed by my quickness as I am aware of its badness. Just the dull facts about a not very interesting man, who only achieved what he did because he happened to be extremely rich. I still have much to do – revision, addition, omission, etc.

Sunday, 25th June

Our garden open today. Just in time, for weeks of perfect weather coming to an end. Towards closing time the Llewellyns came, Bishop

---

* Russian-born Oxford philosopher and historian of ideas (1909–1997).
† Brigid Wright (b. 1928), dau. of FitzHerbert Wright and Hon. Doreen Julia Wingfield, o. dau. of 8th Viscount Powerscourt; m. 1950 Julian Salmond, o.s. of Marshal of the RAF Sir John Maitland Salmond and Hon. Monica Grenfell, dau. of 1st Baron Desborough.
‡ Dodington Park, Gloucestershire, which the Codrington family had been obliged to sell a few years earlier (see *Holy Dread*, 1 November 1982). In 2003 it was on the market again for £15 million.

Bill* looking very ill. We talked of our time at McNeile's [House,
Eton]. He must be one of the last of my contemporaries there. His
favourites were Roger Pettiward, killed as a parachutist in war, and
Reggie Turner, killed in an air crash just after the war. Both Llewellyns
very depressed by ruination of Leighterton [Gloucestershire] where
they now live. Fault of county council which owns the village and has
evicted tenants of old farms, erecting beastly Dutch barn buildings,
visible from Bath–Stroud road.

Last night we attended ceremony to celebrate two centuries of
Lansdown Cresent. The Colonel, who is chairman of the Lansdown
Crescent Association, asked us to dine. We arrived at 6.30. Crescent
barred to traffic by police. Bands played, Mayor made speech, residents
dressed in bonnets and other unbecoming togs which they presume
were worn then. I turned up my shirt collar and wore a white scarf
like a stock into which I put a pin with the Thomson crest, never
worn by me since inheriting it. Colonel introduced me to Chris
Patten[†] the Bath MP, who asked to see my library. Stayed a time
talking. Nice man, ring on centre finger, yellowing teeth, stocky,
Catholic and friend of Rees-Mogg who is godfather to his children.
Affable and well-informed like most Tory MPs today. Told me he
prayed to God for personal things, a fine day, a good dinner, etc. 'How
can you waste his time?' I asked.

Saturday 1st–Monday 3rd July

We go off for the weekend. First motor to Send to stay a night with
Loelia. A sad experience. This dear little spruce house is no longer
spruce but very faded and down-at-heel. One pleasant Australian girl,
without a clue of course. Garden a wilderness. Silver and furniture
unpolished, rooms unswept. Loelia has quite given up. Can one
wonder? Is haunted by poverty, and showed us two love letters written
to her by Ian Fleming[‡] which she is thinking of selling. Her mind is
all right, except that she cannot remember any name. Who was the

---

* Rt Revd William Llewellyn (1907–2001); Vicar of Badminton, 1937–49; Bishop of
Lynn, 1961–72; m. 1947 Innes Mary Dorrien Smith; Eton contemporary of J.L.-M.
† Conservative politician (b. 1944); MP for Bath, 1979–1992; Sec. of State for the
Environment, 1989–90; Chairman of Conservative Party, 1990–92; Governor of Hong
Kong, 1992–97; European Commissioner from 1999.
‡ Novelist (1908–64); creator of James Bond.

man during the war who smoked a cigar? Yes, Winston. In the morning remained in bed. We said goodbye to her in her bedroom.

On the way to Send we lunched at Parkside. An equally sad experience. Garrett bent and white as a sheet. Took me up to Joan's bedroom to see her. Joan lying screwed up on a daybed, fully dressed, fast asleep, snoring, tongue hanging out. I said to Garrett, perhaps we had better return after luncheon when she is awake. What's the point, he said, she won't know you. Doesn't know him.

From Send to Sissinghurst. Very different experience, highly enjoyable visit. Never have I seen the garden more beautiful. Party consisted of Lady Rupert Nevill,* Sue Baring,† Philip Ziegler‡ and dear Richard Shone.§ Lady R. does not charm me. One front tooth badly cemented in, like an over-pointed brick. Ziegler improves as visit goes on. At first faintly furtive and gauche, doubtless shy. But clever and agreeable. Believes Maître Blum¶ a bad woman who has done harm. Is lunching with her and M. in Paris on Monday – think of it. A. and I given The Cottage to sleep in, she in Vita's old room, I in Harold's, sleeping in the bed in which he died in 1968. They would not have been pleased by the hideously vulgar way the rooms have been decorated by the tenant, American literary agent.

Nigel told story of how he was the officer responsible for deporting some Cossacks in 1945, on the orders of Harold Macmillan. At the time he thought it a dreadful thing. The victims were told they were being sent to Italy, and so went unprotesting. He sent in a memorandum criticising the order, and was severely rebuked. Wishes he had had the guts to disobey and face court martial, like William Douglas Home.** I was fascinated and horrified. Nigel is to be a

---

* Lady Camilla Wallop (b. 1925), er dau. of 9th Earl of Portsmouth; m. 1944 Lord Rupert Nevill (1923–82), yr s. of 4th Marquess of Abergavenny, friend and aide of HRH The Duke of Edinburgh.

† Hon. Susan Renwick (b. 1930), dau. of 1st Baron Renwick; m. 1955 (diss. 1984) Hon. Sir John Baring (b. 1928; succeeded 1991 as 7th Baron Ashburton).

‡ Historian (b. 1929), then writing official biography of King Edward VIII.

§ Art historian (b. 1949); associate editor of *Burlington Magazine* from 1979; friend of Eardley Knollys.

¶ As the ex-King's executor, Suzanne Blum had been unwilling to cooperate with Ziegler on learning of his appointment as official biographer (see *Beneath a Waning Moon*, 23 May 1987); but she had been persuaded to meet and help him by Michael Bloch. She was in her ninety-first year.

** Playwright (1912–92), court-martialled when he disobeyed orders on moral grounds.

leading witness for the defence in case to be brought next October by Lord Aldington against Count Tolstoy.* He has invited Tolstoy to live at Sissinghurst if he loses the action and is ruined.

Large luncheon party on the Sunday. Betty Hussey,† much aged but affectionate. Attorney-General and wife.‡ I sat next to Jeremy Hutchinson,§ who is on a committee to improve the museums around London, Chiswick, Kenwood, etc. Richard Shone recommends Sintra for Eardley and me in September.

Saturday, 8th July

Vicar told us the following story. While Master was alive, it was traditional for an annual meet to take place in his honour on his birthday. One year the birthday fell on Good Friday, and the Vicar told him he could not possibly have a meet that day. Whereupon the Duke took up the telephone and put through a call to Buckingham Palace. He asked for the Queen, who came on the line. 'Our Vicar tells me . . .', he began, and told the story. Then a long pause, and the Vicar heard him say, 'Well, if you really think so, Ma'am. That's what the Vicar advises. Seems incredible to me.' He put the receiver down, and said not a word. There was no further question of it.

Sunday, 9th July

Helen Dashwood is dead. I wrote Francis a difficult letter. Couldn't pretend I liked her. So I praised her steadfastness, her loyalty to her

---

* The historian Count Nikolai Tolstoy (b. 1935), whom J.L.-M. had met on 4 November 1981 (*Deep Romantic Chasm*), had published a pamphlet accusing the former Brigadier Toby Low (1914–2000; cr. Baron Aldington, 1962) of personal responsibility in deporting of prisoners of war to their deaths in the Soviet Union in 1945. Aldington sued for libel and was awarded damages of £1.5 million. Tolstoy has since attempted to challenge this verdict, and the European Court of Human Rights has ruled the award to be excessive. Nicolson gave evidence for Tolstoy, but was critical of his later assertion that he had failed to receive a fair trial.
† Elizabeth Kerr-Smiley; m. 1936 Christopher Hussey (1899–1970), architectural historian and sometime editor of *Country Life*; owner of Scotney Castle, Kent (whose gardens she donated to N.T.).
‡ Sir Patrick Mayhew, QC (b. 1929); m. 1963 Jean Gurney; cr. life peer as Baron Mayhew of Twysden, 1997.
§ Jeremy Hutchinson, QC (b. 1915); m. 1st 1940 Dame Peggy Ashcroft, 2nd 1966 June *née* Capel (daughter of J.L.-M's friend Diana, Countess of Westmorland); cr. life peer as Baron Hutchinson of Lullington, 1978.

family and to West Wycombe, her beauty and zeal. Made no reference of course to the bloody way she treated the poor N.T. staff when
they were billeted at West Wycombe during the war – as described in
my diaries, over which she made such a hullaballoo. She was a spoilt,
snobbish and vulgar woman who had to be invited to every lighted
candle, though few if any of the lighters cared for her. She was horrid
to the humble and meek.

Monday, 17th July

Last night Selina stayed, in order to take us to Hardy [Amies]'s* eightieth birthday dinner. I had been dreading it, what with the heatwave and
all. Given by the Faringdons at Buscot Park. About forty. Extremely
posh surroundings and gold plate. I was given a place at the top table,
between Debo on Hardy's left, and Loelia on my left. On Hardy's right
as guest of honour Princess Peg,† that dear and charming old bundle
with large white tombstone teeth like a cook's. Also at our table Henry
Bathurst‡ and Lord Briggs.§ Loelia talked whole time but I could not
hear a word. At one point I took my napkin and wiped food off her
chin. Debo divine, but in unsuitable tomato-coloured dress with high
winged shoulders. Enjoyable on the whole – but oh dear, the horror of
my old contemporaries! Peter Coats a white skeleton. Hardy looking
drained, skin taut and shiny, wearing large black-rimmed spectacles like
a tycoon's. Made speech which was well-delivered but embarrassing.
Stressed his humble, corrected to humdrum origins; then thanked the
Countess of Somebody, grandmother of our hostess, who had given
him patronage fifty years ago; went on to thank Devonshires for welcoming him into bosom of Chatsworth, etc. Call me snobbish, but I
thought all this rather ill-bred. A pity, for he is a dear man who deserves
his swimgloat. Is to be knighted this week.

   On leaving the dining room I watched a small, shrivelled man with

---

* Dressmaker by appointment to HM The Queen (1909–2003).
† Hon. Margaret Geddes (1913–99), dau. of 1st Baron Geddes; m. 1937 Prince Louis of
Hesse (1908–68), who became head of Grand Ducal House of Hesse (Darmstadt) when
the aeroplane carrying his elder brother and children to his marriage in London crashed
with no survivors.
‡ Henry Bathurst, 8th Earl (b. 1927), of Cirencester Park, Gloucestershire; m. (2nd) 1978
Gloria Rutherston.
§ Historian (b. 1921); Provost, Worcester College, Oxford, 1976–91; cr. life peer, 1976.

bent and balding head in front of me. Only when I heard the voice
did I recognise Alan Pryce-Jones.* As voluble and amusing as ever, he
now resembles Harry Melvill,† a shrill old queen. Henry Bathurst
button-holed and bored me with his problems over Alfred's Hall in
Cirencester Park. It will cost £75,000 to repair what was built as a
ruin. Heritage won't help; Landmark Trust might, but would that
mean trippers invading his park? I advised him to trust in John Smith.‡
Noticed his mouth down at the side, as if he had suffered a stroke.
How sickening are the old. Mama was right when she said they should
not be seen, only heard occasionally.

Sunday, 6th August

As a birthday treat, the dear Mitchells motored us to Highclere, not
seen by me before. Another grilling day. We arrived long before
opening time and picnicked in the park, against a wire fence, squatting on hard-baked earth, persecuted by wasps. How anyone can honestly enjoy a picnic beats me. Nevertheless we quite enjoyed ourselves.
House better in photographs than actuality, though a noble picturesque pile in Tudoresque rather than Gothick style. Crowds of visitors. The 1870s Gothic vestibule a noble thing, with Early English
pointed roof and colonnettes of red and blue. Little furniture or contents worth looking at. Napoleon's desk and chair used at Longwood.
Dreary 1930s decoration on bedroom floor. Nothing can be said for
the taste of that deplorable decade. Then to Sandham Memorial
Chapel, not seen by me since Eardley and I negotiated with the
Behrenses. Rather moving, sort of folk-arty Carpaccio chapel.
Building again 1930s, rather nasty and mean.

A female guide at Highclere nearly died with excitement when I
casually remarked that I knew Tilly Losch,§ whose name is not

---

* Author and journalist (1908–2000); editor *Times Literary Supplement* (1948–59); Eton
contemporary of J.L.-M.
† Edwardian raconteur and dilettante, often seen in Oxford during J.L.-M's undergrad-
uate days, by which time he had become an absurd figure.
‡ Sir John Smith (b. 1923; Kt 1988); banker; MP (C) Cities of London and Westminster,
1965–70; Deputy Chairman of N.T., 1980–5; founder of Landmark Trust; m. 1952
Christian Carnegy.
§ Ottilie Ethel ('Tilly') Losch, Austrian actress and dancer (1907–75); m. 1st Edward
James (art patron and Eton contemporary of J.L.-M.), 2nd 1939–47 (as his 2nd wife)
Henry Herbert, 6th Earl of Carnarvon (1898–1987).

mentioned by the present Carnarvons,* but of whom there was a photograph behind a rope. Of course I didn't know her the least well. Tom [Mitford] had an affair with her. She was a real bitch I imagine.

Tuesday, 8th August

To London. Collected Harold [Acton]'s medal from British Academy. Was received by Sec. and Deputy-Sec. Handed medal. What to do with it, and how to get it to Florence? Went to Julian Barrow's† studio in Tite Street at height of afternoon heat. Was so fagged I barely made sense, and did not know how to give praise. Must now write introduction to his exhibition catalogue. Kindly motored me to Paddington, where dear M. had tea with me at station hotel. Brought me enormous book on French Revolution as a present. Said he was now keeping a diary, which he wrote up daily before going to bed, *i.e.*, at 4 a.m. Said he considered himself slow-witted. It is true that he does not have quick responses, but ponders and ruminates. I told him this was his strength as a writer.

Saturday, 12th August

The dreaded eightieth birthday party for Alvilde was a triumphant success, as all the guests assured us. A. herself delighted, which was the main thing. We were lucky with the weather, the long spell of relentless sun, accompanied by drought, having at last come to an end. Yet sunshine on the day, accompanied by strong wind and scurrying clouds. We received the guests on the porch at Sheldon‡ – a difficult climb for the halt, Loelia and Woman having to be escorted on both sides. Champagne for sixty, wandering in the house and sitting on benches on the terrace. Then a painful procession to the stables where we ate at nine tables. A. had Andrew [Devonshire] and Garrett [Drogheda] next to her, I, Patricia Hambleden§ and Rachel

---

* Henry Herbert, 7th Earl of Carnarvon (1924–2001), s. of 6th Earl by 1st marriage and sometime stepson of Tilly Losch; m. 1956 Jean Wallop.

† Painter of portraits, landscapes and country houses (b. 1939), who had recently completed the picture of J.L.-M. in his Bath library featured on the jacket of this volume; m. Serena Harington.

‡ Sheldon Manor, Wiltshire, seat of Major Martin Gibbs.

§ Lady Patricia Herbert (1904–94); dau. of 15th Earl of Pembroke; m. 1928 3rd Viscount Hambleden; Lady-in-Waiting to HM Queen Elizabeth from 1937.

Bridges.* Piano-playing by young BBC man found by Freda, Paul Guinery. A's grandchildren dressed as toreadors, looking hideous. Andrew gave us both a toast in a few words to which A. tossed off a cursory yet rather charming reply as she wrestled with the huge birthday cake. Instead of 'Happy Birthday to You', which she hates, Guinery struck up with 'Rule! Britannia', very jolly. He played the accompaniment for a song which little Kane, aged six, was supposed to sing; but he lost his nerve, so A. took him and waltzed with him. A pretty sight.

I can't say I enjoyed this extremely expensive party, though delighted by its success. Thank God it is behind me – it kept me awake at nights. On reflection, it worked because we were not too ambitious. Unlike Hardy we did not stage a lavish banquet in a rarefied setting. We chose a simple but genuine manorial setting for a squirearchical feast. What with the Gibbs family portraits, antlers, saddles, brick paving of loose boxes, iron posts topped with balls and decorated with trailing ivy and periwinkle, we contrived a rustic, almost a Breughel scene, and an air of jollity which suffused ancient and infant alike.

Chloë and offspring staying two nights, boring me to tears. One has to be careful, for she flies off the handle if provoked. I fear her children will not get a proper education, for she cannot stay put. Is about to take them to the toe of Italy for a month, and thence to Ireland. No plans thought out about where to live.

Wednesday, 16th August

David Beaufort is a fascinating subject for study. We lunched with him today, Daphne [Fielding] the only other guest. Why does he suddenly ask us? He telephoned last night, infinitely polite, so glad, looking forward so much; and then when we arrive today, so pleased, which he can't be particularly. Never refers to the hostile press articles. One last week in the *Mail* stating that he has £100 million, owns 50,000 acres, is investing £14 million in BAT,† leads a separate life to his wife (not quite true), has a son with a drink problem (true). He must be totally indifferent, as he is to comment about Miranda moving into a

* Rachel Bunbury; m. 1953 Thomas, 2nd Baron Bridges (b. 1927), second cousin once removed of A.L.-M., HM Ambassador in Rome, 1983–87.
† British American Tobacco.

house he has had converted for her on the edge of the park. Talks of
so-and-so being frightfully rich, while *he* must be ten times richer.
Casually remarks that the lovely old Turkey carpet in the library, torn
to shreds by the young with their heels and stilettos, cost him £10,000
four years ago, and that a similar one to replace it will now probably
cost him twice as much. He is ruthless yet charming, apparently highly
sensitive to one's feelings, yet would probably not care tuppence if one
dropped down dead at his feet.

   When we left, he pointed out the two cupolae which he has
repaired, re-leaded and repainted, and said he was very irritated with
the Heritage people. He wants the House exempted from death
duties, for whereas ten years ago a large house was assessed as of little
value, today, owing to sheikhs, etc., it is valued at millions. Although
he does not open it to the general public, yet every year thousands
came to Badminton for dinners, meetings, etc., and the great crowds
attending the Horse Trials and other shows benefit from the House,
even if they do not enter it. I agree with him – a historic house ought
to be exempt just like a painting or tapestry.

Friday, 18th August

This morning at 9.30 I answer the telephone and am surprised to hear
Jock Murray's voice. Asks how Bachelor Duke getting on. He wants
to publish it very much. This is nice to know, and flattering. He has
returned the first two chapters with comments.

Saturday, 19th August

The day of parting. A. has been angelic, stocking up with all the food
I shall need in her absence. She says this is the last time she will go
away without me. Kissed her goodbye and restrained tears with an
effort. Folly, silent, sits beside me.

Thursday, 24th August

J.K.-B. came to stay yesterday. Today we went on a jaunt. First thought
of Ragley [Hall, Warwickshire], but on reaching Northleach decided
to go instead to Broughton Castle [near Banbury, Oxfordshire], first
seen by me with Desmond Parsons in 1936. It is still the most romantic house imaginable. English to the core, as Henry James says. I would

rather be the 21st Baron Saye and Sele* than any duke. Both title and house have descended in unbroken line since fourteenth century. Lovely day we had. Too many people, but all well-behaved and nice. Nothing jars outside. Inside looks as if bailiffs had been in. I believe the last peer was pressed for funds and sold much. Some restoration in progress. Beautiful parterre garden laid out in *fleur de lys* style on south side. Perfection, what with moat, gatehouse, church, and gorgeous orange and buff stone.

Saturday, 26th August

J.K.-B. and I lunch with the Fitzboys† for me to meet Dosia Verney‡ after so many years. She looks wonderful, with Grecian features, far better than she did as a girl. She reminded me of how she arrived at Wickhamford during the war, having bicycled in the rain from Worcester, and Mama took her upstairs to fetch some clothes for her to wear. I asked if Mama was nice to her. Fairly, she said. She remembers a large cupboard full of dresses, out of which flew two birds. He, Andrew, charming. A golden youth when last seen, now grey and collapsed.

Sunday, 27th August

Tonight I watched a film about Ian Fleming.§ What a horrid man. I think the actor impersonated him well, looking handsome in that lady-killing, butch yet silently penetrating way of those MI5 men. Ann¶ and Loelia were likewise portrayed fairly, with all the vulgarity of the smart set of those days, amoral, full of sex and Noël Coward sophistication. I find myself shocked by their prodigality and *Côte d'Azur* tastes.

---

* Nathaniel Fiennes, 21st Baron Saye and Sele (b. 1920); m. 1958 Mariette Salisbury-Jones.
† Desmond Briggs and Ian Dixon.
‡ Theodosia Olive Cropper (b. 1921), yr dau. of James Winstanley Cropper (Lord Lieutenant of Westmorland); m. 1st 1944 Frank Barrington ('Barry') Craig (1902–51), artist, 2nd 1955 Dr Andrew Felix Verney (1921–2000), yr son of Sir Harry Verney, 4th Bt. She was a fellow Wiltshire magistrate of Desmond Briggs, and had got to know J.L.-M. before the war when they had both lodged in Cheyne Walk with her cousin Rick Stewart-Jones.
§ *Golden Eye: The Secret Life of Ian Fleming*, with Charles Dance as Fleming, Marsha Fitzalan as Loelia, Phyllis Logan as Ann and Julian Fellowes as Noël Coward.
¶ Ann Charteris (1913–81); m. 1st 1932–44 3rd Baron O'Neill (brother of J.L.-M's friend Midi Gascoigne), 2nd 1945–52 2nd Viscount Rothermere, 3rd 1952 Ian Fleming.

Monday, 28th August

The eighty-second birthday of my beloved Rupert Hart-Davis.* I sent him an affectionate card. Doubt whether I shall ever see him again, perhaps better not. Instead I lunched with the other Rupert – Loewenstein – who was staying with the Warrenders at Widcombe. He joined me in my library and we went to the Royal Crescent Hotel. I must say it is posh, and the mews house in which we ate nicely tarted up in Georgian fashion. People sitting on terrace under blue umbrellas, Mediterranean sky overhead. Food nothing special, vegetables undercooked, good bread-and-butter pudding. I think it cost Rupert about £50. I offered to go Dutch, but was pleased when he insisted. Very easy to gossip with. He told me a friend of his had just married, aged sixty, a spinster of forty. The friend wants to have an heir but is not sure whether he can consummate. I asked if the couple had come to an understanding before matrimony. No, he says. Well then, trouble is in store.

Thursday, 31st August

A. returned from Morocco this evening. Seemed well but tired, and had been robbed again by David [Herbert]'s rascally servants. In her absence I have duly fed the four goldfish [in the garden pond]. Even goldfish have distinctive personalities. They seem quite stupid, for when I chuck in the pellets, they are usually slow to pursue them. The smallest fish makes no effort at all, gets left behind and usually ends up with nothing to eat. The large silver fish is aggressive and with a whisk of the tail frightens off the others while he gobbles the pellets.

Friday, 1st September

Two sad events reported today. First, Peter Scott[†] has died before reaching his eightieth birthday. Many justified tributes. A remarkable, far-seeing man, one of the earliest conservationists of the dwindling

---

* Sir Rupert Hart-Davis (1907–99); publisher, editor, writer; Eton contemporary of J.L.-M.

[†] Sir Peter Scott (1909–89); o.c. of Captain Robert Scott ('of the Antarctic'; d. 1912) and Kathleen, later wife of 1st Baron Kennet; sportsman, artist, naval officer, naturalist and writer; Chairman World Wildlife Fund from 1961; m. 1st 1942–51 Elizabeth Jane Howard, 2nd 1951 Philippa Talbot-Ponsonby.

wildlife, especially birds and fish. I am glad we visited him at Slimbridge at the end of 1987.* He looked frail then. I suppose he was about the age K[athleen Kennet] was when she died. I feel I am the grand survivor when I remember visiting her on her deathbed, poor darling. How proud of him she was. Prince Philip spoke of him on television, paying great tribute. Dosia and I were talking of his first wedding only a week ago.†

The second event very tragic. Uppark‡ burnt down. By a blow-lamp, Midi tells me, informed by her great friend Jean Meade-Fetherstonhaugh, Meg's daughter. When I think of Meg and the Admiral sacrificing themselves and everything to the preservation of that magical house, I ask myself – does God care? Is he a philistine too? Furniture apparently all but saved, chandeliers of course all gone and those wonderful mulberry curtains which Meg restored so pain-fully with her saponaria on which the V&A experts poured such scorn. O the cruelty.

Sunday, 3rd September

In church at Little Badminton today, the replacement Vicar (Tom still being away) gave a sermon about the last war. All the papers are writing about its outbreak fifty years ago. It is glorious weather, as it was then; and oddly, the days of the week are the same. So far away. I think I was at Cheyne Walk, but can't remember quite. A. and I lis-tened to the repeat of Chamberlain's broadcast at 11.15. I certainly heard the original delivered. Moving and well-done, coming from a disillusioned and disappointed man, with none of Churchill's his-trionics. I remember my intense unhappiness and wondering what the future held for me. Vicar today said our declaration of war was abso-lutely justified. I suppose he is right.

---

* See *Beneath a Waning Moon*, 12 December 1987.

† In her memoir *Slipstream* (2002), Elizabeth Jane Howard writes of Dosia Verney as her oldest and closest friend.

‡ William and Mary house in South Downs, donated to N.T. by Meade-Fetherstonhaugh family in 1954, J.L.-M. being involved in negotiations. A remarkable restoration took place following the fire resulting in the re-opening of the house in 1995, the N.T.'s cen-tenary year.

Thursday, 7th September

David Beaufort at dinner said Derek Hill was undoubtedly an influence on the Prince of Wales, and responsible for the Prince sticking those thin pilasters onto the front of Highgrove. We were surprised when he introduced two subjects close to home. First, drugs. He wondered if it might not be better to allow them, so that they might 'find their own price on the market'. The second was mistresses, he telling us that Alfred Beit* wanted one but could not afford one. He asked us whether Alf was really rich at all. As if we would know. D. had just returned from playing golf with the Duke of Marlborough† in Scotland. I'm not sure how much they really like each other, but I suppose dukes find each other cosy company, and talk ducal 'shop'. Caroline looking extremely handsome and dignified, stout but upright. We sat in the little yellow room. Delicious dinner of crab, obtained by Mervyn the Keeper.

The Keats–Shelley Bulletin says Keats suffered from something called cyclothymia – a quick alternation of depression and comparative elation, similar to manic depression but faster in cycle and not as devastating. Of course it is what I have suffered from all my life. Why did I not recognise this before? Because I have never heard the word until today.

Saturday, 9th September

We lunched with Francis Watson‡ at his nice Regency village house in Wilts. Packed with desirable things, as one would expect. Among the other guests Diana, Duchess of Newcastle,§ divorced wife of Pelham who was my Eton contemporary and a cousin of Michael Rosse, who held him in low esteem for selling up Clumber¶ and being

---

* Sir Alfred Beit, 2nd Bt (1903–94), art collector and sometime Conservative MP; m. 1939 Clementine Mitford.
† John Spencer-Churchill, 11th Duke of Marlborough (b. 1926).
‡ Sir Francis Watson (1907–92); Director, Wallace Collection, 1963–74; Surveyor of Queen's Works of Art, 1963–72; m. 1941 Mary 'Jane' Gray (d. 1969).
§ Lady Diana Montagu-Stuart-Wortley (b. 1920), dau. of 3rd Earl of Wharncliffe; m. 1946–59 (as the 2nd of his 3 wives) Henry Pelham-Clinton-Hope, 9th Duke of Newcastle (1907–88).
¶ Clumber Park, Nottinghamshire, seat of the Dukes of Newcastle. The house was demolished in 1938 and the estate eventually became the property of the National Trust.

a 'rotter' in many senses of the word. Nice woman, who began without effrontery, 'I am Diana and I shall call you Jim.' These single duchesses proliferate in the country, and are to be found amongst the intellectual queers, who adore and amuse them. She spoke of the Fitzwilliam family, her grandfather coming from Wentworth Wood-house* where she spent much of her youth. Also asked me if I knew her Uncle Lawrence at the National Trust. I could not think whom she meant. It was Lord Zetland.† I replied that I could hardly say I knew him, though I held him in reverence. He was very grand, stiff and formidable. She said he was a sweet, affectionate man, though proud; that his life was ruined by his wife who was very promiscuous in her amours. He would probably have become Viceroy but for her.

Francis a good host, full of mischievous chat. Showed us a pair of brass ormolu Gothic candlesticks which came from Fonthill, and a water-colour of the Pantheon in Rome which belonged to Catherine the Great. Francis has adopted a Chinese son who has rigged up a temple under the roof. One has to doff shoes to penetrate. This boy full of strange superstitions – won't do this or that on a Friday, makes Francis keep one gate of his circular drive locked so devils can't drive through.

Friday, 15th September

Christopher Chancellor‡ was buried yesterday. I did not go. I shall never forget him taking me aside in the dining room at Alderley one day after luncheon and saying, 'Jim, I have been thinking over the future. When you and I are widowers, would it not be a good idea for us to live together?' I was appalled, unable to think of anyone I would like to live with less. A powerful tycoon, ruthless and ambitious. Must have had a big brain once. By the time I knew him as Chairman of the Bath Preservation Trust, his mind was already slipping. The rows he manufactured made him and his supporters, including me, very

---

* Palladian pile near Rotherham, Yorkshire, seat of the Earls Fitzwilliam. After the Second World War it became a training college, but was purchased in 1999 by private owners who intended to restore it as a residence.
† Lawrence Dundas, 2nd Marquess of Zetland (1876–1961); Secretary of State for India, 1935–40; Chairman of National Trust, 1931–45; m. 1907 Cicely Archdale.
‡ Sir Christopher Chancellor (1904–89); General Manager of Reuters, 1944–59; Chairman, Bath Preservation Trust, 1969–76; m. 1926 Sylvia Paget.

unpopular. He adored intrigue and I think of him sitting over whisky and soda in my Bath library plotting terrible schemes to oust unco-operative trustees and carry off daring plans. Many of his plans were good, and he sorted out the Trust's finances. Our alliance was based on what I wrote about Sir Roderick Jones in *Another Self*.* Christopher also hated him, and eventually replaced him at Reuters after engineering a palace coup. He himself was not sympathetic, and a terrible snob. He once lent us his villa near Pisa, but when he discovered we were having the Graftons to stay, remained as host, and was a great bore. One night there was a thunderstorm and water poured through the roof. Christopher completely lost his head and started shouting at us all hysterically. I thought, can this be the man who ran Reuters and Bowaters? I began to wonder whether he was a bit of a fraud, with feet of clay.

What saddens me more is Barbara Ghika's† death from a knock-out stroke. I did not know her well, or for long, but saw much of her in Rome when she and Rex Warner were courting. We then made a friendship which always lasted in my heart. She was never a beauty, but had much fascination and charm. Was gentle, tolerant, extremely intelligent, with good taste and humour. I picture her sailing down the Corso in a horse-drawn cab with Rex beside her; or squatting on the grass while Rex and I went to look at a church. Always radiant and welcoming.

Sunday, 24th September

Got back last night from Scotland where I stayed for a week with Eardley at the Falls of Lora, Connel Ferry [near Oban, Argyll]. Retraced some ancient haunts. Weather not good. Much rain and several totally grey days, which put me in mind of visits long ago to Aunt Dorothy,‡ walking solitary and wretched and lonely along the

---

* In the penultimate chapter of *Another Self*, J.L.-M. writes of his dislike of Jones (1877–1962), Chairman of Reuters where he was employed in 1935–6, and describes a (possibly imaginary) scene in which he forestalled imminent dismissal by tendering his resignation to Sir Roderick.

† Barbara Hutchinson (sister of Lord Hutchinson of Lullington); m. 1st (1933–46) 3rd Baron Rothschild, 2nd 1949 Rex Warner, 3rd Nico Hadjikyriakou-Ghika, painter.

‡ Dorothy Heathcote-Edwards (d. 1968); m. Alec Milne Lees-Milne (1878–1931). Much affection existed between J.L.-M. and this eccentric aunt, who dressed as a man, smoked a pipe, and became an ardent supporter of another nephew, Sir Oswald Mosley.

road before Arcady or across the moors behind the house. Falls a nice hotel, clean rooms and good food, though no porridge, alas. Saw much of Joan Hewitt.* Now a very old and tiny lady with frizzy grey hair and furrowed face. Neatly dressed in trousers. She was jolly and funny. Her new solicitor tells her she has a nice pile in the bank and must spend it. A relief to know this, for guilt assails me when I see her.

No good walks around Connel. One day Joan took us to Benderloch and beyond. On return we called at Ardnamurchan and looked at Uncle Milne's enormous salmon in glass cases, all caught on the river Awe in the year 1913, several over fifty pounds. On our last day we made an expedition to Iona. Does not arouse any feelings of sanctity. Abbey a well-restored fake, surroundings unattractive and tourist-ridden. Monotonous drive across Mull in bus. As we passed Lismore by boat, I remembered visit there in 1932 to Lady Kinross and dear Patrick.† Dreadful occasion when Patrick and I came upon badly wounded stag which had fallen from cliff to beach. We had nothing to kill it with, and had to drag it to sea and drown it. Haunting experience. We played consequences in the evenings. Never was there such merriment or vulgarity over rhymes.

Thursday, 28th September

I feel smug when I have accomplished all I meant to do on a day's jaunt to London, and disgustingly so when I have entertained the humble and visited the sick. Bought at Austin Reed the waterproof which Eardley wore in Scotland and I much admired. It is pale brown like a pre-war dust coat of the sort which used to be worn in open touring cars, made in Japan, very long, and folds up into a pocket handkerchief so as to be put in a bag the size of a pin-cushion. Had A's umbrella mended at Briggs. Then Igor‡ to luncheon at Brooks's. Is now humbly employed in a travel agency, doing odd jobs in back regions, not in front issuing tickets. Complained to me about his

---

* Aunt Dorothy's close companion during her long widowhood (see entry for 2 August 1991).
† Patrick Balfour, 3rd Baron Kinross (1904–76); author and journalist; his mother was Caroline Johnstone-Douglas, a family connection of the Marquess of Queensberry.
‡ J.L.-M's step-grandson Igor Luke (b. 1965), o.s. of Hon. Clarissa Chaplin and Michael Luke.

inability to get on with girls. He blamed his looks and his voice, but I told him that the fault lay in his manner rather than his appearance. Then I went to see Ros. I saw John Jolliffe and gave him a lift in my taxi. He is writing the life of Clive Pearson.* How boring I thought, but did not say.

Ros still pitiable, but has fallen in love, aged eighty-eight, with a beautiful youth, a distant cousin aged twenty-eight.† Waits for him to telephone. Thinks only of him. He is writing a life of the Dalai Lama.‡ Is being encouraged by Ros in his pursuit of the spiritual. Ros seemed dreadfully flushed. Did she in her blindness paste her poor face with rouge, unseeing? She told me how her first husband, Runciman, who has just died, would not allow her to have a child by him, and forced her to go through the horror and ignominy of having a backstreet abortion. She recalled how we had first met in France. I don't believe that I so fell for her that I exclaimed, 'Too late, too late!', having just married A. Can't be true.

Tuesday, 3rd October

A vicious article by that nasty little man [David] Pryce-Jones§ about Diana Mosley. I telephoned Debo who had not seen it, and thought she might get Frank Longford¶ who loves her to write in protest. Debo is going to America to lecture. On what, I asked? Oh, the dump of course. You are the Queen of Dumps, I said. I told her that A. was in France and going to do the garden of Giscard d'Estaing.** 'Isn't it strange how we are all wanted in our old age?' said Debo. Too late, I replied.

---

* Hon. Clive Pearson (1887–1965), yr s. of 1st Baron Cowdray; industrialist.

† Alexander Norman.

‡ Lhamo Dhondrub (b. 1935); recognised aged two as reincarnation of 13th Dalai Lama; assumed religious and political authority in Tibet, 1950, but forced into exile by Chinese invasion, 1959; awarded Nobel Prize for Peace, 1989. His book *Ethics for the New Millennium*, written 'with Alexander Norman', appeared in 1991.

§ Journalist; son of Alan Pryce-Jones and his 1st wife Poppy Fould-Springer. He had fallen out with the Mitford sisters (except for Jessica) over his book *Unity Mitford: A Quest* (1976) (see *Ancient as the Hills*, 3 May 1974, and *Through Wood and Dale*, 15 April 1976).

¶ Francis Pakenham, 7th Earl of Longford (1905–2001); politician, humanitarian campaigner, writer and publisher; m. 1931 Elizabeth Harman, writer (1906–2002).

** Valéry Giscard-d'Estaing, President of France, 1974–81.

Thursday, 5th October

Went to London just to attend John Murray's party at 50, Albemarle Street. What a civilised house – dear old staircase; first-floor room hung with early nineteenth-century portraits; on stairs K. Clark, Osbert [Lancaster],* John Betj[eman] – and Paddy [Leigh Fermor], survivor among eminent contemporary authors. Peter Quennell, very old, murmuring that this was like the last party in Proust. Conversation with him not easy, as one senses he expects more than one can give. Diana Menuhin† said she and I had known each other longer than most people had known us – for I knew her when she was the not very successful dancer Diana Gould.

Friday–Monday, 6th–9th October

Flew to Stuttgart on Friday, returning Monday evening. Joined small party organised by Derek Hill. We stayed at Brenner's Park Hotel, Baden Baden, where Edward VII stayed, somewhat altered inside since. Extremely grand, comfortable, luxurious and expensive. Weather dark and cloudy, with some rain. Pity, for the setting, bedroom window overlooking arboretum and river below, very fine. Party consisted of dendrologists. A. is the dendrologist, not I, though I enjoy watching them as they pull and pore over leaves and argue about them.

Highlight for me was visit on 8th to Darmstadt to lunch with Princess Peg.‡ Bus drove through narrow gateway of Schloss Wolfsgarten where she lives. Approached through suburbs. No lodges, which were deliberately pulled down by her husband so as to preserve anonymity. Short drive to *circa* 1700 house of dull sandstone. Tall, Dutch-like centre with cupola, and extremities added. Was until 1918 a shooting lodge, where royals could retreat to lead informal existence.

The Princess was on the steps to welcome us, and in the saloon made a pretty little speech. 'Please have a poor man's white lady, or orange juice.' Some pretty furniture, and pair of handsome glass-framed mirrors

* Sir Osbert Lancaster (1908–86); cartoonist, humorist, writer and dandy, of whom J.L.-M., his Oxford contemporary, wrote an affectionate memoir in *Fourteen Friends*.

† Diana Gould, ballerina (1912–2003); m. 1947 Yehudi Menuhin, violinist (1916–99; cr. life peer, 1993).

‡ HRH Princess Margaret of Hesse and the Rhine: see notes to entry for 17 July 1989.

on wall with deep blue borders. On windows the signatures of various celebrities, visitors to Wolfsgarten, had been scratched by diamond. I first noticed that of Adenauer,* carved in 1952. Princess told us that strangers remark on the dirty, broken windows which she must be too poor to have mended. She showed us dozens – Derek of course, Mick Jagger even, Julian Bream.† On other panes our present Queen, Queen Mother, David and Wallis‡ (this pane cracked), Prince Charles, *et al.* And 'Nicky', the last Czar, dated 1895.

A white-gloved footman handed round a tray on which were little slips of paper marked M[ann] and F[rau]. Mine taken at random resulted in my sitting on right of Princess. (Her slip said, 'Die Hausfrau'.) She had Patrick Forde§ on her left, and I had Anthea Forde on my right. I had a long talk with the Princess. During the war she ran the Red Cross in Darmstadt until she and the Prince were confined to the house on Hitler's orders, as her Geddes relations were involved in the British war effort. She never met Hitler, though her wedding certificate was witnessed by Ribbentrop¶ in London. (Her husband was born three months after me.) She said that, after 1918, all royal land, unlike that of ordinary private landowners, was forfeited by the Government, except for the immediate surroundings of a house. It was lucky that, when the Tsarevich** visited Wolfsgarten just before the 1914 war, an area of 150 hectares was fenced off for security reasons, and this was allowed to be kept. Most of the family's revenue came from their huge estate in Silesia, long since lost, but she still has a castle in Switzerland.

After lunch, she escorted us round the house. Several rooms filled with *Jugendstil* stuff collected by last reigning Grand Duke, very ugly I thought. In the park close to the house a very pretty baby cottage in *Jugendstil* built for little Princess Elizabeth, daughter of last Grand Duke and Princess Victoria Melita of Edinburgh (known as

---

* Konrad Adenauer (1876–1967); Chancellor of German Federal Republic, 1949–63.
† Guitar and lute virtuoso (b. 1933).
‡ The Duke and Duchess of Windsor.
§ Patrick Forde, squire of Seaforde, Co. Down (b. 1940); m. 1965 Lady Anthea Lowry-Corry, er dau. of 7th Earl of Belmore.
¶ Joachim 'von' Ribbentrop (1893–1946); German Ambassador to London, 1936-38, and Foreign Minister, 1938–45, whose biography was being written by Michael Bloch.
** Crown Prince Alexei (1905–18); o.s. of Nicholas II of Russia and Alexandra of Hesse.

'Ducky').* This poor little girl, result of a miserable marriage engineered by Queen Victoria and dissolved the moment the old Queen
died, herself died aged eight of diphtheria. No grown-ups were
allowed in the cottage or its tiny garden no matter how naughty the
little girl may have been. Went into the cottage, full of photographs
of the little Princess and the Romanov children. Full of pathos and
sadness.

Princess P. is running a centre at Darmstadt to settle refugees from
East Germany.† Says they are all young and skilled, and therefore most
welcome as there is a shortage of skilled labour in the West. When I
asked if it was not difficult to house them, she said it was no problem
at all.

The 9th we spent at Ludwigsburg [Württemberg], the largest
Baroque palace in Germany, inspired by Versailles. Very fine inner
courtyard of undulating curves, a musical rhythm. Some splendid galleries, full-blood Baroque stucco work of Turkish prisoners *circa* 1730.
Also saw Favorita pavilion, enchanting. Have never seen a more
cynical disregard for fine architecture than the modern buildings, of a
hideousness unparalleled, built right up to the entrance of the palace.
A hospital on the garden side, now being extended. Indeed there
seems to be no planning in Germany. All along the motorways are factories, dotted indiscriminately. The traffic is terrifying, even on
Sunday morning.

Thursday, 12th October

Sat up watching Denis Healey‡ on TV. His eyebrows are like two
horrid stag beetles approaching one another; his teeth, which he
shows much, are bright yellow. One would have supposed a man
seeking the limelight would have more vanity. Appears benevolent,

---

* HRH Princess Victoria Melita ('Ducky') (1876–1936), yr dau. of HRH Prince Alfred
Duke of Edinburgh and Grand Duchess Marie Alexandrovna of Russia; m. 1st 1894 (diss.
1901) Grand Duke Ernst Ludwig of Hesse and by the Rhine, 2nd Grand Duke Kirill of
Russia.
† A flood of these had begun arriving, as the communist East German regime tottered
following the withdrawal of Soviet support. The Berlin Wall came down, and the
German Democratic Republic effectively collapsed as a state, a month later, on 9
November.
‡ Labour politician (b. 1917); Secretary of State for Defence, 1964–70; Chancellor of the
Exchequer, 1974–79; Deputy Party Leader, 1980–83; cr. life peer, 1992.

but is devious I would guess. Fond of music. I dislike public figures who flirt in a common way with women. I don't care for Mr Healey, that's the truth.

Monday, 16th October

Darling Giana Blakiston lunched with me in Bath. Aged eighty-six. Drove herself from Hindon; then left for London down the motorway. Talked of the Devonshire House set, and in particular of Harriet Granville, her great-grandmother. Asked me if the Bachelor had any heterosexual instincts. Surely you mean 'homo', I asked? No, hetero, she repeated.

The *D[ictionary of] N[ational] B[iography]* have sent me a copy of a letter they have received from the killer of Jamesey Pope-Hennessy, sent from Parkhurst Prison. This person threatens to sue for libel on the grounds that he was never charged with murder, and I describe Jamesey as having been murdered in my *DNB* entry on him. I always understood that the case brought was of manslaughter because John P.-H., advised by Lord Goodman,* did not want a sensational trial full of revelations about Jamesey's sex life. They ask if I am willing to alter wording in future editions. I hope I do not get involved in this matter.

Another old friend not seen for a long time, Desmond Shawe-Taylor,† came for the night. We watched Mr Heath‡ being interrogated by Ludovic Kennedy. H. was asked rather bad-taste questions about his sex life which he parried without a quiver of annoyance or give-away. I admired him for this. Did he ever think of marrying? Yes, twice. Why then did you not do so? Were you not really in love? Heath's jowl is appalling, huge and pendulous; how does he shave it? Betrayed that he had a grievance. Out it came, that Mrs T. had never offered him a cabinet post, though tried to get him to accept the Embassy in Washington in order to get rid of him. Desmond said that Heath has twice lunched at Long Crichel, necessitating many police in house and garden. Heath telephoned beforehand to ask if there

---

* Arnold Goodman (1913–95; cr. life peer, 1965); solicitor, known for his skill in handling sensitive matters arising from the private lives of public personalities.
† Music critic (1907–95); co-tenant of Long Crichel, Dorset.
‡ Sir Edward Heath (b. 1916); Conservative politician with musical interests; Prime Minister, 1970–74.

would be any 'pomposos' lunching, odd word to use. On both occasions he was half an hour late, without apologising. Desmond says he is of almost professional standard as a conductor.

We talked of Jamesey, and A. asked Desmond if he had known anyone else who was murdered. 'Only my father,' said Desmond. This was in 1920, by Sinn Feiners. Desmond too young to be much affected, and bears no grudge against the Irish.

Thursday, 19th October

Young man from BBC telephoned, asking if I would join TV discussion on the Monarchy. Roy Strong had suggested me, on the basis of my having written a book about somebody called Lord Esher (pronounced like 'thresher'). I said I wouldn't. Could I suggest anyone else? I mentioned M., and Kenneth Rose. Had never heard of either. Finally asked for my opinion of the monarchy. I said I was 100 per cent in favour. Why, he asked, what made me think they were of any use? I did my best to enlighten the cretin. Shocked that a programme so sensitive can be put into the hands of someone as low grade as this.

Saturday, 21st October

Enjoyable day. Motored to Hambleden for A. to have a quick glance at the young Smiths'* garden which she is doing, and on to the John Smiths at Shottesbrooke [near Maidenhead, Berkshire] for luncheon. Much teasing, because in 1944 I turned down the then lugubrious, rambling, semi-derelict house for the N.T. The change unbelievable. It was then rendered in dreary cement. The Smiths on inheriting have pulled down two-thirds of the house, leaving a neat block with pretty Gothick colonnaded entrance. Rendering gone to reveal deep red brick with purple vitrified headers forming diaper pattern. Very well done within. Large central hall and library on left. Mown swards right up to house, and on entrance side, two oblique avenues. A kempt place, most attractive. Two other couples, the Adamses,† ambassador to Cairo, and

---

* Hon. W. H. B. Smith (b. 1955); er s. and heir of 4th Viscount Hambleden of The Manor House, Hambleden, Henley-on-Thames; m. 1983 Sarah Anlauf.
† Sir James Adams (b. 1932; KCMG 1991); HM Ambassador to Tunisia, 1984–87, to Egypt 1987–92; m. 1961 Donatella Pais-Tarsilia.

Alistair Hornes,[*] author of Macmillan biography and father of Camilla Harford.[†] Talked of Nancy Mitford whom he greatly admires and once met lunching with the Colonel[‡] in Paris. Colonel was expatiating about the superiority of French tanks to German in 1939. Nancy, clearly bored, piped out, 'The trouble was the poor darlings wouldn't bring them out of their garages.' John and Christian both charming. Excellent luncheon, handed round by jolly, blooming lady with whom I had jokes about heaviness and heat of dishes. After luncheon Christian drew me aside and told me blooming lady had six of my books which she begged me to sign. Greatly touched. Saw the church, which is very interesting. Truncated nave and pronounced transept, almost Greek cross. Many mural tablets to Smiths and Vansittarts through whom Shottesbrooke descended. One Smith married a Somerset, and the Plantaganet coat depicted. Extraordinary to find this squirearchical set-up – well-ordered country house, park, dominating church with spire – amid surroundings of unattractive metroland.

When we got back, Julian Barrow came round with catalogue of his forthcoming exhibition. On first page, over my short introduction, illustration of his painting of my Beckford library. Says National Portrait Gallery have made sign of wanting to buy. I said, 'But they do not buy paintings because they are good ones, but on account of the subject', meaning that I couldn't believe they would want me. A. said afterwards that I had been rude.

Monday, 23rd October

At midday to Bath Clinic to have lump removed by Clive Charlton. Was not alarmed, just slightly apprehensive. He talked throughout the operation to keep up my spirits. I felt nothing, just some tugging. 'You may feel a bit funny,' he said when it was all over. I did. Returned to the library to have something to eat, and took Folly for short walk on getting home.

---

[*] Writer and journalist (b. 1925), official biographer of Harold Macmillan (2nd volume of biography appearing in 1989); m. (2nd) 1987 Hon. Mrs Sheelin Eccles.

[†] Camilla Horne; m. 1985 Gerald Harford (b. 1948), then squire of Little Sodbury Manor, Gloucestershire.

[‡] Colonel Gaston Palewski (1901–84), leading aide of General de Gaulle in both wartime and postwar politics; loved by Nancy Mitford; m. 1969 Violette de Talleyrand-Périgord.

Wednesday, 25th October

Clive rang before I set out for Bath. I think he expected to get A., who had gone to London for the day. I parried his irrelevant enquiries as to how I felt, and asked for the result of the test. 'Same as the cheek,' he said, giving the name of the growth. My heart sank. 'I am *not*', I said, 'going to submit to that radium treatment again.' He replied, 'Wait and see.' I thought about this blow all day, but with disappointment rather than wretchedness. Worked away at Chapter Six. Am determined to finish and deliver this book before I am bogged down with treatments. I did tell poor M. over the telephone, which was rather selfish, but I wanted to tell someone, and no one more understanding and sweet than he.

Friday, 27th October

Saw Dr King, who was extremely nice and sensible. He understood my disinclination to submit to further treatment, but said, 'You see, Jim, you are still worth patching up. In other respects you enjoy reasonable health, apart from your eyes, and your brain is still functioning.'

Saturday, 28th October

Darling A. left at seven this morning. Came into my room with Folly and kissed me goodbye. A day of terrible storms, 100 m.p.h. wind. Alex [Moulton] came to dine with me. While I was preparing dinner, the lights went out. Whole village blacked out for two hours. Had some difficulty finding torch and candles, Alex talking the whole time. Said Nigel Lawson* was a shit to waltz off during a crisis. Alex is to give a large luncheon for his seventieth birthday next April. During it, he intends to ask all guests who do not intend to support Mrs T. at next election to raise hands. To them he will say, 'It would be churlish not to let you finish your meal; but when you have done so, will you please leave my house.' Sitting by the gas fire by candle-light, Alex says, 'You look so well. How splendid that that horrid time

---

* Conservative politician (b. 1932), who had just resigned as Chancellor of the Exchequer (a post he had held since June 1983) after disagreements with Mrs Thatcher and her economic adviser, Sir Alan Walters; cr. life peer as Baron Lawson of Blaby, 1992.

of your cancer treatment is well behind you and you are as good as new.' I refrained from telling him the truth.

Tuesday, 31st October

Tony Mitchell motored me to Stowe,* where the National Trust launched an appeal for the park. Beautiful day after early rain; as we drove down the avenue, the sun flickered across the great arch like the lighting at an opera. We gathered at the Temple of Friendship and Concord.† A large crowd including many old friends. We followed George Clarke,‡ the great Stowe authority, on a tour of the temples. I fell ignominiously walking up the steps of one. Given luncheon in a marquee, and listened to speeches begging for a mere £12 million. Dame Jennifer Jenkins a charming woman, straightforward and enthusiastic. Is clearly devoted to the N.T. I sat near her on the top table, between George Clarke and Ralph Verney,§ much aged and bent. Glynn Boyd Harte¶ opposite, speaking warmly of Julian Barrow, my other library portraitist. Headmaster of Stowe and others embarrassed me with praises of *Another Self*. Said they had never laughed so much, that there should be an A.S. Society, etc. What does this mean to me, under sentence of death?

Wednesday, 8th November

Before rising, in that semi-state of sleeping and waking, I now find myself consumed, not by despair, but utter languor and the certainty that I cannot 'carry on' any longer, and must die very soon. Yet exciting things are happening – the Bachelor coming to a close; the prospect of my diaries being dramatised (though I could not possibly

---

* Formerly the seat of the Temple and Grenville families, Stowe in Buckinghamshire became a school in the 1920s. The splendid Georgian landscaped grounds with their decaying temples were transferred to the N.T. in 1989.

† In December 2003 it was announced that this atmospheric folly, long used by schoolboys for romantic trysts, was to be marketed by the N.T. as a venue for 'gay weddings'.

‡ Master at Stowe who wrote a history of its buildings and landscape.

§ Sir Ralph Verney, 5th Bt, of Claydon, Buckinghamshire (b. 1915); chairman of committees concerned with conservation of nature and architecture; brother-in-law of Dosia Verney.

¶ Artist, illustrator and dandy (1948–2003).

attend a performance); and Nick [Robinson]'s offer to publish the first half of my novel* as complete in itself. So odd to have a letter of praise and criticism from my dear great-nephew, almost incestuous. Now Jock Murray has asked me to write a brief life of Sachie. I am not at all sure that I want to do this, and a short biography would involve almost as much research as a long one, and possibly more labour. I would rather write something autobiographical or indeed another novel, which can be taken up and put down, rather than a biography which is ceaselessly demanding.

Thursday, 9th November

Folly and I went into the Bath Hospital. Dr Rees, looking overworked and unhealthy, chatted in the polite way specialists think patients prefer to straight facts. Was not in the least concerned about latest outbreak of malignancy. Suggests we just wait until another lump appears and deal with it accordingly. How do you feel? Fine. That's good – and off I go. F. sitting curled up on passenger seat just as I left her.

Friday, 10th November

Beauforts to dine. A. cooked delicious dinner of chicken and rice, baked apples with jam. We talked of Gladys Guinness† taking up the bottle again. D. said, good, I want her house for Eddie.‡ When Caroline expressed her worries about Daphne [Fielding], D. said, good, you will soon be able to get her certified. Wicked man. D. knows Sir Alan Walters,§ and lunched with him recently. A.W. is very indiscreet, and talks about national finances so learnedly that one does not understand a word. D. believes that Lawson, who started on the right track, went entirely wrong, and Mrs T. was justified in listening to contrary advice.

---

* *The Fool of Love.*
† On 3 February 1980 (*Deep Romantic Chasm*), J.L.-M. related how this formerly 'nice, dull' resident of Badminton village had got drunk and attacked her husband with a knife. She died in 1993.
‡ Lord Edward Somerset.
§ Economist (b. 1926; Kt 1983); economic adviser to Mrs Thatcher, 1981–9.

Saturday, 11th November

I had an odd dream of the time when I was languishing at Wickhamford in the late 1920s during vacation from Oxford, bored and longing to get away. I was at some neighbouring big house and my host was Henry Yorke,* yet the house was not Forthampton [Court, Gloucestershire] but Brockhampton [Hall, Herefordshire], with its staid red brick front. A side wing turned into a high bastioned wall, as it might be one of Knole's. I said to Henry, I never knew this wing existed. I was happy and impressed.

Nick [Robinson] lunched alone with us. Afterwards he and I walked with our dogs on the Slates. He definitely wants to publish my novel, albeit truncated. Of course I am delighted, though I refuse to take an advance. Will accept royalties if there are any. A strange state of affairs, after all the rejections received through Bruce Hunter.†

Thursday, 16th November

A. has finished reading *Bachelor*, and is made dizzy by the dates. Says I must reduce these. I know it is a bad book, lacking sparkle, too factual. Next week I will take two copies to London, to show J[ohn Kenworthy-Browne] and M. J. will, I know, be justly critical. M. may withhold what he really feels.

Saturday, 18th November

I do wish Hugh [Massingberd] would not bang on about an honour for me. Today's *Daily Telegraph* article on Bath refers to me in first and last sentence as a leading Bath conservationist. It is untrue. I have done the minimum for Bath.

Today A. and I lunched with Tanis [Guinness]‡ to meet A's first cousin Michael Menzies and American wife. Other guest was

---

* Novelist (1905–73) who wrote under name of Henry Green, the subject of an essay by J.L.-M. in *Fourteen Friends*; Forthampton (inherited by his brother) was the family seat.
† Canadian-born literary agent (b. 1941); joined London firm of David Higham in 1962 and became J.L.-M's agent following death of D.H. in 1979.
‡ Thrice-married yr dau. (b. 1909) of Benjamin Guinness of New York.

Maureen Dufferin,* who had brought with her some of Ava's last letters written from Burma shortly before his death. This was very sweet of Lady D., who clearly adores him still. The letters full of affection for her, the children and Clandeboye [Co. Down], which he begged her to keep intact for Sheridan. He clearly knew he might be killed. She said he was actually on some sort of secret mission when he died, and orders were on their way for him to return to London. She admitted his drink problem, and that she too drank to excess. I told her that F. E. Smith† was responsible for making that group drink at Oxford. The wicked thing was that F.E. claimed that when drunk his mind improved. This may have been true in his case, but it was not in theirs. The silly young things believed that by drink they would achieve greatness. I liked this old lady. Difficult to see how she was ever pretty. Her face looks as if someone had tried to press it down her neck. Strange to think that seventy years have passed since Tom [Mitford], Ava and I shared the top dormitory at Lockers Park.

Tuesday, 21st November

Back from two delicious days in London, staying at Brooks's. We lunched with Derek Hill at Boodle's to meet Anna-Maria Cicogna.‡ I decided that Anna-Maria was a foolish society woman really, socially sharp but not clever. Talked hot air. Recalled an occasion when Nancy was dining with them, together with Victor Cunard's§ baronet brother. He said to Nancy, 'You can't guess what I've been doing all morning – destroying your letters to Victor.' Nancy's face fell, for her best and most numerous letters had been addressed to Victor. The baronet went on, 'Then there were Freya Stark's¶ letters too.' Nancy

---

* Maureen (1907–98), 2nd dau. of Hon. Ernest Guinness; m. 1st 1930–45 Basil, 4th Marquess of Dufferin and Ava, 2nd 1948–54 Major Desmond Buchanan, 3rd 1955 Judge John Cyril Maude.

† Frederick Edwin Smith (1872–1930), lawyer and Conservative politician; cr. Earl of Birkenhead, 1919. J.L.-M., an Eton friend of his son, sometimes visited his house near Oxford, and observed how his drinking habits influenced the young and clever.

‡ Anna-Maria (b. 1913), dau. of Count Giovanni Volpi di Misurata (1877–1947); m. 1932 Count Cesare Cicogna Mozzoni; prominent resident and hostess of Venice.

§ Journalist (1898–1960); sometime correspondent of *The Times* in Paris and Rome, who spent his last years in Venice.

¶ Dame Freya Stark (1893–1992); writer and traveller.

brightened a little. 'I have kept those because, after all, Freya is a famous writer.'

Coote gave us tickets for Covent Garden to see Berners' ballet *The Wedding Bouquet*. Has a nice period flavour and décor, but does not quite grip. Two other modern ballets in the programme – *My Brother, My Sisters* by Kenneth MacMillan,[*] atonal music by Webern and Berg,[†] perfectly horrid, and *Frankenstein, the Modern Prometheus*, electronic music by Vangelis,[‡] very noisy and vulgar.

This morning I walked to Felix Kelly[§] exhibition. Haunting nostalgic romanticism. Castles on dreamy rivers with ancient steamboats; empty garden chairs, a parasol left behind. At 11.15 I joined M. at O&C Club to watch State Opening of Parliament on TV. Wonderful spectacle, though alas without my new specs I could not see faces. We exchanged typescripts, he giving me his book on the Abdication, and I handing him my *Bachelor Duke*.

Today is the 110th birthday of George Lloyd. To think of it. When I worked for him, he was a sprightly young middle-aged.

Wednesday, 22nd November

Vivid dream last night that I was with Harold and Vita on some kind of walking tour, in India or some exotic land where I had never been. We stopped at a watershed in beautiful and lush country, mountains bathed in sunshine through deep purple clouds. (Scenery inspired perhaps by Felix Kelly's paintings.) I remarked, 'We might as well be in the Lake District.' Whereupon H. and V. gave each other a pitying look, and smiled at me indulgently.

Thursday, 23rd November

To London again. Was called for at Brooks's by Peregrine Worsthorne's[¶] smart car and chauffeur and motored to *Telegraph* offices in

---

[*] Choreographer (1929–92).

[†] Anton von Webern (1883–1945) and Alban Berg (1885–1935); composers of 'Second Viennese School'.

[‡] Pseudonym of Evanghelos Papathanassiou (b. 1943), Greek composer.

[§] New Zealand-born artist (d. 1996), specialising in atmospheric paintings of country houses in their landscapes.

[¶] Writer and journalist (b. 1923; Kt 1991); editor, *Sunday Telegraph*, 1986–89; m. 1st 1950 Claude de Colasse (d. 1990), 2nd 1991 Lady Lucinda Lambton.

Docklands. Ugly block in hideous mess of wasteland and skeletons of future blocks. Met at door by P.W.'s secretary, taken up in lift. P.W. received us in room with glass walls, sun streaming in. A party of eight, the others Frank Johnson,* nice jolly man of East End origins, Tony Hervey, Simon Blow, Geoffrey Wheatcroft,† Ali Forbes and Lucy Lambton.‡ I was treated like an idol, but owing to acoustics of room had difficulty hearing. Liked Worsthorne much, fine shock of white hair, neatly dressed with waistcoat and chain. We sat down to luncheon, not waiting for Lambton who was late. P.W. clapped his hands and said in authoritative tones, 'Please cease *tête-à-tête* talk, I want to hear the views of our guests on the National Trust. Is there a necessity for it? Cannot owners now afford to maintain their own houses? Is it N.T. policy to allow the families to continue in residence?' As soon as I tried to speak, Ali interrupted and talked ceaselessly. Eventually our host clapped again. 'Does not Mr L.-M. think that the aristocracy are returning to power and authority in England and Eastern Europe?' Mr L.-M. did not think. Then Ali made the remark of the day: 'As I once said to Pope Pius XII§ at a cocktail party . . .' I can't understand why I was invited. Rather like the Queen's luncheon parties at Buckingham Palace. Filthy luncheon, hardly edible.

J.K.-B. took me to Covent Garden – *Medea*, which I last saw with Callas¶ in Florence in 1950s. Very bad performance, lacking sparkle and terror. Gave J. my book to read. Now await his and M's verdicts.

Monday, 27th November

Finished M's *The Reign and Abdication of Edward VIII*** last night. It is fair, concise and moving, making a good case for Mrs Simpson and even the King. Today I got a postcard from him saying don't worry,

---

* Journalist (b. 1943); then assoc. editor of *Sunday Telegraph*, later editor of *Spectator*.
† Writer and journalist (b. 1945), former literary editor of *Spectator*, then writing a weekly column in *Sunday Telegraph*.
‡ Lady Lucinda Lambton (b. 1943); dau. of Viscount Lambton; photographer, writer and broadcaster; m. 1st 1965 Henry Harrod, 2nd 1986 Sir Edmund Fairfax-Lucy, 6th Bt, 3rd 1991 Sir Peregrine Worsthorne.
§ Pope, 1939–58 (Eugenio Pacelli [1876–1958]).
¶ Maria Callas (1923–77); Greek soprano.
** Published by Bantam Press, May 1990.

Bachelor is good. Greatly cheered by this. Both of us slapping each other on the back. Have also heard from a Frenchman called Guillaume Villeneuve,* asking to translate *Another Self* into French. I rang Debo this evening about getting *Bachelor* typescript to her to read. She is concerned about Diana's appearance on *Desert Island Discs*, which has become front page news. Even the *Telegraph* has headline 'Lady M. loved Hitler', etc. M. fears she may be treated like Rushdie† and go in danger of her life.

Tuesday, 28th November

Went yesterday to see Paul Methuen's‡ exhibition at Victoria Gallery, Bath. Really excellent his pictures are. Sickert influence apparent in the oils. What a strange man, so abstracted, unworldly, socialist even, not really approving of private ownership, yet, like old Sir Charles Trevelyan,§ convinced that in the circumstances he was the best person to be curator of his long-inherited house. I never knew how much Paul cared for me. At times he was affectionate in a distant way. He was mightily attracted by women. A renaissance man in that he excelled at many things – music, botany, but above all painting.

Today I visited Woman at Caudle Green, getting lost because the steep hill road to the village was closed. Found her alone, looking old, a little haggard and very lame. Brought copy of *Bachelor* for Debo, who arrived just as I was leaving.

Thursday, 30th November

An article in *Sunday Telegraph* quoting those country house owners who have never had it so good. Vulgarians like Francis Dashwood and

---

* See entry for 13 September 1990.
† British novelist of Indian origin (b. 1947), obliged to live in hiding after the Iranian leader Ayatollah Khomeini had called upon fellow Muslims in February 1989 to kill him for having insulted the faith in his novel *The Satanic Verses*.
‡ Artist (1886–1974) who succeeded as 4th Baron Methuen in 1932 and devoted himself to the conservation and management of the Corsham estate in Wiltshire; subject of an essay by J.L.-M. in *Fourteen Friends*.
§ Sir Charles Trevelyan, 3rd Bt (1870–1958); politician and landowner, education minister in Ramsay MacDonald's Labour Governments, who donated Wallington estate in Northumberland to N.T. after long negotiations in which J.L.-M. was involved.

Hugh Hertford* boasting of their cellars-ful of wine, their cuisine, the numbers of their guests, their *douceur de vivre* – and deriding me for writing (where and when?) that the country house is doomed for lack of servants. I might have asked them why it was that dukes needed to sell their treasures, Devonshire his engravings, Beaufort his Georges, Bedford his *Three Graces*. They can't be that rich if they live on capital.

Monday, 18th December

Have been suffering from influenza for past fortnight, and felt rotten. At one point ran a temperature of 103° [Fahrenheit], and could not speak, eat or even walk to bathroom. Today we learned that Joan Drogheda has died. She had been dead to all of us for some years already. Nevertheless sorrow rears its hoary head.

Tuesday, 19th December

Hugh Massingberd rings me up. I know what he wants – a piece for the *Telegraph* about Joan. I say I will oblige, though it may be short. I do it, and of course it is long. All my feelings expressed in it. I am not displeased.

Thursday, 21st December

The shortest day, and a distressing one. Ian Dixon motored us through terrible rain to Joan's funeral, at Royal Chapel by Royal Lodge, ugly-pretty Victorian church with high-raftered roof. Full of friends – Jack Donaldson† behind us, Julian and Gilly Fane‡ in front. Alexandra [Moore], who organised the whole thing, squeezed in beside me, and wept throughout. Joan's tiny coffin raised high in chancel, covered with a cascade of flowers. Most poignant moment was entrance of Garrett, wheeled in by nurse and doctor and hoisted, a lifeless sack,

---

* Hugh Seymour, 8th Marquess of Hertford, of Ragley Hall, Warwickshire (1930–97).
† J.G.S. ('Jack') Donaldson (1907–98); Eton contemporary of J.L.-M.; cr. life peer as Baron Donaldson of Kingsbridge, 1967; Minister for the Arts, 1976–9; m. 1935 Frances ('Frankie') Lonsdale, writer.
‡ Hon. Julian Fane (b. 1927); yr son of 14th Earl of Westmorland (and of J.L.-M's friend Diana *née* Lister); writer; m. 1976 Gillian Swire.

into front pew. Derry read from Gospel. I did not hear one word, nor the Dean of Chichester's address. Dadie [Rylands] read from Wordsworth and Shelley, most moving. I was especially moved by Benjamin Moore, aged six, playing unaccompanied Bach on the violin at foot of his grandmother's coffin. Yet he was not visibly moved, nor was Derry. We then drove to Parkside for tea. I am never happy at these death parties. Fabia Drake* told us that she was Joan's oldest friend, remembered her as a child, attended her first marriage. I asked if her childhood was wretched. Not wretched, she said, but neglected. The servants loved Joan, and were nearly in tears.

Monday, 25th December

What a Christmas. Clarissa and Igor staying with us for five days. I am enraged by this youth, without an idea in his head but extreme young fogey snobbery. Mother sits with Cheshire cat-like grin of adoration. I can never go through such purgatory again. At breakfast Freda rings to say that Lennox is in a deep coma, looking like a beautiful boy, and not expected to survive the day. She is calm, sensible, relieved. Then Alexandra telephones to announce that Garrett died this morning, just four days after Joan's funeral. A. comes into room weeping. He is a great loss to her.† When we left Parkside, he said to me, 'Look after yourself.' I replied, 'That's what I should say to you. Goodbye, old friend.'

Debo rang yesterday, in raptures about the *Bachelor*. Allowing for Mitford exaggeration, I honestly believe she is pleased. A great relief. Much still to do with this book, by which I am now bored.

Thursday, 28th December

The *coup de grâce* was another grandchild plus two greats for the day yesterday. Thank God we are alone again. Even A. is relieved.

Yes, what a Christmas. Lennox died on Christmas Day. Charlotte Bonham Carter‡ also died, and Sybil Cholmondeley, both nonagenar-

---

* Stage name of Ethel McGinchy (1904–90), actress known for her portrayal of *grandes dames* in films and television dramas; m. 1938 Judge Maxwell Turner (d. 1960).
† The Earl, as he wrote in his memoirs *Double Harness* (1978), had been in love with Alvilde as a young man, and counted himself as her oldest friend.
‡ Charlotte Ogilvy (1893–1989); idiosyncratic social figure; m. 1926 Sir Edgar Bonham Carter (1870–1956), colonial civil servant and member of N.T. committees.

ians, and splendid women in their different ways. We both feel unmoved by Lennox's departure, not because he was a cabbage, but because we never quite got through to him. I suppose all saints are intangible.

Today we lunched at Tormarton with the Griggs. The Roy Jenkinses there. He very red in the face, and untidy. Was civil to me, and talked about my diaries. I wish they wouldn't. Asked if I thought Harold [Nicolson] 'important'. He didn't seem to think so, like many today. Asked about my Bath life. When I said A. gave me an egg or a pie for luncheon, he said he would not like that, and would have to go to the pub. His complexion suggests that. As soon as luncheon over, he dashed off with John to play ping-pong in the barn. A very curious mind. Now her I like tremendously – and I understand why the N.T. love her. She looks like a benevolent hedgehog, slightly drooping and hibernating-looking. Has prickles nevertheless, not shown to me so far.

Friday, 29th December

Met Freda at the station. The poor widow; very good and sensible, though distressed by deathbed scene at the hospital. Lennox revived almost miraculously the afternoon before, smiled and showed signs of recognition at the family gathered. Then died peacefully at eight the next morning.

Saturday, 30th December

Nephew Henry [Robinson] motored me to see Audrey. A melancholy visit. She has had several little strokes, and gone downhill. Extremely thin, and can't communicate. Just says yes or no. I tried reminding her of childhood days. During tea, she suddenly touched my arm, and said, earnestly, 'I wish, I wish', and again, 'I wish . . .' I supposed she was trying to tell me something like where she wanted her ashes scattered, or give me some directions which the others would not understand. Then Dale, who had overheard, asked, 'What is it you wish, Mummy?' Slowly she said, 'I wish . . . to be a butterfly.' Now what did this mean? The absurdity of it may have concealed a reluctance to share her confidence with the others. So I begged Dale to find out what she wanted to say, and let me know. Poor Audrey, I cannot wish her to linger on.

1990

They all talk of the new decade, whereas strictly speaking it does not begin until 1991. Whatever happens, it must be my last. This morning I saw poor Dr King, his surgery overflowing with patients who have bottled up their complaints until after the holiday. He told me at once that the swelling in my groin was a hernia; suggests doing nothing unless it gets bigger, or hurts. Great relief.

To London for first time in weeks. I get confused by the din and buzz, particularly on the underground. To Inigo Jones exhibition at Royal Academy. I had seen most of the drawings before, either in John Harris's[*] catalogue or at Chatsworth. J.K.-B. was to lunch at Brooks's, but the club was shut, so we ate in Jermyn Street. Walked to Higham's, but Bruce [Hunter] did not keep our appointment, and I saw a beady girl. To Heywood Hill which was in turmoil, upside-down for three months with dry rot. At five to Paddington hotel to meet M., who arrived from his publishers half an hour late. He is reading Ziegler's Edward VIII manuscript. Says it is mischievous, though extremely clever and astute. M. is keen to write a biography of Jeremy Thorpe.[†] John Grigg thinks it a good idea; but if Thorpe agrees, it may be a *via dolorosa* for M.[‡]

---

[*] Writer on architectural subjects (b. 1931); 1950s protégé of J.L.-M.

[†] Charismatic politician with 'homosexual tendencies' (b. 1929); leader of Liberal Party, 1967–76; tried at Old Bailey for conspiracy and incitement to murder, 1979; acquitted, but career in ruins; m. 1st 1968 Caroline Allpass (d. 1970), 2nd 1973 Marion, Countess of Harewood.

[‡] Prophetic words.

Friday, 5th January

To Garrett's funeral at Windsor, A. going separately from London. Listened on the way to Dirk Bogarde's *Desert Island Discs*. I find him a bit of a fraud; his perpetual feigned humility carries no conviction. Derry at door of St George's Chapel, greeting mourners. Hugo Vickers,* wearing blue sash and medal, conducted me from nave through rood screen into chancel, to seat under Garter canopy. There was A. seated in the stall next to Garrett's, which was left empty, banner removed from canopy and a white notice displayed reading 'The Late Earl of Drogheda, RIP'. It was sensitive of Derry to arrange this for A., whom G. loved, and who must have been his oldest friend. A moving service of the Order: military knights stomping in, scarlet tunics, cocked hats under arms, almost like toy soldiers; choir; Dean of Windsor and Bishop of Winchester in gorgeous robes; representatives of Queen and Royal Family; pale new shiny coffin with G. inside. Most moving moments were the surrender by the military knights of G's banner to the Dean at the altar, and at the end, the coffin followed by Derry and Alexandra with little Benjamin between them. Dadie read from Shakespeare and Bacon and Campion in a voice like a clarion.

While the Moores followed coffin to cremation, we went to the Deanery for drinks. Welcomed by nice Mrs Dean, not knowing us from Adam. I talked to the Bishop of Winchester. He said his cathedral was kept going by volunteers, consisting of retired people, mostly women. Again back to Parkside, this time a stand-up luncheon for eighty. Dadie very complimentary of my *Independent* piece on Garrett. Fabia Drake holding forth to him about her book on Shakespeare. I mentioned Leslie Rowse's[†] forthcoming book. Oh that dreadful monster, said Dadie, he thinks *he* is the Dark Lady.

Wednesday, 10th January

I am having an uninterrupted week in Bath, working on my novel. Nick is taking such trouble editing it that I feel I too must alter and improve. The beginning is embarrassingly awful; the middle better; the end again poor. Oh, what an effort.

---

* Writer (b. 1951); lay steward at St George's Chapel.
† A. L. Rowse (1903–97); historian and Fellow of All Souls. The book referred to is probably *Discovering Shakespeare: A Chapter in Literary History* (Weidenfeld 1989).

Wednesday, 17th January

On Sunday we lunched with Woman. Diana [Mosley] over from France, looking very old, distinguished and beautiful. Usually so free of disapproval of family and friends, she disapproves of her niece Emma Tennant for being so disapproving herself. Emma does not feel the cold and inflicts it almost sadistically on her guests, including Woman who is very delicate. Emma described how she attended the deathbed of Sheridan Dufferin, and made it sound so jolly that Diana said, 'Let's die of Aids'. Was surprised Emma did not disapprove of Sheridan for having Aids.

Today I thought I might write a book about old age: on the one hand the inanities and indignities, the outward senility; on the other, the inner serenity, the ability to understand more deeply, the absence of the distorting influence of sexual feelings. Would have to be amusingly told, if not to be a catalogue of horror. *Yet Another Self*, perhaps? Meanwhile I have written to Jock Murray definitely refusing to undertake Sachie's biography. I do not believe I am up to it, and even if it is to be a brief life, the research and the reading of his ninety-odd books would be a labour. Greatly though I loved and admired Sachie, I found him intangible somehow. And shall I be alive in 1995?

Friday, 19th January

A letter from Bruce Hunter, full of praise of the *Bachelor*, which he has passed to Murray's.

Diana comes for the night, brought by Woman. Coote joins us for luncheon. A. thinks I fuss too much over Diana. Probably true, because of what she meant to me in my extreme youth.* I treat her differently from other mortals. We talked and talked. I said, 'Here we are discussing Proust and Montherlant, just as in the Twenties we discussed Shelley and Keats.' She has a prodigious memory, retains all she has read. Like all Mitfords, she adores her friends, while not being very interested in their problems and domestic concerns. Sweetness on the surface. Remembers slights and grievances, e.g. Nancy's betrayal of

---

* He was infatuated with her from 1926 until her marriage to Bryan Guinness in 1929, having earlier been in love with her brother Tom at Eton.

her to Gladwyn Jebb,* and Woman's lack of sensitivity in writing to her in prison to announce that she had put down her horse and dog. So long ago too. A tigress in defence of her Kit.† Has his large framed photograph beside her when travelling. My affection for her is very deep; my joy in her company exceeds all joys, once the affectation barrier has been pierced.

Saturday, 20th January

We take Diana to luncheon with Sally [Westminster]. There meet charming lady deacon, one Mrs Carter, cousin of Anne Rosse, with genial old buffer husband. She is allowed to give communion, but not consecrate. Also affable schoolmaster called Rory Stuart who lives near Winchcombe and is a great gardener. Then I motor Diana to Bath to see my library, and down to Royal Crescent Hotel where she is collected by the chauffeur from Crichel‡ where she is to stay.

Sunday, 21st January

We motored to Parkside to lunch with dear Derry,§ Alexandra in Russia filming. Were shocked by his appearance. He has been through a dreadful time. Furthermore, trouble with Alexandra over where they are to live. D. adores Parkside and wants to stay there if he can afford the new rent, whereas she would prefer to live with her parents, the Nico Hendersons, at Combe,¶ which he is rightly determined not to do. I asked why Nico failed to appreciate Garrett. He wondered if N. was perhaps jealous of his father's background, standing and good looks.

---

* Gladwyn Jebb, 1st Baron Gladwyn (1900–97), diplomatist; m. 1929 Cynthia Noble (she d. 1990). In 1940, Nancy Mitford had urged him to have her sister Diana interned as a security threat.
† Sir Oswald Mosley.
‡ Estate in South Dorset owned by Hon. Mrs Marten, whose daughter Charlotte was married to Diana's son Alexander Mosley.
§ Now 12th Earl of Drogheda.
¶ Sir Nicholas 'Nico' Henderson, diplomatist (b. 1919); HM Ambassador to France, 1975–79, and USA, 1979–82; m. 1951 Mary Barber (she d. 2004). They had converted three school buildings in the Berkshire village of Combe, one of which had been used by the Moores (see *Holy Dread*, 27 August 1983).

He took A. round the garden, asking her advice on how to reduce it. So sad here, memories of Garrett and Joan so vivid. When I was alone with D., he asked me if his parents had led separate lives. I said I thought not, for Garrett, whatever his harmless little flirtations, was always in love with Joan so far as I could see. He seemed surprised at this. He said that when at Eton he had never brought home other boys, except for a few who knew his parents, because he never knew what mood Joan might be in. Evidently he loved Garrett, whom he considers a great man. G. very philosophical at the end; knew he was dying and didn't mind. Was never told he had lung cancer. G. believed he was a failure. He certainly did not do well for himself financially, never seeking or receiving a golden handshake, unlike other captains of industry.

Thursday, 25th January

A frightful gale blowing as I drove to Bath. At lunchtime A. telephoned from Badminton to announce that the two splendid cedars were down. (The third, mingy one was strangely untouched.) A terrible blow for they were the outstanding features of our otherwise featureless little garden. I left for home. Journey took an hour and a half; roads blocked; was diverted five times. Fearful lashing. The terror of driving between swaying trees. An enormous lorry on its side. At last managed to get home by Grittleton village. A. very calm. Both cedars uprooted. Garden literally cut in half. Apollo statue mercifully spared by one foot. Fence between us and lodge garden obliterated. Heart-rending.

Sunday, 28th January

We dined at the House last night, in the large dining room. Twenty at table, silver spread over snow-white cloth, like banqueting chamber at Apsley House. No particular occasion, just family and friends. Talked with Tony Lambton* afterwards. He has charm, though his

---

* Antony Lambton (b. 1922); s. father as 6th Earl of Durham, 1970 and disclaimed peerages but continued to use courtesy title Viscount Lambton; MP (C) Berwick-on-Tweed, 1951–73, resigning seat and office in Conservative Government after a newspaper revealed that it possessed a film of him smoking marijuana with a 'call girl'; m. 1942 Belinda ('Bindy') Blew-Jones (1921–2003).

dark glasses lend him what Lesley Blanch[*] calls 'sinistry'. Said the Prince of Wales had begun to read too late – one cannot become literate at the age of forty. Told hair-raising stories about sexual relationships in the Hope family between the Viceroy[†] and his brothers. And of Jamie Neidpath, who once picked up Lambton's foot and licked his sole, saying 'That was the best sole I have ever tasted.' Talked of second sons, of whom he said more than you would believe suffered from shoulder chips all their lives. Instanced David Herbert who loathed Sidney Pembroke (which I can't believe), and Andrew Cavendish who loathed his brother Hartington. When we repeated this to David this morning, he told us that Tony L. is himself a second son, his elder brother having killed himself; so is David, whose brother was killed in the war. When A. remarked that most sons would be relieved not to have the responsibility of inheritance, David replied, 'But no man likes to see his brother richer than himself. It all boils down to money.'

Tuesday, 30th January

To London and Chatsworth, travelling first class. At Swindon, nephew Richard Robinson got in and sat facing me. Has become handsomer, and very interested in pedigrees. Christopher Chancellor's memorial service in St Faith's Chapel, St Paul's. Quite a crowd. Sat at back in order to slip away early, but in trying to escape got caught by Johnston family, and was obliged to kiss all the women. Saumarez[‡] came up to me at Brooks's, telling me that 'Young John [Murray][§] says your book is not as boring as you make out.' Then to St Pancras, where I was strangely advised that a return ticket was cheaper than a single to Chesterfield.

Spent two nights alone with Debo and Diana. Absolute bliss. Chat, jokes and laughter in Debo's little sitting room, with long processions to dinner through cold, empty drawing rooms and corridors, and walking in pleasure ground in biting winds. Debo becoming fat, with

---

[*] American-born travel writer (b. 1907) living in South of France, a great friend of the L.-Ms when they too lived there in 1950s; m. Romain Gary.

[†] Victor Hope, 2nd Marquess of Linlithgow (1887–1952); Viceroy of India, 1936–43.

[‡] John Saumarez Smith; managing director of Heywood Hill Ltd, booksellers in Curzon Street.

[§] John Murray VII, heir to publishing house, then running the publicity department.

dewlap; Diana by contrast painfully thin. How I love these sisters. At tea on Wednesday, round tiny table, Debo said, 'Let's stay here forever. Why not?' Why not, indeed. A surge of love for them suffused my whole being.

When Andrew came, the temperature changed. A charming and attentive host – but his companions are impelled to please, and avoid topics. He says that the Queen is quite indiscreet about the Thatchers. She said to one of the equerries at the Palace while awaiting them, 'Don't make me laugh when Denis bows from the waist.' Says royalty all jealous of each other. If you invite one who fails, you may not ask another instead without causing grave resentment.

This visit hardly advanced the Bachelor, and was for pleasure. The nice Librarian Michael Pearman has read the book and suggests an introduction explaining the interest of the B. as a historical figure.

Friday, 2nd February

Debo motored me to lunch with the Sebastian Ferrantis* at Henbury near Macclesfield. This brand new country house is stupendous – Palladio's Villa Capra† in an English park setting. Untoned white stones bought from France, each one labelled they told me. No appendages, just sitting on a rise, with four porticos. Inside plan unusual but satisfactory. Ground floor, low and vaulted, sustains *piano nobile*. No central circular room, but long room from one end to the other, and vertiginous gallery under dome approached from staircase. Most rooms small with high ceilings. Very *luxe* of course, and will improve with use. Decoration snow-white, typical of David Mlinaric and not so good. But whole house a triumph, not to be criticised. He is a jolly fellow, pleased with his achievement. She querulous and grousing about inconvenience from housekeeping point of view. *Il faut souffrir pour être belle.*

---

* Sebastian de Ferranti, er s. of Sir Vincent de Ferranti; Chairman of Ferranti, 1963–82; m. (2nd) Naomi Angela Rae. They built a remarkable new Palladian villa on the site of the old Henbury Hall in Cheshire (demolished 1958) to the designs of Julian Bicknell, based on a sketch by Felix Kelly.
† Near Vicenza, begun by Andrea Palladio *c.* 1550; it consists of a circle within a square, with a portico on each of its four sides, and a domed rotunda interior.

Saturday, 3rd February

Elspeth [Huxley]* lunched with us [at Badminton]. Very spry for eighty-two. Told us she had been commissioned by the widow to write Peter Scott's biography. Thinks he was too decent and dutiful to be true, or to make interesting. But he is a hero, revered all over the world. I was telling her that Peter never liked me, and after K's death shunned me. Much to my surprise, A. suddenly said in front of Elspeth, 'If you don't mind me hazarding a guess why, it was because he disapproved of your affairs with young men.'† So what? I can hardly be said to have led a scandalous life. It is gallant of Elspeth to motor twenty miles to Slimbridge each day to research the Scott papers. Peter never threw anything away. He was a cold fish, his wife Jane leaving him because of his neglect. Never opened a book.

Wednesday, 7th February

A dark day of pouring rain. We drove to Bath Hospital where A. had to undergo a cardiac test. I waited in the car with Folly, as she would not let me accompany her. The test revealed that her heart valve has diminished, impeding the circulation and causing the feeling of faintness she experiences when doing anything which involves effort, like climbing stairs or carrying heavy parcels. The doctor warned that she could let things take their course, which would mean a steady decline, or have an operation to install a new valve. She at once decided on the latter. But it will be a hazardous operation. As she drives me home, I look at her precious silhouette, so beautiful and calm, and am filled with a terrible foreboding.

Thursday, 8th February

A. went to London to attend the Beits' dinner party. I refused to go, but wish now I had accepted, for I don't like her out of reach. I telephoned her specialist, Dr Thomas. He explained that if the state of her arteries proved to be unfavourable, she would be unable to have the operation, and could not live two years. I put the telephone down,

---

* Elspeth Grant (1907–94); m. 1931 Gervas Huxley (d. 1971); writer.
† However, as J.L.-M. was to learn from Elspeth, Scott himself had homosexual inclinations: see entry for 17 May 1992.

aghast. Then I thought, we are both very old, and the chances of either of us surviving much longer are slender. Nevertheless to have such a term put to one's life is upsetting. Later A. telephoned. Listening to her abrupt, no-nonsense voice, I shed tears. I must learn to control them.

Saturday, 10th February

A. back from London, her normal brusque self. Forbids me to commiserate or fuss over her; yet is telling everyone about the forthcoming operation.

The Harfords dined at the House last night, bringing her father Alistair Horne. Also Miranda Morley, David's mistress of many years, sweet and well-mannered. Horne a large, uncouth, burly man, whose daughter will soon resemble him. Little Gerald, whom I much like, is now set on selling his beloved house, Little Sodbury Manor, proclaiming that it is not really a family place, that it is too big and inconvenient, and that the proximity of the Bristol environment is intolerable – he spoke feelingly of the ruination of the countryside, the litter, the erosion of green verges, the havoc caused by urbanisation. I understand entirely of course, though feel the move is dictated by the new wife wanting to get away from the Harford relations. He wants to live in the Welsh border country, near Llanthony Abbey, where he has found a ruinous Welsh manor house to buy and restore.

Monday, 12th February

Bruce Hunter writes that Murray's would be pleased to publish my *Bachelor Duke* – on condition that they can cut it down to 85,000 words. Since I have written about 130,000, this would be a massacre. I have replied to Bruce that I do not consider this an acceptable arrangement. I know the book is too long, but not to that extent. It is now more than two months since I finished the damn thing, and I am fed up with it.

Wednesday, 14th February

To London yesterday, just to give luncheon to Derek [Hill] at Brooks's. He was charming, though his eyes swivelling towards Sir Martin

Gilliat* at next table. Talked of his visit to Mount Athos with Bruce Chatwin, who was so moved by the experience that he could not write about it. He hoped to retreat to one of the monasteries, had he been spared. Derek agrees Bruce's fame has been exaggerated by the press – but what do they not exaggerate when it suits them? Derek full of self-pity – Debo does not like him, never invites him to Chatsworth; Virginia Surtees returned an expensive silk scarf he sent her and refused to overlap with him at a health farm.

Saturday, 17th February

Dined last night with Desmond Briggs and Ian Dixon. Such a kind couple they are. Nothing they would not do for their friends. When I told Desmond that Murray's wanted me to cut the Bachelor by a third, he asked as an old hand to give me some advice. It was to accept Murray's offer, as they were the most suitable publisher for such a book, having first got them to agree to 95,000 rather than 85,000 words. Once contract signed, cut less than agreed – they would not be in a position to argue much. What amoral conduct you are counselling, I said.

Sunday, 18th February

Debo telephones at breakfast to say she is appalled by Murray's request to cut the Bachelor by a third, and under no circumstances must I agree. Diana said the same when she rang from Paris in the evening.

A. and Clarissa return from health farm after one week's starvation cure. A. indeed looking thinner, and smaller. Not sure how good this is. We are still in the dark about her immediate future. The moment Lukes set foot in this house they rush to the telephone and ring up other Lukes, which enrages me. Then torrents of silly gush. But Clarissa sweetly concerned about her mother.

Saturday, 24th February

The John Griggs, Jessica Douglas-Home and Rory Stuart lunched. Successful little party. Alas, the Griggs have sold Tormarton and are

---

* Lieut-Col. Sir Martin Gilliat (1913–93); Private Secretary to HM Queen Elizabeth The Queen Mother, 1956–93.

leaving in April. Jessica talked of Romania, where she is going shortly. Said one can have no idea how cowed the people are, still terrified of speaking openly. All important government posts are still held by ex-communists. John was present at the [Edward] Heath luncheon this week. He sat next to a Sir Somebody who boasted of his part in ousting Heath from the premiership.* John thinks Heath was treated shabbily. It was not his fault that world oil prices soared. Believes he would have done better than Mrs T. had he remained in the premiership.

Sunday, 25th February

We went to London for the Droghedas' memorial concert at Covent Garden. I stayed with Burnet [Pavitt],† A. with Derry and Alexandra. The Sainsburys‡ invited us to the Royal Box, a privilege appreciated by us, Daphne Poole§ their only other guest. Marvellous concert, consisting of extracts from operas and ballets introduced under Garrett, Solti¶ conducting, all soloists giving services for free. Derek [Hill]'s portrait of Garrett displayed in foyer. Dame Ninette de Valois,** over ninety, made a speech from the stage. After the interval, Benjamin Moore played a Dvorak solo on a tiny violin. Most moving spectacle, child not the least shy. Will he be in six years' time? If not, possibly a bad sign. During the next performance he sat on his father's knee and went to sleep. His teacher believes he is a prodigy and will become a star. Afterwards a dinner party at Derry's house. Did not get to bed until 12.30.

---

* Heath had lost the premiership after being narrowly defeated in the general election of February 1974; a year later, he lost the party leadership to Mrs Thatcher after a ballot of Conservative MPs.

† Businessman with musical interests (1908–2002), sometime Trustee of Royal Opera House; friend of J.L.-M. since 1948.

‡ John Sainsbury (b. 1927); industrialist and philanthropist; Chairman, J. Sainsbury plc, 1969–92; Chairman, Royal Opera House, 1987–91; m. 1963 Anya Linden; cr. life peer as Lord Sainsbury of Preston Candover, 1989.

§ Daphne Bowles; m. 1st Brig. Algernon Heber-Percy, 2nd 1952–65 Oliver Poole, sometime Chairman of Conservative Party (cr. Baron Poole, 1958).

¶ Sir Georg Solti, Hungarian-born conductor (1912–97).

** Dame Ninette de Valois (*née* Edris Stannus), dancer (1898–2001); founder of Sadler's Wells Ballet (later Royal Ballet), 1931; m. 1935 Dr A.B. Connell.

Monday, 26th February

Spent day at Greater London Library and Archive in Clerkenwell. Georgina Stonor,* Duke of Wellington's archivist, met me there by arrangement. Strange woman, the perfect Miss. She questioned me about early days of Georgian Group.† Wants me to see Douro,‡ who does not always get on with his father the present Duke but hero-worships his grandfather Gerry. She treats me flatteringly as a survivor, and I like her much. Surprised me by saying, 'I like naughty people. Am interested in their tastes.'

I gave a dinner party at Brooks's – Eardley, M. and Richmond Herald.§ Richmond very bright, and talks a lot. In fact, we talked till nearly midnight.

Tuesday, 27th February

While writing a letter in the morning room at Brooks's, I overheard the following dialogue. Member reclining on sofa to waiter: 'Could you please give that fire a bit of a poke?' 'Yes, my lord duke.' 'Thank you.' I looked round. It was Andrew Devonshire, half-asleep.

Wednesday, 28th February

Roped in by the Colonel to entertain Lady Fforde,¶ a descendant of Beckford. This formidable lady came with her hostess, a mild-manned Mrs Berry, at eleven o'clock. Colonel in a great fluster, with coffee prepared upstairs in his flat. We descended to mine where she talked until nearly one o'clock, though her knowledge of Beckford slight. She has inherited Brodick for some reason, and recognised illustrations in Maddox's book of the ebony chairs which she still possesses.

---

* Hon. Georgina Stonor (b. 1941), dau. of 6th Baron Camoys.
† The Group, which still flourishes, had been founded in 1937 under the aegis of the Society for the Protection of Ancient Buildings.
‡ Arthur Charles Wellesley, Marquess of Douro (b. 1945); er s. and heir of Arthur Valerian Wellesley, 8th Duke of Wellington (b. 1915).
§ Patric Dickinson (see notes to 4 January 1989) had been promoted from Rouge Dragon Pursuivant to Richmond Herald.
¶ Lady Jean Graham (b. 1920), yr dau. of 6th Duke of Montrose; m. 1947 Colonel John Fforde; lived on Isle of Arran.

Her brother is the present Duke of Montrose,* whom I remember at McNeile's house at Eton as Angus Kincardine, huge, burly, fair, handsome, and good at all games. A massive, splendid figure, but stupid. I imagine he looks rather like his sister now. She said he was so bullied at Eton because of his name, abbreviated to 'Kinky', that he called his eldest son by another title. I can't imagine Angus being bullied by anyone.

Thursday, 1st March

Sarah Bradford† came from London to talk about Sachie whose biography she is to write. I expected a precise, correct, middle-aged lady. On the contrary, she is pretty, youngish and flirtatious. She brought a copy of Regy, which I signed as her St David's Day friend. A day to be remembered, for it was fifty-two years ago today that I met Rick [Stewart-Jones]‡ in Queen Anne's Gate. Mrs Bradford is married to the future Lord Bangor of Castle Ward. She is bright rather than deep. I offered her a scratch luncheon, which she bravely accepted. We got on well. Much to be said for saucy ladies.

Poor old Fabia Drake is dead. She deserved a better obituary, for she was an excellent actress. Not two months since she was holding forth to Dadie and me at Parkside, gallantly keeping her flag flying while Dadie was being jokey.

Sunday, 4th March

I am appalled to receive a letter from Sir Peter Wakefield§ of the National Art Collections Fund offering me a 'Life Achievement Award' for services to the Arts and Conservation, to be presented at a dinner in May.

---

* James Angus Graham (1907–92); succeeded father 1954 as 7th Duke of Montrose; lived in Southern Africa; a minister in Southern Rhodesian governments during 1960s.
† Sarah Hayes (b. 1938); m. 1959 1st Anthony Bradford, 2nd 1976 Hon. William Ward (b. 1948; succeeded 1993 as 8th Viscount Bangor); writer. Her *Splendours and Miseries: A Life of Sacheverell Sitwell* appeared in 1993.
‡ Richard Stewart-Jones (1914–57), architectural conservationist; one of the great loves of J.L.-M's life, whom (as described in *Fourteen Friends*) he had met on St David's Day 1938.
§ Diplomatist (b. 1922), HM Ambassador to Belgium, 1979–82; Director, National Art Collections Fund, 1982–92.

Tuesday, 6th March

A's energy over repairing the damage to the garden is amazing. She organises the gardeners, finds craftsmen to rebuild fence and wall, and chases the estate office. Yet what is in store for her? The pathos of it.

Wednesday, 7th March

Took darling A. to The Glen, Bristol, where she is to have artery test tomorrow. Saw her into a pleasant room with all cons, telly, telephone, etc. She at once threw open the window and turned off the heating. Then said to me, 'I would rather you left now.' So off home I went, with Folly.

Thursday, 8th March

Ian Dixon drove me to Bristol. Waited until six when A's heart doctor Vann Jones came to her room. Charming and direct. Made it clear that operation essential. Refusal to have it would mean heart attacks, black-outs, and a life of three years at most. A. thereupon agreed without reservation to have it in two weeks' time. She was so stoical, so serene, so beautiful sitting in bed that I was deeply moved.

Saturday, 10th March

Fetched A. from The Glen. She was already waiting on the doorstep. Once home she was in the garden, directing operations. She did not want me hanging around, so I went to Bath. Telephoned Midi to condole on the death of her brother-in-law Sir Julian Gascoigne.* We bemoan the appalling declension of standards in this country. The world was far better when we were young, we decide like all octogenarians. London was safe to roam around; people were basically honest. Yet our own young lives were both clouded by the fact that, although we came from well-off families, we were obliged to eke on miserable salaries and allowances, which prevented us consorting freely with our contemporaries.

---

* Major-General Sir Julian Gascoigne (1903–90); Governor of Bermuda, 1959–64; Chairman, Devon & Cornwall Commitee, N.T., 1965–75.

Sunday, 11th March

Maureen Dufferin has invited us to dine on 29th to meet the Queen
Mother. Now of course we cannot go. A. would have loved it. 'How
pleased you must be,' she says. We lunch at the House. Caroline back
from New Zealand, a beautiful country, though she was bored by her
fellow dendrologists. Everyone solicitous about A's predicament.
Then we motored to Wincanton to see Audrey in her home. Sitting
like a pillar of salt by herself in large circular room. Knew us. Says 'yes'
to everything, nothing more. Does not seem wretched. Accepts
placidly.

Tuesday, 13th March

At breakfast telephone rings. A. dashes to pick up receiver. I overhear
her say, 'Kind of you to let us know. A merciful release, of course,' or
words to that effect. Who, I ask? Selina, to say Rosamond [Lehmann]
died last night while eating her dinner. Pneumonia. A. quite indifferent as I might expect.* But I loved Ros deeply. Felt pleased that she is
released. But very remorseful that I did not see her last week when in
London. Selina has been more dutiful, visiting and taking little gifts
of chocolates. Darling Ros, with whom I have been more intimate
than with any other woman friend.

Received a charming letter from Sir P. Wakefield, assuring me there
is no ill feeling over my declining award. He doubtless thinks me mad.

Tuesday, 20th March

Joshua Rowley, dearest of men, motored me in hired car to Putney
Green cemetery [for Rosamond Lehmann's funeral]. Outside waiting
room, I talked to Patrick Kavanagh† and Hugo Philipps standing in
the sun. Kavanagh said someone had taken me to task for having
written [in *Independent* obituary] that Ros was a Christian. But she
always strongly maintained that she was a follower of Christ. Hugo
introduced me to his new wife, nice-looking, grey-haired lady. She

---

* Alvilde had broken off relations with Rosamond nine years earlier, as a result of an inci-
dent described in *Holy Dread*, 11 May 1982.
† Writer, poet and actor (b. 1931); m. 1st 1956 Sally Philipps (d. 1958), o. dau. of Hon.
Wogan Philipps and Rosamond Lehmann, 2nd 1965 Catherine Ward.

amazed me by saying she had been reading my letters to Rosamond, amused by my accounts of this, that and the other. So dumbfounded that I could not reply. The idea of my letters to Ros being read before she is buried. We sat in the waiting room, Joshua, Selina and I. Decent but cold, clinical service. Old Wogan* bent double and shuffling, supported by grandson. No emotion anywhere, but some good singing. The harrowing newness of the coffin, so carpentered and glittering – for what? Ros not so big as I imagined. I did not care to look. With head bent I hear a squeaking as though a door behind me opening; looked up and saw the coffin had slid away. Did not weep.

Wednesday, 21st March

Lennox's Requiem at Westminster Cathedral. Again not a bit moved. Was bored. Many pieces by Lennox and some by Michael [Berkeley].[†] Freda had kindly invited me to meet the Cardinal afterwards, but I could not face it, and walked away before the end. Michael read first lesson and Tony Scotland[‡] the Gospel, both beautifully.

Thursday, 22nd March

I take A. to The Glen. Her activity prior to departure was amazing – giving orders to gardeners, buying food galore for me and writing instructions for its preparation, putting daffodils in Clarissa's bedroom. She makes me realise how useless I am.

Friday, 23rd March

Much telephoning from A. Has the carpenter finished the fence? Has the stone mason mended the wall? I meet Clarissa and motor her from Bath to the hospital, where we have tea and cakes with A. She is sitting surrounded by flowers and affectionate messages – the

---

* Having been divorced by Rosamond during the Second World War, he married Cristina, Countess of Huntingdon in 1944 and succeeded as 2nd Baron Milford (the only peer supporting the Communist Party) in 1962.
† Michael Berkeley (b. 1948), er s. of Sir Lennox Berkeley and Freda *née* Bernstein; composer and broadcaster.
‡ Writer, broadcaster and journalist (b. 1945); on staff of BBC Radio, 1970–91.

well-wishers including Mick Jagger and Jerry Hall, which greatly impresses the nurses. I write a note of love to A. and leave it on her pillow. We embrace rapidly. No tears, no emotion.

Saturday, 24th March

A day of anxious waiting. We lunched with dear Sally [Westminster], all kindness. The surgeon rings at 6.15. Very jolly. A total success, no complications. Clarissa threw her arms round me. I poured myself a whisky. Then I had an odd feeling as though of disappointment, can't understand why. We telephoned the good news to friends.

Sunday, 25th March

After lunching with the kind Barlows, we drove to The Glen. A. in special care ward. Sitting, even talking, but tired and fretful. I am amazed she is so well, after dreadful ordeal of four hours. A horrid tube from some artery in her poor face. Surgeon told us she must stay a fortnight. Clarissa returns to London tomorrow, mercifully.

Wednesday, 28th March

When I arrived this afternoon, A. said, 'I am in a beastly mood.' A good sign. Although my only concern should be for her, I have been thinking of myself of late, wondering what I should do were she to die. Would I remain in Badminton, go to live in Bath, or chuck up everything and retreat to a 'home', or a religious institution if they would have me?

Saturday, 31st March

Debo rang last night, as she does constantly now. Said I was very precious to her, possibly the greatest compliment I have ever received. A. is coming home next Tuesday; very cross with me for 'intriguing' with the surgeon to keep her there, for she wanted to come out tomorrow. Surgeon foolishly informed her of my talk with him on grounds of 'openness', another dotty liberal notion.

I dined at the House. The Michaels of Kent. Much groaning before they arrived. She has changed in looks – thinner in the face; hair unnaturally yellow, and frizzy. She sat on David's right, I on his left;

Ali Forbes on her left, Caroline on my right. Princess very affected and flirtatious. After dinner she invited me to sit with her on an ottoman while she talked to me of her new book – on courtesans. She certainly seems to know much about the subject. Much complaint about her publishers. Ali asked her for details of Henri II's penile deficiencies and X's vagina troubles. She warded off these queries. Says Nell Gwynn* was a designing minx, not the open-hearted whore the history books presume. Royal couple did not rise until 11.30, by which time I was nearly dead. He, dear little toy soldier, politely regretted we had not had the chance to talk.

Tuesday, 3rd April

Voice on the telephone asked if I could speak to Princess Michael of Kent. Before I could say yes, she spoke. Was in her motor, barely audible because of the din of the motorway. (Original interlocutor must have been her chauffeur.) We talked for a quarter of an hour about the mistresses and bastards of Charles II. She asked if I could come to lunch during A's recuperation, but I told her I couldn't budge.

I fetched A. from Bristol and brought her home. She was fully dressed and packing when I arrived. For the first time ever, she asked me to drive slowly. On her arrival, she walked straight into the garden; then slept soundly for two hours.

Friday, 6th April

A. gets up, dresses, and wanders about the house, noticing what is wrong. Is depressed, tires easily, and is rather *exigeante* and cross at times.

I have been to the Tormarton sale, bidding £30 for Edwardian butler's tray and £75 for a bust of Lord Palmerston. The first went for £150, the second for £400 (possibly cheap).

I have just read the preface to Volume I of Painter's life of Proust, deeply impressed by what he writes about the difference between fantasy and imagination, and how Proust projected his autobiography into his great novel. This has given me ideas; but at present any sort

---

* Hereford-born actress, mistress of King Charles II (1651–87).

of work is out. And I am not happy when not at work. I pray that my endeavour to get A. back to health may provide the impetus for a new book.

Monday, 16th April

On Good Friday I motored to stay two nights at The Slade with Eardley and Mattei. Much agreeable talk and laughter. Mattei has become older; but the flaring temper of which E. complains was not shown during my visit, during which he was his old sweet-tempered self, charming and whimsical. I admire their carefree mode of life, though it would not suit pernickety me. Mattei's old mother present, a dear old pussy cat. Speaks not a word of English. He is sweet to her, chats and jokes. Eardley smiles and tolerates her benign and unobtrusive presence.

On Easter Sunday I went to Prior's Dean Church. Dear tiny ancient church, white plaster within and some pretty Jacobean monuments. Every pew filled with gentry. Friendly, old-fashioned vicar, a gent like the rest. Flowers everywhere, no Moyses Stevens* poshery, but nosegays of wild flowers in small pots and jars. Some curiosity over me. Who was I? Where was I from?

Called on Janet Stone† in Salisbury on way back. Her house is delightful, so pretty and spruce, filled with good things and memorials of Reynolds. Janet nearly eighty; less Edwardian, and very dear.

Friday, 20th April

Ariane [Bankes] came down to Bath for the day. A delight to see her. She showed me the suggested cuts, amounting to some 15,000 words. I could not take it in and asked for a copy to go through at my leisure – though I wonder if I can rouse myself to show the interest required. All jokes and fun seem to have been excised.

My poor father was born 110 years ago today. I hope his spirit burns bright somewhere, and that he forgives me.

---

* Society florist in Berkeley Square.
† Janet Woods (1912–98); m. 1938 Reynolds Stone (1909–79), designer, wood engraver and artist.

Sunday, 22nd April

Just four of us at Acton Turville this morning, including Vicar's wife and me. Holy Communion means everything to me, yet I have grave doubts about the after-life, in which St John tells us it is imperative to believe. Meanwhile the Pope is right to warn Eastern Europe as it emerges from barbarism not to be seduced by the materialistic and ungodly ways of the West.

I am disillusioned by Mrs Thatcher for several reasons. First, Hong Kong: absolutely wrong to admit half a million Chinese to this overcrowded island.* Second, Poll Tax: absolute disaster.† Third, Lithuania: monstrous and cowardly not to stand up to Soviets.‡ Fourth, absolutely no steps being ventilated, let alone taken, to reduce birth rate. Fifth, Ireland: strong steps should be taken against that devilish island, e.g. dismissing all Irish citizens from England, and imposing sanctions. Sixth, the riot at Strangeways Prison [Manchester]: madness to allow criminals to hold police at bay for a month, whereas troops should have been sent in to sweep prisoners up and out on first day.

David Beaufort called at midday. Oh the charm of that man. Explained why he is selling his Italian cabinet, said to be the finest single item of furniture ever produced in that country. Needs to find £2 million to pay the tax on Master's estate and won't raise it from the sale of land; it would be unfair on the tenants and besides, tenanted land is not so valuable. Hopes Jacob Rothschild will buy it for Waddesdon, which would be better than it going to a dreary museum. Jacob wants to live in the whole of Waddesdon and keep the public out. Good for him – but will the N.T. agree?

---

* Following Britain's agreement in 1984 to return Hong Kong to Chinese rule in 1997, it had recently been announced that up to 500,000 of the colony's six million inhabitants would be allowed to settle in the UK.

† The introduction from that year of a 'community charge' to finance local government, theoretically to be paid by every citizen, had led to rioting in London in March 1990.

‡ The Republic of Lithuania had unilaterally declared independence from the Soviet Union in March 1990, though Moscow refused to relinquish sovereignty and attempted to continue to exert control through military and economic pressure until August 1991.

Tuesday, 24th April

That charmer James Knox* came to see me in Bath to talk of Robert Byron. Very good-looking; slight; little cow-lick on side of hair. White teeth, white skin, white cuffs, thin white hands. Comes from Ayrshire; knows Arthur and Cunninghame relations.† Very keen on Robert, left job on *Spectator* to concentrate on biography. Can he write? Is clearly intelligent, with a quick grasp. We spent an agreeable three hours chatting, the recorder whirring the whole time. I fear I said too much. I enjoyed his visit, and think he was pleased.

Sunday, 29th April

Took Folly for walk in Westonbirt Woods, while A. sat in the sun in the car. Never have I seen more bluebells and speedwell, or primroses in drifts; but trees in bad state, hundreds having been blown down in January gale, their dead, chopped trunks lying in piles.

In church this morning, instead of attending, I read the Commination Service. The phrase 'Too late to Knock' struck me as a good title for a last volume of memoirs.

Sunday, 6th May

Motored to Huish Manor Farm to lunch with Candida and Rupert Lycett Green. Large party for John Betj[eman]'s old friends to see the library she has built to house his books. Certainly a charming large room. We did not eat till two. I found standing all this time tiring, making converse with strangers. Luncheon in the barn, long table seating fifty. I was happily placed, opposite Candida and between Myfanwy Piper‡ and Catherine Palmer,§ *née* Tennant. Myfanwy delightful. I asked what her name meant. 'My darling', she said. Catherine unrecognisable, now a sweet and dowdy wife and mother. The moment luncheon was over I kissed Candida and sped away.

---

* Writer and artistic consultant (b. 1952); sometime publisher of *Spectator*.

† J.L.-M's mother's sister Doreen Bailey had married a Cunninghame and his own sister Audrey had married an Arthur, both families being distantly connected to J.L.-M's maternal grandmother Christina Thomson, daughter of a house of Glasgow merchants.

‡ Myfanwy Evans; m. 1935 John Piper, artist (1903–92).

§ Hon. Catherine Tennant (b. 1947), yr dau. of 2nd Baron Glenconner; astrologer and writer; m. 1976 Sir Mark Palmer, 5th Bt (b. 1941).

Thursday, 10th May

To London for day after long interval. Chief objective to deliver revised typescript to John Murray's. A thrill to be published at last by this Rolls-Royce of publishers. Then to Agnews for John Ward* exhibition. Good full-length portrait of Princess Anne, making her mysterious and beautiful, with that lovely complexion peculiar to the Royal Family. At Brooks's, John Saumarez Smith told me that my brother Dick† once walked into the shop and said *Another Self* was a tissue of lies. I think a good title for a sequel would be *A Tissue of Truths*.

Saturday, 12th May

Dear Billa comes to stay for two nights, our first guest this year. Full of chat about the Prince of Wales, with whom she is going to stay next. Says that presents are expected, which seems strange. She has saved up to buy a water-colour for £300. As though the royal walls were not groaning with them. But she gets presents in return.

Elspeth Huxley rang up to say she has been reading K. Kennet's diaries. Mentions of me during late Twenties and early Thirties, going to Switzerland with her. She paid for me, I think. Elspeth assumes she loved me, for I was good-looking then. I don't think so, though she liked young men in a wholly platonic way. E. says she fantasised about the innumerable men she imagined to worship her, wondering whether to marry Kennet or T. E. Lawrence.‡ Now we do not believe Lawrence would have proposed to any woman. All fantasy.

Tuesday, 15th May

Yesterday I drove Billa to Highgrove. We swirled off the main road down a tarmac drive. At newly-built, stone sentry box, smiling policeman asked our business. I said I was chauffeur to Lady Harrod. Politely he telephoned through to enquire. By the farmyard, a second police-

---

* Portrait artist (b. 1917; RA, 1956).

† Richard Lees-Milne (1910–84); m. 1936 (as her 2nd husband) Elaine Brigstocke (1911–96).

‡ Soldier, writer and archaeologist (1888–1935), 'Lawrence of Arabia' (said to have been a friend of J.L.-M's uncle Robert Bailey – see *Beneath a Waning Moon*, 12 May 1986).

man stopped and inspected us before letting us through. A brand new barn in mediaeval style being erected; a meadow filled with glistening white sheep, very picturesque and Samuel Palmer-like.* At the front door, B. got out and was greeted by a smiling, youngish equerry. I got her luggage out of the boot and dumped it on the newly-built portico steps; then exchanged a friendly word with the equerry, embraced B., and drove off. What I could glimpse of the garden and park was most attractive.

Billa telephoned before dinner, overbrimming with content. She had been alone with the Prince. Said the house very correct inside; good furniture, no fantasy. The P's own room rather touching, filled with books he had no time to read, and decent water-colour landscapes (not his own). It rained the moment they stepped into the garden. We have not had a drop since March. He held a large umbrella over her head, telling her it was a delight to be with someone who really knew about gardens. She was in ecstasy.

Wednesday, 16th May

Nigel Nicolson lunched with me in Bath. Always a delight to see him. He is so full of chat. He sails into the room like a gigantic man-of-war, noticing nothing. He is compiling a book about all the houses known to have been stayed in by Jane Austen. Next work will be a selection of the letters exchanged by Harold and Vita. He is very happy that his son Adam† has overcome his qualms about inheriting the Carnock barony and the fortune of his cousin David.‡ Nigel is worried about the forthcoming BBC dramatisation of *Portrait of a Marriage*.§ They are concentrating exclusively on the Trefusis affair,¶ whereas the book's message is that the marriage was a happy one. 'I never thought the BBC would behave like this,' he says. This shows

---

* English Romantic artist (1805–81).
† Only son (b. 1957) of Nigel Nicolson; writer, notably on walks and architecture; m. 1st 1982–92 Olivia Fane, 2nd 1993 Sarah Raven.
‡ David Nicolson, 4th Baron Carnock (b. 1920), to whom Nigel, his first cousin, was heir presumptive.
§ Nigel Nicolson's book about his parents, which dealt candidly with their homosexuality and created a sensation on its publication in 1973.
¶ The book certainly centred on the 'elopement' in 1920 of Vita and her lover Violet Trefusis (*née* Keppel, 1894–1972), and the efforts of their respective husbands, Harold Nicolson and Colonel Denys Trefusis, to get them back.

naïveté. Nigel asked why the backs of Georgian town houses, such as those in Bath, are so untidy. I explained that most of the untidiness was caused by additions of bathrooms, WCs and waste pipes by later generations. He was relieved to hear this, as he believes the Georgians could not go wrong tastewise in either architecture or furniture. He hates modern painting.

M., when I told him Nigel had been lunching, wondered whether N. might have been prime minister by now, if his Bournemouth constituents had not got rid of him.* I think not.

Saturday, 19th May

Vicarage Fields are in their full blowsy beauty, despite the lack of rain. Covered with rashes of golden buttercups, and hawthorn never so abundant. To my delight I have heard many cuckoos these past days. They like these spaces dotted with decaying oaks and the distant Allen Grove. How I adore this cruellest of birds.

Sunday, 20th May

We lunched with Liz Longman† on the far side of Moreton-in-Marsh. The longest expedition so far for A., who stood up very well and thoroughly enjoyed it, as did I. The Gibsons staying.‡ Also Sir Edward Ford,§ whose distinguished smiling face I recognised but whose name I did not catch; I hope I did not make a fool of myself by discussing Sarah Bradford's biography of George VI, for he was the Queen's private secretary. Pat [Gibson] told me that John Smith was resigning from the Landmark Trust, his creation, owing to persistent lack of cooperation from Lord Montagu of Beaulieu's¶ Heritage Trust. Lord M. an unattractive man, obstinate and lacking humour.

---

* Nicolson sat as Conservative MP for Bournemouth East and Christchurch from 1952 to 1959, but was 'deselected' on account of his opposition to Sir Anthony Eden's Suez venture in 1956.

† Lady Elizabeth Lambart (b. 1924), er dau. of Field Marshal 10th Earl of Cavan; m. 1949 Mark Longman (he d. 1972).

‡ Richard Patrick Tallentyre ('Pat') Gibson (1916–2004); director of companies; cr. life peer, 1975; Chairman of N.T., 1977–86; m. 1945 Elisabeth Dione Pearson.

§ Courtier (b. 1910); Assistant Private Secretary to the Sovereign, 1946–67.

¶ Edward Montagu, 3rd Baron Montagu of Beaulieu (b. 1926); writer, motorist and land-owner; Chairman, Historic Buildings and Monuments Commission, 1983–92.

Pat tried to make him see sense, but no response. Hugh Grafton, equally stuffy and unimaginative, was present and tended to side with Lord M. Pat is on a committee chaired by Roy Jenkins to advise on future of British Museum Reading Room. Says the new British Library people very autocratic and jealous. They have already removed the King's Library to hideous new building at King's Cross. It should have remained where it was, for George III gave the books and commissioned Smirke* to build the King's Library to contain them. Pat also told me how heartily he dislikes Nicholas Ridley. When confronted about a proposal to drive a new motorway through a N.T. property, Ridley merely said, 'We must live with motorways these days and learn to put up with them,' turned on his heel and left the room.

Saturday, 26th May

The drought is appalling. No rain since March. Mrs Thatcher's 'environment' speech is not to be scorned, though Friends of the Earth and other fundamentalists deride it for not going far enough. But she understandably says we must wait and see whether other nations cooperate. They won't, of course – can't even agree a common policy on highjackers and terrorists. And no one has yet suggested concerted action against population growth, though this is the root cause of all pollution, and would involve measures which, though unpopular, it would be possible for governments to enforce.

Sunday, 27th May

This afternoon I drove to Clifton-on-Teme to see Elaine[†] in her new dwelling. A bungalow in a 'genteel' neighbourhood, but comfortable and convenient. Simon[‡] near and yet not too near. Filled with her furniture, much of it old and good. E. is very philosophical, and accepts her lot. Talking of her husband and son, she said the

---

* The British Museum Reading Room and King's Library was the work of Sydney Smirke (1798–1877), brother of the Museum's main architect Sir Robert Smirke (1781–1867).

[†] J.L.-M's widowed sister-in-law (1911–96), until lately resident in Cyprus.

[‡] J.L.-M's nephew Simon Lees-Milne (b. 1939), o.c. of his brother Dick and Elaine *née* Brigstocke; m. 1st 1962–74 Jane Alford, 2nd 1976 Patricia Derrick.

Lees-Milnes lacked ambition. True enough. She told me she had discovered some accounts kept by my father, which show that when he bought the Wickhamford property in 1907 – manor house, garden, cottages and fields galore – he paid £2,300. At that time he and my mother were living on £4,000 a year, and my Uncle Robert[*] advanced him some of the capital required for the purchase.

Wednesday, 30th May

A. telephoned me in Bath yesterday to say that Sally [Westminster] had suffered a massive stroke and was in Frenchay Hospital. I collected A. and we drove there. We were the only visitors, Brigid Salmond having been and gone. We sat awhile by Sally's bedside, holding her hand and talking to her gently. No response. She looked strangely pretty and young. I wondered what was going on in that dear head. Dreams? Nightmares? Just blessed nothingness I hoped. We drove away, extremely sad. As soon as we returned home, the *Telegraph* rang, asking for an obituary. How could they have heard? I reluctantly agreed, after unsuccessfully appealing to Elspeth [Huxley], who is a sort of cousin of Sally. Today at breakfast the hospital rang to say she had died in the early morning.

Friday, 1st June

The much-anticipated day on which I drive A. to Cornbury [Park, Oxfordshire] where she has been commissioned to do the garden. She endured it very well. Charlbury such a pretty village with still a remote feel. A lovely place where I first went in 1930 or even 1929 when Woman was engaged to that black stick Togo Watney.[†] Beautiful Webb-like gate piers between twin lodges. Drive leads straight to Nicholas Stone's stables which one thinks may be the house, but one swerves to the left and stops outside pair of shut gates at foot of steps to the terrace. Then the Hugh May façade of honey ashlar. Robin

---

[*] Robert Bailey (1882–1917); only brother of J.L.-M's mother; ed. Eton and Magdalen College, Oxford; a clerk to the House of Commons; killed in action. A great hero to J.L.-M.: see entry for 21 August 1990.

[†] Watneys lived at Cornbury for several generations: Oliver Vernon ('Togo') Watney (1902–66) m. 1934 Christina Margaret Nelson (whose sister married 2nd Baron Moyne as his 2nd wife).

Cayzer* a charming young man, formerly in Life Guards, a mixture of Mickey Renshaw† and Thomas Messel. Knows a lot about plants and trees, and loves the place. It should be a pleasant job for A., if not too arduous. We walked all round pleasure grounds of fifteen acres. He showed us the famous Hugh May chapel over which John Fowler had a row with Lord Rotherwick‡ who wished to convert it into a squash court. Yet somehow the chapel is not nice, much of the wainscot and carving probably bogus. Carved on the west front of the house were the words *Deus Nobis Haec Otia Fecit. Otia* presumably means leisure, enjoyment, recreation, delight.

Tuesday, 5th June

Brigid [Salmond], looking a sad lady with her one eye and somewhat creepy countenance, took me to Cheshire [for Sally Westminster's funeral] in her sumptuous Citroën. Reached Eccleston Church at 11.30. Intensely gloomy Victorian edifice of liver-hued sandstone. The Duke of Westminster§ officiating and seating people, decent-looking but not clever. A man sat next to me and said good morning. It took me some time to recognise John Sandoe.¶ Kept my eyes off the pall-covered coffin, borne away at the end by six bearers. Then a buffet provided for whole congregation in village hall. Many folk from these parts. Could not hear, and had nothing to say.

On way home we called at Worthenbury church [near Wrexham], which I rightly remember as one of the finest small Georgian churches of its kind. Marvellous box pews, the Puleston** ones facing

---

* Hon. Robin Cayzer (b. 1954), er s. and heir of 2nd Baron Rotherwick (whom he succeeded as 3rd Baron, 1996); m. 1982 Sarah McAlpine.

† Michael Renshaw (1908–78); journalist and traveller, whom J.L.-M. found 'always entertaining, tremendously giggly, and of course socially sophisticated' (*Through Wood and Dale*, 9 March 1978).

‡ Hon. Robin Cayzer (1912–96); succeeded father as 2nd Baron Rotherwick, 1958, and inherited his shipping companies.

§ Gerald Grosvenor, 6th Duke of Westminster (b. 1951).

¶ Chelsea bookseller.

** The 1st wife (m. 1848) of J.L.-M's maternal grandfather Henry Bailey (1822–89) had belonged to this family of Flintshire gentry, which died out early in the twentieth century. The Puleston estates, including their seat of Emral Park near Worthenbury, had been inherited by J.L.-M's half-uncle Crawshay Bailey (1853–1935), who changed his name to Puleston but died without issue.

each other at east end, each with fireplace. Splendid wall tablets, one commemorating my grandfather's marriage to Louisa Puleston. I felt very exhausted on return. Jeremy Fry* came to dine. At the funeral he was almost in tears. Heard the news while on the Danube and rushed home. We talked of nothing but Sally, who emerges as almost an immortal because of her goodness, sweetness and courage.

Wednesday, 6th June

How time has passed. We became Gloucestershire residents in 1961.†

Saturday, 9th June

To Chatsworth for two nights. Missed train there from Gloucester and arrived late for dinner in a great fluster. On return journey, Debo delivered me into care of ticket man at Chesterfield station and told him to look after me, as I was slightly dotty. Ariane came down for the day to help me select illustrations for the *Bachelor*. So attractive, sweet and clever. A joy to have her, and she was a great success with the Devonshires. Debo showed me a Royal Appointment for Bed and Breakfast she had received from the Prince of Wales. This shows humour.

On my return, A. and I dined with Miranda Morley. Lovely house and garden made for her by David out of three Badminton cottages. I sat next to Miranda, who is easy and amused. Charming party, the others being a granddaughter of Beaverbrook,‡ Charlie Morrison, and Colonel Parker Bowles.§ The last assured me the army could destroy IRA by rounding up 120 well-known suspects. Most other nations would do so, certainly the French.

Sunday, 10th June

Debo rang to say that Lord Carlisle thinks he has identified portrait of 6th Countess at Castle Howard. Also that Diana [Mosley] got a

---

* Inventor and businessman (b. 1924); m. 1955 (diss. 1967) Camilla Grinling.
† When A.L.-M. gave up her French tax residence and purchased Alderley Grange.
‡ William Maxwell Aitken, 1st Baron Beaverbrook (1879–1964); newspaper owner and politician.
§ Andrew Parker Bowles (b. 1939); m. 1973 Camilla Shand (diss. 1994, in which year he retired from army with rank of brigadier).

rousing reception last night from two hundred old BUF* men at a dinner given in London in honour of her eightieth birthday.

Derry and Alexandra came for the day. We took them to Alderley garden which was open in the afternoon. Love of this house surged through me. Garden rather overgrown and romantic. Has a secret feel, though A. criticises it for being too full of shrubs. The poplars and limes we planted are now enormous. We peered inside the house, where the same quality prevails, but not so attractive as without – overcrowded and over-opulent.

Friday, 15th June

To London for Nick [Robinson]'s marriage to the taciturn Alice [Webb]. Quite a little party of thirty assembled at Chelsea Town Hall. Richard the best man, resembling a pale stick caterpillar. Alice swathed in a diaphanous white shawl and wearing my mother's diamond pheasant brooch. Dear Nick, when he inclined his head, showed a spot of baldness in the middle of his crown; this and the occasion mark the end of his youth. But he was so charming and attentive to me, as were the brothers. We walked to a restaurant in the King's Road. Food very good, but being early we had to stand for an hour in low-ceilinged hot basement. Spoke to Alice's father, a good solid craftsman. He talked of his father, stained-glass maker and pupil of John Betjeman's idol architect Ninian Comper,† and of his great-uncle Sir Aston Webb.‡ I like this craftsman association. It is right for Nick, and one to be proud of. Whole occasion rather a strain because of my difficulty hearing, and being 'bothered in the head'.

I went on to see Ariane at John Murray's to go through the Bachelor illustrations, and took her to Brooks's to see Archer Shee's§ portrait of the young B. She is so sane and sensible as to what is suitable and what not. Then for a cup of tea with M., who is getting rather fat in the face. He glanced at the proofs of my novel which Nick handed me in return for my two inadequate presents – a glass vase, and a pottery plate by Quentin Bell.

---

* British Union of Fascists.
† Sir Ninian Comper (1864–1960); artist and architect, specialising in church decoration.
‡ Victorian architect (1849–1930), whose work includes the façade of Buckingham Palace and Admiralty Arch.
§ Sir Martin Archer Shee (1769–1851); artist, President Royal Academy 1830–50.

Saturday, 16th June

We dined at the House. Just the Beauforts, Jeremy Tree* and Dominic de Grunne. David told me how he hated being alone with Master, to whom he had nothing whatever to say. Admitted he was the dumbest, most conventional man ever born. After dinner I sat with de Grunne, handsome and civilised Frenchman. I asked him if he was still a priest. He said once a priest always a priest; he was entitled to give extreme unction, though it would be bad taste for him to administer communion. What decided him to leave the Benedictines was Vatican II, the jettisoning of Latin and the traditional trappings, and the Papacy's rejection of birth control.

Sunday, 17th June

Billy Henderson and Frank Tait lunched. Frank is a well-informed man, quick, amusing and a good story teller. Talking of how French queers adopted their young lovers to enable them to inherit under the *Code Napoléon*, he said that Osbert Lancaster once drew a cartoon of a midwife carrying the swaddled baby Alan Searle up to Willie Maugham† saying, 'Good news, it's a boy.'

Thursday, 21st June

The summer solstice, and as cold as Christmas. Went to London for the day, Peggy mentioning as I left the door that there was a photograph of me in the *Daily Mail*. I returned proofs of my novel to Nick's office in Shepherd Street. Then to Murray's where I discussed further illustrations with the adorable Ariane. Then to Spink's exhibition of twentieth-century artists – Paul Nash, Duncan Grant, Gilbert Spencer. After lunching at Brooks's with George Dix, I went to see Midi in Cranmer Court, taking two minute bunches of sweet peas costing £12.20. Poor Midi has clearly had a stroke. Moving slowly with a steel frame; face pulled down to one side; voice so thin and low

---

* Racehorse trainer based at Beckhampton, Wiltshire; yr s. of Ronald Tree MP of Ditchley Park, Oxfordshire, and Nancy Lancaster, interior decorator.
† The novelist and dramatist W. Somerset Maugham (1874–1965) bequeathed much of his estate to his companion Alan Searle under French legal arrangements which were challenged by his daughter Liza.

as to be almost inaudible. We drank tea and chatted. Her memory still good, for we discussed when we had first met. She thought it was at Admiral Volkoff's Russian restaurant in South Kensington, when I was dining there with Johnnie Churchill. I thought it was at Swinbrook when she was staying there with Nancy [Mitford]. We kissed goodbye very fondly. I wonder if I shall see her again.

Sunday, 24th June

Nico Guppy* came for luncheon. A large teddy-bear with deep voice and precise diction. Told us his eldest boy, aged twenty-six, is now a commodity millionaire, with enough money to see him through life.† Began buying and selling at Eton; got a double first at Magdalen. Nico full of curious information: that Napoleon III invented the colour magenta from the mixture of mud and blood on the battlefield of that name; that Haiti once had a black monarchy, of which there still exist dukes of Marmalada and Limonada.

   A. took him to the memorial party in Sally's garden, while I met Bevis Hillier in Bath. He wants me to contribute to Sotheby's magazine of which he has been appointed editor. Also interviewed me for second volume of his John Betjeman, but I fear I was little use. It was one of my bad days, and he was not a good interrogator – polite and flattering, but too slick for me. He must have thought, 'This man is gaga.' Indeed, I sometimes feel that my mental processes are like a faulty electric wire, which sometimes flickers into life, and is sometimes detached.

Friday, 29th June

Last night we watched the Queen Mother's ninetieth birthday ceremony on Horseguards Parade. Marvellously organised and drilled it was, and very moving. She did not look her years, but pretty and sweet. One must admit she is the perfect actress. Behaviour throughout the

---

* Underwriting member of Lloyd's, then undergoing difficulties owing to the insurance crisis.

† Darius Guppy, who had become a celebrity after acting as best man at the wedding of his Eton friend Earl Spencer (brother of Princess of Wales) in 1989, had in fact made his recent fortune through an insurance swindle for which he was eventually sentenced to six years in prison.

long ordeal flawless. She had to stand for an hour or more under the canopy with the sun in her eyes, waving that tiny hand and bowing appreciatively. A joyous spectacle.

Terence O'Neill* is dead. M., brought up in Northern Ireland when Terence was Prime Minister there, sees him as a tragic figure who was destroyed when he tried to overcome local prejudices. I have known Terence since he was a child, and never thought him very clever. He had the same sense of humour as his sister Midi; screwed up his face in silent laughter. Otherwise conventional; no wide range of interests; none of the charm of his brother Brian; shy and reserved. He was a prisoner of war, which must have accentuated the reserve. Brian and Shane were killed in the war; Timmy died soon after. Only poor Midi remaining – just.

Saturday, 7th July

Hugh Montgomery-Massingberd comes from London to spend day here. He wants to write a profile of me to coincide with the publication of my novel next month and my birthday. Alvilde takes to him warmly; likes his good manners, his hesitancy, his wide knowledge and cleverness. While she watched Wimbledon, he sat with me in the small room before the gas fire, for it was a perishing day. Has read the book. Asked questions about my extreme youth and what I remembered of the First World War, and the German prisoners working on the farm. I trotted out the old and worn memories. But he is a good, casual-seeming interrogator, and makes talk easy. After he left, I told A. that I now rather dreaded publication of this novel. She replied, 'Well you do ask for it, don't you?'

Saturday, 14th July

Although I have never cared much for Nicholas Ridley, I am sorry for him.† He got carried away in talk with Dominic Lawson – just as I

---

* Hon. Terence O'Neill (1914–90); Prime Minister of Northern Ireland, 1963–69; cr. life peer as Baron O'Neill of the Maine, 1970; m. 1944 Jean Whitaker (sister of J.L.-M's friend Billy).

† Ridley had been forced to resign from the Government after casually remarking to Dominic Lawson, editor of the *Spectator*, that European Monetary Union was 'a German racket designed to take over the whole of Europe'.

did the other day with the *Daily Mail*. The pity is that he retracted what he said about Germany, which deprives him of the sympathy of those millions who agree with him (not including myself). Meanwhile he is being hounded by his many enemies – and I detest the baying of hounds. Caroline [Beaufort] reminded me that she once met him lunching with us at Alderley, when he came into the room wearing his wife's shoes, which was meant to be funny but wasn't. I had forgotten this silly incident.

Sunday, 15th July

In our snobbish way we lunched today with the Michaels of Kent instead of going to Sally's memorial service at Wickwar. But the service was given contrary to her wishes, for she was a total unbeliever; and I did go to her funeral in Cheshire. So we lunched with the Prince and Princess, though I warned A. what this luncheon would be like, and indeed it turned out to be exactly like the two last I attended on my own.

We arrived punctually at one. Met by her in the downstairs hall. Much friendliness, embraces moderated by A's bob and my bow. I had taken the precaution of bringing straw hats. They were needed, for the heat was stifling. Drinks under mulberry tree on lawn. Usual strange assortment of guests. A nice decent couple called Biddulph, he a son of Mary Biddulph,[*] unknown to us and to our hosts. It transpired the secretary had invited them by mistake. Lynn Seymour,[†] dancer who has just played Marie Antoinette in a film; Lady Northampton, *divorcée*.[‡] Luncheon was outdoors in the sun, and even under our hats the heat was terrific, the flies tiresome.

The Prince's manners beautiful as always. He is becoming less shy with me, and tells nice tales of 'my grandmother' and 'my great-uncle'. They have been in Hungary visiting her grandmother's castle, now a terrible computer factory, all coffins in the family mausoleum vandalised. She is determined to build a small property nearby for themselves. The Princess sets out to please and entertain. Her taste is good – lovely china, and two charming silver wine carafes in the shape

[*] Mary Birchall (1909–91), gardening friend of A.L.-M.; m. 1938 Major Anthony Biddulph (1910–84); had two sons, Simon (b. 1942) and Jasper (b. 1946).
[†] Ballerina (b. 1939).
[‡] See notes to 26 February 1989.

of Chianti bottles. But there is a feeling that everything is just a little unreal and Ruritanian, and may dissolve. She was sharp with the poor young footman, borrowed from Buckingham Palace, when he trod on the cat's paw carrying heavy trays in the sweltering sun. Told me she was having a row with the publisher of her book. She asked me if she ought to consent to newspaper serialisation – 'not that I need the money'. I cautioned against, as they always highlighted the scandalous. 'There's nothing scandalous about my book,' she said of her history of royal mistresses.

Thursday, 19th July

We dine with the Westmorlands* alone. David W. is a friendly, jolly man who talks a great deal, but is not boring. Always full of information – he gave me the inside story of the Ridley interview affair, which he got from George Jellicoe.† He is perplexed as to how to ensure that his Westmorland treasures – family portraits, silver etc. with 'W' engraved – remain with the holders of the title. Burghy‡ has no son, just a daughter, while Burghy's younger brother Harry§ has a son. How can David ensure that these things eventually end up with Burghy's nephew rather than his widow? As we drive away, A. reminds me that David is a courtier – Master of the Horse, no less – and that like all that breed he is genial, welcoming, at pains not to appear exclusive, brimming with fun and jokes, yet in reality full of reserve, and conscious of distinct limits beyond which trespass would be frowned upon. I find these people good company despite such limitations.

Monday, 23rd July

The heatwave persists and drought threatens. Even the foxes fail to leave their earths. We dined at the House. I sat between Caroline and Clementine Beit, the latter now enormous and square. Waxing furious, she attacked Diana [Mosley] for having praised Hitler in her

---

* David Fane, 15th Earl of Westmorland (1924–93); Master of the Horse, 1978–93; m. 1950 Jane Findlay.
† 2nd Earl Jelllicoe (b. 1918); Lord Privy Seal, 1970–73 (resigning over 'call girl affair').
‡ Anthony Fane, Lord Burghersh (b. 1951); er s. and heir of 15th Earl of Westmorland (whom he succeeded, 1993).
§ Hon. Harry St Clair Fane (b. 1953).

'absurd' appearance on *Desert Islands Discs*. Perhaps Clementine suffers from guilt for having been Bobo's* associate in Berlin before the war. 'It's all very fine for you to laugh,' she says. 'It is no laughing matter that Diana brought such shame on Aunt Iris and Uncle Tommy.'† It was just that notion which did make me laugh, though I was too polite to say so. Somehow I can't indulge in recrimination about political allegiances of half a century ago. And what about Stalin, faithfully supported by the majority of my contemporaries among the intellectuals? Clementine also said that Alfred now hates being called 'Alf'. I said I would in future refer to him as 'the sacred river'.

Yesterday we lunched at Barnsley Park. Some fifty assembled. Two hours of sheer banality, during which I heard not one single remark worthy of remembrance. It is ghastly that I never see intellectuals and spend so much time with idiotic society people – though our host, Charles Faringdon, is decent and good-natured. How rich the rich are today. Grandest house, enormous garden and park, wine flowing. Is 'society' on the edge? Can it last – and should it?

Thursday, 26th July

The huge old chestnut tree overhanging Essex House has been causing us much alarm since a large branch fell a fortnight ago during an afternoon of total calm. Today a gang of three came and demolished most of it. The youngest member, a sturdy blond with long fair hair knotted at the nape, was the steeple-jack. We were fascinated by his daredevilry and skill. He hauled himself up by a harness, talking to his companions below as he went. Like a monkey ran from branch to branch, felling branches small and large with a motor-saw. I never took my eyes off him, yet could not see his face. Handsome, said A.

---

* Unity Mitford (1914–48), fourth of the Mitford sisters, who became enamoured of Hitler and shot herself in Munich when Great Britain declared war on Germany in 1939.
† Clementine was the dau. of Hon. Clement Mitford, eldest son of 1st Baron Redesdale. Her father having been killed in action 1915, the second son, Hon. David Mitford (1878–1958), father of 'the Mitford girls', succeeded as 2nd Baron in 1916. The 1st Baron's younger children included the unmarried Hon. Iris Mitford (1879–1966), who devoted herself to good works, and Hon. Bertram 'Tommy' Mitford (1880–1962), who succeeded his brother as 3rd Baron in 1958.

Tuesday, 31st July

Desmond Briggs lunches with me in Bath. Thinks my library the most beautiful room of its type he has ever seen. Tells me that he edits every novel Simon Raven[*] writes.

Wednesday, 1st August

I motor to Upper Slaughter [Gloucestershire] for funeral of my second cousin Alice Witts.[†] The heat so overpowering that I doubted I would get there, and wondered what would happen if I succumbed en route. Pretty old church in picturesque setting, already packed. At the door I told the usher that I wanted to sit at the back; but when I gave my name he said a seat was reserved for me in front, in a pew behind the sisters. Service lasted nearly an hour. I thought I would die. Address lauded the Christian virtues of Alice, who was thoroughly decent like all the Wrigley women – a devout churchgoer, a good wife and neighbour. How shocking they must have thought us Lees-Milnes, in their eyes raffish if not downright wicked. Church walls covered with mural tablets to Wittses, mostly reverends and generals. I could not face the tea to which we were invited at the old house, now a hotel. I felt but little sorrow for Alice who was sadly dull, but would like to see something of Edith before we both die, and have written suggesting as much.

Thursday, 2nd August

August is once again proving a dangerous month. Brightest, sunniest weather, as in 1914, 1938, 1939, 1940 . . . Now the Iraqi aggression, which is world-shaking.[‡] The unbroken heat brings with it an invisible worm of fear.

---

[*] Novelist (1928–2001), who drew heavily in his writings on his own devil-may-care early life.

[†] Alice Mary (1902–90), eldest of the five Wrigley sisters; m. 1929 Major-General Frederick Vavasour Broome Witts (1889–1969), whose forebears had been Rectors and Lords of the Manor of Upper Slaughter for three generations.

[‡] To international uproar, Iraqi forces had invaded and occupied Kuwait in the early hours of that day, Saddam Hussein proclaiming the territory annexed as the nineteenth province of Iraq.

Monday, 6th August

My eighty-second birthday. Heralded by Hugh Massingberd's interview with me in yesterday's *Sunday Telegraph*, which I can't fault for
kindness and understanding. A. gave me *The Oxford Companion to
French Literature*, a green jersey and a white dust-proof jacket. A luncheon for seven – Caroline [Beaufort], Woman, Billy [Henderson] and
Frank [Tait] – and Nick, who came down from London bearing the
first six copies of the dreaded novel [*The Fool of Love*], which looks
very well. Billy very aged and frail. We agreed that with the best will
in the world we could no longer sparkle or even keep up.

Tuesday, 7th August

Peter Coats has died. Scarcely a surprise. Hugh Massingberd in the
Telegraph has written an obituary which is cruel but accurate. He was
an inordinate snob, who whenever I saw him would take me aside and
bore me with talk of Lockers Park, Eton, or affairs he had had in the
past. He was elegant, affected, sophisticated and handsome. And vain,
desperately wanting to be loved and admired. He never forgave me
for criticising Chips [Channon] in my diaries. Indeed I did not admire
Peter or have much regard for him, and Chips was a whore-monger.
I recall sitting with them in Belgrave Square during the war, when
they urged me to accompany them to dances with young men and
thought me prudish when I refused. Peter took his garden writing
seriously, and his study of royalty.

Thursday, 9th August

To London for the night. Still intolerably hot. At London Library,
Douglas Matthews told me he had already begun indexing the
Bachelor, and thought he might find the European royalties difficult.
Peter [Coats] would have helped him. Went to see poor Midi, who
has had a fall in hospital, and looked awful. Bamber arrived before I
left, looking handsome in pale trousers and open-necked striped shirt.
Laughs a great deal, without much meaning in the laughter. Is
working on a new British Encyclopaedia, writing half the entries
himself. I said I supposed it would keep him busy for the rest of his
life. Not at all, he replied, he meant to finish it in two years. Eardley
and Richard Shone dined with me at Brooks's. Richard full of fun and

information as always; talked of modern art, and how he preferred Balzac to Dickens.

Next morning I called on M. after breakfast, unseen for some weeks. He gave me a pewter hip flask with a facsimile of my signature engraved on it along with my telephone number. When I asked how he had got the signature, he replied, 'from the first letter you sent me'. Most touched, though unsure how to use this precious gift. I brought him a copy of *The Fool of Love*. Then to John Murray's where I went through illustrations with Ariane. How she enchants me. Jock [Murray] joined us for sandwiches, jolly and jokey. I watched Ariane, the dutiful, admiring subordinate, responding deferentially to the spate of jokes. Jock showed me Paddy [Leigh Fermor]'s manuscript, a spider's nightmare of corrections which he goes over again and again. Jock says Byron's are the same. He says a Byron letter will fetch as much as £3,000 if unpublished, otherwise only half that amount. Jock showed me letters from his friend Axel Munthe,* who told him how bored he had become by his weekly audiences with King Gustav.† When the King arranged for him to be buried in the royal mausoleum, Munthe was horrified to think he might continue to be bored by the sovereign for all eternity. After his death, his son secretly disposed of his corpse at sea, and an empty coffin was interred in the mausoleum. When I left, Jock said, 'Now do one thing for me. Make a list of all those friends you want invited to the party I shall give for the publication of *The Bachelor Duke*.' Terribly kind, but the last thing I want is a cocktail party.

In asphyxiating heat, I stumbled to Burlington House to see the Edwardian paintings exhibition. A pretty poor lot, barring Sargent and Nash. Then crossed the road to Fortnum & Mason. While I was waiting for the lift a woman with a jolly face and charming smile turned to me and said, 'Am I right?' It was Mrs Nuttall, widow of my recently discovered half-brother. A delightful lady, a Mrs Miniver;‡

---

* Swedish doctor and writer (1857–1949), who became physician to the Swedish Royal Family, and spent much of his life on Capri; known for his autobiography *The Story of San Michele* (1929).

† Gustav V Adolf, King of Sweden, 1907–50 (b. 1858).

‡ Character created by the writer Jan Struther (Joyce Anstruther [1901–53]; m. 1931 Andrew Maxtone Graham), the ideal English wife and mother with sharp observations on everything and enormous zest for life. She first appeared in the Court Page of *The Times* during the 1930s; a book based on her chronicles, published after the outbreak of war, became a transatlantic bestseller; and the film which followed in 1942 was similarly successful and of great propaganda value to the Allies.

very slight accent, which might be Australian or North London. Over tea, she was able to tell me more than I already knew of my father's affair with her mother-in-law, the Crompton Hall coachman's daughter. Said that her John minded the bastardy much when a boy with his mother in Sydney, and made her buy a wedding ring and pretend to be a war widow. No future in this connection, and after an hour I was relieved to depart for Paddington. But I liked her.*

Tuesday, 14th August

Walking in the park, without Folly for once, I discovered traces of a former ride to the north of the House, still perceptible through the over-growth. The ancient oaks very silent; how redolent of history if one could consult them. When I told A. that I had no further book in mind, she suggested I should write a history of Badminton and the Beauforts. But I don't much care for the Somerset family, don't want to embark on more dukes, fear getting embedded in another long book which I might not finish, and would prefer to write another novel, if the present one has any favourable reception.

Tuesday, 21st August

I wonder how many people recall the birthday of an uncle who died seventy-three years ago. If only my Uncle Robert had lived he would surely have guided my feet into the way he saw most fitting for me, have encouraged my desire to learn, have smoothed my relations with my father, have taught me to be filial and not reproachful, have inculcated courage in me and turned me into a more worthwhile character.

---

* Going through the effects of John Nuttall (b. 1907), an Australian banker, following his death in February 1990, his widow and stepson were intrigued to come across papers suggesting that he had been the illegitimate son of J.L.-M's father George Lees-Milne. (His mother, Katherine Nuttall, had been the coachman's daughter at George's property of Crompton Hall near Oldham, and had emigrated with her son to Australia in 1916.) They had written to J.L.-M. in an effort to find out more about the connection, enclosing photographs which showed a strong family resemblance.

Wednesday, 22nd August

The gravity of the present Iraq situation is appalling and I don't see how war can be avoided. The West may be underestimating Saddam's power to wreak havoc in the form of a global catastrophe. I admire Mrs T's courage but question the wisdom if not the ethics of fighting Iraq. Few wars bring anything but disaster, and posterity may judge this one as cataclysmic and futile as the Kaiser's.

Thursday, 23rd August

In the car this morning I run into hounds in the village. I stop patiently and wait. The Master, Ian Farquhar, comes up to the window and we chat politely. I ask when they will start cubbing, feigning interest and goodwill. Two discreet huntsmen, in square billycock hats and green, traditional livery, touch their hats and thank me. Well, I like all this tradition, just as I like the old builder saying, 'Yes, Sir', 'No, Madam'.

Sunday, 26th August

A memorable dinner last night at the House, at a round table on the terrace by the south-east conservatory, watching the lights in the windows come on. We took Burnet [Pavitt] who is staying with us. Only the Beauforts and the Brands.* Table of glistening silver candlesticks, early Georgian, casting flashes of light from glass hurricane shades as we ate grouse. The seven of us waited on by three. The *luxe* of the whole thing.

This evening we listened to the repeat of a radio programme about Virginia Woolf,[†] first broadcast in 1956, narrated by Dadie and including Vita reading passages from Virginia's letters to her. It gave us both a turn to hear Vita. How to describe that lovely, deep tremolo, like an old Spanish church bell, slightly cracked, full-throated, full of the warm south, as though smouldering into passion? I think nothing evokes the memory of a writer so much as the voice, not even the original manuscript of words written. Virginia's voice resembles

---

[*] Michael Brand; m. 1953 Hon. Laura Smith (b. 1931), dau. of 3rd Viscount Hambleden and Lady Patricia Herbert.
[†] Novelist and publisher (1882–1941); lover of Vita Sackville-West.

Vita's, though less full-blooded and emphatic. The same clear articulation of the educated Edwardian lady.

Wednesday, 29th August

One Peter Mandler came to interview me about a book he is writing on the history of public access to country houses.[*] I had at first declined to see him, but then he sent me a copy of his book *Whig Government*, by which I was impressed. He had already seen Howard Colvin,[†] who barely unbuttoned, and John Summerson,[‡] who was full of information of every kind, including details of his successes with women. When Mandler asked Summerson how well he knew me, he replied, 'We have always got on, but he is too patrician for me.' I began to worry about what Mandler might have heard about me, and was alarmed to see the ubiquitous tape recorder, though as usual I soon forgot about it and said too much. He asked me when and by whom I was first inspired to love country houses. I mentioned John Betjeman, Osbert [Lancaster], Gerry Wellesley, Robert Byron, and my colleagues at the National Trust and the Georgian Group. Oh, he replied, I thought it was at Oxford when you experienced the awakening at Rousham.[§] Kept pulling me up. Although he made a favourable impression, I did not enjoy the interview, which I fear was not much of a success for him.

Tuesday, 4th September

The diaries of Benjamin Haydon,[¶] edited by John Jolliffe, are full of period incidents which would have been a help to me in writing *The Bachelor* had I read them sooner. A tragic man, who might have made a decent living as a portrait artist, but insisted on painting vast

---

[*] *The Rise and Fall of the Stately Home* (Yale, 1997).

[†] Sir Howard Colvin (b. 1919); architectural historian.

[‡] Sir John Summerson (1904–92); architect and architectural historian.

[§] In *Another Self*, J.L.-M. claims that his interest in architecture was 'awakened' when, as an Oxford undergraduate, he was invited to dinner at Rousham on the Cherwell, and watched in horror as his drunken host and fellow guests started vandalising the house and its contents.

[¶] Artist (1786–1846), whose diaries had been published by Jolliffe under the title *Neglected Genius*.

historical canvases no one wanted, and became penniless. Every entry a moan about how his great art unappreciated. Except that I am not penniless, have I not the same failings and grievances? I am very upset not to have received any reviews of my novel, and not even one letter from a stranger.

Having made a copy for myself, I am sending my unpublished manuscript diaries up to 1978* to Rota to sell with the rest of my papers. Why am I exposing myself gratuitously to eternal obloquy, when I could destroy the lot and keep my reputation unscathed? Is it vain of me to suppose that my papers may be of some interest two hundred years hence, as those of an ordinary man of his time who kept his letters and recorded his own insignificant and not very estimable life?

Wednesday, 5th September

We made an expedition to Wickhamford. While A. sat with Folly in the car, I went into the church. Two nice elderly ladies therein, looking around. The head one told me they visited it once a year. I told her I did too. When she said I seemed to know a great deal about it, I explained that I had been born and brought up there. 'You are not James Lees-Milne, by chance?' she asked. When I confessed to this, she clasped her hands, bowed, and said, 'Well, I never.' When the dear things left, I inspected the panels of the box pews, which are Henry VII or earlier. Paid my respects to this beloved building and Reynolds [Stones]'s lovely tablet commemorating my parents.

We then called by arrangement on Frederick Mason and his wife at Ashcroft, a bungalow the far side of the Sandys Arms. He wrote to me recently to say he had been employed as the boot boy at the manor from 1924 to 1927, at 12 shillings a week. He is one year younger than myself, and remembers how I used to sit with a pile of books under the mulberry tree while brother Dick messed about with his motorbike. He is tiny (from early lack of nourishment perhaps), rather toothless, well-dressed, with very nice manners. Wife a dear, dressed in her best. They declined our invitation to come with us to a tea shop in Broadway, and insisted on giving us tea in their parlour, a room which they admitted they used rarely, as neat as two pins with hideous

---

* They were edited by J.L.-M. himself during his lifetime and published by John Murray as *A Mingled Measure* (1994), *Ancient as the Hills* (1997) and *Through Wood and Dale* (1998).

suite in orange and gold. Delicious home-made sausage rolls. He talked much about the servants at home – Copeland the Cockney butler, and Paddy the Irish groom who used to bet on my father's horses (Mason taking the betting telegrams to Badsey post office, running across the fields). He referred to my father as 'the boss'. I would have loved to know what he really thought of my parents, but could not ask.

Saturday, 8th September

Tony Scotland and Julian Berkeley* to luncheon. Both delightful. Julian has lost his giggly, looking-into-stomach habit, and is now adult, gentle, soft-spoken and wise. Tony his usual bubbling self. Said the director of Radio Three now urges announcers to make personal comments on the music they present – surely a mistake. He talked of the book he is thinking of writing about his adventures in Europe during a three-month sabbatical. He agreed with me that one should not go into too much detail about experiences, but rely on understatement, suggestion and innuendo.

We dined with Charlie and Rosalind Morrison at Luckington, another enjoyable reunion. Charlie says the proceedings in the House of Commons over the Gulf crisis this week showed the chamber at its best. All contributions deadly serious, even Kinnock's first-rate. Saddam is totally unpredictable, and no one has the slightest idea what the outcome will be. He talked to me of the overpopulation problem, which is at last sinking into the minds of ministers, including Chris Patten. Poor Charlie is on the 'hit list' both of the IRA and the Animal Rights people, and spent this afternoon with the police, who warned him of bombs not only under his car but in his rubbish bins. He will be glad to step down as an MP at the end of this Parliament.

Monday, 10th September

To London, to deliver to Rota's my diaries from 1953 to 1978, along with the letters I have accumulated in recent years. At Brooks's, when

---

* 2nd son (b. 1950) of Sir Lennox Berkeley and Freda *née* Bernstein; musician; founder of Berkleyguard Automatic Security Systems, and defender (like his father) of the traditional liturgy of the Catholic Church; lived with Tony Scotland at Ramsdell near Basingstoke, Hampshire.

John Saumarez Smith made no mention of my novel, I did not refrain from telling him that a film producer had asked for a copy to see if he might make something of it. To Burlington House for Monet exhibition. Fascinating variations of the same view repeated – the poplars, mists and sunrises and sunsets. How did he paint? By stepping backwards after each stroke? What sort of eyesight did he have? For within two feet the canvas is unintelligible. Jamie Fergusson dined at Brooks's. He exhorted me to write a book about what he called 'my babies' – that is, those houses which the National Trust acquired largely throught my efforts.* But I have to overcome my current apathy, and sense of disappointment at the total ignoring of my novel, before I can write again. Jamie looking most distinguished – tall, collected, morose, companionable, clever.

Tuesday, 11th September

To Knole as the guest of Pavilion, publishers of Gervase [Jackson-Stops]'s forthcoming book on country house perspectives. In the train, Gervase spoke to me of his stammer for the first time, saying it was now a constant embarrassment to him. Indeed, as he showed us around Knole, the pauses were appalling. He had to give up a lecture the other day and hand the text to someone else to read. An admirer is sending him to an establishment in Virginia next month for a cure. I advised him to stop lecturing and speechifying, a waste of time anyway.

I had a long talk with Nigel who is appalled by the television version of *Portrait of a Marriage*.† He says the 'seduction' of his mother by Violet is horrifying. He has written an article for *The Times* criticising the production, and is going to America for six weeks to avoid the consequences. Nigel really ought to have known what he was letting himself in for with the modern media.

Thursday, 13th September

My French translator Guillaume Villeneuve spent the day, coming all the way from Fontainebleau by car. I had tried to put him off, but he

---

* As described below, he wrote it in 1991 and it was published by John Murray in 1992 as *People & Places*.
† See entry for 19 September following.

was most insistent on meeting me. He was not the established literary man I had envisaged, but youngish and touchingly modest. The day not a great success. Our luncheon in a Bath wine bar was filthy; I took him to see Dyrham, which turned out to be closed; then I gave him a cup of tea at home and took him to see the House, which was shut up, David and Caroline both being away. Although conversation was not easy, as his spoken English is not much better than my French, we ended friends. Spoke to me of his background. Only child of separated parents; father from Mauritius (hence swarthy appearance); devoted to mother. Familiar story. Said he always felt an outsider, whatever the company. Asked me direct questions, to which I gave hesitant answers. Has read all my books and can quote long passages by heart, illustrating my views on politics, religion and all other matters. I was touched that he had come all this way just to see me. He told me he had a mania for neatness and tidiness; preens and polishes all day long; can't abide anyone being in his flat for long because of the disorder engendered. Guillaume – I suggested we use first names as he already knows me so intimately – is one of those foreigners fascinated by English literature, architecture and social distinctions, like Stuart Preston.

Wednesday, 19th September

Tonight on BBC 2 the first part of *Portrait of a Marriage*. A. refused to watch and went up to bed. I turned on to see a (recognisable) impersonation of Vita in her actual Tower Room at Sissinghurst, huddled over a bottle of gin (she only drank sherry), dead drunk. Then a series of flashbacks – Vita playing with Violet in the Knole galleries; Vita and Harold getting married; Lady Sackville,* looking like a common tart with red hair, explaining her husband's sexual inadequacies to her dinner table while three liveried footmen stood silently to attention. Then V. driving her car in Kent on the right-hand side of the road, passing a horse-drawn cart, making the horse rear, getting out to bark a haughty apology. Harold portrayed as a feeble, whingeing wimp, like a bank clerk with Hitlerian moustache; shown writing with left hand.

---

* Victoria Sackville (1862–1936); illegitimate daughter of 2nd Baron Sackville and Pepita, a Spanish dancer; m. 1890 her cousin Lionel Sackville (1867–1928), who, following a sensational succession case, was deemed to have succeeded 1908 as 3rd Baron; mother of Vita Sackville-West.

Then back to V. swigging gin in the tower, her manner unbelievably haughty. Then Harold confessing at her bedside that he cannot sleep with her as he has caught the clap, and blubbing. I turned off, disgusted that these two distinguished, beloved friends should be so degraded and misrepresented in a film which will presumably be watched by millions. Nothing to suggest they were creative artists, with a life of the mind.

Monday, 24th September

Stayed last night with dear Burnet [Pavitt] in Montagu Square. We talked about our ailments, this being the favourite topic among octogenarians. This morning to Brian Fothergill's* memorial service at St James's Church, Islington, drear late Victorian outside, prettily decorated with glowing colours within. I read the lesson, Chapter 12 of Ecclesiastes, very slowly but not, I think, too badly. Good address, better than I could have done, and a reading from *Strawberry Fair.* Returned to the house for a drink, where I exchanged words with Brian's charming nephew Miles, Simon Blow, the nice queenly High Church priest Father Gerard, and Virginia Surtees.

Kenneth Rose lunched with me. Was friendly and flattering, saying how much he felt at ease with me, etc. Yet began by criticising my novel for being too contrived and improbable; then disparaged Harold and Vita; then said Douglas Matthews overrated as an indexer. Carping at this and that. And oh dear, what a toady.

Saturday, 29th September

We go to stay with Derry and Alexandra at Parkside for two nights. The pleasure of their company rather diminished by the presence of three children, delightful in themselves but claiming their parents' constant attention. A. given Joan's bedroom, I Garrett's. Somewhat painful; too recent. (True, we were put up in Harold's and Vita's rooms at Sissinghurst – but they have been dead more than twenty years.) Dear Garrett's toothbrushes and toilet water still on shelf and other

---

* Historical writer (1921–90) with strong interest in architectural history, who had treated several of J.L.-M's favourite subjects, including the Jacobites and William Beckford, and like him had twice won the Heinemann Award.

personal things around. Yet his spirit benign and welcoming – A. not so keen on Joan's.

Sunday, 30th September

Derry arranged with the Castle for us to be shown round Frogmore this morning by Hugh Roberts,* deputy keeper of the royal works of art. Delightful man like most courtiers. Said the Queen had had to be consulted, and give her approval of us. This house most evocative of past inhabitants. Marvellous restoration of original contents, includ ing curtains, carpets and even chandeliers. Rooms restored are of three main periods – Queen Charlotte; Duchess of Kent; Queen Mary.† The last the least tasteful, it must be said. The Gallery restored to resemble a plate in Pyne's *Royal Residences* [1819]. A wondrous and moving display.

Monday, 1st October

We motor to Petersham Lodge, Richmond, stopping on the way at Chiswick. Here is another example of restoration on the grand scale. A marvellous recreation, for unlike Frogmore, the house and garden at Chiswick constitute a work of art created at one period, by Lord Burlington‡ and William Kent.§

Petersham, where the Loewensteins have now been living for a year, is very luxuriously appointed. I was envious of Rupert's mag-nificent library, which has every convenience; likewise his bedroom and dressing room. Yet the house is too posh and overdone. The yellow drawing room with its gilded furniture gives a feeling of being empty and unnatural. The floor of the staircase hall is of shiny black marble; it should be of stone. The building a fake from top to bottom, the interior completely reconstructed by the Ls at huge expense. A

---

* Deputy Surveyor of Queen's Works of Art, 1988–96 (Surveyor from 1996; b. 1948; KCVO 2001).
† King George III bought Frogmore House and its grounds in 1792 as a pleasure retreat for his wife Queen Charlotte (1744–1818). In 1841, Queen Victoria presented it to her mother, Victoria, Duchess of Kent (1786–1861), as a residence. The future King George V and Queen Mary lived there as Prince and Princess of Wales from 1902 to 1910.
‡ Richard Boyle, 3rd Earl of Burlington (1694–1753); statesman and architect in the Palladian style.
§ Artist, architect, furniture designer and landscape gardener (1685–1748), who worked closely with Burlington from their first meeting in 1715.

large garden by metropolitan standards, in fact an untidy little park. Portuguese couple, butler handing out cocktails. Princess Margaret a frequent visitor. Too snobbish they are; but loveable.

Tuesday, 2nd October

I join Eardley in West Halkin Street and we set out for Spain. Whereas I have one suitcase with wheels, he has two without wheels plus shoulder bag. In the chaos of Victoria and Gatwick, he struggles with these impedimenta without a murmur, aged almost eighty-nine.

At Malaga we are met by E's friend Aart Kruisenbergen who drives us for two hours to Cortijo Llano, ten miles north of Ronda [where they were to stay as paying guests]. The Costa Brava is horrific. When A. and I motored here in the 1950s, it was an unspoilt coastline with a few fishing villages. It is now a hideous example of man's inhumanity to mother earth. A relief when we climb out of this muck into the dry, brown mountains, under a full moon.

The Cortijo is in the depths of real Spanish country. It is an old farmstead, recently and extremely well converted by our hosts. Site of a monastery with remaining arched cloister; two paved courts; swimming pool. All snow white, the whitening an annual task done traditionally by the women. Fine views over the ubiquitous brown fields, blue mountains in distance. Inside the house is charming in all respects. Very good cooking by Michael Cox, Anglo-Argentine and Spanish-speaking. Aart is huge, resembling David Burnett* in his energy and geniality. Makes me laugh more than anyone I can remember. Three English youths staying our first three nights, handsome, clever, bedint, and earning huge salaries. All complain of Thatcher; but they are her children all right. Very casual, like most young today; get up late, expect cooked breakfast at eleven, don't say if they will be in to luncheon. When they leave, we realise how much we liked them.

Thursday, 4th October

After tea, Aart takes me to Ronda, from where I telephone A. Such a relief to hear her dear voice. We walk around the centre of Ronda,

---

* Publisher (b. 1946) of J.L.-M's *Some Cotswold Country Houses* (1987), for whom J.L.-M. (as revealed in *Beneath a Waning Moon*) had conceived a great affection during their tours to inspect the properties which formed the subject-matter of that book.

which I last visited in 1958 and seems little changed. Aart buys jam and little sweet cakes from Franciscan nunnery by means of a revolving cylinder tray, which means he never sees the owner of the gentle but firm voice. But he knows her well even without seeing, and they have their little jokes. We descend into the valley and look up at the fortress town, crossing the famous bridge, a stupendous structure straddling a gorge. From here the Reds during the Civil War hurled numerous victims into the abyss.

We visit the large church of Santa Maria Mayor, which has two colossal reredos of gilded convolutions at either end of nave, which is strange. Grand domed crossing supported by giant columns of Renaissance Corinthian before the high altar. Some recent mural paintings done in 1980s in derivative Carpaccio style, nice subdued colouring, not unpleasing. This church momentarily revived my interest in church architecture, and might have produced an element of spiritual resurgence too had it not been completely empty. A spiritual vacuum in everything we saw. No incense; no signs of devotion; no black pools of old women praying prostrate before altars. Makes me exceedingly sad, remembering the Spain of thirty years ago. The national spirit seems likewise extinct.

Saturday, 6th October

It is suddenly extremely hot, with a fierce sun. After luncheon, E. and I walk to the woods. Stupefying beauty. Ancient holm oaks bearing acorns; view of blue mountains like Persian tiles, suggesting scenes by Lear. Beautiful landscape is difficult to describe in words, best depicted in paintings and music. Yet Dorothy Wordsworth and Virginia Woolf somehow managed it. E. carries his heavy paintbox and stool. One wonders why he needs to come all this way to study landscape, for his paintings will be indistinguishable from those he does in Hampshire – the same vivid contrasting colours of very little subtlety in outline and gradance. Our hosts greatly admire his work, which they display with prominence and pride.

Sunday, 7th October

We take our hosts to luncheon in a village called Villaluenga del Rosario. It went through a terrible experience during the Civil War, when every single inhabitant was butchered by the Reds. Our tavern, a vaulted crypt, was the village prison and scene of unmentionable cruelties. We ate excellently, a bouillabaisse followed by the tenderest roast lamb. The drive there was through a dramatic cork forest. The cork is not the bark apparently, but a sort of fungus which grows on it. When this is stripped, the tree is left a brilliant terracotta colour, almost Cardinal scarlet. After seven years or so the fungus returns, and the tree becomes grey again.

Tuesday, 9th October

Aart motors us to meet some diggers on the site of a Bronze Age settlement. The diggers all young, hacking away with large implements. Result of their activities to date not impressive to the untrained eye. They were charming and enthusiastic but struck me as ignorant amateurs; I hope they won't wreck this isolated and extremely beautiful site. Then we drove across the valley to look at the Roman amphitheatre, which really was impressive – a semi-circle of stepped seats excavated along with part of the stage.

Wednesday, 10th October

Aart motors us to lunch with Janetta Parladé* at San Pedro just off the coast. A long, twisty drive. Stopped in Ronda to buy presents – black soap for A., a wretched little purse for Peggy – and to cash cheques. Our ten days here are costing 60,000 pesetas, just £40 a day for immaculate service, delicious food, and every attention desirable.

Alcuzcuz is a grand Spanish villa belonging to the (today) absent husband Jaime, said to be Spain's leading decorator of international repute. Indeed, I could not decide whether his house was recently decorated in the Edwardian style, or is a 'genuine' house of 1910. Walls hung with interesting paintings of inter-war and post-war period, including a portrait by Janetta of Robert Kee.† Rooms jammed with furniture – easy chairs covered with bits of Turkey carpet, sociables, leather-seated fenders, Edwardian lamps and shades.

---

* Janetta Woolley (b. 1922); Englishwoman brought up in Spain; m. 1st Robert Kee, 2nd Derek Jackson, 3rd Jaime Parladé.
† Writer and broadcaster (b. 1919), last mentioned by J.L.-M. on 20 July 1986 ('a terrible breaker of women's hearts').

Janetta, who is Angela Culme-Seymour's* half-sister, and has been
Derek Jackson's wife and Andrew Devonshire's mistress, is a once-
beautiful, sophisticated, intellectual moll, rather like her intimate
friend and neighbour Magouche.† She frightened me to death on the
two or three times I met her (E. says the last time was when we both
stayed [with Frances Partridge] at Ham Spray in early 1950s). Is now
a bad seventy, straight hair pulled back like a skull-cap, one drooping
eye, raddled skin, hollow chest and bulging stomach. But nice and
welcoming and undoubtedly clever. Very anti-Christian, which upsets
me rather. She destroyed the chapel in the house – 'I can't abide such
things . . . had to take away cartloads of saints.' Fanny Partridge staying
and the only other guest present. She has long been a sort of mother
to J.

Delicious luncheon eaten outside at 2.30 – *foie gras* with truffles, fish
in *brochette*, chocolate cake. We went indoors for coffee to escape the
swarms of wasps. Looked round house, peered at pictures, watched
grey parrot in courtyard dancing to Fanny's dancing, walked through
garden filled with exotic plants from other continents collected by
Jaime, thinking how much it would have been appreciated by A.
Fanny delightful, vigorous as ever at ninety. Her striated face so deeply
furrowed one wonders how it keeps together. No body to speak of,
yet the dynamo buzzes. Shrill and plaintive voice made lively by constant laughter. Accepts no statement without probing and questioning; always needs to investigate meanings. When I said my nanny told
me never to make wasps angry, she smartly replied, 'I always make
them angry – being stupid they are more easily destroyed.'

Thursday, 18th October

Mrs Dalley‡ comes to Bath to interview me about Diana Mosley. An
attractive woman who looks eighteen, but tells me she has children.
Difficult to talk about the living. She is fascinated by D., but does not

---

* Famous siren (b. 1912), whose husbands had included two friends of J.L.-M, Johnnie
Churchill and Patrick Kinross.
† Jean Magruder (b. 1921); American-born social figure; m. 1st Arshile Gorky, Armenian
artist (who coined the name 'Magouche'), 2nd Jack Phillips, 3rd Xan Fielding (formerly
married to Caroline Beaufort's mother Hon. Daphne Fielding).
‡ Jan Dalley; literary editor of *Financial Times*; her biography of Diana Mosley appeared
in 2000; m. 1985 Andrew Motion.

regard her as a saint. Suggests that D's cultural interests, love of music, etc., all inculcated by [her brother] Tom. She wanted to know about Tom, but he has receded into the mists. Luckly she didn't ask to see Diana's letters to me, now in Mr Rota's custody. When she asked to see David Pryce-Jones, he replied, 'Why do you want to write about that evil woman? She is a witch.'

Wednesday, 24th October

Last night Dale telephoned to say that poor little Audrey had died at 3.30 in the hospital. She developed a slight cough, then faded away. Dale was with her, holding her hand. No mother could have had a more devoted daughter. I rejoice that she went peacefully, yet feel desperately sad, my grief tainted with the usual remorse. For I was often unkind to Audrey; she irritated me and I snubbed her, an unforgivable thing. She was as good as gold, and never harboured an ungenerous thought or did a mean thing, which cannot be said of me. And let's face it, goodness is greatness; nothing else counts for much in the sight of God. I shudder to think of the many occasions when I was horrid to her. I never responded to her harmless whimsies, e.g., that I call her 'Minty'; I was self-righteous over her husband Tony,* on whose account she suffered torments; I was never generous or protective towards her as I should have been. Before she married Matthew, I remember Ralph Jarvis[†] fancying her, which I discouraged for no better reason than that I thought her too simple for him. I am now the last of the Wickhamford family, and feel like a plant torn out of the earth. Although Audrey was not at all religious, yet she seemed to be disembodied somehow, a spirit rather than a terrestrial being.

Thursday, 25th October

To London for the day. J.K.-B. lunched at Brooks's. Angus Stirling[‡] came and sat with us. Very distinguished-looking, one of nature's ambassadors. Much exercised by a move among the membership to

---

* Cecil ('Tony') Stevens (d. 1972).
† Colonel Ralph Jarvis of Doddington Hall, Lincolnshire; Eton contemporary of J.L.-M.; merchant banker and wartime secret service agent; m. Antonia Meade.
‡ Director-General of N.T., 1983–95 (Deputy Director, 1979–83); (b. 1933, Kt 1994).

ban hunting on N.T. land. If this goes through, it will deter landowners from giving their estates to the Trust in future, and make great inroads on the country way of life. I feel divided myself, for instinctively and rationally I do not approve of hunting; yet I believe that it renders more good than evil. John accompanied me to Spink's to see exhibition of Lucien Pissarro* sketches and drawings. I would love to have one, but huge prices demanded. His manner of conjuring up climate is wonderful. I can't see much difference between Impressionism and Post-Impressionism.

To tea with M., who was very affectionate, and had bought a strawberry cake. He has developed a curious trick of turning his head to one side when emphasising a point. I fancy he will become very eccentric with the years. He gave me the first chapter of his Ribbentrop biography to read.

Tuesday, 30th October

This afternoon A. accompanied me to Audrey's funeral at Bagendon. Nice little service in this pretty church. I tried hard not to be moved, but of course was, especially when her tiny coffin passed me in the aisle. Could not bring myself to go to the graveside. Try as I might, all memories of our childhood at Ribbesford and Wickhamford surged, days when I was as close to her as she always was to me. She is to be buried next to Prue and Ted.† How much would the poor darling have relished Ted's eternal company? Then tea with the Henry [Robinson]s at Moorwood. I suppose I ought not to be ashamed of weeping. How I admire Dale, who was wonderfully controlled.

Wednesday, 31st October

To London again, for Peter Coats's memorial service at St James's, Piccadilly. A real society event, church packed. All the boys officiating, Tom Parr‡ and Hardy Amies. An isolated, elegant figure standing in the

---

* French-born artist (1863–1944), son of the Impressionist Camille Pissarro, who lived in England from 1890.

† Audrey's dau. by her 1st marriage, Hon. Prudence Arthur (d. 1976), and her husband Major Edwin Robinson, MC, of Moorwood House near Circencester (d. 1985): parents of the Robinson brothers.

‡ Interior decorator (b. 1930); Chairman of Colefax & Fowler.

vestibule. It was Espie Dodd,* the heir. Then came George Dix, who sat with me. A good service with excellent address by Paul Channon,† who pointed out that Peter was not just a socialite but a hard worker, who served the Raj, made a contribution to gardening and wrote fourteen books. I ran into all the world on the way out. An elderly man touched my sleeve and said, 'Well, Jim, do you know who I am?' I prevaricated, saying that I knew his face. 'No,' he replied, 'it is the other way round. I am Teddy Voules.'‡ He could have knocked me down with a feather. 'You are cheating,' I said, for we made a pact never to acknowledge each other if we met in public. I asked him to lunch with me, but he couldn't, and we separated. An unsettling encounter, for I have not written to him for years or replied to his letters.

I ruminated over this posh service. The very same hymns – 'All Things Bright and Beautiful' and 'God be in my Head' – I had been weeping over not twenty-four hours earlier, at Audrey's funeral in the little Cotswold church. But today I was singing them without a qualm.

I met Kirsty McLeod at Fortnum & Mason to talk about Sibyl Colefax.§ Another clever, pretty young wife¶ who has taken to writing biographies. Her eyes so swimmingly beautiful that I could not look into them. I impressed on her that Sibyl, though a good woman, was deadly earnest and lacked humour.

Tuesday, 6th November

To London, to lunch with Dr Hooker** at Royal Society of Arts. Arrived rather early at the Adelphi and wandered around. Saw house in which Sir Richard Arkwright†† lived, and another in which Robert

---

* Australian architect.

† Conservative politician (b. 1935), o.s.of Sir Henry 'Chips' Channon and Lady Honor Guinness; Sec. of State for for Trade and Industry, 1986–7, for Transport, 1986–9; cr. life peer as Baron Kelvedon, 1997.

‡ Herbert Edwin Mervyn Voules (1905–91): see entry for 27 June 1991.

§ Sibyl Halsey (1874–1950); m. 1901 Sir Arthur Colefax, QC (d. 1936); London hostess, famed for her 'lion hunting'; founder (1931) of a firm of decorators (later Colefax & Fowler). J.L.-M. had written much about her in his 1940s diaries. Kirsty McLeod's biography *A Passion for Friendship* appeared in 1991.

¶ She m. 1978 Christopher Hudson (b. 1946), writer and journalist.

** Dr Michael Hooker (1923–2004); director of educational trusts.

†† Inventor of the Spinning Jenny (1732–1792).

Adam, Galsworthy and Barrie lived. Strange to reflect that even in my young days large houses in the centre of London were lived in from top to bottom by not very rich individuals.

Hooker took me round the Society's house before luncheon. I knew the building from old times. Well kept up, but quite without taste; fitted carpets, dreary upholstered easy chairs, nothing worth looking at except Barry's canvas walls. We were joined for luncheon by the Secretary, Lucas, and Norris McWhirter.* The last immensely likeable and told me of two fascinating links with the past. As a boy aged eight he knew Alice Liddell (Alice in Wonderland) aged eighty. When a little older, he and his twin Ross squirted water over Rudyard Kipling, who was reading *The Times* on the balcony of a Swiss hotel; the twins' father made them write a letter of apology and deliver it to the great man, who was amused. McWhirter confirmed that left-wing and anti-Thatcher bias is rife at the BBC, not among the high-ups but the producers and interviewers. He asked what I was writing now. Nothing, I said, though the *Bachelor* was coming out in the spring. He thought it might make a TV programme and said he would mention it to Ian Curteis† at dinner. Good of him.

Tuesday, 13th November

Have just watched Sir Geoffrey Howe‡ on television speaking damningly in the House of Mrs Thatcher. The attacks on the poor woman from her own side do not augur well for the Conservatives' chances of survival. Personally, I think she is right to go cautiously over Europe – though I believed in the ideal of a continental federation during the war, under the influence of Robert [Byron].

---

* Writer, publisher, broadcaster and philanthropist (1925–2004).
† Dramatist and scriptwriter, on staff of BBC (b. 1935); m. (2nd) 1985 the novelist Joanna Trollope. He had expressed admiration for J.L.-M. when they met on 29 July 1985 (*Beneath a Waning Moon*).
‡ Conservative politician (b. 1926); Foreign Secretary, 1983–89; resigned as Deputy Prime Minister and Leader of the House of Commons, 1 November 1990, owing to disagreements with Mrs Thatcher over 'Europe'; cr. life peer as Baron Howe of Aberavon, 1992.

Saturday, 17th November

I have been reading Georges Cattaui's* *L'amitié de Proust*. Very percep-
tive it is, though flowery. Georges identified himself with Proust, of
whom he always talked with adoration. I was intellectually incapable
of discussing Proust at the time, and paid little attention. I wish I could
tell him now how good I think his little book is.

Wednesday, 21st November

I feel sick at the way poor Mrs T. is being hounded. She looks on the
verge of a breakdown, yet won't give in, despite the advice of her followers to do so. M. is in a rage that she should be treated like this by
the scum of the Tories.

Thursday, 22nd November

Mrs Thatcher fell this morning. The great and glorious woman has
resigned. The media are now full of her praises, as are her enemies.
Really, the lack of loyalty and integrity among politicians is unbelievable. Even A., the least politically-minded of beings, says she has not
been so upset since Kennedy's murder. Mrs T's speech in the House
this afternoon was one of the most admirable displays of courage I
have ever witnessed. Making light, pulling no punches, teasing,
damning, edifying, exhorting; a splendid display of nerve and dignity.

Sunday, 25th November

The country is plunged into a state of shock, and the Tories into
dismay and shame. The greatest Prime Minister this century toppled
for no good reason, by pygmies.

We had the Badenis[†] to luncheon. He talked of his recent
audience with the Pope. Tactlessly I asked him whom he was

---

* Egyptian Jew, author of three books on Marcel Proust, who was unrequitedly in love
with J.L.-M. in the 1930s (at which time he was on staff of Egyptian Legation in London),
and whom J.L.-M. (as recounted in *Caves of Ice*) visited in 1946 in Switzerland, where he
had become a Catholic priest.
† Count Jan Badeni (1921–98); wartime Polish aviator; High Sheriff of Wiltshire, 1978–9;
m. 1956 June Wilson.

representing. 'Old Poland,' he replied. They talked in Polish. Jan says there is something about the Pontiff which transcends charm or even holiness and is almost supernatural. I said I experienced similar feelings with Pius XII, and supposed that one's awe of the office induced it. No, he said, it was a special gift. He said the Vatican is just as splendid as ever. Nothing is second-rate or shoddy. Halberdiers, Swiss Guards, flunkeys at every turn. He then said to me, 'You must come back to the Church,' as if I had left it because of the lack of panoply. There is an Oundle master who is trying to persuade me likewise.

Monday, 26th November

To London for the night. Struggled to Mortlake to lunch with Vicky Ingrams.[*] She was waiting for me at the bus stop, a little, bent old lady but with the same whimsical eyes. Late Victorian house at the end of a row, approached by iron bridge over railway line, trains hurtling past every five minutes. She gave me a delicious nursery lunch of soup, *ragoût* and creamy pudding. Talked of her doctor father who was sixty when she was born and died in 1923. She remembers as a child seeing the green file in which reposed all the letters from John Brown to Queen Victoria. Its contents were eventually destroyed. She is confident that the Queen slept with Brown, and thinks it possible they were married. Two of Vicky's four sons are alive, Richard[†] (of *Private Eye*) the favourite. Disclosed that her married life had been awful. I remember disliking Leonard Ingrams, who was rude and offhand. He was jealous of every man she spoke to, including the milkman. When he discovered she had become a Papist and was going to Mass, he turned her out of the house and even tried to divorce her. But she nursed him devotedly during his final illness.

On return from Mortlake I went to 26 Rutland Gate, which I remember as the Redesdales' house sixty years ago, for the *Under the Shadow of Vesuvius* exhibition. Interesting collection of Neapolitan paintings, some of them in ravishing eighteenth-century frames. Wonderful pictures of eruptions, liquid lava descending like rivers and threatening villages.

---

[*] Victoria Reid (1909–97), dau. of the royal physician Sir James Reid; m. 1935 Leonard St Clair Ingrams (d. 1953).
[†] Journalist (b. 1937); editor of *Private Eye*, 1963–86, and of *The Oldie* since 1992.

Brinsley Ford gave a dinner party at 14 Wyndham Place. One was told to arrive punctually at 7.30, when Brinsley rapidly conducted his guests round the dark and cold house, which is in fact three houses, or rather one house and the first floor of the two adjoining. What a collection! Walls crammed with marvellous things. Then dinner for ten. I sat opposite Nathalie Brooke,* direct, funny and clever. After dinner I encountered Lady Reigate,† who found me as dull as I found her. She said that all the politicians were secretly thankful that Mrs T. had gone, because she listened to no one. Brinsley is the ultimate connoisseur. Tall, hollow-chested and pot-bellied, with his long inquisitive nose and quizzical little eyes, he misses nothing and notices anything of *vertu* that may be lurking in unexpected places. He is respected all over the continent for his vast knowledge and sound advice. The Prince of Wales has engaged him to spend £20,000 a year on buying pictures for him. He knows so many young artists that he hardly notices the deaths of old friends.

Sunday, 2nd December

Am reading *Wenderholme* again. The story grips me, unlike *The Antiquary*. Mrs Ogden, the rough diamond, is said to have been based on my great-great-grandmother Alice Crompton,‡ though P. G. Hamerton§ denied this is a letter to her son Henry Travis Milne. Novelists always make such denials, but I can't believe that Granny Crompton was quite so illiterate as Mrs O.

My Bath neighbour Kenneth Hudson was asked by a French friend how he felt about Mrs Thatcher's fall. He replied, 'Just as you felt when Marie Antoinette was guillotined.'

A man from the National Trust called this afternoon, Adrian something [Tinniswood], saying he wanted to talk about a book he was doing on country houses. I did not like the sound of him, and when

---

* Countess Nathalie Benkendorff; granddaughter of last Imperial Russian Ambassador to London; m. 1946 Humphrey Brooke, Secretary to Royal Academy, 1951–68.

† Emily Cross of New York; m. 1940 John Vaughan-Morgan, MP (C) Reigate, 1950–70, cr. life peer as Baron Reigate, 1970.

‡ She was nevertheless a remarkable woman, who founded one of Lancashire's leading cotton mills, and remained a keen shot into old age.

§ Artist, essayist and novelist (1834–94).

he arrived, with shaven head, sandy moustache and earring, I felt no better disposed. But after a few minutes he revealed a keen sense of humour, and I melted. He laughed at the right jokes.

Monday, 10th December

Walking through Bath this afternoon, almost dark at 3.30, I looked through uncurtained windows at the interiors of Queen Square, Gay Street and Brock Street. Every single building is now an office with strip lighting. Not a vestige of Georgian decoration to be seen; only the façades left. What has happened to the people who used to live here? Why have they been driven from this beautiful classical setting? What is the point of it all?

Saturday, 15th December

Another successful little luncheon here, all cooked and arranged by A. The John Smiths and the Duff Hart-Davises.* John attended the meeting of the N.T. Council at which hunting discussed. Though himself pro-hunting, he was concerned that Dame Jennifer seemed to disregard the motion carried by the antis. Christian [Smith] full of charm. She surprised me by saying she had almost no English blood – her father of German-Jewish descent, her mother half-Cuban.

Friday, 21st December

The shortest day of the year. Motoring to Bath in thick fog required an eye on the ball. At Bath Preservation Trust party I saw several old friends. John Jolliffe said that Brooks's ought at least to give a dinner to us unpaid contributors to the new history. He told me that the average age of the club's eighteenth-century founders was twenty-four. Lees Mayall,† full of cheer and wine, is writing a monograph on Eddie Gathorne-Hardy,‡ but lacks data. No contemporaries left. Difficult to say much now about his vast knowledge of books.

---

* Duff Hart-Davis (b. 1936), writer and journalist, son of Rupert Hart-Davis; m. 1961 Phyllida Barstow.
† Sir Alexander Lees Mayall (1915–92); diplomatist; m. (2nd) Hon. Mary Ormsby-Gore, dau. of 4th Baron Harlech.
‡ Hon. Edward Gathorne-Hardy (1901–78), 2nd s. of 3rd Earl of Cranbrook; bibliophile (his yr bro. Hon. Robert [1902–73] being even more famous in this regard); notorious for homosexual escapades; brother of Lady Anne (b. 1911), who was engaged to J.L.-M. in 1935 and m. 1938 the bookseller Heywood Hill (d. 1986).

Anecdotes numerous but ephemeral. He had an abysmal character, living and jesting at the expense of others, and an even worse reputation, only just managing to stay out of prison.

Before driving home in the dark, I sat in my library with the lights on, imbibing the opulence of the rich colours – the yellow curtains, the green lampshades, the silver and brass lamp-stands, the mahogany, the gilding, the bindings of the books. I love this room, which I ought now to leave and get rid of. And I felt lonely and empty, without purpose, no book ahead of me, unable to get down even to the short article I am supposed to be writing for *Country Living*.

Sunday, 23rd December

Coote Lygon, who is staying with us, told me that, during her childhood and early youth at Madresfield, they had family prayers daily in the chapel. When her father was present, he read them. When he was absent, the Vicar officiated. After Lord Beauchamp was obliged to go abroad, the prayers continued. By this time only the children were in residence, Lady Beauchamp having been taken by her brother Bendor to live at Saighton Grange. The Vicar continued to officiate, and Coote played the organ. This continued right up to 1939. None of the children was religious. All drifted away. I was surprised to hear this, as I imagined that family prayers only survived in middle class families after Edwardian times. I recollect that the Chutes still had them at The Vyne [Hampshire] during the last war; but then they *were* rather middle class. I asked Coote if Lady Beauchamp was deeply shocked to learn of her husband's peccadilloes. No, she said, her mother was extremely simple and never understood what homosexuality meant.[*]

Coote also spoke of Zita and Teresa [the Jungman sisters],[†] who

---

[*] Coote's father, the Liberal statesman 6th Earl Beauchamp (1872–1938; m. 1902 Lady Lettice Grosvenor [d. 1936]), was obliged to resign his offices in 1931 and flee abroad to avert an imminent scandal arising out of his homosexual life, which his vindictive brother-in-law 'Bendor', 2nd Duke of Westminster, was threatening to make public. Only when near to death could he safely rejoin his family at Madresfield Court, Worcestershire. Evelyn Waugh's portrait of Lord Marchmain in *Brideshead Revisited* carries echoes of the affair.

[†] Teresa ('Baby') Cuthbertson and Zita James, daughters of the socialite Mrs Richard Guinness by her first husband, Dutch-born artist Nico Jungman. As girls in the 1920s, the sisters attracted attention through their ribald antics, and started a craze for masquerades and treasure hunts at country houses; they were now among the last survivors of the 'bright young things'.

have sold their house and moved to Aynho.* They first applied for rooms in a convent, and were presented with a questionnaire. The first question was, 'Are you incontinent?' They had no idea what this meant, but imagined it must be a good thing and answered, 'Yes, very'. Both were refused admission.

Monday, 24th December

Coote motors us to Chatsworth for Christmas, Woman and Madeau Stewart† the other guests. Delicious food and *grand luxe*. Folly a worry, for she hates the Ds' dogs. Andrew returns from a luncheon with the Mayor of Derby. In his hearing, a vicar, asked by the Lady Mayoress if he had any children, replied, 'No, my stipend is too small.' To which the Mayoress replied, 'I am sorry you have medical troubles.'

Tuesday, 25th December

Rain and bitter cold. Only we and the Ds make it to church in the morning. We sit in the front row of the nave, under the multicoloured marble pulpit. Good sermon by old Mr Beddoes who reads two poems by Hardy, who claimed to be a non-believer yet had a strong sense of animal creation.

Before dinner, we were summoned to assemble at the Christmas tree in the south corridor. The indoor servants then arrived, and presents were distributed by Debo. 'Now Henry, yours from the Hartingtons.' He steps forward. 'Thank you, Your Grace.' 'And Mrs Carr.' Steps forward. 'Thank you, Your Grace.' All very simple and unpatronising, yet a trifle embarrassing. Away they go, and we return to the drawing room.

Sunday, 30th December

We lunch with Lady Harlech at the instigation of Selina who is staying with her. A typical example of a rich American with 'taste' buying a

---

* Country house in Northamptonshire, former seat of Cartwright family, converted into sheltered accommodation.
† Miss Madeau Stewart; cousin of Mitford sisters.

simple farmstead and tarting it up out of all recognition. Conservatory added; little barn given marmalade-stained doorway and neo-Georgian windows *à la* Clough Williams-Ellis.* Rooms thrown into one, all mod cons and heated through the floors. Lady H. an ugly woman with sharp pointed chin. Clever and bossy. We sit at a large round table and eat deliciously.

I mentioned to Selina what Coote had told me – that Evelyn Waugh's last years, though he would not admit it, were made miserable by the loss of faith consequent upon Pope John's disastrous Vatican Council II; that this contributed to his being so bad-tempered and difficult and may even have killed him. Selina showed the insensitivity of the non-believer by saying, 'But Evelyn ought to have been happy not sad to have lost his faith.' I tried to explain that it is not so, when a man loses what he found for himself.

---

* Welsh architect and conservationist (1883–1978).

1991

We have rather a grand luncheon party to which come the Beauforts, the Loewensteins, and Archduke Ferdinand of Austria.* Not terribly enjoyable. Caroline shouts; David spouts gossip; Josephine's talk is dull and pointless. Rupert who can talk doesn't, attending obsequiously to the Archduke. In the sitting room after luncheon, I try to steer conversation to the Austro-Hungarian Empire. Do you live in Austria? Yes, a flat in Salzburg. I suppose your family were unable to live in Austria for some time after 1918? No response. I offer chocolates, wondering how many one could eat before feeling sick. 'Five,' suggests the Archduke. End of contact.

Rupert told us that poor little Tony Pawson,† to whom he was devoted, died on Boxing Day. A noble figure, in that he insisted on joining the army in 1939 when he might have continued to live abroad with Arturo Lopez‡ and thus inherited his millions. As it was, he led a hand-to-mouth existence for the rest of his life. Rupert is organising a memorial service and desperately whipping-in.

I am re-reading *The Bachelor Duke* in preparation for the dreaded luncheon the Devonshires so generously offer to give at Chatsworth for booksellers. I have found a few misprints, and many infelicities in syntax. I fear it is not a good book, and that I cannot write now.

Reading through old family letters chucked helter-skelter into the bottom drawer of the Sheraton bureau, and trying to sort them for posterity (who are they?), I come across a pathetic little torn notebook in which Mama, a few months before her death [in 1962], wrote

---

* Archduke Ferdinand Karl Max Frank Otto Konrad Maria Joseph Ignatius Nikolaus, also known as Count von Kyburg (b. 1918); nephew of Karl I, last Austro-Hungarian emperor.
† A. J. Pawson (1917–90).
‡ Wealthy bisexual Anglo-Chilean living in Paris and New York (d. 1962).

directions as to how she wanted her possessions divided between us three. Touching little requests. Jim, do keep this, not that it is valuable, but I remember it at Coates. And apologies for being cross and difficult when she feels so ill. And the agony of having Alice (whoever that was) foisted upon her when she longs to be alone. O the sadness of it.

Friday, 4th January

Rupert Loewenstein called to inform us that his mother-in-law Miss was dead. Burglars had again broken into her house in Chelsea. The paper boy found the front door smashed in, and Miss dead on the floor. Not known how long she had lain there. The incident may have happened while we were lunching on New Year's Day. Murder suspected, and the house sealed off by police when Josephine arrived. May those responsible for this heinous deed rot in hell.

Sunday, 6th January

Yesterday I was unaccountably cheered by having written a silly little article for *Country Living* which I thought would be beyond me. Too serious for such a mag. Then today I read a short review in the *Telegraph* of the reprint of my *William Beckford*, referring to my 'jerry-built prose'. This has plunged me down again. I am an object of contempt to young critics, who regard me as *passé*. I shall certainly never write another book, to be insulted in this manner.

Clarissa staying the weekend, brought by her lover Billy. She tells us that every full moon he becomes a different character, abstracted, moody and somnolent – a 'lunatic', so to speak. This may explain the slightly odd look in the eyes which Oenone noticed in him.

Monday, 7th January

To London town for the night. Invited to luncheon at Murray's, smoked salmon sandwiches and orangeade. Ariane fetched me from the waiting room, greeting me with an embrace. Young John is immensely *bien*, handsome, correct, courteous and old-world. A fairly useless meeting, to establish what few press contacts I have. They claim to be pleased with the book. The Chatsworth party is off, to my relief; but the Murray's one is on.

To Sotheby's, to see the silver given by Elizabeth I to the Czars in the Kremlin. Barbaric stuff which I don't covet. Then to tea with Jack Rathbone,* now installed with his nice furniture in luxurious flat in Ladbroke Terrace. He is looked after by an outrageously cissy servant, as nice and attentive as can be. Jack making rather more sense than a couple of years ago. Doesn't know who is alive or dead, but has surprisingly lucid memories of the past. Chain-smokes cigarettes which he throws away after a few puffs. Says the lighting-up is what gives pleasure. Whole place stinks of Virginia tobacco.

Joined Eardley at West Halkin Street who motored us to dine at Richard Shone's flat in Holbein Place. Flat pristine like a new pin. Richard gave us a good dinner of roast mutton. Showed us photographs of Parisian views by Sisley,† whose biography he is writing. Says his friend MacGregor‡ at National Gallery is the perfect administrator, even if his judgement of paintings is unreliable.

Tuesday, 8th January

No. 1 bedroom at Brooks's, recently re-papered and hung with Piranesi prints, could not be cosier or more bachelorish. Derry breakfasted with me. Has settled into a very handsome middle age. I love him and wish he were my son. Says he and Alexandra still cannot agree over Parkside, which he loves and she, encouraged by her father, hates. Told me he hated Bertie Abdy,§ not for being his mother's lover but because he was mean in demanding from Derry the full price of a small drawing he saved up to buy when he was an undergraduate. He never spoke to Bertie again.

To *Patronage Preserved* exhibition at Christie's. I didn't want to spend £10 on the catalogue, but Francis Russell¶ insisted on giving me one, saying 'you have done so much for such treasures', etc. At Brooks's ran into David Hildyard,** who spoke affectionately of Myles but said relations were strained. Myles's son as well as all his nephews and nieces are

---

* John Francis Warre Rathbone (1909–95); Secretary of N.T., 1949–68.
† Alfred Sisley (1839–99); French Impressionist artist, born in Paris of English parents.
‡ Neil MacGregor (b. 1946); editor, *Burlington Magazine* (of which Shone was Associate Editor), 1981–6; Director of National Gallery 1987–2002.
§ Sir Robert Abdy, 5th Bt (1896–1976).
¶ Director of Christie's (b. 1949).
** Sir David Hildyard (1916–97); diplomatist; yr brother of Myles H. of Flintham Hall.

naturally in awe of this bullish, red-faced creature, who prefers people who have confidence and cheek. The irony is that, as a child, Myles was just as shy and tongue-tied in face of his own father, the judge.

Thursday, 10th January

M. thinks just as well we are going to war, the world is so rotten. Whether the air will be cleared remains to be seen by those who survive the holocaust. We should never have got into this situation; but we must not now give way to the monster.

I drove to Kemble [near Circencester] for Miss's funeral. A grey and drab affair; no music for psalms; colourless church. All the Loewensteins assembled. Rudolf* now bald and bearded with wire spectacles, looking like Edward Lear. Parson delivered some excellent words about Miss, composed by Konrad.† I wonder whether the whimsical, shrewd, inscrutable Konrad is not brewing novels as world-shaking as Proust's. Was obliged to walk bare-headed in the cortège to the cemetery, getting frozen, and then join the tea at Wild Duck Inn, Ewen. Rupert and Josephine said my letter was the best they had received. I strolled to Ewen House where Uncle Robert and then Aunt Deenie‡ lived. Little changed since we used to go there in the 1920s – a nice, straightforward old farmhouse with barn entry to court. No frills, and pretty walled garden in front.

Saturday, 12th January

Bright, cold weather after days of gales and floods. We lunched with the Johnstons at Shellingford. An air of well-being about this charming old house, gabled, roughcasted, Stuart in feel. Susanna matronly and improved in looks. A[lvilde] threw her stick into the corner on entering dining room, followed by Sylvia [Chancellor], Coote and me vicariously (for I had left mine in the car). I sat between Sylvia and Rosie.§ Lily arrived late with a boyfriend of such outstanding beauty

---

* Brother Rudolf Amadeus Loewenstein OP (b. 1957).
† Prince Konrad Friedrich Loewenstein (b. 1958).
‡ Doreen Cunninghame (d. 1952); widowed sister of J.L.-M's mother.
§ Rosie Johnston (b. 1964) had gone to prison in 1986 for supplying heroin to her Oxford friend Olivia Channon, daughter of the cabinet minister Paul Channon, who had died of an overdose: J.L.-M. (as described in *Beneath a Waning Moon*) had given her moral support at that time.

that I gasped. Beautifully dressed too in blue velvet suit and patent-leather shoes. I tried not to stare but took frequent surreptitious glances. Rosie now working for an opera company. Her recent boyfriend a Guinness grandson of Diana Mosley, whom she admires tremendously. Sylvia about to be ninety, but as amusing as ever. Said to me, 'I was born dilapidated.' Disparaged Bamber Gascoigne for lacking profundity.

Tuesday, 15th January

Tonight at midnight we shall know for certain what seems ineluctable. It is clear that Saddam is bent on war, while the Western countries have done all in their power to prevent it. He seems mad to defy the United Nations, unless he really has some secret weapon. The only hysteria in Britain seems to be an obsessive listening to the news with its repeated platitudes. There is none of the jingoism of 1914 or even the Falklands, rather a sense of resignation. If the world survives, I suppose the outcome may be some system of universal peace-keeping in future.

Thursday, 17th January

I turn on news at 7 to learn that the Allies have bombed Baghdad, with no casualties to us. I later speak to M. who watched the bombing throughout the night on television, moved to tears with excitement. How different from 1939, when all was mystery and concealment of facts; now even troop movements are mentioned.

Saturday, 19th January

The euphoria is over, and we are warned that the war may last four months. Israel has been attacked and persuaded to refrain from retaliation, but she will certainly strike back if attacked again. Then the Arab world may shift and the Alliance dissolve, so we are warned.

It being a fine and sunny Saturday we decided at breakfast to make an expedition – to see Eliza Wansbrough at Broughton Poggs and Hardy Amies at Langford. Found Eliza much the same at ninety-four, mind all right if slightly forgetful. Front door unlocked. We chatted for an hour. Hardy on the other hand much aged and standing with difficulty. Yet still plays tennis, bent. Like all successful men he presides over an entourage – his doting sister Rosemary, his assistant Ken, the posh maid Helen. I had a glimpse of the church. Very splendid, Saxon I suppose, with unusual east windows. The two roods by the porch also remarkable. A wall tablet dated 1697 reads, 'Within this little Howse three Howses lie.' Wish I had more time to examine. Must return at leisure.

Monday, 21st January

To London. Murray's not interested in my 1941* diary, but keen for me to do a book on N.T. country houses. I warned that two others are tackling this hackneyed subject, but agreed to have a go, without contract or obligations. Went with J.K.-B. to see *The Three Sisters* featuring the three Redgraves,† my first theatre for years and not a great success. Could hardly see in the subdued lighting, though J's opera glasses helped. Could not follow the text unless I could see the actors' lips. Too much farce for so serious a play. We ate deliciously afterwards in what John calls Chinatown – the now pedestrianised Gerrard Street. Back to Brooks's at midnight.

Tuesday, 22nd January

To British Museum in hopes of seeing the Venetian St Mark. Too late, alas; it was removed yesterday and is now in Brussels. Instead I visited the Elgin Marbles. Something cold and clinical about the vast Duveen Gallery. Figures more mutilated than I remember, presumably the state in which Lord Elgin found them.‡ In a crazy moment, I bought a gold-headed cane in a Jermyn Street window for £50. Not gold of course but some shoddy substance. I always wanted a gold-headed

---

* While recuperating from illness at Wickhamford in the summer of 1941, J.L.-M. kept a detailed diary whose style owes much to Virginia Woolf whose novels he had been reading in hospital.

† The sisters Vanessa (b. 1937) and Lynn (b. 1943) and their niece Jemma (b. 1965).

‡ Henry Bruce, 7th Earl of Elgin, when British Ambassador at Constantinople in 1801, having obtained the consent of the Sultan (then ruler of Greece), had the East Frieze of the Parthenon removed and transported to his house in Scotland (though he finally sold it to the British Museum for rather less than the operation had cost him). The substantial damage to the marbles was almost certainly caused by his workmen. Controversy has raged ever since as to the propriety of their removal and whether they should be returned to their original place.

stick for my Bath umbrella stand to contrast with the two silver heads. Tired of London, unlike Dr Johnson, I took the train home at midday.

Saturday, 26th January

Charlie Morrison, with whom we dined, said that Mr Major was a great success. Everyone liked him, and even the Labour Party found it hard to be beastly to him.

Sunday, 27th January

Elspeth [Huxley] lunched. Full of gloom about the flooding of the Gulf with oil by the demon Saddam. She showed me an entry in K. Kennet's diaries in which she writes that she 'picked up a beautiful boy', and then describes his pyjamas and what he was wearing at breakfast. I remember K. talked like this, and that 'picking up' did not quite mean to her what it means today.

Wednesday, 30th January

Diana M. and Woman called and we all lunched with Caroline at the House. I sat next to Diana and had the greatest difficulty hearing. She says she can't begin to hear unless she can see her interlocutor's face and watch the lips. Yet she is remarkably quick at catching words and innuendoes. She had been to the Loewensteins' party Monday last. They gave two, one (to which we were invited) for the arties and the other (including Diana) for the smarties. Diana sat with Princess Alexandra, whom she considers the most beautiful woman alive, but whose life is made a misery by the horrid daughter and husband.* The parents live in dread of what is coming next.

---

* Marina Ogilvy (b. 1966), daughter of Sir Angus Ogilvy and HRH Princess Alexandra of Kent, had been the *enfant terrible* of the royal succession since appearing on the cover of the fetish magazine *Skin Two* dressed in rubber, wearing a crown and surrounded by corgis. In 1990, after conceiving a child out of wedlock, she gave media interviews making candid revelations about her parents, who were pressing her to marry the father, the photographer Paul Mowatt. The couple were married later that year but the marriage quickly ran into difficulties, ending in divorce in 1997.

Saturday, 2nd February

We are in a spell of great cold. I have started on my new book, which is not proving too difficult. Have done the piece on Brockhampton [Herefordshire], and am now tackling Blickling [Norfolk]. Nice to be occupied again. Am writing by hand, and a nice elderly Miss Anson from New Zealand who lives in Lansdown Terrace will type for £7 an hour.

I went for a walk in the snow at dusk. At first the picture was one of unrelieved grey and white; but suddenly the sinking sun emerged, bathing the scene in blue and yellow. What would the Post-Impressionists have made of this?

Tuesday, 5th February

Nasty 'mare last night. I was at some college where the students were given an essay to write by a certain time. Time came. We were all assembled in a large room to read our contributions. I was in a great scare of the headmistress, and endeavoured to hide behind a grand piano lest I be called upon. Woke just before the dreaded moment, by which time it was no longer a mere essay demanded of me, but some-thing more in the nature of a sexual performance.

John Saumarez stayed the night, abounding in gossip, enthusiasm and talk of books. He had come from Cheltenham where he exam-ined the Emery Walker* library which has at last been acquired by the municipality. He had long and tiresome dealings with the owner Elizabeth de Haas, who I am surprised is still alive.† Harry Horsfield‡ was in love with her after Mama's death, and even then she seemed aged and delicate, though I suppose she is younger than me. Although she has sold the library for a large sum, she continues to live in the empty Walker house in Hammersmith Terrace.

---

* Fine printer (1851–1933) who worked with William Morris at the Kelmscott Press, and in 1900 co founded the Doves Press with T. J. Cobden-Sanderson.
† Elizabeth de Haas (1928–99) inherited Emery Walker's house and its contents from his daughter Dorothy.
‡ Worcestershire gentleman and Great War aviator who married J.L.-M's widowed mother in 1953 – though they soon separated.

Wednesday, 6th February

I have decided that, when on the road, I do not steer so much as aim. As one does shooting with a barrel gun at a flying bird. I am rather a good aimer, like George V. But one can miss. When I see a car approaching on a narrow lane I measure to myself whether and by how much margin I may avoid collision. This seems to work; but as my right eye is almost blind, I do make mistakes in parking.

Sunday, 24th February

When I spoke to Jock Murray on Thursday, he said he had something important to tell me, but not then, having had a hard day dealing with Candida [Lycett Green] and Paddy [Leigh Fermor]. Oh dear, I thought, he is going to tell me, as Nigel [Nicolson] had to tell Harold, that I am gaga and that the first instalment of my N.T. book is gibberish. This evening he rang. He said, 'You know Freddie Stockdale,* who produces opera in country houses.' (I don't.) 'He is a great friend of Ariane. Well, they are afraid to approach you directly, but they have asked me, as your old friend, to tell you that they want to write your biography.' I was aghast and replied, 'You must be mad. I have never heard anything so preposterous. It's out of the question.' Jock laughed and said he understood my reaction, adding, 'But you wouldn't oppose the idea out of hand?' Yes I would, I replied. Just imagine being interviewed by dear little Ariane whom I adore, and a man completely unknown to me, about my love life, my relations with my father and mother, my inmost thoughts. I discussed it with A[lvilde]. She said why not, someone will do it one day anyway. I don't believe this for one minute, and have written to M. to warn him as my literary executor.†

Monday, 25th February

Woke to the news that the ground battle in the Gulf had begun.‡ I wonder what makes British soldiers fight this war. They are fairly sophisticated, and can't be fired with a desire to free Kuwait. Like the

---

* Frederick Minshull Stockdale (b. 1947), yr s. of Sir Edmund Stockdale, 1st Bt; writer, and founder of Pavilion Opera (see entry for 2 December 1992).

† A biography by Michael Bloch is due to be published by John Murray in 2006.

‡ The offensive was instantly successful: Kuwait was liberated on 27 February and President George Bush declared a cessation of hostilities the following day.

majority of Brits, they probably disapprove of war unless it were to defend their own shores. I am amazed by their loyalty and courage.

Tuesday, 26th February

A beautiful day; mild too. My first whiff of that elusive, disturbing spring which used to cause me such distress – that far-off enticement by unseen sirens towards *Wanderlust*. In the garden here, a bunch of primroses is out; lots of snowdrops; no crocuses yet, but euphorbia in flower, and one violet.

We dined at the House, just the four of us. Caroline complained she was the only duchess who had not been painted, and wanted a full-length of herself. David said he was perfectly agreeable. We suggested her son-in-law Matthew [Carr]. C. objected, saying he had made Anne look 'like a houri'. A drawing of Anne was produced, the first work of Matthew I had seen. Simply excellent, giving her an air of hawk-like power and intellect. C. said she didn't think it reflected her own character. Of course not, we said, he would depict you as you are. 'I don't want to be depicted as I am,' C. replied, 'but as I was when young and pretty. I want someone to do a portrait of me from a photograph of twenty-five years ago.' In that case, said David, he would not pay for it. He asked me whether the upper classes spoke with regional accents a century ago. I said many of them did, instancing Tennyson's Lincolnshire burr.

Wednesday, 27th February

To London for the day. Lunched with Hugh Montgomery-Massingberd at Travellers'. Admired the dining room which has been richly redecorated by Gervase and others, canary, red and gold on pale yellow ground. Hugh very greedy, ate one of my cutlets as well as his own. Is going to write front page of Saturday's *Telegraph Review* on *The Bachelor*. No need to talk to me, he said. 'I know you so well I shall just invent your replies. Do you mind?' 'All the same to me,' I said. He said his fascination with the stage and the green room had become a mania of which he was almost frightened. Not actresses but actors he is interested in – their vanity, their patter, their history.[*]

---

[*] As he has fascinatingly explained in his memoir *Daydream Believer* (2001).

Hugh looking spruce, if not exactly slender, in smart blue London suit.

Struggled in pouring rain to National Trust offices in Queen Anne's Gate. Had a security tag attached to me. Shown by secretary to Martin Drury's room, where until 5.30 I looked through old files on Blickling and Attingham [Park, Shropshire]. Odd to be reading my correspondence with the Berwicks* of half a century ago. When Martin came in, he asked if I recognised the tall lampstand. It is the one I was photographed under as Historic Buildings Secretary, sitting at the same writing-table before the same inkstand. Robin Fedden and Bobby Gore† retained these items, which are now historic souvenirs. Martin charming. We arranged a tour of N.T. properties in June.

In pouring rain to Paddington. While I was waiting for the train, a voice on the loudspeaker suddenly commanded everybody to leave the station instantly. A huge crowd was herded out into the rain. After twenty minutes, we were told by police to make our way to Ealing Broadway by means of underground from Lancaster Gate. We tramped to L.G. through sodden streets, only to be told that the station had had to be closed because of the crowds. Despair set in. Luckily a taxi drew up to where I was standing. I seized it, and with three others was driven to Ealing Broadway. Driver extremely helpful and kind, would not take more than £3 from each of us for the long ride. Chaos at Ealing Broadway, but as soon as I reached the platform a train came in, bound for Taunton. I slipped into first class carriage and took last seat. Changed at Swindon and got home at 9.15, thinking myself very lucky. People so kind and good-natured during these crises. I was reminded of war experiences in trains during air raids.

Talking of obituary-writing, Hugh M.-M. said, 'It is not one's friends' virtues but their foibles which endear them to one.'

Thursday, 28th February

Youngish lady from *Observer Magazine*, Ena Kendall, inteviewed me for her series *A Room of One's Own*. Would not have Lansdown Crescent, which she says has been overdone. So we sat in my little room at Badminton. A nice, polite, but not over-bright version of

---

* Attingham came to the N.T. on the death of 8th Baron Berwick in 1947 – largely owing to the initiative of his wife, who lived there until her own death in 1972.
† J.L.-M's successors as Historic Buildings Secretary of N.T.

Luisa Nicolson.* Unless I am interviewed by someone more intelligent than myself, I flag. Besides, was dead tired after yesterday's experience. Nice photographer fussing around the room with vast camera and screen. Flicked away at me slumped in deep armchair. Polaroid showed an ancient gentleman with head craned forward in the way the old have. To my alarm she wanted to know the history of every object in the room. Did you inherit that clock? And you say Robert Byron gave you that Greek pot? No, Patrick Kinross? How do you spell his name? Is that a portrait of your father? No, great-grandfather? By whom? Raeburn?† Who was he? And so forth, as if my humble possessions were at Chatsworth. I dread burglary in consequence, though Miss K. assures me she has done this series for seven years now without any disasters so far.

Wednesday, 6th March

I went to Hanbury [Hall, Worcestershire] at invitation of Jeffrey Haworth,‡ who thought I would be interested to see the improvements being effected. Nice of him, but they depressed me to extremes. Horribly drizzly day and Hanbury surroundings *triste* and *morne*. The house entirely gutted except for Thornhill staircase and ceilings.§ Floors up, walls stripped to plaster, not a vestige of furniture to be seen. This house which I love has lost all its magic, and indeed its antiquity too. It might now be a building of any date. Sad, sad, sad. There must be something deeply wrong with the National Trust, spending so prodigally on this building, which has no endowment, and which was restored in 1952 by an anonymous benefactor for an enormous sum. Why within thirty years should another drastic restoration be necessary?

I saw the church, with its fine Vernon monuments. Emma Vernon's gravestone is poignant, she having asked to be buried 'next the coppice'. Is this where she illicitly trysted with the curate? Then on

---

* Luisa Vertova; m. 1955 (diss. 1962) Benedict Nicolson (1914–78), er s. of Harold Nicolson and Vita Sackville-West.

† Sir Henry Raeburn (1756–1823); Scottish artist, friend of J.L.-M's great-great-grandfather Robert Thomson (1771–1831).

‡ N.T. Historic Buildings Representative for Severn Region, 1981–2002 (b. 1944).

§ Sir James Thornhill (1675–1734) had decorated the walls and ceilings of this part of the house with mythological frescoes.

to Norgrove Court, last seen and photographed by me in April 1939, doubtless with Rick [Stewart-Jones]. Then a simple farmhouse; now lived in by a nice fellow who makes stained glass, and too much tarted up.

M. telephoned, back from South Africa. Says Cape Town getting shabby after years of economic sanctions, public services running down. Restaurants and night clubs packed, the whites indulging in an orgy of *après nous le déluge*, but the streets no longer safe to walk because of marauding black gangs.

Saturday, 9th March

Front page of *Telegraph Review* ablaze with colour picture of Bachelor and article by Hugh Massingberd. A wonderful notice, which I hope will produce more results than the one he gave my novel last year. Debo and Hardy Amies rang to congratulate.

Sunday, 10th March

We lunched with the Acloques* at Alderley. How I love this house and garden. Seeing this couple who have now been here fifteen years, bringing up a son and twin daughters, and thinking that we were here fifteen years, almost makes me wish we too had a son and heir, and could have remained. The garden, with its view of the wooded hill above Ozleworth Lane, is a dream of beauty and tranquillity. The Acloques have some splendid things. The house is too tarted-up, but never mind; they adore the place, and he is a good gardener.

This morning a review of *The Bachelor* in *Sunday Telegraph* by Philip Ziegler. Favourable and polite, yet he clearly thinks the B. a wimp.

The prospect of Murray's party on Wednesday is like a rat gnawing at my vitals. I have nightmares of being hemmed in by a multitude of faces, recognising no one, hearing nothing, panicking.

---

* Guy Acloque; m. 1971 Hon. Camilla Scott-Ellis, dau. of 9th Baron Howard de Walden. They had bought the house from A.L.-M. in 1974 and maintained the garden she had created there.

Wednesday, 13th March

The dreaded day. Found the Sarge* at Brooks's lunching with his handsome French protégé Didier.[†] They accompanied me to a silly 'Cupid and Venus' exhibition at Wildenstein's. I lay down during afternoon to prepare self for coming ordeal, then collected A. from Lansdowne Club and we went together to Murray's. Although the two rooms were packed – apparently more had accepted than ever before – I actually enjoyed it. Numerous friends old and new, plus critics and celebrities. Everyone enthusiastic about the book and congratulating. Many came with book in hand asking for signature. One woman asked me to write, 'To Jacqueline Onassis[‡] from J.L.-M.' Instead I put, 'For J.O. and *by* J.L.-M.' Long talks with Graftons and Hutchinsons. Much photography, I suspect for *Tatler*. ('Jennifer'[§] there taking notes.) Certainly I have never before been fêted in this way. At nine Jock gave a dinner at Brown's Hotel for eight, Devonshires, Murrays, Ariane, Gervase [Jackson-Stops] and L.-Ms. I praised God that it was all over and had been without embarrassments, feeling rather pleased with myself.

Tuesday, 19th March

Despite heavy cold, I went to London for the day to continue reading N.T. archives. Two piles of *The Bachelor* in Hatchards' window. Gave luncheon at Brooks's to Hugh Massingberd and John Martin Robinson. Cost over £50. J.M.R. took us afterwards to Spencer House. Of course most beautifully restored and decorated at lavish expense by Jacob Rothschild. Filled with good furniture mostly bought by [Christopher] Gibbs[¶] and [John] Harris; fine wood-

---

* Stuart Preston.

[†] Didier Girard (b. 1964); French scholar interested in English eccentrics, then writing a doctoral disseration on J.L.-M's Eton contemporary Edward James; he later edited a French edition of the works of William Beckford.

[‡] Jacqueline Bouvier (1929–1994); m. 1st 1953 John F. Kennedy (1917–63; President of United States, 1961–63), 2nd 1968 Aristotle Onassis (1906–75).

[§] 'Jennifer's Diary' was the society column written by Betty Kenward (1906–2000), notorious for its carefully graded lists of those attending various parties and ceremonies: it originally appeared in *Tatler* from 1944, then in *Queen* (later *Harpers & Queen*) from 1959.

[¶] Christopher Gibbs (b. 1938); antique dealer and collector, member of N.T. committees.

carvings copied from Althorp. Yet what is the result? Mallett's shop.*
We got out at 4.15, too late to return to N.T. Cold worse and almost
collapsed on return home.

Friday, 22nd March

To Chatsworth by train. Got there at 6.45, just in time to change into
black tie for performance of *Entführung* in Painted Hall. I sat between
Debo and Mistress Cutler, Master Cutler† wearing gold and brilliants
collar badge on Debo's left. A most novel and interesting performance
by Pavilion Opera. We sat amongst them and their rudimentary props.
No orchestra, just a pianist. But outstanding singers, superb costumes,
stupendous setting under Laguerre ceiling. Altogether an unforget-
table experience. Devonshires and audience of millionaire shopkeepers moved off to immense banquet in Bachelor's dining room (costing
£1,000 a cover), while I slunk off to first floor dining room to enjoy,
solo and free of charge, delicious spread from hot plate. The astonishing *train-de-vie* of Chatsworth.

Monday, 25th March

Left Chatsworth this morning after a lovely visit. Saw much of Feeble,
who is full of gossip and fabricates the strangest stories with her sister
Anne [Tree].‡

Every other left-hand page of the Chatsworth visitors' book bears
the Prince of Wales's signature. He stayed for three nights lately. I
asked Debo how he spent his time. He disappears unaccompanied for
long solitary walks across the moors. A fairly unhappy man, full of passionate beliefs, over-sensitive, trusting, anxious to learn. Has no
friends among his family, apart from Queen Mother whose departure
will be a terrible wrench. Not many men friends; Colin Amery§ drafts
speeches and advises, but hardly an intimate. His friends mostly
women, including Candida [Lycett Green].

On Sunday, Robert Innes-Smith and Mrs lunched.¶ I liked him

---

* Mayfair antiquaire.
† Sheffield dignitaries.
‡ Lady Anne Cavendish (b. 1927); m. 1949 Michael Tree, painter (1921–99).
§ Architectural historian (b. 1944); architecture correspondent of *Financial Times* from 1979.
¶ Writer, publisher, genealogist and journalist (b. 1928); m. 1954 Elizabeth Lamb.

much. He edits *Derbyshire Life*. Is pleased with *The Bachelor* and will review it. Produced from his pocket a lock of the 5th Duke's hair cut from head by Bess the widow. Auburn, like the Bachelor's. After luncheon, Debo and I went to the Stables to sign our books. Quite a queue when we got there. Someone to help us by handing the books and repeating the names we were to write inside. Several asked me to put 'To Mum and Dad on their silver wedding day', or 'With love from Peg to Bill', etc. I consented with a gracious laugh, protesting I was not the suitor. Apparently several of the staff have bought the book, expensively priced at £20.

Wednesday, 3rd April

And now Graham Greene[*] is dead. I only met him once, staying at Long Crichel [Dorset]. Eddy [Sackville-West] was fond of him because of Catholic connections. But he was certainly an unconventional Catholic, portraying every member of the faith as a drunken, fornicating sot. At Long Crichel, he spoke little but drank much. He always protested he was not one of the great novelists, and was probably right.

A. being in France, Folly and I were alone after Easter with Clarissa and her fancy boy Billy, who is a decent fellow, extremely good-looking and stupid. Asks countless questions without listening to answers. 'What exactly do you mean by squirearchy?' 'Is the aristocracy no longer rich?' Then Clarissa: 'Jim, do tell Billy about the man who lived at No. 19 before you.' 'You mean Lord Strathcona?'[†] She was thinking of William Beckford, of whom she knew nothing and he had never heard.

The book progresses. Today I finished the chapter on Charlecote [Park, Warwickshire]. The garden here is well ahead of season, just like last year. Crown imperials out, and primroses everywhere. A. telephones that cowslips are out at Fourchette.

Thursday, 4th April

Bamber telephones this afternoon. 'I have got news,' he says in his cheery voice. 'It is good. Mother had a stroke a week ago, but is now

---

[*] Novelist (1904–91).
[†] Donald Howard, 4th Baron Strathcona and Mount Royal (b. 1923).

rather better. Actually she was better yesterday but has relapsed a bit today.' Really, he is extraordinary. Apparently Midi is dying, for I asked, 'Please tell me, Bamber, should one hope for recovery or not?' and he replied, 'Well, I would give her a fortnight. I am sure she would be glad to see you on a good day. Do ring up when you are next coming to London.' Darling Midi, lying there gazing into space. Yet Bamber is not heartless. What is he?

Saturday, 6th April

Drove myself to Stourhead [Wiltshire]. Met by Dudley Dodd. Introduced to nice caretaker and wife, ex-policeman and genteel lady. They all accompanied me round the house, which looks the same, but is better kept. Polished and scrubbed. Dead somehow. Eagerly they drank in anything I had to say about the place in the old days. Lunched upstairs with Dudley in his flat to meet the Henry Hoares.* Only he appeared, she sitting on the bench today. Caretakers remained which inhibited conversation a little. Henry Hoare an elderly man who, to my surprise, was charming and gentle, unlike his horrid, scowling, prickly father Rennie.† He said his stepmother, recently stroke-ridden, was brought up in the West Indies in a shack by the sea. Rennie swept her off her feet at the end of the war and took her to England on the *Queen Mary*, to live in what he described as his little house. While on the Atlantic a cable arrived announcing deaths of Sir Henry and Lady Hoare,‡ so on landing they drove straight to Stourhead. New wife appalled by size and responsibilities; had no idea how to cope, and never did.

Henry Hoare admitted that his father resented the N.T., and I sensed that he too had reservations about it, though he was too polite to say so. He asked if I was responsible for banishing the St George

---

* Henry Cadogan Hoare (b. 1931); banker, Chairman, C. Hoare & Co., from 1988; m. (2nd) 1977 Caromy Maxwell Macdonald.

† Henry Peregrine Rennie Hoare (1901–81); m. 1st 1931–41 Lady Beatrix Cadogan, 2nd 1941–46 Anne Troyle (formerly wife of 5th Baron Ebury), 3rd 1947 Dorothy Hairs of Jamaica. He inherited that part of the Stourhead estate which had not been donated to the N.T., along with the right to live in the House, from his distant cousin Sir Henry.

‡ 'They died on the same day, 25 March 1947, without either realising how ill the other was. On that day the Stourhead estate, garden, house and contents, became the [National] Trust's property . . . all but the outlying farms which were left to Rennie Hoare.' (*People and Places*, Ch. 5.)

Hare* paintings to the attics. Probably, I said, with Eardley; but I agreed they ought to be displayed downstairs now, slave girls in chains and all. We went up to look at them. Full-length of Lady Hoare looking like Lady Macbeth, and one of Harry on his twenty-first birthday in cricket flannels – typical Edwardian *jeunesse dorée* and gentlemanship.

Dudley rather eccentric, long and languid, with smiling sallow oval face. His flat full of modern paintings, a good sign, and stuffed pets, not so funny.

Tuesday, 9th April

Acquaintances fall off the perch. A.W. Lawrence[†] at an advanced age, and Bill De L'Isle.[‡] Latter one of the most courageous men I have known. Intensely inquisitive, yet cagey about the exploits which won him fame. Was she a worthy wife, with her dislike of Penshurst? Bill inherited the Shelley baronetcy, though no one seemed aware of this except genealogists. Pity he dribbled so much.

Selina who dined with us said that when she had finished [Evelyn] Waugh's life she would start on Rosamond [Lehmann]'s. She said she was relying on me to let her have Ros's letters to me. I murmured that I hoped they had not gone to Yale with the rest of my papers, aware that they probably have. I'm not sure how much I want Selina to see Ros's letters, which are sure to contain much about the differences between A. and myself in the past. And Selina gossips.

Wednesday, 10th April

In London Library, someone came up to me to say that Reresby [Sitwell] had lent him a copy of my *Heretics*[§] to read at Renishaw. Said he, 'It made me feel absolutely sick.' What is an author to reply to such a remark? I said nothing.

---

* British artist (b. 1857) specialising in erotic (especially lesbian) subjects.

† Younger brother (1900–91) of T. E. Lawrence ('of Arabia'); first encountered by J.L.-M. on 20 March 1944 (*Prophesying Peace*).

‡ William Sidney, 1st Viscount De L'Isle, VC (1909–1991), of Penshurst Place, Kent; m. 1st 1940 Hon. Jacqueline Vereker, dau. of 6th Viscount Gort, 2nd Margaret, widow of J.L.-M's cousin 3rd Baron Glanusk.

§ J.L.-M's first novel *Heretics in Love*, published by Chatto & Windus in 1973, which dealt with incest, homosexuality and necrophilia, among other peculiarities.

Worked all day at N.T. papers, then to see Midi. Terribly down-casting experience. Midi lying on back with mouth open and teeth out, unrecognisable. More like a corpse than anyone I have seen. Kept mumbling as if wishing to say something, but words unintelligible. I did not know what to say. She knew me, held up an arm which looked like a stick, and gave a ghost of a smile. Eyes staring, blank and water-ing. A terrible sight to see. What have we humans done to deserve such an end? I took her warm hand, pressed it and slunk away. Poor darling Midi, my oldest woman friend.

Saturday, 13th April

Julian Barrow has been here yesterday and today painting A. and me in the drawing room. Such a charming man. Told us he and his broth-ers all brought up as Quakers, but broke away. One brother contem-plates returning. Picture fairly promising, but we fear A's head too big for her body. Tomorrow he will try to rectify.

Wednesday, 17th April

Lovely sunny days, all things bright and beautiful. Yet I have horrid nightmares. On Monday dreamt I had to take Ros by car right across London and went mad working out the route. On Tuesday found myself climbing a twisting staircase at Brooks's and having to crawl on my hands and knees, dangling over the abyss. Why the stair treads went into reverse I can't think, but the experience was frightening.

Friday, 19th April

Have finished R. B. Martin's life of Gerard Manley Hopkins.[*] Admirable. He shows an understanding of the tormented soul. I had not realised that Hopkins went mad at the end through lack of love. Martin gives Robert Bridges[†] full credit for his valiant loyalty and belief in Hopkins's poetry. Bridges has not had a good press since 1918.

---

[*] Poet and Jesuit priest (1844–89): Martin's biography was subtitled *A Very Private Life*.
[†] Hopkins's poetry was unknown to the public until an edition of it was brought out in 1918 by his friend Robert Bridges (1844–1930), then Poet Laureate. Bridges, a first cousin of A.L.-M's father, is now considerably less fashionable than Hopkins.

Reading through reviews of *The Bachelor*, I feel I have been treated better than my subject. The general view is that he was a bore. In fact he was extremely funny, and his character complex and interesting. It is my fault for failing to reveal him.

Sunday, 5th May

We dined with the Norwiches at Castle Combe. Christopher Miles,[*] film producer, and wife the other guests. Miles seemed taken by my idea of making a film of *The Aspern Papers*.[†] I'm not sure there hasn't already been one; I certainly remember a play with Beatrix Lehmann.[‡] Mollie said John Julius much upset by horrid profile of him in the *Telegraph*, calling him a lightweight, middle-brow writer. J.J. very devoted to Queen Mother. Says she is the best of the lot and doesn't have to be prompted ever; remembers not only everyone she has met, but what their interests are. A phenomenon.

Sunday, 19th May

Spent five nights in Venice, staying with Anna-Maria Cicogna in her palazzetto on Dorsoduro. Did not greatly enjoy it in spite of her kindness, the delicious food, and the good company of the Thorneycrofts.[§] Venice has become stale for me. I have no desire to see the sights. I am in search of nothing, so nothing reaches me. It seems wrong that I should be indifferent to this queen of cities with its ineffable beauty.

I returned to the news that Midi had died. Though no surprise this saddens me deeply, for she was my beloved friend of more than sixty years. I vividly recall our first meeting in the drawing room at Swinbrook, perhaps as long ago as 1926. As she was a friend of Nancy, I feared she would be frighteningly sophisticated; but not at all. She

---

[*] Professor of Film and Television at Royal College of Art, 1989–93 (b. 1939); he made a number of television series with Lord Norwich, including *Love in the Ancient World* (1996).

[†] Novella published by Henry James in 1888, about a literary historian in search of the love letters written by a deceased poet to his surviving mistress.

[‡] English actress specialising in macabre roles (1903–79).

[§] Peter Thorneycroft (1909–94); politician, Chairman of Conservative Party, 1975–81; m. (2nd) 1949 Countess Carla Roberti, dau. of Count Malagola Cappi of Ravenna, Italy; cr. life peer, 1967.

was friendly, amusing and amused from the first, and we became intimate. I have laughed with her more than with anyone. Alas, latterly I became irritated by her constant questioning. But she was the loyalest of friends, always concerned about me, sympathetic about my family problems and later my marriage problems, always sympathetic. Not intellectual, but intelligent; devout in her way, which was my way too. It was thanks to me that she and Derick moved to Mount House,* and for fifteen years she was my companion in walks through the fields and woods of those glorious slopes. Bamber asked me to give an address at her funeral; but I told him I couldn't, because I was too fond of her. He understood, which was sensitive of him.

Wednesday, 22nd May

I walked through Vicarage Fields hoping to hear the cuckoo in the big wood. Too late, alas. I thought how quickly time now flies. To write a letter takes me an age. It is always time to go to bed, time to get up.

Thursday, 23rd May

Dear Midi's funeral. Woman, awaiting operation and walking with greatest difficulty, came with us to Alderley church. The approach very beautiful and lush, and the two bright green larch trees, Jim and Alvilde, now enormous and flourishing. The church, so pretty with the grey groins and gold brackets we had painted, was packed with relations from London. Touching service. Bamber read the first lesson too fast, Veronica the second too inaudibly. Address given by Merida Drysdale,† Julian Gascoigne's daughter. Charming and apt, read with such emotion that she almost broke down. I knew I was right not to have attempted it. Bamber gave a sit-down luncheon at Petty France Hotel for everyone in church. I sat with Nathalie Brooke, who thanked the Almighty for her friendship with Midi, who was life-enhancing.

---

* At Alderley, where they became neighbours.
† Merida Gascoigne (b. 1933); m. 1956 Andrew Drysdale.

Saturday, 25th May

A. gave a party for sixteen gardeners. Tables out-of-doors. Rain kept off. Garden looking splendid. Apart from Melanie Cairns and the two retired '*Mädchen*'* from Sissinghurst, all the gardeners were young men, and mostly queer I should say. Mostly head gardeners to great houses, calling each other Nick, Mick, Jack, etc. Clarissa [Luke] and Pat O'Neill† also present. I am fond of old Pat for the sake of Rory and past glories of Cap Ferrat, which I never really enjoyed at the time. She is incensed by a vicious article about her mother in one of the glossies, alleging that Enid murdered all four of her husbands.‡ Enid used to say this of herself in jest, but the author of the article takes it quite seriously.

Friday, 31st May

Ariane telephoned this morning, I supposed to confirm her arrival tomorrow. Not at all; it was to announce that Murray's had made her redundant from next week. She asked to be excused staying with us, which I completely understood. The news came without warning and was a shock, though she says that all her friends, whatever their employment, are being sacked right and left, and that Murray's, like all publishers and booksellers these days, are wringing their hands. She will continue to work with authors whose books she already has in hand, which I suppose includes me, unless Murray's change their mind about publishing me.

---

* Pamela Schwerdt and Sibille Kreuzberger, who went to Sissinghurst as head gardeners in 1959: see *Deep Romantic Chasm*, 26 August 1981.

† Sister of A. L.-M's deceased friend Rory Cameron (1914–85) of La Fiorentina, Cap Ferrat; owner of a stud farm in South Africa, where the L.-Ms had stayed with her in 1983 (see *Holy Dread*).

‡ Enid Lindeman of Sydney, NSW (d. 1973); m. 1st 1913 Roderick Cameron of New York (d. 1914), 2nd 1917 General Hon. Frederick Cavendish (d. 1931), heir to 6th Baron Waterpark (their son succeeding as 7th Baron), 3rd 1933 (as his 3rd wife) 1st Viscount Furness (d. 1940), 4th Jan. 1943 (as his 2nd wife) 6th Earl of Kenmare (he d. Sept. 1943).

Monday, 3rd June

Noticed in *Times* list of deaths that of Berkeley Villiers* who was the first boy to seduce me at McNeile's [House, Eton]. I remember the incident extremely well, I aged fifteen at most. In the middle of the performance Michael Rosse, then his great friend, came into Berkeley's room and like the perfect gentleman he was fetched something he had left on the mantelpiece without turning his head in our direction. Michael never referred to the incident in later life, nor did B.V. whom from time to time I ran across. A prissy, affected fellow. I never had the opportunity to talk to him and would have liked to. The smell of his Roger & Gallet Carnation Soap never fails to remind me. Thrilling, alarming, wicked-seeming and delicious it was.

Wednesday–Thursday, 5th–6th June

Martin Drury, a charming man and perfect for his job, took me on a two-day tour of Midlands. Lower Brockhampton our first call. This beautiful setting much the same. The old Manor lies snug behind the gatehouse, farmyard still next door and good old smell of pigs. Delightful volunteer lady administrator received us, treating me like something pre-historic from the Ark. Much-fingered copy of *Caves of Ice* lying on long table. The Hall is now rented by insurance company as offices. Fitted carpets, telephones in every room. Still traces of what went before, original door hinges and fireplaces *à la* Pritchard. Bluff caretaker assured us that the house was haunted by a child of nine, who bangs doors, opens windows and sneezes in the night.

Thence via Hanbury Hall to Little Moreton Hall [Cheshire]. Hanbury has advanced since my last visit, but Little Moreton swathed in polythene sheets from gallery roof to ground. Not possible to get any idea of what it now looks like. New compartmentalised garden on east front, too well-kept for the dear old farmhouse I remember.

---

* Lieut.-Col. (Francis) Berkeley Hyde Villiers (1906–91); kinsman of Earl of Clarendon; sometime senior executive of ICI; married an Austrian; art collector at his house near Kidderminster. J.L.-M. had referred to him anonymously in his diary for 13 November 1947 (*Caves of Ice*), after meeting him at a concert: 'X, and I suppose his wife, were in the box. His proximity made me feel self-conscious. I must have been no more than fifteen . . . when I met my "undoing" from his hands . . . I rather enjoyed it, though of course pretending not to.'

Here joined by Julian Gibbs* who took us to stay the night at their nice, plain rectory in Shropshire. A dear couple, he a simple soul like his father Christopher but without the business acumen, she, picture restorer, more sophisticated and beguiling, very pretty with dark hair and fresh complexion, and slightly Tartar cheekbones from Greek mother.

We continued to Charlecote, dismayed at appalling ruination of Shropshire landscape by motorways, pylons, factories in fields. Welcomed by nice custodian and given coffee by Edmund Lucy† in his studio. A charmer, his face Alice's, his frame and slouch Brian's. I coveted his paintings of Venice, and wish I could afford one. He gets irritated by the public milling outside his window, and is happier here in winter. Then to Coughton [Court, Warwickshire]. Much the same, but too many cars in front of house. Met husband of Robert Throckmorton's‡ niece who is heiress to contents. She evidently believes that I talked her grandmother into donating Coughton.

Sunday, 9th June

We lunched with Chiquita [Astor]§ to meet the Jenkinses. Roy (as he now is to me) said that to understand the value of money in 1941 one has to multiply by forty. When I said that my great-aunt Isabel¶ lived in No. 5 Royal Crescent, Bath with cook, parlourmaid and house-maid on £600 per annum, he admitted that no one would get far on £24,000 today. I had to keep off politics, for both were ready to bash Thatcher. When I said, in retort to his mockery of House of Lords debates, that the Lords showed more wisdom than the Commons in

---

* Son (b. 1949) of J.L.-M's former colleague Christopher Gibbs (d. 1985), Assistant Secretary of N.T., 1935–66.

† Sir Edmund Fairfax-Lucy, 6th Bt (b. 1945); artist; life tenant of Charlecote Park, Worcestershire, bequeathed by his grandfather to N.T.; m. 1st 1974 Sylvia Ogden, 2nd 1986 Lady Lucinda Lambton.

‡ Sir Robert Throckmorton, 11th Bt (1908–89), whose mother, Lilian, Lady Throckmorton (*née* Brooke, d. 1955), had set in motion a long legal process resulting in the donation of Coughton to N.T.

§ Ana Inez Carcano; m. 1944–72 Hon. John Jacob Astor (d. 2000), 4th son of 2nd Viscount Astor. (See entry for 6 January 1992.)

¶ Isabel ('Eny') Nesbitt, unmarried sister of J.L.-M.'s paternal grandmother. As a boy, he dreaded having to visit her gloomy house, but she won his heart by sending him books and ten-shilling notes, and he was the only relation to attend her funeral in the 1930s.

opposing the trial of old war criminals, he agreed the idea was ridiculous and wrong, adding that it was started by Mrs T. Jennifer is gentle, wise, moderate in her views and infinitely sympathetic, far more so than he. When I told her of my shock at the ruination of Shropshire, she said it had all happened within the past ten years – *i.e.*, under the Thatcher régime. Roy is easily bored. I could see the film across his eyes and the fidgety hands while I was trying to reply to a polite question he had put to me. Talking of atrocities in Europe since 1939, both Jenkinses insisted the Germans were worse than the Russians. Now this is just not true; they were of equal horror; but it is a socialist article of faith that Hitler must have been worse than Stalin.

Wednesday, 12th June

I stayed with Jean Lloyd* at Clouds Hill [Hertfordshire] for two nights, not having been there since George Lloyd died in 1941. I became his private secretary exactly sixty years ago. Clouds Hill, named after T. E. Lawrence† who died the week he moved in, has been transformed by David and Jean from an ordinary vicarage to a Jane Austen residence, with 'georgianised' windows. I brought and gave Jean a photograph I took of G.L. standing in front of the house in an absurdly uncountrified suit. Debo also staying the night. I was given a wonderful welcome and treated like a reincarnated dinosaur. Jean not much changed from her wedding. She was pretty then, if no beauty. Daughter Laura‡ who is a social worker came to dinner the second night to meet me, seeming rather embarrassed by her mother's upper class manner and views. G.L's room and writing desk still retain many pictures and objects which for years I kept in order. The butler Wright said that Charlie,§ the son who committed suicide, was an angel. Everyone adored him. 'Life was just too much for him,' he said with a tear in his eye.

---

* Lady Jean Ogilvy (b. 1918), dau. of 11th Earl of Airlie; m. 1942 David, 2nd Baron Lloyd (1912–85).
† Lawrence had a cottage of that name in Dorset, now a property of the N.T.
‡ Hon. Laura Lloyd (b. 1960).
§ Hon. Charles Lloyd (1949–74); o.s. of 2nd Baron Lloyd; see entry for 2 December 1992.

Thursday, 13th June

Filthy weather, wet and cold. Debo leaves for an agricultural show at which she is to sit next to Mrs Thatcher. Jean drives me to Shaw's Corner. Pretty curatress could not believe that I visited G.B.S. fifty years ago. Charming old butler and gardener of forty years' standing. The house less hideous than I remember; admittedly ugly, but orderly and convenient. Well-kept, the old hats still on display. How long can they survive the dusting and fingering?

Friday, 14th June

Ariane lunched with me at Franco's restaurant. She is reconciled to her dismissal from Murray's and remains on good terms with them to work on a freelance basis. Keenly interested in my book which she will still edit.

Tuesday, 18th June

To Sissinghurst for the night. Nigel had asked Arland Kingston,* the N.T. regional agent, to meet me, along with Anthony Hobson. We all lunched in the restaurant. I remember Arland as a very young member of staff in my day; very handsome still, as well as clever and bright. He said burglaries at N.T. properties had lately increased twofold.

Nigel motored Anthony and me to Smallhythe.† Same isolated situation on edge of the Level with Isle of Oxney to the south. Charming Mrs Weare and husband custodians. Just the right type, being stage-connected, and very knowledgeable about Ellen and Edie. House beautifully kept. Pretty cottage-like garden on north side. We went on to Rye to see Lamb House.‡ I would like to live in this town. Unspoilt,

---

* Joined staff of N.T., 1961; Regional Director for Kent and East Sussex 1973–93 (b. 1935).
† This small but ancient Kentish property, subject of a chapter in J.L.-M's book, had belonged to the actress Ellen Terry, whose daughter, Edith Craig, wished to preserve it as a shrine to her. J.L.-M. visited it on behalf of the N.T. in 1938 and was 'wholly captivated . . . I have seldom walked through rooms more nostalgic of a particular owner.' After its acceptance virtually without endowment, Vita Sackville-West kept a benevolent eye on Miss Craig, who lived eccentrically with a group of lesbian friends.
‡ Residence of Henry James, whose niece-in-law donated it to N.T. after Second World War.

overlooking the Level which can't be built over because of flooding. Mrs Martin, late tenant of Long Barn,* which she showed me over when I was writing my *Harold*, is the N.T. tenant. Nice, clever woman. Showed us round house, upstairs where the public do not go, and round garden. Large garden, lawns and brick walls, like the Meteyard painting we have of Mrs Meteyard there, sitting in deck chair. Relics of Henry James accumulate as the house is visited by thousands.

Betty Hussey came to dinner. We embraced tenderly. She has become a very old lady, but her voice and laughter unchanged. She told me how she commissioned Henry Moore to erect a sculpture on an island in the moat at Scotney. She sold jewelry to pay for it, but Moore would take no money out of admiration for Christopher. After his death however the executors wrote to her that as it had never been sold, it now belonged to his estate. However, after much wrangling she got their consent to keep it on more or less permanent loan.

Wednesday, 19th June

Anthony leaves Sissinghurst early for a funeral. I wander round garden, sun half out. Actually heard a cuckoo towards the lake. Greatly enjoy being with Nigel. He brushes aside obstacles, and gets things done. Telephones Batemans, Kipling's house, to warn we were coming. Telephones Max Egremont† to ask if we may lunch at Petworth [West Sussex]. Batemans unchanged, and coping with huge influx of visitors. We go quickly over the house, and on to Petworth. On greeting us, Max says the butler is away today, and we shall eat in the kitchen. Lady Egremont repeats this when she receives us in the Rococo drawing room. I wonder if this is a dig at me for something I wrote in my beastly diaries? What a charming couple they are. He is grand yet simple, unlike his horrid father John and portentous great-uncle Leconfield.‡ She is very easy and intelligent. Nigel and I whisked round the state rooms, enabling me to refresh my memory of the

---

* Property at Sevenoaks, part of Knole estate, lived in by Harold Nicolson and Vita Sackville-West prior to their purchase of Sissinghurst in 1930.

† Max Wyndham, 2nd Baron Egremont and 7th Baron Leconfield (b. 1948); writer and farmer; m. 1978 Caroline Nelson.

‡ Charles Wyndham, 3rd Baron Leconfield (1872–1952), with whom J.L.-M. (as described in his diaries) had some unedifying wartime encounters to discuss the future of Petworth.

pictures and architecture. The N.T. are spending millions on redecorating the vast North Gallery because the Egremonts don't like John Fowler's vivid orange walls. Enjoyable conversation over luncheon. Which authors do we consider will be read in a hundred years? Which living politicians do we respect, if any? Nigel drops me at a wayside station. I get a train for Waterloo, and am home in time for dinner.

Friday, 21st June

Bevis Hillier comes to interview me for his magazine, and to talk about John Betjeman. I warm to him. He is sensitive, perspicacious and understanding. We think alike on many things. I give him a copy of *Round the Clock* and drop him back to his expensive hotel, paid for by Sotheby's.

Sunday, 23rd June

This morning Folly, who had not seemed well of late, was making funny little noises, and could hardly stand. We were both very worried and telephoned Riley the vet, who told us to bring her in at midday. We agreed that, if he advised it, we would let her go. A. had to prepare luncheon for Hardy [Amies] and Rosemary, and I dreaded going alone, so A. telephoned Ian [Dixon] who like a brick accompanied me and Folly, waiting in the car while I carried her in. Riley took a grave view and thought her case hopeless – spinal trouble with no hope of cure – so I took the decision. He gave her an injection while I held her in my arms; I then bolted, brimming with tears. Ian motored me back. I said to A., 'I have long known that, after you, the creature I love best is Folly.' She said, 'It is the same with me. I think we made the perfect trio.' After fifteen years of close companionship I feel empty, as though rats had consumed my innards.

Monday, 24th June

Obliged to go to grand luncheon at American Museum [at Claverton near Bath] for thirtieth anniversary of its foundation. I sat at top table next to Natalie Keffer* and Patsy Jellicoe.† Boys of Downside School

---

* Wife of John Keffer, Chairman of Trustees of American Museum.
† Patricia O'Kane; m. 1944–66 2nd Earl Jellicoe.

played jazz, deafening. I was bored to tears. Patsy, old and rather witchlike, told me she had been mugged by two white men in Eaton Square where she lives. She had returned from dining somewhere and parked her car in the square. The men threatened her and seized her bag. This is now a common occurrence in London.

I see Folly everywhere – in my car, at No. 19 despite my removing all her dear relics. The silent little presence, so forceful, demanding, uncompromising about the time for her dinner, her walk, her desire to go to bed. Her different barks indicating different emotions – for wishing to go out, fear, suspicion, detection of intruders. So wise in her responses, so clever in sensing our moods. And what wrings the heart is the memory of her affectionate little habits – laying her head on my shoulder, nosing my leg from behind to indicate she was there. Never bearing resentment; sometimes irritating, never boring. And her morning welcome of me when she slept with A., and would jump on my bed and lick my face. She was a catalyst, a joy, someone to talk to, always the best companion. How to bear the house alone now when A. is away?

Thursday, 27th June

I see in *The Times* that my pen friend Teddy Voules has died. I feel curiously sad, and am glad that, not having written to him for a year, I sent him a letter a month ago. A., though understanding, thinks me foolish because I was constantly complaining about his spate of letters, which I eventually gave up responding to. And yet, there was a good old man, older than me even, presumably lonely, who hitched on to me and poured out anecdotes of his uneventful past which to him was Elysium owing to the people he had met and the grand princesses he had known through the person he liked to call his 'mistress' – Princess Marie Louise.* He was a nice man and I am touched that he liked me *in absentia*. I always told him that he wouldn't like me if he met me, and we had but one momentary encounter, at Peter Coats's memorial service last year.

---

* Her Highness (the last recognised member of the British Royal Family to be allowed that designation) Princess Marie Louise (1872–1956); granddaughter of Queen Victoria (daughter of HRH Princess Helena and HH Prince Christian of Schleswig-Holstein); m. 1891 (annulled 1900) Prince Aribert of Anhalt; resided at Schomberg House, Pall Mall, where she indulged her love of gossip.

Tuesday, 2nd July

A hot day, but tolerable. I lunch with Admiral Currey[*] and nice wife in garden flat in Great Pulteney Street. He is the great-grandson of Colonel Currey who was the Bachelor Duke's agent at Lismore. Feels aggrieved that Paxton[†] was given so many perks and favours whereas the Curreys were far more protective of the Duke, behaving strictly honestly and loyally. They must have been irked by the interference of Paxton, their educational inferior. Nice people these, the salt of the earth.

Thursday, 4th July

The new Podium in Bath is wonderful. Pleasing if erratic architecture. I don't mind liberties being taken with the classical, so long as the result is gracious and traditional. I went to the new reference library here, up the moving staircase. Service at once. Old people sitting comfortably reading every newspaper and periodical. We are blessed as a nation in that culture is laid on for the masses, if they want it.

Saturday, 6th July

Heat now insufferable. Tom and Rachel Bridges stay a night. Very nice and correct. I like her, who perhaps talks too much. But she is clever, and her heart in the right place. Both keen conservationists in Suffolk, he chairman of this and that. Like his father Edward,[‡] he speaks when he has something to say, and talks as if to a committee meeting, with a flat voice, and occasional savage emphasis, with twist of mouth. We imagine the weather is set fair, and leave cushions etc. out on the terrace. At midnight I see lightning, followed by a cascade. In tidying up I realise how tired and confused I am. Can hardly bear it, and want to die.

---

[*] Rear-Admiral Neville Currey (1906–98); ADC to HM The Queen, 1958; m. 1941 Rosemary Knight.

[†] Architect and landscape gardener (1803–65), whose experience of designing magnificent greenhouses for the Bachelor Duke led him to create the Crystal Palace for the Great Exhibition.

[‡] Edward Bridges (1892–1969), Cabinet Secretary; cr. Baron, 1957; son of Robert Bridges, Poet Laureate 1913–30, and father of Thomas, 2nd Baron (b. 1927; m. 1953 Rachel Bunbury), diplomatist; 2nd cousin of A.L.-M.

Tom says that a good biography of his grandfather the Laureate is about to come out,* also a new collection of Hopkins's letters.† Thinks R. B. Martin quite wrong to suggest that Hopkins was in love with Dolben.‡ Is in a quandary about his grandfather's library, containing all his working books, with notes and annotations. His father Edward meant this to be preserved intact, but his mother left it jointly to her four children. It is in Tom's custodianship in Suffolk, but he cannot afford to buy out his three sisters.

They leave at four and we retire to bed, worn out. We agree they are both very nice and clever, but too earnest. He signed the visitors' book for both of them, 'Tom and Rachel Bridges'. We could have written that ourselves.

Monday 8th–Tuesday 9th July

By train from Bath to Bodmin, changing at Bristol and Plymouth. Welcomed by Michael and Elizabeth Trinick§ and motored to Newton House for cold luncheon in kitchen. Michael takes me to Lanhydrock. Beastly day, mist and drizzle. House shut today but Michael conducts me around every room alone. We draw back blinds as we go along. He is justly proud of the house and what he has done. Another late-Victorian specimen. He has ingeniously pre-served the crinkly brass electric light switches by putting them on hinges which swing open revealing the horrid modern switches which are now mandatory. Who else would have thought of this refinement? In the late Lord Clifden's¶ bedroom, bottles on his dressing table of Bay Rum and Eau de Portugal from Trumpers, no longer obtainable.

On our return at six, two N.T. boys join us for drinks – Michael's successor [Jeremy] Pearson,** shy and nice, and Giles Clotworthy,†† frisky and facetious. An old colonel to dinner, who tells a funny story

---

* Catherine Phillips, *Robert Bridges: A Biography* (OUP, 1992).
† Catherine Phillips (ed.), *Gerard Manley Hopkins: Selected Letters* (OUP, 1991).
‡ Digby Dolben (1848–67); poet, loved by Hopkins; died by drowning.
§ G. E. M. Trinick (1924–94); served N.T. from 1953 to 1984 as land agent, later Historic Buildings Adviser, for Cornwall (of which county he later became High Sheriff).
¶ Francis Agar-Robartes, 7th Viscount Clifden (1883–1966); bequeathed Lanhydrock, Cornwall and most of his fortune to N.T.
** N.T. Historic Buildings Representative for Devon and Cornwall from 1988 (b. 1951).
†† Joined Cornwall staff of N.T. 1983 (b. 1944).

of how he had gone into Hatchards and told a terrified young lady assistant that he had come for *You Bloody Women* – in fact a book about three Englishwomen in the Boer War protesting against the concentration camps.

Next day Michael motors me to Cotehele.* Told me that, when the last Lord Clifden† succeeded his brother, he received letters addressed to him as Lord Mendip, summoning him to sit in the House of Lords. He returned these to the post office, marked 'not known at this address'. Michael had to explain to him that the Clifden viscountcy was Irish, and it was by virtue of the Mendip barony that he held his seat. At Cotehele he shows me the Quay, the docked *Shamrock*, the Mill grinding away – all features developed by Michael – then garden and house, all in mint condition, almost too tidy. He has opened the kitchen, every detail thought out, a spit brought from some demolished house in Plymouth. A wonder of a man, really a treasure to the National Trust.

Saturday, 13th July

This morning A. confessed she was lonely without her constant companion. I already knew this – I could hear it in her voice yesterday when she called to her wild doves at the end of the garden. I know I am not often a bright companion for her, and anyway out most days when she needs companionship. Her need of animals is very great. We discussed a cat, but neither of us really likes cats, though I was flattered when one of the Trinicks' came to my room while I was dressing and roosted on the pillow. And it may be awkward for us to get another whippet, even a middle-aged one from the Dogs' Home. We can do nothing anyway until the autumn.

We lunched with the Warrenders. I put on my summer suit, though all the others were in shirt-sleeves. Kenneth Rose staying. He said what a killer of a good story Rhodes James‡ was. He thought my diaries would be remembered when all my other books were forgotten. I said I hoped not. Was much impressed by Robin's affection for

---

* Tudor house donated to N.T. by Edgcumbe family.
† Arthur Agar-Robartes (1887–1974); s. brother 1966 as 8th and last Viscount Clifden (the remainder to Barony of Mendip passing on his death to 6th Earl of Normanton).
‡ Robert Rhodes James (1933–99; Kt 1991); writer and politician; MP (C) for Cambridge, 1976–87.

his son, who returned from abroad. Left me in the drive after our arrival to greet the boy, and talked vivaciously with him during and after luncheon.

Monday, 15th July

The Trinicks to tea in Bath, which was nice. A. came over to meet them. Then I went to PCC meeting in Badminton Village Hall to discuss women priests.* Vicar vehemently against. Penny Wood and Dorothy Lane, both on Synod, in favour. Object to find out what the rest of us thought. To my surprise, the majority were in favour. I declared myself so, though deprecating pursuing the matter at this delicate juncture in history of C. of E. Was told that every moment in the history of the Church was delicate. I nevertheless feel that, since recruits to the clergy are now hard to come by, and females are naturally more devout than males, we must admit them sooner or later. Vicar upset. I must have it out with him. Then home to greet Mrs Astor and Lady Lloyd, who asked themselves this morning. A. and I both tired by these absurd women, to whom we could barely be polite. Jean is conventional and affected; as for Chiquita, *tête de moineau*.

Tuesday, 16th July

Writing about my old days at the N.T., I seem almost to be as much on the move as I was then. To London again, spending the whole day in N.T. archives room reading files on West Wycombe. The behaviour of both Johnny and Helen Dashwood was pretty bad, hers indeed appalling. I found the minutes of N.T. Executive Committee for March 1936, one of which read: 'Mr J. Lees-Milne has been appointed Secretary of the Country Houses Committee at a salary of £300 p.a.' By cab to Ariane's party, losing the way. Found Fanny Partridge in the street, equally lost. Nice little house in modest row, Ariane making great and successful efforts. A. arrived with the Hutchinsons, followed by Jamie Fergusson, looking tired and unshaven. I gave him a

---

* The General Synod voted to ordain women priests the following year, almost 500 clergy leaving the Anglican ministry. The first women were ordained at Bristol Cathedral in 1994.

book which had belonged to my great-grandfather (his great-great) Alexander Nesbitt,* dated 1862, which I hope he will treasure.

Saturday, 20th July

Dear Freda [Berkeley] staying. We had the Jonathan Scotts to luncheon. She clever and formidable, a JP, etc. He rather like Tom Bridges, slight, aquiline features, the same grim mouth. He is about to give up the chairmanship of Export of Works of Art Committee. Says the Government has no concern. Mrs Thatcher was indifferent, the present minister Renton† is unhelpful. Funds reduced – usual thing. Of the works which the committee recommends should not be granted export licences, only between 5 and 10 per cent are prevented from going. The Romans buy only English furniture, which leaves every day by the lorry-load. He is in despair. I like him.

Monday, 22nd July

We go to La Fourchette for two nights. Met at Charles de Gaulle [airport] by Jagger's new agent. Airport modernismus but good I think for the purpose and the convolution of concentric arrival and departure lanes on stilts impressive; also airport runways which go over motorway. Motorway very clean compared with ours, and suburbs less shabby, turn-of-the-century apartment blocks at Neuilly not ignoble. Once we leave Orsay the country very dull to Amboise, fields and prairies full of short-stemmed sunflowers. Something rather dreadful about the battery-production of these noble blooms associated with Vandyke and Charles I.

La Fourchette is paradisal though A. very upset by idleness and neglect of head gardener. Nevertheless extremely beautiful thanks to her splendid layout, terraces and hornbeam hedges cut open at the waist so that one can see into the parterre while walking down the gravel paths. As it was stifling hot, I rose early the first morning to walk around the policies, through the axial-pathed coppice. Poor A. trudges up and down the terraces after the gardener whom she hates

---

* London hide merchant, whose daughter married J.L.-M's grandfather James Henry Lees-Milne, his son having married James Henry's sister.
† Timothy Renton, Conservative politician (b. 1932); Minister for the Arts, 1990–92; cr. life peer as Baron Renton of Mount Harry, 1997.

and who is surly towards her. Bravely she tackles Mick [Jagger] and Jerry [Hall], neither of whom knows one plant from the other and who would clearly be content with a blaze of colour. But she explains that she will be held responsible by those visitors who come here and know, and that the present arrangement is a waste of his money and her time and effort. I could sense that Mick was slightly bored with her discontent, and moreover does not like to make scenes and sack. But she wins the day.

Mick arrived just after us, having flown in from Los Angeles. Ugly, pig eyes, obscene mobile mouth, trim body for nearing fifty. Fascinating rather than attractive. Charming when he smiles. He is restless like all the rich. Stalks swiftly across the room with determined, severe air. Took me and his brother to see Leonardo da Vinci's house which was shutting as we arrived. Just as well; horrid restored *François Premier*. In the car which he drove at furious pace he was attacked by terrible sneezing fit. Pollen I fancy, for I have a throat-ache here. He has a certain dignity. Extraordinary voice ceases to be common when one is accustomed. Brother younger, good-looking and nice, but not bright. Jerry a good hostess, kind, puts herself out, wants one to be happy. Not strictly beautiful, save for eyes, mouth and hair like spun honey. They don't read, but flip through books; conversation is not sustained. Yet he is quick and clever.

Friday, 26th July

Four people attending a Beckford congress at Bristol University call this morning to see the library. Stuart's protégé Didier Girard and fellow Frenchman; my Indian professor from Canada, Dr Varma,* bringing copy of his book *A Transient Gleam*; and female professor from Cambridge, extremely ugly with large specs and fuzzy hair. All nice, especially Didier, whose enthusiasm for Beckford is touching – stirring his coffee with a Beckford spoon he was in seventh heaven. I shall leave my Beckford spoons to him.

We lunched with Selina, Geoffrey Wheatcroft complaining of the treatment of himself and Worsthorne at the hands of Max Hastings.†

---

* Devendra P. Varma (b. 1923); authority on Gothick novels (and admirer of those written by J.L.-M): see *Beneath a Waning Moon*, 21 August 1985.
† Journalist and military historian (b. 1945); editor *Daily Telegraph*, 1986–95, *Evening Standard*, 1995–2002; stepson of J.L.-M's friend Osbert Lancaster; Kt 2002.

Then dined at the House where the Beits staying. Alfred eighty-nine and almost bent double, but his wits are still about him and he is as full of information and desire for same as ever. Clementine described Sebastian [Walker]'s funeral attended by hundreds from all walks, he beloved by all who worked for him.

Monday, 29th July

Another expedition. Hugh Massingberd greets me on platform at Grantham [Lincolnshire]. It is torrentially hot. He opens the roof of his car, and lends me his panama. As we leave the town I say, 'That little corner shop might be Mrs Thatcher's birthplace.' 'It is,' Hugh tells me, pointing out nice little neo-Grecian Methodist chapel opposite. We get to Marston at 1.30. Henry Thorold[*] is an amazing spectacle, long flaxen hair falling over temples, belly like a pregnant elephant, walking not on the soles of his shoes but the sides. A young couple called Thorold from South Africa call without warning. He talks to them in a friendly, condescending fashion, and sends them to eat in a pub. They return while we are eating a massive lunch prepared by Hugh, and share our strawberries. We talk about churches and genealogy, and are then shown round the house and garden. Henry tells us about the wonderful couple who look after him and even decorate the rooms for him. Their taste is naturally ghastly.

Accompanied by Henry, we drive, seemingly for hours on small roads, to Gunby.[†] I am delighted with this dear old house. Had forgotten it stands within a substantial park. Hugh's wife[‡] there, whom I had not met before – delightful, good-looking and distinguished, but painfully thin. Very sweet, but strange. Looks adoringly at Hugh. They seem very happy. I like her much. We have a large tea on the steps of the west front in blazing sun, I still sweltering under Hugh's hat. Then we amble around the walled garden, which is very pretty,

---

[*] The Revd Henry Thorold (1921–2000); squire of Marston Hall, Lincolnshire; bachelor antiquarian and writer of guide books; sometime housemaster and chaplain at Lancing College.

[†] Hugh Massingberd recalls: 'For a jaunt across the vast, remote county, I unwisely recruited the great local antiquarian Henry Thorold, to join us . . . All too audibly, at various stops, Jim persisted in referring to Henry as "the dear old boy", even though Henry was thirteen years Jim's junior.' (*Daydream Believer*, pp. 177–8.)

[‡] Caroline Ripley (b. 1947), er dau. of Sir Hugh Ripley, 4th Bt (1916–2003); fashion model; m. 1983 Hugh Massingberd as his 2nd wife.

in full midsummer bloom. And into the wilderness, and the church-yard where we pay our respects to the Field Marshal and Lady M.-M. I press £5 note into the eleemosynary box out of love for Gunby and them. We then dine very late in the kitchen off good food bought by Hugh from Marks & Sparks, for wife neither cooks nor eats. At 11.15 I say I must go to bed. Hugh then motors Henry all the way back to Marston, not returning until 1 a.m.

Tuesday, 30th July

At 8.30 Hugh brings me a delicious breakfast on a tray. Until one o'clock I read the Gunby Papers and look round the house. Hugh drives me to Langton where we look at the church – perfection, eighteenth-century original pews facing each other like college chapel pews. Dr Johnson* worshipped here while staying with Bennet Langton,† and John Betjeman visited and admired. Hugh lunches with me at the Massingberd Arms at Ormsby, very remote. He is strongly Lincolnshire-minded. We call at Hainton and are greeted by Mrs Heneage,‡ who leaves us to look quickly round the house. Huge, eighteenth- and twentieth-century-ised in good taste by that SPAB architect whose name I used to know. Arrive at Flintham [Hall] for tea. I rejoice to see Myles [Hildyard], looking a sight with blotchy complexion and parti-coloured boiler shirt. We have tea in the library. It and the conservatory in which we later dine are splendid Victorian specimens. Myles has done wonders with this house. All portraits cleaned, furniture sparkling. Likewise the garden is very good indeed. All better than when I last was here. Myles is to Nottinghamshire what Henry and Hugh are to Lincolnshire. I could not have been treated more kindly by this beloved old friend. He gives me to read Esdaile's book about George Crawshay§ who, staying at the rectory here in the

---

* Samuel Johnson (1709–84); man of letters and lexicographer.
† Squire of Langton, Lincolnshire (1737–1801); Professor of Ancient Literature at Royal Academy and friend of Dr Johnson, who observed to Boswell that 'earth does not bear a worthier man'.
‡ Roberta Wilkinson; m. 1978 James Heneage (b. 1945), squire of Hainton Hall, Lincs.
§ Of Haughton Castle, Northumberland (1821–96); thrice Mayor of Gateshead; m. 1847 Eliza Fife; great-grandson of Richard Crawshay (1739–1810), the 'iron king' of Merthyr Tydfil, whose sister was the mother of J.L.-M's great-grandfather Sir Joseph Bailey, 1st Bt.

1840s, fell in love with one of the Thoroton* daughters. Of course, says Myles, there could be no question of so middle-class a man marrying a Thoroton. I mention that I am George Crawshay's third cousin once removed – a fact he makes me write in the book. Rather odd the disparity of but one generation after a century and a half.

Wednesday, 31st July

Spent morning going round the house with Myles, stopping before each picture or relic and hearing its story. A country house like this is my natural element – blinds down, the sun percolating mischievously through crannies, the sense of a green world shut out, the musty smell of ancestral belongings, the blind stare of their faces on the walls. Myles takes me to Newark station. I read *Du côté de chez Swann*† all the way to Charing Cross. At Paddington I take a taxi to Ledbury Road to charming Mr Blackburn's shop of mezzotints and framed engravings, like an eighteenth-century picture gallery, and buy for £300 an engraving of Beckford's father the Alderman. Coveted a beautifully-framed coloured engraving of the library at Syston [Old Hall, Lincolnshire] by Vulliamy,‡ which I cannot afford at £800.

Friday, 2nd August

Mrs (Barbara) Saben called on me in Bath to talk about poor Joan Hewitt's last days. She astounded me with the news that Joan, whom I imagined to be as poor as a church mouse, and whom I have reproached myself with not helping more these past thirty years, left nearly half a million pounds. She came into the money from a sister in 1976 and it was augmented down the years by a clever stockbroker. She never knew what to do with the money and never changed her mode of life. Wore clothes from second-hand shop; never did anything to alleviate the grinding conditions in her hovel. Yet was generous; gave Mrs S. £1,000 without turning a hair. She has left me

---

* The surname of Myles Hildyard's long-established Nottinghamshire family was originally Thoroton; his ancestor Colonel Thomas Thoroton of Flintham Hall assumed the name of Hildyard in 1815 on marrying the niece and heiress of Sir Robert Hildyard, 4th and last Bt.

† First book of the great novel of Marcel Proust.

‡ George John Vulliamy (1817–1886); architect.

Uncle Milne's gold cigarette case and match-box and his dressing case, by instructions of Aunt Dorothy; these things, along with Aunt D's own jewelry, were left to Joan in the first place so she might 'pop' them if she ever had need of money, which she refrained from doing all the years she knew penury.

Tuesday, 6th August

Yesterday A. left to stay with the Johnstons at Lucca, and Eardley arrived in the evening to stay with me. Today A. rang on my birthday. She is having hot sunshine, whereas here it is dark with threatening rain. Gerry Noel* wrote to say he and his wife staying in Bath, and I asked them to tea. Haven't seen them since forty years ago in Rome. A decent, sixtyish man, squat, square and short, with extremely good manners. Speaks to me as though I were Graham Greene. Is still on the board of the *Catholic Herald*, and Hon. Sec. of the luncheon club† founded by Ben Nicolson‡ (born this day, 1914) and Philip Toynbee.§ Asks how many books I have in my library. E. good with them, and a help. We walk round A's garden which they greatly admire. He is surprisingly nervous, fiddling with paper-knife. I like him.

Wednesday, 7th August

Eardley and I dine with Alex [Moulton], who makes himself very agreeable with his good and jolly manners. Upstairs in his working room he shows us his calculations – blackboard with hieroglyphics in chalk, meaningless to us, and little quick notebooks crammed with diagrams of motor-car chassis, etc., beautifully scrawled, reminding me of Professor Richardson's¶ rapid sketches of architecture which I

---

* Hon. Gerald Noel (b. 1926), yr s. of 4th Earl of Gainsborough; writer and journalist; editor, *Catholic Herald*; m. 1958 Adele Were.

† The club, which met for many years at Bertorelli's restaurant in Charlotte Street, was founded in 1953 and celebrated its half-centenary in 2003.

‡ Benedict Nicolson (1914–78), er s. of Harold Nicolson and Vita Sackville-West; art historian; Deputy Surveyor of King's Pictures, 1939–47; editor, *Burlington Magazine*, 1947–78; m. 1955–62 Luisa Vertova.

§ Writer and journalist (1916–81).

¶ Sir Albert Richardson (1880–1964); Professor of Architecture, London University, 1919–46.

so admired. We came away wondering if Alex is a genius, not knowing enough to form an opinion.

Saturday, 10th August

Eardley departed yesterday morning, rather to my relief. I was aware of something indefinably snubbing in his manner, a dismissiveness of my enthusiasms, a lip-curling disapproval of my writing (as when I showed him some chapters of my N.T. book), a contradictory manner as if determined never to admit that I can have an original thought or make an amusing remark.

I lunch with Bob [Parsons]* at Newark. Liz Longman, the Guy Hollands and Henriette Abel Smith.† He is welcome to these county ladies, who see him as a nice old thing, not of their class, but harmless and acceptable, almost as the Guermantes‡ saw Swann I fancy. I sit next to Joan Holland but try not to look at the gold fillings and particles of potato visible in her open mouth. I make conversation and then dry up, mesmerised by my own ineptitude like a rabbit by a stoat.

Return home to give Bamber and Christina Gascoigne tea in the kitchen. They are real people. Christina is like Virginia Woolf, beautiful with a gentle calm face. Speaks little; feels much. Loved the garden and referred to the plants as if they were humans. Bamber brought me Midi's little gift – very pretty card case made of papier mâché, inlaid on back, painted with Martyr's Memorial on front. I kissed it when he handed it to me, a foolish gesture, but spontaneous. When I mentioned that I disliked all-male dinners such as those of the Dilettante Society, he agreed. 'I would love them,' said Christina.

Tuesday, 13th August

A sweet letter from Eardley, saying he loved his visit which was just as much fun as the old days. Whereas I, if not actually horrid to him, certainly felt horridly about him at times. There was a moment in the

---

* American architect (1920–2000); tenant and repairer of Newark Park, Gloucestershire, N.T. property, where he lived with Michael Clayton.
† Henriette Cadogan (b. 1914); m. 1953 Sir Alexander Abel Smith; Lady-in-Waiting to HM The Queen.
‡ The great aristocratic family in Proust's novel.

car when we almost had a row, and I just managed to control myself. The fact is that E. is only really interested in his painting, The Slade and Mattei – just as I am now only interested in my writing, Badminton and Alvilde.

Saturday, 17th August

Dined with the Norwiches at Castle Combe. Mollie is very pretty, and fun alone. John Julius makes me feel inferior, not by his manner but his accomplishments. He is organising a V&A exhibition about the Queen, preparing to tour Japan, finishing his history of the Byzantine Empire, presiding over 'Venice in Peril', writing introductions to three books, and constantly appearing on television. He also cooked the pudding.

Monday, 19th August

Kind Tony Mitchell motored me to Attingham. Spent whole day there under guidance of Betty Cousens, the efficient and charming representative who manages the N.T's historic buildings in these parts. The house makes a splendid impression from the bridge, vastly spread out to impress the world with the new lord; yet the architecture does not bear examination. Spent morning going over state rooms. Rather barren, otherwise very good. Since the [Shropshire Adult] College left in 1986, the Trust has been repairing furniture and redecorating along most conservative lines. Snack lunch under East colonnade in the wind. Met Julian Gibbs, new area organiser, and Mrs and Mrs Walker who are studying and cataloguing the miniatures and landscapes respectively. Continued during afternoon in nether regions and upstairs, and drove to look at the mausoleum in the park for which I in a sense was responsible. I think Gerry Wellington first suggested a mausoleum with deer grazing from Constable's painting in National Gallery. The large rear courtyard has been brought back to what it was, and is probably the best feature of the exterior.

The Russian coup is alarming,* and might lead to world war if not controlled, and the usurpers try to revive the Iron Curtain. There

---

* The attempt to restore the old order ended in total failure and led to the final collapse of Communism in the Soviet Union.

might also be an unprecedented swarm of refugees to the West. China would doubtless support the revived Soviet communist party, and countries like Iraq would gleefully join in a war against Western values. These dreadful calamities always begin in August.

Tuesday, 20th August

I motor self to stay the night with Christopher and Francesca Wall* at The Apple Orchard, Bradenham. Charming their house has become, walls crammed with paintings. Friendly welcome, though C. rather morose. Daughter and new husband Charles Ernle-Erle-Drax, nice young man, not outstandingly bright. Dine in garden by candle and mosquito, sitting in uncomfortable low chair, but fun. I hope they did not think me rude when I asked to go to bed at ten.

Wednesday, 21st August

Extremely hot day. Join Christopher in the morning at the office in Hughenden. Went round the house, like all N.T. houses immaculately kept.† Has anyone been living here since Dizzy died? No one seemed to be when I first visited from Oxford in 1930 with Arthur Rathbone,‡ he being a friend of Major Coningsby Disraeli's sister Mrs Calverley. I remember Coningsby stalking about the library wearing a skull cap, bored by us visitors. Sister pale and prim. Christopher accompanies me in afternoon to West Wycombe. Dashwoods away. Great number of public going round in parties every twenty minutes. C. escorted me at our leisure. Many changes since I was here during the war, mostly for the better. Francis, with financial assistance from the Government, has transformed the whole place from seedy dilap-idation to poshness, just missing a *House and Garden* standard of fash-ionableness. He has done well in restoring the original marbling of dining room and hall. Temples restored. Saddest thing is Francis's

---

* Christopher Wall (b. 1929), N.T. Historic Buildings Representative for Thames and Chiltern Region, 1956–94; m. 1961 Francesa Fummi (b. 1935; her mother Lady Cynthia was the sister of David Lindsay, 28th Earl of Crawford, Chairman of N.T., 1945–65).

† Hughenden was the seat of the Prime Minister Benjamin Disraeli, Earl of Beaconsfield, from 1847 until his death in 1881, when it passed to his nephew Coningsby. Coningsby's sister sold it to Mr W. H. Abbey, who presented it to the N.T. in 1946.

‡ Arthur Benson Rathbone (1853–1933); member of Liverpool shipping family.

development on far side of valley, mean terraces of worst sort visible from drive as one approaches front door.

Friday, 23rd August

We drive to Chatsworth, five ghastly hours stuck in Bank Holiday queues on the M5. Elysium on arrival. The two Feray* brothers staying. Like a continuous party at the Guermantes'; never have I heard so much *Almanach* talk.

Andrew spoke of Uncle Harold [Macmillan]†, who appointed him Minister for the Colonies, for which he had not the slightest qualification, out of pure nepotism. Andrew loved him but wishes he had not engineered his recall from Africa during the war after his brother Billy was killed – he could never face his regiment again for shame. Standing on the terrace outside the Blue Drawing Room, watching the flow of public through the garden, Andrew said wistfully, 'You see, there will never be communism in this country.' 'No,' I replied, 'because Chatsworth already belongs to them.'

One evening after dinner, Debo – wearing the most stunning dress designed by herself and made by a Chatsworth lady, a cutaway black chasuble and bunched lawn sleeves such as the bishops wear sitting on their bench in the House of Lords – showed us her insect jewelry. From a huge red case shaped like a butterfly she poured presents received from Andrew in the form of every sort of butterfly and insect, some made for her, some old. Such dazzlement I never saw. 'Surely I am not such a bad husband?' remarked Andrew.

Feeble talked to me about Bevis Hillier, whom I defended. She said that never, never would she talk to him, nor would Candida who was looking for another biographer. Why on earth? Because he had insinuated that John had had an affair with Auden, which John denied when asked. I suggested that this must have been the result of some misunderstanding, for Bevis was a very decent man.

Andrew spent much of the weekend closeted in his library, glued to the Russian news. He is overcome by the turn of events, and thinks

---

* Jean and Thierry Feray; unmarried French brothers, both experts in architectural conservation, who lived together in the rue Cambon, Paris and died together (1999) in a car crash.
† Harold Macmillan (1894–1986), Conservative prime minister (1957–63); m. 1920 Lady Dorothy Cavendish (aunt of 11th Duke of Devonshire); cr. Earl of Stockton, 1984.

Yeltsin* very sinister. M. rather wishes the coup had succeeded as it would have kept those fractious republics in order. As things are, Russia must now be a perpetual worry, what with nuclear arms and the flight of refugees.

Debo said that on the anniversary of O. Mosley's death Diana goes into purdah, her voice on the telephone taking on the sorrowing tone of a Victorian widow.

Thursday, 29th August

Today, Mama's birthday, I have received a present of an expensive bottle of brandy from Lord Westbury,† who thanks me for my wonderful contribution to a book on Historical Dinners. I have never heard of this book, and am not aware of having contributed to it. To unpack it from piles of white fluffy balls took hours. I can't repack and post.

Tuesday, 3rd September

These are glorious late summer days, like those one (no doubt faultily) remembers of yore. A. has a special buddleia by the raised terrace corner upon which so many butterflies congregate that one might suppose there was no dearth of these creatures in England. Rare red admirals, tortoiseshells and peacocks galore, and an infinite variety of whites. The best year for ages.

Thursday, 5th September

To London for the day, working in N.T. registry until tea time. Rushed through the Hatchlands‡ file, and finished it and the archive research for my book. So engrossed that I felt no pangs of hunger, though I had breakfasted at seven. Worked at full steam, reading letters and taking notes – not brain work, but requiring intense concentration. Felt happy. Called on M. for tea, just returned from Paris where

---

* Populist politician (b. 1931) who dismantled the Communist system in Russia, becoming first President of Russian Federation, 1992–2000; hero of the events of August 1991 (during most of which he is now said to have been in an alcoholic stupor).
† David Bethell, 5th Baron Westbury (b. 1922).
‡ See entry for 11 September 1991.

his beloved Maître Blum has miraculously recovered from her accident. He is now engrossed in his *Ribbentrop*. Walked with me to Paddington. *Eheu*!

In the train, an extremely handsome and pleasant young man was sitting in the reserved seat opposite to mine. At Reading, the seat next to his became vacant and was taken by a very pretty girl with a sweet smile who had been standing in the passage. For a time there was no sign of recognition between them; but when the girl rose, the young man said to her, holding out money, 'Will you please get me a coke?' Yes, she said, and smiled. When she returned with the coke and a sandwich for herself, they began an animated conversation. Their eyes were sparkling with desire and that peacock-preen look which lovers assume. When I got out at Chippenham they were still deliciously flirting – or so it seemed, for I did not hear what they said. I could not make out whether they knew each other before meeting in the carriage. I assume not, for surely the young man, who was gallant and attentive, would have given up his seat to her? Do the young instantly assume intimacy of this sort? I left them with an unuttered benediction.

Saturday, 7th September

O lack, lack, lackaday. Was about to sit down to luncheon, the old Coopers* here, when telephone rang. A. said that Mattei wanted to speak to me. At once I feared that something must be wrong with Eardley, for Mattei never rings me up. 'I have to tell you', he said, 'Eardley is dead.' A week ago he had palpitations at The Slade. Motored himself to London, saw doctor, took pills, seemed to recover completely. But no reply when Mattei telephoned yesterday, and none this morning, so he went round and let himself in with spare keys. Found E. slumped half on floor, half on bed, his blue eyes open. Doctor came and said E. must have died instantly. But how instantly? Poor Mattei is dreadfully upset. And I? What do I feel? I returned to the kitchen where we ate and I tried to tell stories and make jokes. What is life?

---

* Sean Cooper, gardener and designer of garden furniture, and wife Evelyn.

Sunday, 8th September

Eardley hated churches; would seldom visit one, even to sightsee. Hated religion, a subject we never discussed. The other was his health. And how beastly I was when he stayed last month. Walking down the Centre Walk, I strode ahead, deigning to turn my head from time to time. He was without doubt my best friend these fifty years, for we met at the National Trust towards the end of 1941. All those wartime and postwar years when we visited properties together, laughing, gossiping; he forever patient and tolerant, someone I could always turn to in moments of near-desperation; and we went abroad together year after year. Latterly a change in us both, no doubt. Old age and bad temper. Yet he wrote to me how much he enjoyed his visit. After Communion this morning, while the Vicar was talking of his summer at Lake Como,* I kept saying, 'Yes, how interesting', my thoughts concentrated on E.

Monday, 9th September

Have finished *Paradise Lost*. It was a grind in anticipation more than in reality. Middle sections boring; end ones retrieve the sublimity of the earlier. At times the story grips. How much did Milton believe? What did he mean by it? Was it considered shocking by Commonwealth folk? I believe it was not published until the permissive years of the Restoration were well established.

Tuesday, 10th September

I experienced the Sainsbury Wing of the National Gallery this morning, and could not but be attracted by it. Much liked staircase girder ceiling. Awkward site for architect. Some rooms askew. Pictures most beautifully hung, at right level for me and so I hope for all. Gripped by familiar friends in new setting. Richard II diptych most moving, white hart lying peacefully on bed of rosemary stalks and wild flowers, surely reflecting the King's gentle character. The Middle Ages were not sentimental about animals, yet this picture, like the famous Cluny tapestries, makes one wonder whether this was invari-

---

* He had a seasonal appointment as the Anglican chaplain there.

ably so. Richard II a tiny central figure – indicating his retiring nature, wishing to eschew the limelight? Young and plain yet beautiful face; kneeling attended by larger saints; background of G. Bellini's St Jerome; the walled city; blue hills far away.

John Saumarez Smith for luncheon at Brooks's. He is overjoyed that Andrew Devonshire has bought 51 per cent of the shop [Heywood Hill]'s shares, saving his bacon. Most satisfactory solution, and another interest for Andrew. Then to Tate Gallery for the Constables. Far too large an exhibition. Somehow the great six-footers are pompous rehashes of the first inspired little canvases of twenty years earlier. J.K.-B. and nephew Nick dined at Brooks's. Nick charming and handsome, never a banality even when discussing art subjects which are not his.

Wednesday, 11th September

By train to Leatherhead. Met by Christopher Rowell* who drove me to Polesden [Lacey near Dorking] to look through some papers and see Mrs Greville's† tomb. We went on to Hatchlands [near Guildford], where Alec Cobbe‡ took us round. Curious sallow face, deep dark eyes. Something of a genius there. Amazing the opulence of the rooms compared to the sparsity of Goodhart-Rendel's§ time. Jamie Fergusson caught me at Brooks's and persuaded me to write a supplement to the two obituaries of Eardley in today's *Independent*, dealing with his N.T. side. I wracked my brain and scribbled in train home, typing out before going to bed.

---

* N.T. Historic Buildings Representative for Southern Region, 1986–2002 (b. 1952).

† Margaret McEwan, illegitimate daughter of the brewer William McEwan; m. 1891 Hon. Ronald Greville, yr s. of 2nd Baron Greville. She bequeathed Polesden Lacey to the N.T. on her death in 1942.

‡ Richard Alexander Charles Cobbe (b. 1945); artist and designer, arranger of pictures and interiors for N.T.; m. 1970 Hon. Isabel Dillon. In 1987 he became tenant of Hatchlands, which he redesigned in theatrical style, filling it with his family pictures from Newbridge House, Co. Dublin and his collection of early keyboard intruments.

§ Harold Stuart ('Hal') Goodhart-Rendel (1887–1959); architect, donor of Hatchlands to N.T.

Monday, 16th September

To London for Eardley's funeral. Kind Fred Oppé* hired a car to take us to Putney Vale Cemetery from Coleherne Court, but I had greatest difficulty getting cab to him in pouring rain and arrived worn out. No emotion whatever during service in dehydrated, ice-cold, antiseptic chapel. Sat with Burnet [Pavitt] and Fred. Hymns, which E. would have hated. His coffin brought in and dumped on slab which mercifully did not glide away theatrically. A little posy placed on it by Mattei before service, which would have pleased E. Fanny Partridge there, and E's niece Anne and her husband the General. Also Joan Cochemé† whom I recognised just in time, and who asked if she could have a photograph of her portrait of me. Lunched with Fred at Brooks's and returned straight home. How sad I feel. I already miss E. There is no one who possesses my entire confidence now.

Thursday, 19th September

To Bolton Abbey. Just me and the Devonshires, a large shooting party having dissolved. Andrew, who owns three of the most beautifully situated country houses in England, speaks of how fortunate he feels to have been allowed to keep them, along with all his possessions. He feels a strong sense of *noblesse oblige*, attending public dinners, etc.

Friday, 20th September

Debo drives me to Wallington [Northumberland] in her beautiful fast car. We call ourselves 'partners', in the modern parlance. When I offer to pay for petrol, she will not let me. 'We are multis,' she says, raising a finger. Having spied Wallington across Wansbeck Vale, we eat delicious grouse sandwiches in the car. At the house, the Regional Representative's secretary introduces herself and accompanies us. She means to be helpful but is a nuisance, and very ignorant. We escape from her to see the garden, situated half a mile from the house in the Scotch manner. Rooms well-arranged and well-maintained, better

---

* Director of advertising firm (1914–95); pre-war friend of J.L.-M., and his fellow lodger with Rick Stewart-Jones in Cheyne Walk.
† Artist specialising in portraits of children; widow of Jacques Cochemé, Mauritian biologist who had worked for UN.

than when I first came here in Sir Charles [Trevelyan]'s day. Landscape is unspoiled agricultural land, rather unromantic. Best thing about outside is the vast courtyard at rear of house, with arched cupola'ed entrance tower, as at Attingham.

We drive on to Roxburghshire to stay with Emma and Toby Tennant. They live in a primitive farmhouse near Newcastleton, square plan, 1823. Very rough inside, and cold. My bed has no back to it, and one tiny pillow; no bedside lamp, or plug in the basin. They seem immune to rigours. Emma is a sort of Quakeress with her neat but simple dress and cropped, greying hair, and deeply-held principles. Very intelligent and on the whole right-minded. Toby a large, good-natured, round-faced farmer. She shows us her flower paintings. Are they any good? I can't tell.

Saturday, 21st September

I go with Debo and the Tennants to Netherby, where we picnic in the churchyard off a table tomb. Graveyard, beside swift-flowing river, packed with perpendicular grey stones. We walk across swing bridge into park and look at a crenellated folly which the Landmark Trust have bought. They intend to make it into a residence – quite unnecessary in my view, which will spoil this splendid riverside site with drive, car park, poles, wires, etc. We leave Tennants and motor to Appleby-in-Westmorland, lovely little obscure town. To the castle to see the great hall with huge triptych portrait of Lady Anne Clifford,[*] one of Debo's heroines.

Sunday, 22nd September

At breakfast, Andrew got on to religion, which he says he can't swallow. Debo and I attended 10.30 service. Long sermon about the man who slunk into the back seat of a party and was advanced to the front through humility rewarded. Whereas Debo, followed by me, pushed through the congregation straight to the front pew. We came out first and bolted. Amanda Hartington singing in the choir, surpliced and all. Has a very sweet face. Modest certainly and retiring, but has presence. She will be immensely popular, I surmise.

---

[*] Remarkable woman of her time (1590–1676) who restored and rebuilt many churches and castles in Cumbria.

Took train from Leeds at four, which travelled at snail's pace and arrived at Gloucester 1½ hours late. British Rail deserves to be liquidated.[*]

Wednesday, 25th September

Spent day with Guillaume Villeneuve, my French translator. He is a touching little fellow and I cannot but like him much. Fancy his motoring from Fontainebleau just to spend a few hours with me. Brought first copies of *Un Autre Moi-Même*. I am not sure about the title, or the melancholy 1920s photograph on the cover. I try to appear delighted and am indeed appreciative of his trouble. He drives me to Stourhead which he wishes to see, and we walk into the gardens and round the lake. A glorious late afternoon, few visitors. He knows me better than I know myself, being familiar with every word of my four diaries and *Moi-Même*. Quotes what I said, what I thought, how I acted. Most strange. Confided in me about his unrequited passion for a youth of twenty-one. Lives entirely upon translating. Wants to tackle Walter Pater,[†] but I discourage for no French will be bothered with him now. I feel almost paternal towards him, for there is something vulnerable about him. I like his humour, his brightness and sympathy, his curiosity for all that is beautiful and civilised. Was moved to embrace him on parting. He is anxious for me to present myself at some Parisian bookshop and meet French writers, but I tried to explain I cannot do this. Yet I ought to help him, for he needs the money.

Sunday, 29th September

On Wednesday evening when I got home I found a butterfly with closed wings perched on one side of the frame of Robin Ironside's painting in my bathroom. Its head hangs downwards, its forefeet gripping the wooden frame; it sticks out at an angle. I left it and asked Peggy not to disturb. At first I thought it must be dead for it did not move. On the other hand, if dead it would surely relax grasp and fall

---

[*] The Conservative Government were proposing to split up and 'privatise' British Rail (achieved by the Railway Act, 1993).

[†] English critic and essayist (1839–94); Oxford mentor of Oscar Wilde.

to the floor. It is still there. I believe a peacock, for it is large. A. says it is hibernating. It doesn't mind my switching on the light above the wash basin.

Yesterday Tony Scotland and Julian Berkeley lunched, and Nick the gardener[*] to meet them. Tony told me that Michael Berkeley isn't musical in the sense that Lennox was, in that he does not live for music every moment of the day. He turns it on and turns it off. Tony talked of his new book about his recent travels in China in pursuit of the pretender to the Imperial throne.[†] Found him, a nice, gentle man in his seventies, not clever, living in one squalid room after a life mostly spent doing menial jobs. Was adopted by last Emperor when a boy of two. Tony says living conditions in the provinces are indescribably filthy and uncomfortable. T. such a sympathetic man, and Julian greatly improved. Indeed extraordinarily handsome, and has lost that giggling, slightly furtive manner. Is now confident, and very explicit and precise in talking to us about our burglar alarm and his suggestions.

Monday, 30th September

Baba Metcalfe called on me in Bath this morning, accompanied by the N.T. East Midlands Representative and a lady costumes expert, she having just visited the Costume Museum to select four of her mother's Worth dresses for exhibition at Kedleston. Kissing on both cheeks on the doorstep, and a good deal of Copper society talk in front of the others. Anecdotes about Lord Curzon's houses – Kedleston [Derbyshire], Bodiam [Castle, Sussex], Tattershall [Lincolnshire], Hackwood [Hampshire], Montacute [Somerset] – and how lucky 'Daddy' got rid of some of them before he died. Told me that Peter Thorneycroft, sitting alone in the Venice flat where we go on Sunday, was 'sprayed' by intruders so that he passed out while they rifled Carla's jewelry in her bedroom. Jolly! Baba in full possession, gallant and gay. A splendid woman.

---

[*] Nicholas Lambourne, head-gardener at Badminton: see entry for 1 February 1992.
[†] *The Empty Throne: The Quest for an Imperial Heir in the People's Republic of China* (Penguin, 1993).

Wednesday, 2nd October

Mattei lunched at Brooks's. Sweet as always, but broken-hearted. For
him, Eardley was England. The doctor told M. that E. had the heart
of a young man. Yet it stopped. E. left directions that his ashes were
to be scattered 'near The Slade'. So like him, says M.; of course I scattered them *at* The Slade. E. had to see M. at least once a day, if only
for a few minutes. This is what kept him going. For years he produced
a painting most days, showing it to M. for his opinion. M. now has
to go through these, selecting and destroying.

*From 6 to 15 October the L.-Ms were in Venice, staying with Anna-Maria
Cicogna.*

Sunday, 6th October

First thing of all, a toddle into Salute church after tea. Dusk. Wish to
sit on steps and watch lights glimmering across the water. But effect
spoilt by glaring arc lamps trained on church for benefit of sightseers
on other side of Canal. So enter church for moment's contemplation.
Dense shadows, and by high altar handfuls of candles (real, not electric) burning. Few jeaned youths respectful but not praying. No one
prays. From choir behind presbytery come whispered strains of
angelic singing which I remember on previous visit, from a disc tape.
Not a whiff of incense, but a dribble of holy water in the stoup,
beneath exquisite bronze of the Baptist by I forget whom.

We are given by Anna-Maria [Cicogna] the flat which the
Thorneycrofts have. Extremely comfortable and *bien*. Wake often, but
dead quiet. Since burglary,* reinforced door with complicated lock
installed, four turns of Chubb key.

Monday, 7th October

First morning. No Venice legs. We sally aimlessly to Piazza, parting in
front of St Mark's. I wade through a liquid flood of grey pigeons.
These sacred birds ought to be exterminated. Raised boards in front
of entrance, already preparing for *acqua alta*. Am pushed by dense
throng down central nave. Ropes rightly prohibit straying over

---

* See entry for 30 September 1991.

mosaics – but the agony! Can see nothing even with magic spectacles. Panic ensues, claustrophobia. Have to leave, retreating against the surge; smell of sour clothes. Anna–Maria says ceiling lit up from time to time, and the mosaics recently cleaned are marvellous. But you can never avoid the tourists, except in Jan. and Feb.

Having failed to see Tiepolo ceiling in Pietà church, for the nave is roped off at entrance, I force a passage along the Schiavoni and sit within Gothic colonnade under Doge's Palace (where Ruskin complained of Venetians defecating). Have tepid cappuccino for 9,000 lire. Robbery. Cannot distinguish 10,000 from 100,000, dyslexia or some such terminal folly.

Deep sleep in afternoon. To Mass in Salute. Sit half-way; watch white nuns in habits, so disciplined, demure and aristocratic in movement. Youth in jeans reads Gospel. Through my magic specs able to see beautiful illuminated reredos sculpture of Our Lady brandishing a torch at the Plague retreating. By whom? Sermon drives me out. Gautier's abandoned ladies, like Edwardian courtesans, sprawling over entrance.

At the Dogana one feels the lord of Venice – lights twinkling on either side of water – until two ballet dancers (I suppose) do *pas de deux* and exercises. Amused by exhibitionism of it in full view of Venice, as it were, but in dusk.

Tuesday, 8th October

Downpour. Driven out of flat by the servants, we go to Scuola de S. Giorgio by vaporetto. I forget way. A. forges ahead, saying she knows it, although she hasn't been here in years – and she does. The humour of Carpaccio. But is it intentional? The toy lion on a string; the Friars fleeing like swallows into the distant church; the dragon, head pierced by cruel shaft, led by youthful saint; the little fluffy dog in the library, books on the floor as in my library. Or are we laughing at his naivety and not with? The full-face whippet makes me think this is where Modigliani* derived his oval, attenuated style.

Pouring, puddles, impossible to keep dry. We paddle to San Zaccharia to see the Bellini, so clear and bright. Our Lady's robe of lapis lazuli.

---

* Amedeo Modigliani, Italian painter and sculptor (1884–1920).

The three of us paddle off to tea with the Decazes* at Palazzo Polignac. Met at garden door by footman in smart yellow jacket. Cross dark overgrown garden in courtyard. Put into lift the far side of long underground room at which gondola arrived in old days. Another footman, old but smiling, greets us on piano nobile. Melancholy and crepuscular light. Huge Venetian lanterns casting but a glimmer each. Walk tiptoe in fear of slipping on shiny, marble floor to 'salotto'. From behind sofa, Duchess smiling and showing gums leaves silver tea tray and shakes hands. The genial Duke, wearing subfusc suit, rises awkwardly from recumbent attitude – has sciatica – from another sofa on right of raised fireplace. Facing windows, a gallery enclosed by semi-drawn curtains made of nondescript, sub-fusc tapestry-like stuff, from which dark portraits of seventeenth-century ancestors hang from claret-cloured ropes with tassels against beige neutral silk walls. Whole aura is typical *fin de siècle* (or *commencement du 20ième siècle*). We fall into place, I on sofa to left of amiable Duchess who dispenses tea to all but me, whom she forgets. I talk merrily while she pours and I hand round cups. A plate of horrid *petits fours* are bandied about. I take what I fancy to be a little round pink iced cake and turns out to be an evil-smelling fishcake.

Three women enter. One, enormous woman with baby-face, swathed in yellow satin, is a widow, Mrs Morley-Fletcher. The other two are English and both apparently deaf and dumb, totally inanimate. I talk to the yellow satin one. I say I knew her husband. She looks blank and asks how and when. I say we must have been at school together. She looks blanker still. I ask how old he would be if alive today. She says, 'rising fifty. He ran a famous art gallery.' I say, 'Perhaps it was his father I knew.' It turns out it may have been his grandfather. She asks if I have been to the Celtic exhibition. I say I don't much care for that sort of thing, but ask about the exhibits. She offers to fetch catalogue and leaves room – I suspect an awkward means of escaping from me. I sidle up to the Duchess and start another conversation. She is so tongue-tied with shyness that she leaves her seat and disappears. Yellow satin returns with not a catalogue but a folder, from which she produces no pictures but a history of the Celts. One dumb

---

* Elie, 5th duc Decazes and 5th duc de Glucksbierg (b. 1914; nephew and heir of A.L.-M's intimate friend Winaretta, princesse de Polignac [1865–1943]); m. 1937 Solange du Temple de Rougemont (b. 1917).

lady comes between us, engaging my attention with a pale smile. I ask her how long she is staying in Venice. She gives another languid smile as if deprecating necessity for words. So I say, 'If I were you I would visit the Palazzo Rezzonico.'* She thrusts a paper and pencil at me, I write the name on the paper and smile back. All this while I hear Alvilde having an animated talk with the jolly prone Duke amid gales of laughter.

We walk home in the rain and a complete black-out. As we fumble with the lock of our door, the street lights come on again.

Wednesday, 9th October

Sunshine today. A. and I set out from Salute on vaporetto. No one to buy tickets from. Get off at S. Tomà, walked to Frari. Have come without magic specs, so see nothing beyond a hedge: the Titian *Assumption*, so beautiful, invisible to me. Then find, see and am captivated by the little campo of S. Giovanni di Evangelista Scuola, with beautiful screen entrance. Never seen before. Exquisite. Walk back.

After luncheon, A. and I take public bus from Salute to Lido just for the ride. Soft-sharp afternoon autumn light. Water not blue, but dove green. Cold on deck when not in sun. On Lido we look at shoddy round building of Mussolini time, some sort of military memorial. Disenchanted, we take next vaporetto home.

Thursday, 10th October

Before retiring last night we make tentative plans with Anna–Maria to go on an expedition today and lunch out. But this morning she telephones that the weather is not right, and excursion is off.

We take vaporetto to Ca'd'Oro and walk to Miracoli church. Half of the front is shrouded under cascade of perspex. Within workmen in 'restauro', and strong smell of cigarette smoke. Much hammering accompanied by piped choral music. I am pleased that the Americans are restoring what the French restored ten years ago at great cost. Yet this church seems denuded of all sanctity.

---

* Mid 17th-century palazzo owned by Robert Browning's son in late 19th century: the poet died there (1889), and several artists, including Sargent and Boldini, set up studios there. It was bought by the municipality in 1930s and became the Museum of Eighteenth-Century Venice.

In campo of S. M. Formosa we drink coffee in the sun and revel in the beauty of this domed church, the elegant Baroque campanile and palazzi. Inside of church dull. But the Greek Cross plan very noble; the architecture more Florentine than Venetian. Baroque touches here and there. Over entrance a pair of handled urns, one of which, beheld in solitude against the baby-blue sky from where we drink our cappuccini, looks an exclamation of detached profanity and not a part of a sacred whole.

A. and I dine with John Hoarsbeen, a nice little American who used to inhabit a mezzanine floor of the Albrizzi Palace, now in what he calls 'the slaves' quarter'. In spite of elaborate explanations how to find, we take ages. When about to return home in despair we come upon it. Apartment nondescript. Peggy Willes* staying with him. Taken to restaurant for excellent dinner. Accompanied by Hoarsbeen to vaporetto stop through infinitude of *calle* and *campi* unknown, all swept and garnished (though near midnight). Peggy, walking on my arm, says one feels freer of muggers than in London. Canal strangely quiet and tranquil. Only sound the lapping against the wooden floating raft of waves from a passing barge piled with planks and garbage.

Friday, 11th October

Walk from Ca'd'Oro bus station to Gesuiti, losing way en route. See open door of, and enter Oratorio dei Crociferi for first time ever. Recently restored, this tiny oratory, walls painted by Palma il Giovanne of whom hitherto I have thought little. A treasure casket on lines of Carpaccio Scuola. Anna-Maria says for so boring a painter she would not cross the street. But she's wrong here. As fine as Veronese. I tell her a Cicogna duke or senator depicted. She said the wrong branch.

Step across to Gesuiti. It is one of the few Venetian churches all of a piece, like the Miracoli. I am more impressed than on my last visit here, a few years back when writing *Venetian Evenings*. Exquisite beauty of green-damask-hung walls and columns, gilding more mustard than gold. But the high altar and the heroic figures of the crossing by little known sculptor Giuseppi Torretti exquisite and brimming over with elegant vitality. Rococo of course, not Baroque.

---

* Margaret Willes; J.L.-M.'s editor at Sidgwick & Jackson in the 1980s, subsequently Head of Publications at National Trust.

Condition of interior improved. I no longer see large crack in left transept which worried me hitherto.

Weather forecast bad – much rain and wind. *Acqua alta* in prospect.

A.-M. has a dinner party. We are 7, Lord and Lady McAlpine* and the Astas. Lord McA. looks like a genial pig. Shaven or bald head, square, short square body, enormous belly. Very ugly (whereas wife handsome except for over-large teeth). Is clever and quick, speaks Italian freely. I have long talk with him after dinner. Was Treasurer to Conservative Party; one of Mrs T's right-hand fingers. Adores her. Was with her when she told Denis they had sacked her. Denis said, 'Good for you, they are all shits.' Only Parkinson remained loyal. The rest were traitors. West Green House blown up by IRA two weeks after he & wife left it. Had they remained, would undoubtedly have been killed. He is still a target & so lives permanently in Venice. Has built a house beside Arsenal. Little girl goes to school with nuns of Salute. He comes here every weekend luggageless. Loves H. of L[ords]. Says Labour Party will be hard put to abolish for it works supremely well. The hereditary peers are 'peerless' in their devoted, voluntary work on committees. Is much in favour of hereditary system. Says they are a different race, unbiased, fearless, without axes to grind.

Lady McA. affected, laughs too much, exposing terrifying fangs. Mrs Asta, Donatella, nearly 50 (?), perhaps most handsome woman ever seen. Lovely figure, animated gestures, laughter like a Chopin barcarolle, flawless profile. Has lingering sadness over death of son in motor accident. He, Paolo, a jolly Anglophile, shoots grouse in Scotland, likes a spot of whisky. Leaves early to bid for something at Christie's by telephone, being gentleman dealer.

Sunday, 13th October

Pours in night. Flood in Salone. Sirens shriek from motor-boats along the canals, warning of *acqua alta*. They are like the air raid warning wails during the war. We *have* to cash cheques at American Express. Land at S. Marco, *calle* so under water that we return to boat and go by Piazzetta. Tables and chairs of cafés aswirl. Manage to keep dry

---

* (Robert) Alistair McAlpine (b. 1942); director of building firm; Treasurer of Conservative Party, 1975–90; m. (2nd) 1980 Romilly Hobbs; cr. life peer as Baron McAlpine of West Green, 1984.

till American Express, then tiptoe into office. Sirocco blowing. Suddenness of flooding is astonishing. The pointed prow-like platform of the Dogana totally under water.

We are due to lunch with Rose Lauritzen* but she telephones at midday that the water over the gum-boots of her son Freddy. Although we have been lent by A.-M's little maid some flimsy plastic bags and rubber bands to attach to our shoes, they show no signs of being firmly fixed. Streets littered with old plastic when water subsides, which happens within 6 hours. Streets again miraculously dried out. Since no visible sign of drains it is hard to understand where the water goes to. Of course the tide withdraws the flowing water, but the stagnant lakes likewise disappear before the dark comes.

We go to San Marco after 6 for service of Rosary followed by Mass which seems interminable and sorely tries A's patience. Strange antics. A beautiful fair-haired lady wearing white silk robe to the ground and black stripes from shoulders down both sides of skirt appears from behind altar and seats herself on golden throne. She says nothing. Does she represent Our Lady, whose month is October as well as May? After very long sermon, we leave. Object (achieved) to see the mosaic vaulting illuminated. A golden sheen of ineffable galactic beauty.

Monday, 14th October

The Reresby Sitwells and Rose Lauritzen come to our apartment for a drink before luncheon. Reresby may be a bore who talks too much, but he is an affectionate fellow. Penelope very handsome, straight features, *de haut en bas* manner. She is very outspoken about her mother-in-law Georgia, 'a bad, very bad woman', who always treated Reresby like dirt. Regarding Sarah Bradford, Sachie's biographer, she says that neither she nor Reresby have read her biography of George VI. R. says to me, 'I have your *Venetian Evenings* and your *Bachelor Duke*, neither of which I have read.' R. shares the role of Sachie's literary executor with his brother Francis, with whom he doesn't get on. Sachie left mountains of papers, but those of his works still in print bring in precious little revenue.

---

* Hon. Rose Keppel (b. 1943); yr dau. of Viscount Bury, er s. and heir of 9th Earl of Albemarle (whom he predeceased, 1968), and his 1st wife Lady Mairi Tempest-Vane-Stewart, yst dau. of 7th Marquess of Londonderry; m. Peter Lauritzen.

Tuesday, 15th October

Nightmare day. At ten we leave for airport by taxi at 100,000 lire, *i.e.*, £50. Row over trolley, some air officials refusing to let us take one until a friendly female in uniform intervenes. After waiting some time we are told plane to Pisa cancelled because of bad weather. On ascending metal stairs A. falls and badly wounds right leg.* Bleeding will not stop. Steward has no bandages. In desperation, I tell them that A. a bleeder (true to some extent), whereupon they send for airport doctor. He comes, unsympathetic and officious. We decide to chuck Pisa and fly straight to London, and after much difficulty change tickets. Then doctor refuses to allow her to fly because of her alleged haemophilia. We are obliged to telephone A.-M. who most kindly, if unenthusiastically, allows us to return for the night (she has Nathalie Brooke coming to stay). Meanwhile ticket changed back to Pisa tomorrow. Another taxi of 100,000 lire. A.-M. solicitous, sends for her doctor, but in the course of much fussing (which infuriates A.) she succeeds in fusing lights in our apartment. So we spend night without light, heat, or hot water. Although Venice is a magical city, and the only one unspoilt since my childhood, I shall not come again.† It has lost its savour for me.

Wednesday, 16th October

At last we set off to Pisa. Plane delayed 2 hours. Chloë [Luke] meets us, motors through packed streets (the day's third rush hour), through ghastly new suburbs (indeed, road practically a continuous suburb), to Lucca. We pass rampart walls, so beautiful and stalwart and containing, and reach Lammari, where Chloë and children squat in end house of an old terrace, semi-farmyard setting, semi-suburb. But conditions unbelievably primitive, chaotic, uncomfortable, nightmarish. Given delicious luncheon at 2.30 with children, girl rather porcine, boy pretty but missing some teeth. Afterwards to Hotel Hambro, a kind

---

* Note by J.L.-M. added on 1 September 1992: 'This accident may have been the original cause of the septicaemia and dreadful illness from which she very nearly died in March 1992.'
† He came again the following year (see 2–9 October 1992), and on a number of further occasions.

of Skindles* for adulterous weekend couples, scrupulously clean. Deplorable taste, but we relish the comfort and cleanliness.

I dine with John [Fleming] and Hugh [Honour] at Torofi.† They fetch and return me in brand new posh German car. Unwonted air of wealth. (Strange to think that, when I first knew them, they hadn't a bean. We motored from Naples through Calabria and round Sicily, they staying in such dreadfully scruffy inns that I went alone to some superior hostelry.) John has lost much weight, looks healthy and distinguished, sparse white hair. Hugh still tall, youthful figure, greying hair, now middle-aged and very handsome. House heaven. Space, good rooms, lovely things. Portrait copy of Lawrence's Canova given by Canova to Lady William Russell and now given by Georgiana Blakiston to Hugh. So clever both are. So kind and friendly. Every opinion weighed, dissected, discussed. They have risen to a unique height in the world of intellect by combined work, work, work and true scholarship. Admirable institution they have become, figures in the literary history of the twentieth century, surely.

Their gossip free from malice now. Harold Acton has succeeded in cocking a snook by his achieved position as best known and richest Florentine in city where his father not accepted by the Lady Sybil Lubbocks and Keppels. John Pope-Hennessy does have a heart, as proved by his (platonic) relationship with Michael [Mallon]‡, who has brought him happiness. J.P.-H. means more to them than any friend in vicinity. Joan Haslip a good old trouper, maddening to some. Lives on her books, and is hard up, obliged to sell Japanese painting given to her by J.P.-H. Susanna Johnston adorable, but proprietary. John surprises me by expressing disapproval of Nicky and Susanna's tolerance of their children conducting love affairs under parental roof. Shows lack of circumspection and discipline. I ask, 'But you would not disapprove of two young men sleeping under your roof?' That's different, he says. We are not their parents. Children never resent parents' prohibitions in the home. Susanna also earns disapproval over

---

* Hotel at Maidenhead, Berkshire whose staff had been famous for their willingness to provide the 'evidence' of adultery which was often necessary for divorce before the reform of the law.

† Hugh Honour (b. 1927) and John Fleming (1919–2001); writers, separately and together, on art and architecture.

‡ American art history scholar (b. 1960); personal assistant (eventually heir) of Sir John Pope-Hennessy.

encouragement of daughter Rosie's book about her prison experiences. 'I hate all change, but all change,' John declares.

Thursday, 17th October

I sit on terrace reading Dostoevsky while at another table A. discusses with Chloë and her house-agent and friend, intelligent man, how to acquire the adjoining house and at least prevent it falling into hands of some very common, jumped-up I-ties. At midday Chloë motors us to Pisa airport. She is very deft at the wheel of her little car. Is looking very pretty indeed with beautiful fair hair and glimmering lights. I sit in back with Kane, dear little boy, who sleeps. On our arrival he wakes up and with much efficiency finds us a trolley for our luggage. The situation of C. and her two children is exceedingly 'how',[*] because they are genuinely pleased with their *train-de-vie* which strikes us as deprived as that of the humblest peasants.

Sunday, 20th October

Venice was an imperfect experience on the whole. Nasty weather. Anna-Maria a silly society lady, concerned with clothes and nonsense, though kind and generous to us. Venice is the only city which never disappoints, however 'stale' it may become; it is undoubtedly the most beautiful, the most magical city in the world. It has so far survived, and there is not one ugly building to be seen in it.

I have decided that, whereas an old person may become a friend of a young person, a young person cannot be a friend of an old person. It requires working out; but I think I am right.

Yesterday we went to Hanbury, which I wished to see now the contents have been put back after the major refurbishment. Crowds, which made the occasion sorrowful. It is over-decorated. No longer a squire's country house. Pretentious curtain-hanging, and not quite right – shallow pelmets and garish fabrics. I was reminded of what David Crawford[†] once said to Christopher Wall at Hardwick [Hall, Derbyshire], that within a generation there would not be a soul left who knew what a country house really looked like.

---

[*] A word from the private language of Harold and Vita, meaning pathetic.
[†] David Lindsay, 24th Earl of Crawford (1900–75); Chairman of N.T., 1945–65.

Monday, 21st October

To Norfolk by train. Stop in London to see Schinkel* exhibition at V&A (nicely empty), and give lunch at Brooks's to Stuart Preston (sober and delightful). Merlin Waterson† meets me at Norwich and motors me to Holt. Charming man, fascinated by Lord Lothian.‡ Much talk about his goodness, his visionary outlook, his idealism. Thinks he has been greatly maligned by association with the Cliveden gang,§ whereas before the war he announced that Hitler, whom he visited twice, was impossible to do business with.

Tuesday, 22nd October

Billa [Harrod] motored me to Blickling where we spent the day. The Administrator [Howard Eaton] approached us with outstretched arms and said, 'I am taking you under my wing.' Quick as lightning Billa, with whom I had hoped to go round house alone, said, 'Not too much wing, please.' I feared this nice man, bearded like St Luke, would be affronted, but he joined us at the end of our tour and took us to see the conservation department. The bedrooms at Blickling are just like the pre-war bedrooms to which one was ushered on arrival. Whole house beautifully arranged and kept. Everyone most kind. David Napier,¶ the fund-raiser, gave us lunch at Buckinghamshire Arms. Administrator gave us tea. We then met the Representative, John Madison,** red-head, charming and clever like all N.T. staff.

   Billa, having misunderstood me when I told her over the telephone

---

* Karl Friedrich Schinkel (1781–1841); Prussian architect.

† Joined staff of N.T. 1970; Historic Buildings Representative, West Midlands and Wales 1970–81; Regional Director, East Anglia, 1981–2002; Historic Properties Director from 2002 (b. 1947).

‡ Philip Kerr, 11th Marquess of Lothian (1882–1940); Liberal statesman, whose speech to Annual Meeting of N.T. in 1934 inspired setting-up of Country House Scheme of which J.L.-M. became Secretary, and who bequeathed Blickling, his Jacobean house in Norfolk, to N.T. on his premature death (at which time he was British Ambassador to United States).

§ 'Set' which revolved around Waldorf, 2nd Viscount Astor and his wife Nancy at their seat of Cliveden near Maidenhead, Berkshire, generally associated with 'appeasement' policy of 1930s.

¶ N.T. Fundraiser, East Anglia, 1987–2001 (b. 1943).

** Artist (b. 1957); N.T. Historic Buildings Representative, East Anglia, 1981–92.

that she would be bored with my solitary company for two evenings, invited Sylvia Combe and young Desmond MacCarthy* to dinner. I was dog-tired when we got back from Blickling, but recovered after an hour in bed, and dinner (partridge) was enjoyable. Sylvia still pretty and youthful with smooth face, though she must be over eighty. MacCarthy a delightful, jolly, clever, plain young man, friend of Richard [Robinson]. As Billa spoke of how my Lord Esher book had affronted some members of the Brett family,† I asked Desmond whether he was hurt by the exposure of *his* grandparents' lives in *Clever Hearts* [by Hugh and Mirabel Cecil]. Not at all, he said, for there was no malice in the exposure of his grandfather's love affairs, which amounted to little when all was said and done.

Sitting alone with Billa in the drawing room, we talked about the paucity of friends and how we must keep in touch. She is bright, entertaining, and passionately concerned about the environment, her current worry being a proposed by-pass road around the village, she putting listed cottages before the spotted toad whose habitat might be adversely affected.

Sunday, 27th October

George Dix staying one night, looking far better and thinner than before his prostate operation. Staying this weekend with four differ-ent friends in the locality – someone at Oakley, the Ben Harfords at Ashcroft, us, and the Michael Briggses at Midford, with whom we left him this afternoon. And before Oakley, he stayed with the Ferrantis at their new Palladian house in Cheshire. He talks incessantly and is rather tiring. Driving to church with him this morning at Acton Turville, I recalled that Wyndham Ketton-Cremer‡ once said to me that kneeling beside an old friend at the altar rail brought about an affinity which nothing much else kindled in old age. George and I agreed that the beauty of this short service was ineffable, and we

---

* Grandson (b. 1956) of the eminent literary critic Sir Desmond MacCarthy (1877–1952); inherited Wiveton Hall, Norfolk, from his mother, Pamela *née* Buxton.

† J.L.-M's *The Enigmatic Edwardian* had described in some detail the unorthodox passion of Reginald, 2nd Viscount Esher for his younger son Hon. Maurice Brett, revelations which had caused some embarrassment to Maurice's descendants.

‡ Writer (1906–69); bachelor squire of Felbrigg Hall, Norfolk, which he bequeathed to N.T.

did not understand why every Christian did not want to go to Communion every Sunday.

Wednesday, 30th October

To London. Saw exhibition of George IV treasures from Carlton House at Queen's Gallery, Buckingham Palace. Really magnificent things, of stupendous opulent taste. Bought expensive catalogue and revelled in each exhibit. Then to Fanny Partridge, who had been involved in motor accident with Mary Dunn* last Thursday. She seemed remarkably well, though apparently Mary in very bad state. We talked of Eardley. Walked back to Brooks's to give dinner to Burnet [Pavitt] and J.K.-B. A success, J. full of information which I think impressed B.

Thursday, 31st October

Invited to State Opening of Parliament by Patric Dickinson. Walked there after giving breakfast to Nick, who is thinking of building a house near Tisbury. Arrived punctually at ten o'clock, queueing at Norman Arch. Ladies in best clothes. In Royal Gallery found Patric with co-heralds, looking out for me. Given seat at back, near entrance to Robing Room. A joy the whole thing, pure *Alice in Wonderland*. May the beauty, tradition and symbolism be preserved forever. Much to look at during hour before ceremony began. Duke of Norfolk[†] like genial teddy bear talking to daughters in row below me, they straightening his shaggy robes. Men in black tailcoats, medals round necks. Then the toy soldiers, Queen's Bodyguard of Yeomen of the Guard, their hatbands seemingly interwoven with wild flowers, marching through to Prince's Chamber. Then Gentlemen of Arms, swan plumes waving from helmets, march through slowly, canes tapping rhythmically on carpet. Then Cap of Maintenance, Sword of State and Imperial Crown borne in, the last on a cushion by a page under escort. Then the Crown borne by Lord Great Chamberlain, the handsome young Lord Cholmondeley, looking slightly awkward and not

---

* Lady Mary St Clair Erskine (1912–93), dau. of 5th Earl of Rosslyn; m. 1933–44 Philip Dunn (he s. his father 1956 as 2nd Bt; he and Lady Mary remarried 1969 and he d. 1976).
† Miles Fitzalan-Howard, 17th Duke of Norfolk (1915–2002); Hereditary Earl Marshal, Premier Duke and Earl.

carrying himself quite straight. Princess Margaret in dark velvet, Duchess of Gloucester looking distinguished. The Queen's three ladies, Fortune Grafton* in middle looking old and tired, flanked by fat Mrs Dugdale,† and Lady Airlie‡ looking very distinguished with bare back and fine high diamond collar. Queen looking bored, in spectacles, but splendid. A rustle as she enters, but no lights lowered or raised. Lord Chancellor§ robed in gold and black, the old robes of the peerage. Most males rather ugly. Heralds little better, except for naughty Terence McCarthy, Bluemantle Pursuivant, with his jolly, wicked face. I had a word with him when I arrived, he already tipsy at 10 a.m. He is a great embarrassment, Patric whispered, much as they love him. Hubert Chesshyre¶ also handsome though over fifty, and charming to talk to, which I did at stand-up luncheon at College of Arms to which Patric drove me afterwards in hired car. There I stood first on one foot then the other until hernia started playing up and leg ached.

The Royal Gallery is frankly ugly, all glittering gold, with that cheap, cardboard quality in which the mid Victorians sometimes indulged. But I am haunted by the fluttering (for it was a stormy morning and the wind blew straight up the stairs into the antechamber) of the swan feathers, snow white alternating with mauve grey; and the bustiness and aplomb of the Queen as though she did this daily, her voice a little deeper than usual in keeping with the dignity of the ceremony.

Saturday, 2nd November

Jane Westmorland is beautiful, but her conversation can be extraordinary. At dinner she complained to me how boring the television programmes were. I said I seldom looked at TV unless there was something particularly interesting, which A. usually drew to my

---

* Fortune Smith; Mistress of the Robes from 1967; m. 1946 11th Duke of Grafton.
† Kathryn Stanley (1923–2004; DCVO 1984); m. 1956 John Dugdale (1924–94; KCVO 1994); Lady-in-Waiting (formerly Woman of the Bedchamber) to HM The Queen from 1985.
‡ Virginia Ryan of Newport, R.I. (b. 1933); m. 1952 David Ogilvy, 13th Earl of Airlie (b. 1926; Lord Chamberlain, 1984–97); Lady of Bedchamber to HM The Queen from 1973.
§ Lord Mackay of Clashfern (b. 1927); Lord Chancellor, 1987–97.
¶ Chester Herald of Arms, 1978–95, and Secretary to the Order of the Garter, 1988–2003.

attention. She said there ought to be interesting things all the time. I said I would rather not watch TV all the time because I preferred reading. She then said there were few good books. I replied rather haughtily that, when one considered all the books published down the ages, there were always a great many of interest left for one to read. Did she, for example, care for Trollope? No, she said, she had no time for Trollope, nor for Dickens, though she thought George Eliot rather nice. She said that she and David had been to Subacio, but had not been able to find a guide book. I gave up. The Queen has just made David a GCVO* for being her Master of the Horse for twelve years.

Saturday, 9th November

Patricia [Hambleden] and David Herbert lunched, also Daphne [Fielding]. We made a sad old party of octos, yet weren't sad but mer-ryish – though both David and Daphne about to undergo nasty oper-ations, while Patricia looking bad colour and face broader from cortisone. Queen Elizabeth said to Patricia the other day, 'We must keep struggling on as best we can.'

Tuesday, 12th November

In London, I went to Damas's shop in Burlington Arcade to buy a present for A. on our Ruby Wedding Day. I found a pair of earrings with rubies round a small diamond, £835, and a garnet bracelet. In the end I chose the earrings, which I fear A. may find mingy. The bracelet was not that, but struck me as rather gloomy. Lady in shop said she might exchange if she wished.

Lunched with Hugh Massingberd at Travellers'. He told me that, when he first became a member aged twenty-one, he chose to spend his annual fortnight's holiday in the club, immersing himself. Hardly went out. Roamed around and read prodigiously in the library. Became a nineteenth-century member. Then to see British Portrait Exhibition at National Portrait Gallery, most of the exhibits already known to me. What is there about the human face that one finds so fascinating? I fancy most portrait lovers are iconodules. Then to Brooks's to give tea to M., not seen for weeks and looking healthier

---

* Knight Grand Cross of the Royal Victorian Order.

than for ages – nice white teeth and clear complexion. He told me that, if he reaches a point of difficulty in his writing, he sleeps on it, and the problem which exercised him has resolved itself by the morning. Yes, I said, sleep leaves the brain refreshed. He said that wasn't quite what he meant, rather that the problem is worked out by the unconscious brain and the solution presented to him on waking. Surely not possible?

Saturday, 16th November

Today we lunched with the Richard Robinsons at the Old Mill, to see Julian Barrow's conversation piece of us two hanging. Visit spoiled by constant yelling of their child, a pretty little girl. I will never lunch again with my great-nephews, nor allow them to bring their bloody children to us. They can come and see us on their own, and I shall not go to their houses so long as their children are present.

Monday, 18th November

Tomorrow is our Ruby Wedding Day for which A. is making tremendous preparations, though we are merely having a few friends to dine. She said at breakfast how disappointed she had been by our honeymoon in November 1951, after that rather dismal wedding at Chelsea Registry Office, only attended, as I recall, by Harold and Vita, Freda and Lennox. We went to see my Aunt Deenie at Stow-on-the-Wold and then my mother, both in a bad way. Neither liked A. which put me in an embarrassed mood, I not having the character to rise above such things. Then we stayed the night at the Lygon Arms in Broadway [Worcestershire], whereas we should have gone abroad (in November?) to some delectable Mediterranean shore. It was a cloud upon our marriage, one of several that I now prefer not to dwell upon. She admitted that honeymoons were perhaps only really for young newlyweds, and we had after all enjoyed several 'pre-moons' during the preceding two or three years.

Tuesday, 19th November

We got out the best silver we have, scrubbed and polished, and prepared kitchen table for nine, rather a squash. Guests were the Droghedas, Michael and Isobel Briggs, Nicky and Susanna Johnston, and Caroline [Beaufort]. It went all right, except that A. was worn out before it began. Dinner held up because Derry, who came by road, had to meet Alexandra's train, which was late for some reason. Caroline sensibly slipped away without goodbyes; the others stayed until 11.30, too long; Droghedas staying the night upstairs. No memorable conversation. I dislike artificial celebrations on the whole. A matter between us, and I believe we are made happy by it.

Thursday, 28th November

To Hokusai* exhibition at Burlington House. I remember Raymond Mortimer once telling me that he was one of the world's great artists. I dare say he is, though few of his drawings or pen-and-ink sketches survive. A great many people viewing too few and too small exhibits, though I managed to get a general idea. How he must have enjoyed his pencil running away with his hand into Baroque waves and curls. How odd that at the furthermost ends of the earth this artist, quite unknown to artists in the West, was like them depicting flowers and waterfalls.

Richard Shone lunched at Brooks's. He is devastated not to have been left the slightest memento by Eardley, after all the years during which he strove to help him get some recognition for his paintings, which in truth R. considers worthless (though he admits they do have some admirers). Nevertheless he loved E. Ran into Fred Oppé who joined me to see the Toulouse-Lautrecs† at Hayward Gallery. Rare for me these days to go round an exhibition with another, and Fred's company was very welcome. For the first time I really appreciated this great artist. Unlike Renoir, whose models all have the same faces, Lautrec superbly portrays.

Friday, 29th November

Terence Morrison-Scott‡ has died. With his handsome face, cheerful smile, upright figure and distinguished presence, he was the perfect English gentleman, and always seemed to me immortal. Was my exact

---

* Japanese artist (1760–1849).
† Henri de Toulouse-Lautrec (1864–1901); French artist.
‡ Sir Terence Morrison-Scott (1908–91); Director, Science Museum (1956–60) and Natural Science Museum (1960–68); Eton contemporary of J.L.-M.

contemporary at Eton. I fear I wrote too gushing a letter to the widow, whom I met but once.

Saturday, 30th November

St Andrew's Day. Memories of watching from the Wall [at Eton] the boys' striped shirts so indistinguishable from mud, and through the sweaty, steamy air below, the scrum of odorous bodies.

We had a nice little luncheon party – Chrissy Gibbs, Colin Amery, Rosalind Morrison and Brigid Salmond. Had a long talk with Colin, who looks much older but is charming in an Anthony Blunt sort of way. Thinks few of the other art critics much good, Giles Auty* and Lord Gowrie† being exceptions. We talked of National Trust houses, for he is on the Arts Panel. Also chairman of Lutyens Society which has been given Goddards, where I once stayed with Christopher Gibbs, deceased.‡

Listened to one of the Reith Lectures, about how it was possible for scientists to believe in God. The lecturer explained that the feet of the common sparrow are a fraction shorter in the south of England than the north of Scotland – just as the black man in Africa is longer-legged than the white man in Europe, which explains why he runs faster. Some time in the nineteenth century, the sparrow was intro-duced to North America. Now, about a hundred generations later in sparrow terms, it has been discovered that identical differences in feet-size have developed between northern Canada and southern USA. I marvelled so much over this fascinating information that I fell asleep, only waking after the BBC had shut down.

Wednesday, 4th December

Selina lunched with me in Bath, on her way to see a daughter of W. W. Jacobs§ who was a childhood friend of Evelyn Waugh. She said there was no doubt that the aristocratic intelligentsia was the most

---

* Art critic of *Spectator*.
† Alexander Hore-Ruthven, 2nd Earl of Gowrie (b. 1939); Minister for the Arts, 1983–85; Chairman of Sotheby's, 1985–93; m. (2nd) 1974 Adelheid, Gräfin von der Schulenburg.
‡ See *Beneath a Waning Moon*, 7 June 1985.
§ Novelist and short story writer, author of *The Monkey's Paw* (1863–1943).

desirable milieu in the civilised world; that it was not snobbish to want an entry, but a sign of sensibility and intelligence. Well, we have all known that, but she put it in a charming and forceful way which surprised me. I said 'You were born into it.' No, she replied, for her father, though an earl, had little money and no country house.

I walked four miles by the Cherry Orchard last Sunday, and was not the least weary. Every inch of the way I was reminded of some incident with darling Folly. It was here that she returned to lick my face when I fell in the mud; there that she waited for me to wave my arms and show her the way whereupon she would turn a circle and bolt ahead. *Eheu lacrimae!*

Saturday, 14th December

This has not been a good week. Have a nasty cold caught forty-eight hours ago from Coote, who stayed a night. Can't think why she came; she stayed in bed the whole time, except for a few hours graciously bestowed in our hot sitting room, she streaming. I have been in a rush finishing off retyping and copying my MS which I take to Murray's on Wednesday. Actually I enjoy typing when fingers not too cold.

Am reading in Painter's biography of Proust about the frightful misunderstanding between Proust and his mother. She, knowing that death is not far off, wishes to warn him without alarming him, and asks brightly, 'If I were to go away for a long time, and possibly not return, how would you manage?' Fearing to confirm her anxiety, or show how much he would mind, P. replies in a casual way, 'I would do fine, I wouldn't turn a hair.' With the result that both were made miserable. A vain attempt to achieve content by downright lying. I must say I was unaware of the depths of Sodom to which Proust descended, the cruelty too.

Wednesday, 18th December

To London for the day, hoping not to be held up by bloody Irish terrorists who brought all rail traffic to a standstill day before yesterday. All went well. Dropped two heavy packages of MS at 50 Albemarle Street. If they turn it down, I don't think I shall mind all that much. Took my gold watch to a dear old man in South Molton Street who said he might be able to mend it if I didn't mind spending money on new parts. I said I would pay almost anything to have it going again;

a few years' reprieve, I begged. Lunched at Brooks's, at centre table upstairs. Joined by John Keffer who had bought his wife a Renaissance silver stirrup. He said now our dogs were dead there was no excuse for us not to stay with them in Sussex. He left and I was joined by Holland-Hibbert, who said, it is a frightful bore but I now have another name, Knutsford.* His mother was a Fenwick, sister of Constantia Arnold who is eighty-six and motors herself to shop in Chipping Norton. In London Library I was on my hands and knees at bottom shelf looking for a novel by George Gissing when a voice beside me said, Can I help? I said I was looking for the best-known of Gissing's novels, of which I had forgotten the title, though I would know it when I saw it. '*The Private Papers of Henry Ryecroft*,' he said instantly, and fetched it for me. He reminded me that I met him at Attingham this summer, where he was making an inventory of the miniatures, by name Walker.† Nice man.

At 5 I went to Misha's for a mug of tea to meet his friend Andrew Roberts,‡ author of *The Holy Fox*. Very clever young man indeed though nothing remarkable to look at, podgy with thin fair hair. Asked me if I thought Lord Halifax went to bed with Lady Alexandra Metcalfe. I shouldn't think so somehow, I replied. We talked of Professor Lindemann,§ for he is now writing about Churchill's entourage. Interested in Tom Mosley, the Avons,¶ etc. Very respectful, but plied me with questions I was unable to answer. Produced from his pocket a copy of Harold Vol. II. Would I sign? I suddenly couldn't remember if his name was Andrew Roberts or Robert Andrews, so left it out. He is a candidate for Brooks's and wants my signature.

---

* Michael Holland-Hibbert (b.1926); s. cousin as 6th Viscount Knutsford, 1986; High Sheriff of Devon, 1977–8; member of N.T. committees.

† See entry for 19 August 1991.

‡ Writer (b. 1963), who, like Michael Bloch, had lodged with the legendary landlady Sadie Barnett at 9 King's Parade, Cambridge; his biography of Edward Wood, 1st Earl of Halifax (1881–1959; Viceroy of India, 'appeasing' Foreign Secretary, wartime Ambassador to USA), *The Holy Fox*, had, to much acclaim, been published in 1991 by Weidenfeld & Nicolson.

§ Frederick Lindemann (1886–1957); German-born Oxford physics professor, scientific adviser to Winston Churchill; Paymaster General, 1942–5 and 1951–3; cr. Viscount Cherwell, 1956.

¶ Sir Anthony Eden (1897–1977); Conservative Prime Minister, 1955–57; m. (2nd) 1952 Clarissa Churchill (b. 1920), sister of J.L.-M's friend Johnnie Churchill; cr. Earl of Avon, 1957.

Thursday, 19th December

Grant McIntyre* rang me as soon as I arrived in Bath, to say he had read half of *Donors & Domains* in bed last night and is delighted with it. Looks forward to discussing it with me in new year. Well, this is the best Christmas greeting I could have had, and such a quick response too. Told M., who has had a similarly rapturous reception of the first half of his *Ribbentrop*. So both of us are pleased.

Friday, 20th December

To Bath Preservation Trust party at No. 1, Royal Crescent. While struggling with plate in one hand and glass of orangeade in other, I am cornered by that egregious bore Peter Greening, Chairman of Architecture Panel, who is a fervent Papist. Literally drives me into a corner and talks about his recent pilgrimage to tomb of Pope John XXIII, who is his hero, he says. 'He is not mine,' I say. 'I don't like him. He destroyed the Catholic Church with Vatican Council II.' He replies, 'At your dying hour I'm sure you will send for a Catholic priest.' 'No such thing,' I shout at him, adding that Vatican II and the IRA have destroyed any allegiance I might once have feigned. This may have been going a bit far, but to be spat upon by a man who has been guzzling garlic-drenched canapés is too much.

Sunday, 22nd December

While reading *Portrait of a Lady* – and I don't much care for the heroine Isabel – in a dreadful flash I suddenly saw no future whatsoever. My book is finished. I have no plans for another. The past stretches behind me longer than ever. The future is like an inch-long white ribbon before my nose.

Saturday, 28th December

Igor comes to stay on Christmas Eve. On Xmas Day, as we drive to luncheon at Stancombe, he asks, 'Are the Barlows aristocratic?' I tell him not to be snobbish, and that this is not a question one asks of anyone's friends. Interminable questions. 'How old are these

---

* Director of John Murray, 1987–2003, and J.L.-M's editor there (b. 1944).

Cotswold houses?' 'Do you think Tracy will make a good Duchess?' Having read my account of meeting and losing Theo[*] in that ridiculous book *Memorable Dinners*, he claims that he too has lost dozens of girls by writing his name and address on a piece of paper, failing to give it to the girl, and finding it in his pocket next day.

Today we lunch at Dyrham [Park, Gloucestershire] with the Mitchells, taking Igor who makes himself very agreeable, is well turned-out and looks distinguished even. The other guests the Peter Levis,[†] both of whom I like much. He has had a small stroke, but is mentally alert and full of anecdotes. Is three-quarters way through biography of Tennyson. She is plain, with projecting teeth like the eaves of a medieval cottage and eyes like a bloodhound's. She said that Robert Heber-Percy would never meet her husband, he was so anti-semitic. Horrible man he was.

---

[*] Mysterious man whom the young J.L.-M. (as recounted in *Another Self*) met in London and with whom he formed an instant romantic attachment – though they accidentally returned their exchanged addresses to each other in the course of parting embraces, so never met again.
[†] Peter Levi (1931–2000); Jesuit priest (to 1977), Oxford classics don, archaeologist, writer and poet; Professor of Poetry at Oxford, 1984–89; m. 1977 Deirdre *née* Craig, widow of Cyril Connolly.

1992

Wednesday, 1st January

I say *hares*, hear Big Ben strike, say *rabbits* and turn out the light. Then a night of terrible 'mares, though I ate little at dinner, and had but one glass of cider. In one of them, I find myself crossing the road in front of the V&A at snail's pace, clutching a little dog to my bosom. A very fast sports car suddenly hurtles towards me. I put out a desperate hand – and wake.

Sunday, 5th January

Margaret Anne Stuart staying at the House brings at midday a charming, cultivated Italian nobleman. We presume he is the new *beau*, though Caroline thinks he prefers men. The Mitchells lunch, and ask us why we do not rent the adjacent cottage for a couple to look after us. We ought to think of such things, for the time draws near.

Monday, 6th January

We hear from Elizabeth Longman that Chiquita Astor has suddenly died, having just returned from Argentina in the best of form. Poor good silly little Chiquita, whom we have known since her father was at the Embassy in Belgrave Square during the war.

We watch a film on TV about chimpanzees. These ugly little brutes are shown to be very family-minded, even sharing food with their favourite relations. Then there is the blood-lust which drives them to hunt rival monkeys, chasing them up trees and making them fall to the ground where their mates tear them limb from limb. A. loves these nature films, but I find them disturbing. As David Attenborough[*] says, we derive from these creatures, whose civilisation is just a step behind ours.

---

[*] Sir David Attenborough (b. 1926); broadcaster and naturalist.

Tuesday, 14th January

A. and I go to London together. Whereas her ticket for London only costs £27, mine to Chesterfield via London and back costs £24. Dotty.

To Brompton Oratory for Chiquita's requiem. Large congregation. So much to admire – the sumptuous colouring, the Baroque statues. Lovely music of Fauré. All in Latin; so much better not to understand the words but just follow the symbolism. At the end, a very old man read an address, not mentioned in the order of service. I just caught references to Chiquita's beauty as a young girl at the Argentine Embassy during the war, and to Emerald [Cunard],* and wondered if I knew the speaker. When I asked David Beaufort as we walked away together, he said, 'But it was Peter Quennell.'

Walked away to Cheyne Gardens to lunch with Isabel Napier.† She is eighty-six and a little woolly in the head, otherwise unchanged, Sunningdale 1930s. Bought a nice water-colour of hers for charity, a river in Scotland. Then to V&A to see exhibition 'The Art of Death'. Disappointing, mostly old prints, and the subject a little too near the bone.

We went to party given by [George] Weidenfeld‡ for Nigel Nicolson's seventy-fifth birthday, at long table in Groucho Club. I knew I would not enjoy it – hot, noisy, having to stand beforehand – but went for sake of A. I sat between Sue Baring and Ros's grandson Guy Philipps.§ Weidenfeld made a polished speech which I rather envied; and Nigel a witty reply, announcing that he was embarking on a biography of George III.

Wednesday, 15th January

To Chatsworth, where I am given a tiny bedroom on top floor overlooking court. Diana [Mosley] staying, with son Ali and wife Char.¶

---

* Maud Burke of San Francisco (1872–1948); m. 1895 Sir Bache Cunard; London hostess.
† See notes to 24 June 1988.
‡ Austrian-born publisher (b. 1919), who founded Weidenfeld & Nicolson with Nigel Nicolson in 1948; cr. life peer, 1976.
§ Hon. Guy Philipps (b. 1961); er s. of Hugo Philipps, 3rd Baron Milford (whom he succeeded as 4th Baron, 1999) and 'Mollie', Viscountess Norwich.
¶ Alexander Mosley (b. 1938); Paris publisher, er s. of Hon. Diana Mitford by her 2nd marriage to Sir Oswald Mosley; m. 1975 Charlotte Marten.

Ali delightful and extremely intelligent, though unacquainted with nature and the country, Debo says. Char busy editing Nancy [Mitford]'s letters, from eight thousand of which she must select five hundred or so. Is pretty, friendly, babyish manner, slightly affected and insinuating. Here I over-eat, sleep better than at home, and walk within the Kremlin walls.

Friday, 17th January

Two Sotheby's men lunch [at Chatsworth], James Mitchell, breezy and buoyant and telling me how pleased he is to renew an acquaintance which I have to dive into the memory to extract some clue to, and Lord Something Kerr,[*] small, docile man divorced from Grafton daughter. They leave after luncheon, and two visitors arrive for week-end, Dudley Poplak[†] and Lanto Synge.[‡] Former South African, decorator of the Prince of Wales's houses. He shows us photographs of a house near Cape Town he has just done up, which both Debo and I deem awful. He talks about reincarnation, his pet subject. Debo says the P. of W. is coming tomorrow, and asks me to stay on. I hesitate, saying I had better get home. Then regret missing opportunity to observe at close quarters.

Saturday, 18th January

Again at breakfast Debo says 'Why not stay on?' so I say yes, gladly. Truth is I don't want to be thought pushing where royalty is concerned.

After tea we all wait in the drawing room, uneasily. Escorted by Andrew and Debo, the Prince enters in breeches, stock and stockinged feet. Andrew whispers that he has had a good day [hunting], so thank goodness will be in a good temper. We stand in a circle. To me he says politely, 'Nice to see you again.' He proffers a hand, I grip fingers and bow. He subsides on to a sofa and whispers confidences to Debo. Then retires to change for dinner. We all rise, bow and curtsey,

---

[*] Lord Ralph Kerr (b. 1957), yr s. of 12th Marquess of Lothian; m. 1st 1980 (diss. 1987) Lady Virginia FitzRoy, dau. of 11th Duke of Grafton, 2nd 1988 Marie-Claire Black.
[†] Interior designer (b. 1930).
[‡] Antique dealer (b. 1945); great-nephew of J.M. Synge, Irish poet and playwright.

then relax. At dinner I sit between Synge, young-old man who has little to say to me, and Diana, fully engaged with Andrew. I hear the Prince opposite talking to Debo. When women leave the table, Dudley talks to the Prince about reincarnation, to Andrew's displeasure. Conversation turns to world situation. Prince laments that Christians are so disunited. Was upset by the outcry which prevented him accepting the Pope's invitation to attend a Catholic Mass. Says he dearly loves the Italians, 'who are so nice to me'. He seems harassed and unhappy; also shy, with nervous mannerisms. We move to yellow drawing room, where Debo has displayed John Webb drawings of Whitehall Palace and Henry VII's bible. We flip cursorily through these most precious things. Prince goes early to bed, whereupon everyone relaxes. There is no doubt that royalty causes constraint. When in my bath I decide that my remaining on here has not had much reward; that the last few hours have been of dross.

Sunday, 19th January

Henry [the butler] calls me at 8.15 to say that breakfast will be earlier this morning, at 8.45. I hurry. On my way down meet the Prince issuing from centre bedroom. We greet and walk to dining room. He hopes I slept well. I thank him, wish him the same, and add, 'I believe you had a good day yesterday, Sir.' He says Yes, and there were no 'antis' for a change. Breakfast of all the men, joined by Debo. She must have thought I was not asserting myself, for she said, 'Sir, we owe more to this man for the preservation of country houses than anyone.' For rest of breakfast we have a jolly talk. I feel this very sweet man is deadly serious and worries more about the devastation caused to the world's face than any other problem. He says he feels John Betjeman's mantle has fallen on his shoulders. This is rather touching, but alas he is too ignorant, groping for something which eludes. I somehow feel that all his interests and commitments and speeches and writings are too much for him, that he may have a breakdown. And the sadness of his marriage. No one to share thoughts with. After breakfast Andrew said that, had the Princess been present, we could never have had the interesting conversation we had this morning.

When I leave, Andrew accompanies me downstairs to front door, arm round my shoulder, and says I am always welcome at Chatsworth. Stands in the drive in the cold while Alan motors me off, waving arms, hands to lips. Alan carries my luggage to the platform, rather shocked that I am travelling third class.

Thursday, 23rd January

Dudley Poplak has sent me a book by George Trevelyan[*] on reincarnation and other psychic matters. A sort of erudite madness. The truth is I don't know how much I want to re-establish contact with friends of long ago. There would be little left in common, and juvenile links and affections would surely be outdated.

Monday, 27th January

Grant McIntyre lunched with me in Coffee Room at Brooks's. Very nice man indeed, young middle-aged, with second wife and four children. The expense of their education, he wailed. He is full of suggestions for the introduction I have to write to *Donors & Domains*. I like him so much. A tribute to Murray's.

Wednesday, 29th January

It is not from lack of admiration but I suppose lack of affection that I don't go to John Sparrow's[†] funeral in Oxford today. He always seemed to be there when I went to see Harold, who liked him much and respected his mind.

Saturday, 1st February

Sad time for A. who is losing Nick [Lambourne] the gardener. He leaves tomorrow for France where he has been appointed head gardener at Villandry,[‡] seven French gardeners under him. We had him to a farewell dinner on Wednesday. Though he looks frail and delicate, he is always on the brink of laughter, brisk in movement, quick as lightning and interesting to talk to.

---

[*] Sir George Trevelyan, 4th Bt (1906–96); er s. of Sir Charles Trevelyan, 3rd Bt, donor of Wallington to N.T.; furniture maker, Alexander teacher, schoolmaster, and Warden (1947–71) of Shropshire Adult College, Attingham Park; interested in the beyond.

[†] Warden of All Souls' College, Oxford, 1952–77 (1906–92).

[‡] Renaissance château with famous gardens in Indre-et-Loire.

Saw Churchill programme on TV. Odious man with his cigar, self-adulation and melodramatic rhetoric which sounds affected today. Tehran and Yalta disgraceful episodes, handing over Eastern Europe to Soviet empire.

I am upset by the baiting of the Queen. Horrid articles criticising her by all the intellectual commentators – John Grigg, A. N. Wilson,[*] Ludovic Kennedy, now even Hugh Massingberd in the *Spectator*, who complains that her courtiers are not of the stature of Stamfordham, etc. These people do not realise how destructive they are.

Thursday, 6th February

Renée Fedden is dead. When I tell Debo, she asks if R. 'liked the ladies'. I reply that she certainly liked one lady – Rosie Hinchingbrooke[†] – but after all, most people like something or other. Renée was inscrutable, with her handsome Levantine face and beguiling French accent. When Robin died we swore eternal friendship, but never saw each other again. She adored Robin, shared his mountaineering interests, kept up with him even after they separated. She was a great friend of the famous lady cooking writer.[‡]

My list of famous drunkards of my generation includes Evelyn Waugh, Henry Bath,[§] Patrick Kinross, Gavin Faringdon and Henry Yorke. Coote would not admit to me that they were more than heavy drinkers.

Friday, 7th February

Last night we watched the film about the Queen for the fortieth anniversary of her accession. She is perfection, with her little understated asides of wit, and such tact. Humorous, sensible, wise, wise. No intellectual could put up with her unenviable life. How lucky we are to have her.

---

[*] Writer and journalist (b. 1950); literary editor *Spectator*, 1981–4, *Evening Standard*, 1990–97.
[†] Rosemary Peto, artist (1916–98); m. 1934 (diss. 1958) Victor Montagu, Viscount Hinchingbrooke (1906–95), who succeeded 1962 as 10th Earl of Sandwich but disclaimed peerages, 1964; lived with Renée Fedden from 1974.
[‡] Elizabeth David (1913–92).
[§] Henry Thynne, 6th Marquess of Bath (1905–92); father of Duchess of Beaufort.

Tuesday, 25th February

We got back from our trip down the Nile yesterday, both utterly exhausted. Sunshine all the way, and not too hot. Excellent Cook's boat, with first-rate guide and scholarly Egyptian lecturer. The impression one gets is that Egypt is heading for disaster. Population increase appalling, one Egyptian born every second. Since our last visit in 1975 the building development along the banks of the Nile has increased tenfold. We moored at Luxor alongside 150 other boats. Tombs packed with sightseers, paintings and carvings suffering. And is the Nile drying up?

We made friends on the boat with delightful couple, John and Jill Horsman, who live and farm in Suffolk. He won the prize for the best-administered farm according to 'environmental' methods, and has inherited Drimnin in Glenmorven [on the Sound of Mull] from a widowed aunt, just as I inherited from Aunt Dorothy.* I told him that I used to walk to Mass in Drimnin when staying at Killundine when the Miss Gordons lived there. They invited us to stay at Drimnin in September. To my surprise, he said the Highlanders were by no means the honest and loyal dependants we supposed. They were idle, unreliable in the owner's absence, and resented all 'Sassenachs'. Surely things have changed, or was Aunt Dorothy rooked by the Macallum family?

Sunday, 1st March

St David's Day. What memories [of Rick Stewart-Jones] of more than fifty years. Today we were both taken by Daph[ne Fielding], in Caroline's car driven by Don the chauffeur, to Coote's eightieth birthday party in a vast restored barn near Wantage. In spite of 150 nice people, mostly friends and acquaintances, it was not very enjoyable. The wait awful, the din indescribable. I perched next to Sylvia Chancellor, looking splendid at ninety-one in brown two-piece with tall felt hat and veil. To my surprise I was seated on Coote's left at top table, Tony Martin on her right; I have never felt myself to be very intimate with her, but suppose I was the oldest man present. When

---

* J.L.-M.'s widowed aunt Dorothy Lees-Milne lived during the 1930s on the Killundine estate in Glenmorven, eventually moving to Ardachy House which she bequeathed to him on her death in 1965.

Dominick Harrod* approached, I said to Andrew Devonshire, 'That man ought to be Chancellor of the Exchequer.' Dominick replied that he kept propped on his desk a postcard I once sent him praising his intelligence and acumen. Andrew asked him what measures he would take if Chancellor. He said, lower taxes, lower interest rates.

Tuesday, 3rd March

This evening at about 6 I hear a blackbird; open front door and listen. It is calling its mate presumably, but such a song betokens spring and stirs something dormant within me, and makes me want to cry. The sound is of running water over pebbles.

Saturday, 7th March

We have the Hart-Davises and the Westmorlands to luncheon. I suspect poor David is not long for this life. He wheezes, and has to stand up to breathe. Duff is ghosting the autobiography of General de la Billière,† who he says is the nicest of men but no highbrow. He has to stop himself introducing learned quotations into the text. Duff stands to do well out of it, for the General is a national hero. He says Rupert is well and working on his next volume of autobiography.

We dine at the House. David [Beaufort] gloomy about world's future. Is sure that within a few years everyone who is 'comfortable' will need a permanent security guard, as in Brazil. Agrees that the great menace, next to the population explosion, is Muslim fundamentalism. Thinks the present Pope a remarkable man, who brought about the fall of world communism; but the irony is that the world is a more dangerous place than before the fall of the Iron Curtain, with nuclear proliferation, the rise of nationalism, and the flood of refugees from East to West.

On Tuesday 10 March, A.L.-M. felt unwell, with a pain in her left leg. The following day she felt worse, and became delirious. The L.-Ms' GP Dr King was summoned, and called for an ambulance to take her to the Bath Clinic,

---

* Journalist and broadcaster (b. 1940); Economics Editor, BBC Radio, 1979–93; s. of J.L.-M's old friend 'Billa', Lady Harrod.
† General Sir Peter de la Billière (b. 1934); Commander of British Forces in Gulf War of 1990–1.

where she was diagnosed as suffering from a streptococcus virus which had attacked her leg and kidneys and was threatening her heart. On the 12th she was transferred to the intensive care unit of the Royal United Hospital. She was now in a coma, and the doctor in charge put her chances of recovery at 50 per cent.

J.L.-M. had grown close to his wife in recent years, and was distraught at her sudden collapse and the thought that he might be about to lose her. He continued to keep his diary 'to mitigate somewhat the agonising worry . . . the worst misery I have ever endured'. For the next few weeks it consists largely of medical bulletins and accounts of her distressing condition, while noting the kindness and concern shown by many friends. On Sunday the 15th, the Vicar of Badminton said a Mass for her recovery. J.L.-M. was touched to see the Duke of Beaufort's mistress Miranda Morley among the tiny congregation: 'It is always the sinners who have the most generous souls.'

At this time of crisis, two women descended to stay with him at Essex House. The first was Freda Berkeley, herself widowed a year earlier, whom he welcomed as 'a pillar of strength and support'. Less welcome was his stepdaughter Clarissa, who returned from the South of France with her boyfriend Billy. 'Alas, alas, if only she could be kept away. But she must come, and I must receive her.' J.L.-M. had to admit that Clarissa was solicitous towards her mother, spending long hours at her bedside — though he thought it just as well that A.L.-M. was unconscious, as she would have been maddened by her daughter's baby-talk.

J.L.-M. had gone so far as to contact A.L.-M's solicitor and start thinking of funeral arrangements, when he was amazed to be telephoned by the hospital on the 21st with the news that she was 'waking' from her ten-day coma. He was still more amazed to find her sitting up and talking away in French, a language she had not spoken regularly for thirty years. 'The change is stupendous.' A few days later, however, she suffered a relapse. On the 26th the doctor warned that the virus was attacking the replacement heart valve installed two years earlier, and J.L.-M. would have to decide whether to authorise intensive treatment with antibiotics which risked leaving her brain-dead, or let things take their course. With a heavy heart, he chose the latter alternative, quoting in his diary

> Thou shalt not kill, but shouldst not strive
> Officiously to keep alive.*

---

* Arthur Hugh Clough, *The Last Decalogue* (J.L.-M. has changed the original 'needst' to 'shouldst').

That night he dined at Badminton House. 'David visibly upset, saying he had grown to love A. deeply . . . Not a cosy evening in spite of their sweet kind efforts.'

However, during the following days A.L.-M. again rallied remarkably, and by the beginning of April it looked as if she might recover to lead a reasonably normal life.

Thursday, 2nd April

The head-doctor Dr Hall saw her this morning, so I went to hospital with Freda to lie in wait. Imagine our amazement when he sallied out of her room to say, 'Well, it is almost a miracle. From death's door she is doing well. Heart and valve perfectly all right, also kidneys; the knee infection gone, the swelling being septicaemic arthritis. She can put on clothes tomorrow, and go to a convalescent home quite soon . . .' F. and I were *bouleversés*, not knowing what to feel or where to look, fearing to rejoice. When we got home I went for a two-mile walk along Luckington Lane, picking primroses growing in the ditches over the streamlets to take to A. next morning.

Friday, 3rd April

I take Freda to station. Never could I imagine a better friend or greater consolation in unhappiness than she. Then to A., complaining much and very sleepy. Sit beside her while she sleeps.

Grant McIntyre comes at 1 for a snack lunch. I surrender to him my corrected copy of N.T. book, now to be called by title of my original choice, *People & Places*. We go through the photographs with which he is pleased. I like this charming, shy, clever man more than ever.

Saturday, 4th April

To A. at 10, she demanding things I have not brought and rejecting those I have. Good signs. I arrange with her hairdresser to come tomorrow at 2.

Monday, 6th April

Mrs Weideger,* American lady writing about National Trust, called in Bath by appointment made before A's illness. Smart, well-dressed woman, bringing huge poodle on leash. Said that Commander Rawnsley† – the dreadful man is still active, it appears – criticises my period at the Trust for being 'obscured by homosexual and snobbish elements'. He also accuses Bobby Gore of supplying vintage wine to his upper class friends and plonk to lower grades. And Len Clark,‡ busybody on Trust committees, describes Robin [Fedden], Bobby and myself as 'courtiers of the establishment'. I have always been aware of having enemies in Trust circles.

The boyfriend Billy has gone into a deep depression; sits silently, head in hands, speechless, with curtains drawn, gazing at television and not taking in, a spectre at the table. Clarissa explains that such moods may last two months. Thank God they both leave tomorrow for a few days. C. is being very good with her mother I must admit. It is now my intention to devote my entire life to A., subordinating all other interests.

Wednesday, 8th April

A. is better still. Really in good form, reading letters of commiseration received during her illness, though too quickly to convince me that she properly takes them in. She had her first meal today of meat and veg. When I got home I walked for a mile up Luckington Lane to throw off cobwebs, and after supper listened to Vivaldi's Flute Concerto Op. 10, most wonderful.

---

* Her book was *Gilding the Acorn* (Simon & Schuster, 1994).
† Commander Conrad Rawnsley (1907–97), grandson of a co-founder of the N.T., and director of its successful 'Enterprise Neptune' to save a thousand miles of unspoilt coastline, had issued a violent public attack on the organisation in the autumn of 1966, claiming that it was run by aristocrats for aristocrats and ignored 'the leisure pursuits of the people as a whole'. He was heavily defeated when he proposed radical reforms to the N.T's constitution at an EGM in February 1967 – though his criticisms did encourage a trend of substantial changes over the ensuing years.
‡ He was the link between the N.T. and the Youth Hostel Association, and much appreciated by both institutions.

Friday, 10th April

This morning I turned on TV news to hear about the predicted Labour victory.* When they spoke of re-election of Tories, I at first thought a joke, and turned to wireless for confirmation. It just shows that the majority of the population is now middle-class aspirant, for it is the money in their pockets which governs the way people vote.

Saturday, 11th April

On leaving A., Freda and I drive to Castle Combe to dine with John Julius and Mollie [Norwich]. In the spring evening sunlight their little house is very enviable, set in its secret dell where no officious journalists or teasers can find him. J.J. says it is a treat to hear Princess Margaret sparking up the Queen. The Q. then plays Princess M. up, and both are incredibly funny and witty, parodying pompous royal pronouncements of long ago.

Monday, 13th April

Freda returns to London and I to my library. Feel desperately lonely. I realise that I was never lonely in the past because I knew A. was there twelve miles away and I was going to rejoin her in the evening. However I shall see her this evening in hospital. Finish letter-writing and think of beginning my piece on Sachie [Sitwell] for *DNB*.

Wednesday, 15th April

It was five weeks ago today that A. was taken to Bath Clinic. During the afternoon Princess Michael telephones, full of sympathy and asking me to lunch on Sunday at Nether Lypiatt. Charming of her and I accept, though it will be Easter Sunday.

Thursday, 16th April

Clarissa and Billy come to stay, self-invited. Over dinner I tell C. that her mother, now she is in full possession of her wits again, is irritated by her attitude, lovey-dovey stuff interlarded with endless 'darling

---

* The general election on 9 April confounded the pollsters by returning John Major's Conservatives to power with a majority of 11.

Mamas'. Clarissa bursts into tears and leaves the room. I am left with the boyfriend, who by way of making conversation asks me whether I don't think a little selfishness is a good thing. No, I say, any more than cruelty and spitefulness are good things.

Saturday, 18th April

At 1.20 Princess Michael rings me up in Bath to ask why I have not turned up for luncheon. Horrors! I grovel and say I thought she said Sunday; indeed, I was puzzled that she should have asked me on Easter Sunday. She is charming and assures me I will be welcome tomorrow, although they will have a large family party. Why do I get involved with these people? I have been reading her *Cupid and the King*. A poor show for a Royal to write such half-baked pseudo-porn.

Sunday, 19th April

I get to Nether Lypiatt with plenty of time to spare. A smiling young pansy butler greets and takes coat and ushers. Party consists of father, mother, son[*] and daughter;[†] also the Princess's mother, charming and distinguished Madame Zippari who talks little but listens. And a nice, jolly, bright American couturier called Roberto Devorik, friend of the family. Luncheon in dining room with rare plates in every panel of the white-painted wainscot. Princess kisses me and accepts peace-offering of expensive chocolates. 'Oh, more chocolates, how kind.' Indeed the table groaning with Easter eggs, chocolate rabbits, etc. The poor children bored throughout, as we sat from 1.30 to 4 while the Princess discoursed, almost lectured, on the subject of Mariolatry, how the rise of culture coincided with the enslavement of women and its fall with their emancipation, the current age of women's lib being the age of the yob. She quoted from Aristotle, early Church fathers, Renaissance sages, down to present day. Then told us about a book she is reading about the Duke of Clarence,[‡] suggesting that he did not

---

[*] Lord Frederick Windsor (b. 1979).
[†] Lady Gabriella Windsor (b. 1981).
[‡] HRH Prince Albert Victor, Duke of Clarence and Avondale (1864–92); er s. of Albert, Prince of Wales (the future King Edward VII); died soon after engagement to Princess May of Teck (the future Queen Mary). Much speculation has surrounded the demise of this weak and debauched character, who appeared far from suitable as future monarch.

die of typhoid as supposed but was murdered as he had secretly married a Roman Catholic. (How can they believe this tosh?) She gave me a copy to take away, along with two bottles of her own home-made jam. She is kind, well-intentioned and affectionate. But of course bossy, picks on daughter who may later turn against her. Boy is handsome and clever with excellent manners, hopes to get scholar-ship to Eton. Prince Michael adores the children who clearly worship him. We had everything but crackers on the table, a kind of mid-European, Orthodox Easter. Princess Michael still beautiful with remarkable clear skin and fair hair, very fresh and appealing. How good they were to welcome me, a comparative stranger, in their Easter midst.

Monday, 20th April

I reflect upon love, and how it can never be fully reciprocated. A child loves its mother without wishing to possess her. The mother loves her son knowing he can never respond in like measure. Of two lovers, one always fails to respond sufficiently to satisfy the other. In after years, the affection of one always falls off, leaving the other bereft. In age one grows apathetic. Is A. growing apathetic about life generally, and her hold on it? We talked this morning about the garden, and whether she wants the woman Andrea to come for one whole day or two half-days.

Dined tonight alone with the Westmorlands. I repeated what the Princess told me yesterday about the Duke of Clarence. David threw cold water on this by informing me that he had a collection of letters from the Duke to his great-grandmother Lady W. with whom he was passionately in love at the time he was engaged to Princess May. Would be happy to let me see these. David talked of the perilous state of the monarchy. If a referendum took place now, it would just scrape through; doubtful a generation hence. He feels the Queen ought to start paying tax on her private wealth, and subsidise the younger royals out of her pocket rather than the Civil List.*

---

* In December 1992 it was announced that the Queen had volunteered to pay income tax, details being worked out the following year between her representatives and the Conservative Government. She also agreed that the younger royals should henceforth be supported by herself rather than the Civil List.

Tuesday, 21st April

While I was sitting with A. this evening, a nurse told her that she could have her own room if she wanted. A. immediately said No, she preferred to stay where she was. Before this illness she would never have said such at thing. But the darling is right. She would be lonely shut up in a little room, whereas in the ward there is perpetual coming and going.

Friday, 24th April

So the days pass, one like another, no weekend breaks to punctuate. I go to Bath every day, see her in the morning and the evening, fetch the things she asks for, try to work during the afternoon in my library. I hold desperately on to my wits as a man holds on to his hat while crossing a desolate moor in a whirlwind. I am all right left to myself, but frustrated by the chores with which A. normally copes, especially dealing with gardeners. And I have hardly had the chance to look at the garden this glorious spring, with crown imperials fully out and even cowslips. It is no earthly pleasure to me, but has to be kept going for darling A., who may never see it again. I must not beef but count my blessings, as I used to say to myself during the war at times when the overhanging clouds seemed to darken every pleasure.

Saturday, 25th April

Derry motors from Combe and I take him to the hospital. A. really pleased to see him, and we talk. He has now rented Parkside for two years to rich Germans. I dine with the Norwiches. Mollie's second Philipps son,* immensely tall like his father, and perky girlfriend. John Julius says that George Dix is obsessed by his clothes. He leaves half a dozen suits in their house in London, and the same number in the houses of friends in other cities. He has his shirts washed by the shops which make them, and spends the greater part of his time visiting tailors, shirtmakers, and hosiers, and brushing and pressing what he has to hand.

---

* Hon. Roland Philipps (b. 1962); editorial director of Macmillan (later Managing Director of John Murray); he had in fact m. 1991 the 'perky' Felicity Rubinstein (b. 1958), literary agent.

Tuesday, 28th April

This morning I receive a letter from Prince Michael requesting advice
for a speech he is to make about the future of architecture to the Royal
Fine Arts Commission. Since they have been so kind to me I feel
obliged to comply. Besides I am glad to.

Francis Bacon is dead.* I always thought his subjects obscene, the
effluvia of a tortured mind. Yet his technique and juxtaposition of
colours superb. Jim Richards† also dead. Long obituary in *The Times*,
of which he was architectural critic. I always thought him a bit of a
fraud, with his sly, slushy way of speaking. He was a Marxist fellow-
traveller in the bad old days, and Betjeman teased him for that, which
he did not relish. He was always nice to me and wanted to talk about
Rick [Stewart-Jones], being one of the Cheyne Walk gang – 'that
refined brothel', as Robert [Byron] used to call it.

Nick [Robinson] came to dine. We had finished the shepherd's pie
and were about to begin on the strawberries when the telephone rang,
and a voice said that A. had had a fall, but I was not to worry. I said
that since they saw fit to tell me at 9.15, I did worry. Angelic Nick
motored me to the hospital where A. was fast asleep, face serene and
so pretty. We decided not to wake her. We left on tiptoe, I gulping
with sorrow, and returned to Badminton for cake and coffee.

*The following day, A. was moved to Malmesbury Hospital for her convales-
cence. This was an inconvenience for J.L.-M., involving as it did a twenty-five-
mile drive from Bath.*

Sunday, 3rd May

Freda and I lunched at Newark Park. Most boring party of architectural professors and dreary wives. F. said how lucky she considered
herself knowing the friends she does, and not these dry pedantics
whom fate might have thrown her amongst. How lucky we both are
to have friends such as John Julius, with his bright social manner and
banter.

---

* Artist (1909–92).
† Sir James Richards (1907–92); architectural critic, writer and historian; Architecture
Correspondent of *The Times*, 1947–71.

Thursday, 7th May

The doctor in Malmesbury reads me a letter from the doctor in Bath to say that A. now seems to have no infection of the leg or any other part, and he sees no reason why she should not in time recover to her condition before this devastating illness, and walk again. Almost too good to believe.

In state of elation I take train to Paddington for my first night in London for more than two months. Object of visit the Pavilion Opera's *L'Elisir d'amore* at Brooks's. I take Freda in lieu of poor A. Very good indeed, perhaps slightly too noisy for the small rooms. We then have a not very good dinner, sitting at a table with Lionel Sackville's brother and shy wife. Derek [Hill] came for a drink before Freda arrived, and catalogued the smart friends he had been consorting with.

Friday, 8th May

In the morning I go up the street to John Murray's to hand in final typescript to Gail Pirkis.* Why Gail, I ask, so cold, misty and Scandinavian? She says short for Abigail. Nice young woman, married with children, and good over punctuation. Extravagantly I buy expensive cardigan made of silky wool, and some French socks. Lunch alone at Brooks's. I catch an afternoon train and motor from Chippenham to Malmesbury. So I have not missed a single day's visit to A. since her illness began two months ago.

Saturday, 9th May

Derry telephones. I tell him that it worries me that A. doesn't read. He says she never *has* read. I think about this, and agree he is more or less right. He said his grandmother Drogheda never read a book in her life, and didn't need to. Some clever women don't, yet understand the things which we readers glean from books.

Saturday, 16th May

Lunched with Gerda at Stancombe. Nicky [Barlow] and Austrian friend present. The friend, very *racé*, is an artist, and showed us photographs of his works. I looked at the blotches, trying to identify. 'Limbs?' I queried. 'They are carpenters' tools,' he said. 'That's a

---

* Managing Editor, John Murray, 1987–2003 (b. 1957).

screwdriver.' It looked to me like a penis, and a rather horrid one at that. Gerda whispered to me, 'He's a prince, but doesn't use the title.' She is full of solicitude and affection.

I drove to Malmesbury and stayed about an hour. Then drove to Bath. Having opened door of flat I went to fetch something from motor. Front door slammed behind me, keys within. No other inmate present at No. 19. Had to motor home to Badminton to fetch spare keys. Then to Union Street for Clarissa's picture opening. One large room, formerly part of Owen & Owen's shop. Clarissa stunning in white dress. Paintings well-hung – Billy's work – but mostly rubbish. Young artists milling self-consciously. C. introduced 'my stepfather' to sub-editor of *Daily Telegraph*, one Connell.* I bought a little painting of three Turkish women like Byzantine icon, and left. Felt like Lady Catherine de Bourgh swanning in and out. When I got home I estimated I had motored more than 100 miles this afternoon.

Sunday, 17th May

Lunched with Elspeth [Huxley], who asked my advice. She had discovered that Peter Scott was passionately in love with a Cambridge friend called John. When John became engaged, Peter was distraught. He wrote to a third friend, Michael, that John's marriage meant the end of existence for him. John is still alive. Should Elspeth mention the affair in her biography? Should she reveal that her hero had feet of clay? But why clay, I asked. It makes him more human than I thought he was. One might have expected the affair to have been platonic in that pre-1914 way, although Peter's widow maintains this was not the case. However Elspeth does it, it is sure to be well done.

Tuesday, 19th May

James Methuen-Campbell† came to tea, bicycling from Corsham. He is a cousin of the dreaded John,‡ and great-nephew of Paul whose

---

* Jolyon Connell; deputy editor, *Sunday Telegraph*; subsequently founder and editor of *The Week*; m. 1989 Lady Alexandra Hay, sister of 24th Earl of Erroll.
† Grandson (b. 1952) of Hon. Robert Methuen (yst bro. of Paul, 4th Baron Methuen) and Hon. Olive Campbell (only dau. of 4th Baron Blythwood); inherited Corsham estate on death of John, 6th Baron Methuen, 1995; heir presumptive to 7th Baron Methuen from 1998; writer and musicologist.
‡ John, 6th Baron Methuen (1925–95); nephew of Paul; scouting enthusiast.

memory he venerates. Nice man of thirty-five, plain oval face reminding me of Terence O'Neill, similar self-deprecatory manner. Has been
music critic of *The Times* and other papers, and written a book on
Chopin. His biography of Denton Welch* comes out this autumn. He
met dozens of people who remember Denton, including a doctor
with whom D. was passionately in love. Doctor did not reciprocate,
but was fond of him. After D. died, doctor married a woman who
goes into a towering rage whenever D's name mentioned. Really, the
idiocy and jealousy of which women are capable.

Thursday, 21st May

I dined with the Morrisons. It would be difficult not to fall in love
with Rosalind if one were younger. She said the Lygons† had made
an offer for Madresfield (they already own a life interest in 60 per cent
of the contents) and the Danes had to decide whether to accept. If
they refuse, Ros will not have the chance of getting the estate for
another thirty years, the Danish grandson of old Lady Beauchamp‡
being still fairly young. If they do go to Madresfield they will sell this
house which they have made so delightful and pretty. They know few
people in Worcestershire, yet Ros longs for her native seat. Charlie
delighted to be free of Parliament. He conveyed good news that his
father§ is at last repairing the marvellous boathouse which Alderman
Beckford built at Fonthill and which I tried so hard years ago to get
this philistine old man to save from perdition.

---

* Novelist and diarist (1915–48).
† Probably a reference to the trustees of the estate of Rosalind's grandfather, 7th Earl
Beauchamp, the Lygons having died out in the male line.
‡ Else 'Mona' Schiwe (1895–1989); m. 1st C. P. Doronville de la Cour of Copenhagen
(d. 1924), 2nd 1936 Viscount Elmley MP of Madresfield Court, Worcestershire
(1903–79), who s. father 1938 as 8th and last Earl Beauchamp; her only child was a daugh-
ter by 1st marriage.
§ John Morrison (1906–96) of Fonthill House, Wiltshire; Conservative politician, MP for
Salisbury, 1942–64, Chairman of 1922 Committee, 1955–64; MFH, 1932–65; m. 1928
Hon. Margaret Smith (d. 1980), yr dau. of 2nd Viscount Hambleden; cr. Baron
Margadale, 1964.

Friday, 22nd May

A. home at last after ten weeks, driven from Malmesbury by efficient lady officer called Bridget. I pushed her in her wheelchair around the garden, which looked green and lush and I think pleased her. Not only is she immobile, but she can do practically nothing for herself. Things are out of reach, telephone has to be answered by me and she asked if she wishes to speak. By end of day I was absolutely whacked, having gone up and down stairs a million times. Dreadful to admit, but by 10 p.m. I showed irritability, and told her she was very demanding. Awful of me, but true.

Tuesday, 26th May

Tropical weather for past week. A. doing wonderfully. I have to recognise that I am no longer an independent being. My day begins at 7.15 when I rise, draw back her blinds, empty her commode, descend to fetch her orange juice. Having shaved and dressed myself I boil her egg, lay tray, carry her breakfast up to her in bed. Then dear Peggy comes and gives her a bath.

Saturday, 30th May

And so the days go on. Dreadful for her not to be able to fetch a book from a shelf, a cushion to sit on the terrace, anything. I confess there are moments when the devil gets into me and I am tempted to take revenge on her in little ways. I lack all intellectual stimulus, and physical exercise apart from endless climbing of stairs. I am miserable at not being able to get down to work. In between her calls for aid I have been trying to finish Sachie's *DNB* entry. Much trouble to make it concise. I asked the editor to allow me more than 750 words; she has conceded 900, but I have still not got down to that figure. Am sending draft to Francis [Sitwell] to check.

Tuesday, 2nd June

To London for the day. In morning to exhibition of Sickert and followers at Parkin Gallery. Sickerts far beyond my pocket, but was temped by a Sylvia Gosse* drawing for £325, and Lord Clare's lock

---

* English artist (1881–1968).

of Byron's hair. Guillaume Villeneuve and Hugh Massingberd lunched with me at Brooks's. The former very proud to meet the latter, asking him if he had a book he wanted translated. Hugh looking healthy and wise. Is very upset about Brympton d'Evercy, Ponsonby-Fane* having told him he is obliged to throw in the sponge. Hugh minds more about this magical place than any house left in private hands.

Had to dismiss Hugh to go to Murray's. We settled all the illustrations, which will be quite fun I think. Jock breezed in, having just spoken to Bevis Hillier about Vol. 2 of his Betjeman.[†] J.B's womenfolk very proprietary of his reputation, and extremely jealous both of each other and poor Bevis.

Wednesday, 3rd June

Susanna Johnston came to tea. A. who used to hate the beverage now clamours for it at 4.30. Susanna told the following tale about the eccentricity of rich women. Drue Heinz[‡] has bought Old Fyfield Manor, three miles from the Johnstons. S. had Steven Runciman staying, and invited Mrs H. to dinner, supposing she was at Fyfield. In fact she was at her London house, but accepted, and was motored by her chauffeur. First thing next morning the Johnstons' daily woman discovered handkerchief embroidered with ladybirds under the chair on which Mrs H. had been sitting. A moment later, Mrs H. rang up, to say she had left it behind and ask if S. would have it delivered to her at Heathrow at 11.30. S. replied that she had no chauffeur, but would send it by post. Mrs H. protested that she never went anywhere without the handkerchief, which protected her from misfortune, but S. did not relent. On her return, Mrs H. telephoned to say that every misfortune had indeed befallen her; she had mislaid her ticket and broken her leg.

---

* Charles Edward Brabazon Clive-Ponsonby-Fane (b. 1941); m. Judy Bushby. As related in his book *We Started a Stately Home*, he and his wife valiantly restored his family seat of Brympton d'Evercy, Somerset after it had been vacated by a girls' school, and tried to run it as a tourist attraction, but were finally obliged to sell.

† Published 2002 as *John Betjeman: New Fame, New Love*.

‡ Drue Maher; m. 1953 as his 2nd wife Jack Heinz II (1908–87), Chairman of international food company H. J. Heinz; benefactress of literature and the arts.

Thursday, 4th June

Misha has seen the rival biography of Ribbentrop, though it is not out for another month. It is unbelievably bad, and M. suspects Weidenfeld are publishing it out of spite after M. removed his own book from them and took it to another publisher. M's *Ribbentrop* is to be published on the same day as my N.T. book – 22nd October.

Friday, 5th June

The population explosion has suddenly become a fashionable topic, whereas until recently it was unmentionable. I have been trying to warn about it for years, but we Leeses are not good at making our voices heard. My grandfather refused a baronetcy for fear he would have to make speeches; my father and uncle claimed to have discovered the principle of wireless telegraphy at Crompton, but failed to follow it up.

Selina dropped in to tea. Told us that friends of hers, newly married couple, went to stay at Stanway,* where they discovered a bunch of whips and some razor blades spread on the pillows.

Friday, 12th June

Very sad to read obituary of Shelia Birkenhead.† She was the nicest woman in the world, with whom I used to sit on the Keats–Shelley Committee. Plain but always smiling, genial and clever with the talent of making everyone feel they were a success. She wrote some good books. Adored Freddie and their son Robin,‡ and never quite got over the latter's sudden death while playing rackets.

Reading the biography of Peter Pears, I am amazed by his relationship with Britten. They were both professional partners and lovers, and achieved the ideal union of mutual interests and passion. Each contributed to the other's prowess and fame.

---

* Lord Neidpath's house in Gloucestershire.
† Hon. Sheila Berry (1913–92), dau. of 1st Viscount Camrose; m. 1935 Frederick Smith, 2nd Earl of Birkenhead (1907–75); Chairman of Keats–Shelley Association, 1977–92.
‡ Robin Smith (1936–1985); s. father as 3rd and last Earl of Birkenhead, 1975.

Sunday, 14th June

We lunched at the House, A's first meal away from home. She walked from the motor through the House to the east lawn where we ate under two enormous umbrellas. Unfortunately David lost his temper with Caroline for muddling the seating arrangements. C. said not a word in return, and we shunted round, looking down our noses at our feet. My neighbour, friend of Anne and Matthew [Carr], said that a famous New York decorator had had a room copied from my library in Bath. Must have been from Julian Barrow's painting, I think.

A's sole interest is now the garden – her own, not others'. She doesn't seem interested in anything else. She sits with a pad on her knees, making notes of orders to give the gardeners.

Monday, 22nd June

Midsummer already, but cold. Went to London to return corrected proofs to Murray, along with postscript. So the book is at last done. Young John came into the room and made polite conversation, saying he had read and enjoyed. Then J.K.-B. and Jamie Fergusson lunched at Brooks's, not a great success. Jamie, very spruce in new suit and haircut, thought Murray's were in a precarious condition and living on expectations from Paddy L. F. I fear Jim L.-M. will not help them much. Their great asset is their freehold of No. 50. How tragic if they had to sell.*

Wednesday, 24th June

Hugh Massingberd rang to announce that Johnnie Churchill died yesterday, and ask if I would write a short appreciation. Dear Johnnie, so eccentric and absurd. What memories – of Didbrook and Stanway in 1928,† and Rome in 1931 during the royal wedding.‡ We used to laugh endlessly. He never grew up. Was always clowning, 'the

---

* In 2002, the family sold the firm (to Hodder Headline) and kept the house.

† As J.L.-M. relates in *Another Self*, he and Johnnie Churchill crammed for Oxford with the eccentric Vicar of Didbrook and Stanway, 'benefices in the patronage of Lord Wemyss'.

‡ Presumably the marriage on 8 January 1930 of Prince Umberto, only son of King Victor Emmanuel III of Italy, to Princess Marie José, only dau. of King Albert of the Belgians.

parlour-trick man' as Lady Chetwode called him. He irritated my
father at tennis, for he would not take the game seriously, yet generally won. Always signed his letters to me 'Chunluli' after some foreign
hotel porter's misreading of his surname. He was affectionate and
unwise; a gallant lover; a terrible boozer which made him difficult to
meet in later years, for he would embarrass one in a stuffy club with
his outrageous behaviour. Yet his blue eyes spelt honesty and courage.
(His uncle Winston once assured me he was full of guile, but I didn't
then and don't now believe it.)

Tuesday, 30th June

Motored in terrific heat to Johnnie's funeral at Bladon [by Blenheim
Palace, Oxfordshire]. Church full of strangers in dark suits. No familiar face. Goodish address. Two Crewe grandchildren read extracts, but
too hurriedly, as if wanting to be done. Followed coffin to graveyard,
passing graves of Lord Randolph, Winston and our Randolph,* all
with placards for convenience of tourists. Johnny buried against far
wall next to his last love. I could not face beano at The Bear,
Woodstock. Instead drove to Asthall to look at the Manor, so beautiful looming over the Norman church. Then stopped at Swinbrook to
see Tom [Mitford]'s memorial, 'a very perfect son and brother', and
Nancy's little gravestone, her name and mole insignia almost obliterated by moss and elements.†

Wednesday, 1st July

Today the *Sunday Telegraph* asked me for a paragraph on my favourite
country house. I said that I would have chosen Stanway, had not Hugh
Massingberd already praised it last Saturday; instead selected Moccas

---

* Lord Randolph Churchill (1849–95), yr s. of 7th Duke of Marlborough, Conservative
politician; his son Sir Winston (1874–1965), Prime Minister and indomitable war leader;
Sir Winston's only son Randolph (1911–66), J.L.-M's Eton and Oxford contemporary.
† Two Oxfordshire properties inhabited by Mitford family between the wars. In 1919 2nd
Baron Redesdale bought the Jacobean Asthall Manor on the river Windrush, where
J.L.-M. stayed as a schoolboy with his friend Tom. It was sold in 1926, and Lord Redesdale
built Swinbrook House, described by his grandson Jonathan Guinness as 'an unremark-
able, rather insipid square building in Cotswold stone, such as councillors might have
erected as a cottage hospital' (*The House of Mitford*, p. 289). It was sold in 1938.

[Court, Herefordshire] for its remoteness and melancholy. I wrote rather a silly letter to Sally [Ashburton],* excusing myself for having been such a hopeless godfather. Explained that her christening and upbringing in the C. of E. coincided with my becoming a Catholic. As I subsequently left the R.C. church, this hardly justifies my neglect.

Friday, 3rd July

Spent much of the day in Bath pasting old snapshots of Johnnie Churchill into my photograph book. When I got home, Thomas Messel rang to announce that Anne Rosse died at midday. Heart attack, aged ninety. No surprise, nor do I feel any particular sadness. Funeral next Thursday at Womersley [Park, near Doncaster], all arranged by Anne. A. mentioned that Hugh Massingberd had rung earlier, doubtless wanting an obituary. A., who never liked her, said I would have lots to write, mentioning her considerable horticultural knowledge, and sparkling personality which could never be ignored. Yes, I said, but I hope I won't be asked.

Saturday, 4th July

Motored with A. to Moorwood for cosy tea with Henry in the kitchen. Very nice being alone with him, Suzy having taken the children to a party. We both enjoyed it. Moorwood is a real family house with an attractive air of well-being. Nice family portraits. Children's toys and dogs give a dishevelled feel. On the way there we stopped at Bagendon churchyard to see the stone Dale has raised over Audrey's grave. Very good shape and lettering, altogether full marks. Next to Prue's, already rendered illegible by lichen. No matter, can be cleaned off.

Monday, 6th July

Drove with A. to Mary Keen's rectory at Duntisbourne Rous. Woman came over, and reminisced about Biddesden† and Roland

---

* Sarah ('Sally') Churchill (b. 1935); o. dau. of Johnnie Churchill and Angela Culme-Seymour; goddaughter of J.L.-M.; m. 1st 1957 James Colin Crewe, 2nd 1987 John Baring, 7th Baron Ashburton.
† Biddesden House near Andover, Wiltshire, where Diana Mitford lived during her marriage to Bryan Guinness.

Pym* painting there for Bryan [Guinness]. Rectory has austere late Georgian front with amusing not-in-keeping porch by Gambier-Parry† who lived here. Plain rooms inside. Mary showed me the adorable little Saxon church behind the house, a real gem (seen before) with strange undercroft entered from outside, now under chancel. Was it an earlier church, built over, like Santa Maria in Cosmedin, and that over a catacomb? Were the first churches in this country at all like the Roman? Mary a sensitive, calm, no-nonsense, intelligent, undemanding woman, with much charm for me. Her son William,‡ down from Oxford, likewise charming. Is playing Hamlet with OUDS§ in Edinburgh next month, but has decided against stage career because actors are such tiresome people. The country round here too beautiful for words, and this hamlet quite unspoilt.

On our return the telephone rang. Jamie Fergusson. 'How are you, Jim?' 'I know what you are wanting.' Yes, an obit. of Anne Rosse immediately. Couldn't say no.

Tuesday, 7th July

This morning's paper reports that Bryan Moyne, of whom I was speaking yesterday with his ex-sister-in-law, has died suddenly. A good and gentle husband – too gentle for Diana – whom it was impossible not to like. He was a great patron of writers and artists. Sad that he himself never created anything of substance. Produced far too many children, but since they were all beautiful and well-bred he may be forgiven.

Wednesday, 8th July

To Eton for the day to meet Michael Meredith,¶ who met me on the steps of Timbrall's House (which was Slater's when I was up, and has been much improved since then). Delightful man, bachelor house

---

* Old Etonian bachelor artist (b. 1910).
† Thomas Gambier-Parry (1816–88), collector of 14th- and 15th-century Italian art, whose grandson donated much of his collection to Courtauld Institute.
‡ William Walter Maurice Keen (b. 1970).
§ Oxford University Dramatic Society.
¶ Head of English, housemaster, and School (later College) Librarian at Eton (b. 1936); President of Browning Society.

master, brimming with enthusiasm and a great expert on literary anecdotes and holographs. Has formed the finest collection of Browningiana, including rare photographs and possessions of the poet, all paid for out of his income as a schoolmaster. Boys away on holiday, for which I was glad. He gave me luncheon in the cheerful dining room. He said that Martin Charteris and Eric Anderson formed a perfect combination the like of which Eton may never see again. Why, I asked, was Martin so remarkable? Because of his enthusiasm, and wise adoption of all good schemes. Meredith seemed genuinely delighted with my gift of lockets of Byron's and Dickens's hair, and especially with the authenticating letters from Augusta Leigh and Georgina Hogarth. By the time we had seen the School Library and looked at the treasures he had kindly got out to show me, it was 4.30 and time to return.

An enjoyable visit and I feel I have found a new friend. Meredith is not an Etonian himself I fancy, though he is dedicated to the school, and has undoubtedly done wonders for the Library, which he loves. Said his brother was a master at Stowe, where they have had much trouble since the school went co-educational. When girls get to sixteen or seventeen they become tiresomely flirtatious and cause much mischief; sex behind bushes and abortions ensue. Luckily Eton has not yet committed itself, the Headmaster against.

Thursday, 9th July

To Anne Rosse's funeral at Womersley, the *Independent* having published my obituary yesterday which I fear the family will not have liked overmuch. By train to Doncaster with the Thomas Messels, from where we taxied to Womersley, where mourners assembled for stand-up luncheon. Martin* looking like Mervyn the Badminton gamekeeper, florid-faced, thickset and boisterous in charming puppylike way; William Rosse† by contrast frail and slight, and very Irish. Having not seen them for so long, I had little to say to them, though they were very sweet to me. Lucy Snowdon a darling, and William's

---

* Hon. Martin Parsons (b. 1938); yr s. of 6th Earl of Rosse and Anne Messel; lived at Womersley.
† William Brendan Parsons, 7th Earl of Rosse (b. 1936); er s. of 6th Earl and Anne Messel.

wife nice and unassuming. Service done in great theatrical style of which I approved. Tony [Snowdon] had arranged a marvellous display of white flowers in front of the Bodley roodscreen. Two priests, one Irish swinging a censer. Anne's coffin invisible under a golden pall smothered with wreaths and raised on a catafalque. Three lessons read by the three sons, all beautifully. John Cornforth gave a long address of which I heard little, being the far side of the nave. People said it was good, but what I heard sounded rather conventional to me. He is a stiff pudding. Six young men, one a grandson wearing pony tail, carried the coffin slowly down the nave through the west door, across the graveyard into the grounds of the house, where they put it into the hearse, a handsome, streamlined, modern motor. From her own front door Anne was driven away for the last time, with great dignity and in total silence. Moving moment.

This sympathetic, unknown, beautiful, simple old house within its white limestone park walls has no land left to speak of, and is too large one would suppose for the impoverished Martin and his family. I shall never go there again. I had a last look at Anne's little boudoir wherein she lived during the war, with Oliver's dazzling portrait of her, and the great, stiff, rather gloomy neoclassical room redolent of 'that splendid monster Lois', as Anne's friend Phoebe Davis described Lady de Vesci.[*]

Friday, 10th July

Michael Meredith told me that much has lately been discovered about Shelley's time at Eton. Far from being miserable as Medwin[†] would have us believe, he was happy and led a normal boy's life. He fought other boys in that horrible way which was then expected, and won a fight against a boy whose father was a tailor. I said fights were not expected in my time. He said they had ceased in the mid nineteenth century. Sometimes boys fought each other to the death.

---

[*] Lois Lister-Kaye (1882–1984); m. 1st 1905 5th Earl of Rosse (d. 1918), 2nd 1920 5th Viscount de Vesci (d. 1958); mother of Michael, 6th Earl of Rosse (d. 1979).
[†] Thomas Medwin (1788–1869); cousin and biographer of Shelley.

Sunday, 12th July

At luncheon, Caroline spoke of her father's[*] death and funeral. When he knew he was dying, he ordered the doctor, 'Slaughter me, slaughter me!' He was buried, according to his directions, in an orange-coloured shirt. He also directed that he should not be cremated in an expensive wooden coffin with elaborate fittings, but wrapped in a sack. In the end they put him in a coffin made of inexpensive, hewn wood. He also wanted his hearse to be driven at not less than 60 m.p.h. to the crematorium, but the undertakers refused, deeply shocked. The mourners tried to capture the spirit by weaving about the hearse in their own cars.

All Thynnes are wildly eccentric, Alexander[†] perhaps more than the others. C. says that, having sacked his brother,[‡] he will undoubtedly do strange things to the house. Some years ago he sent her an extract of his much-vaunted autobiography accusing her of permanently harming his whole psyche by bossing him in childhood. He asked her to sign a document agreeing not to sue him for defamation, which she gladly did. She says he is not a bad fellow, and passionate about his beliefs and theories; would go to the stake for them, rubbish though they be. I confess I find the Thynne antics very unfunny and silly. Caroline is crazy too, for at sixty-four she has committed herself to going on an Outward Bound course involving such hair-raising feats as being suspended on a rope across a precipice.

Anne had the distinction of having two sons who were earls and three grandsons who were viscounts or barons at her funeral, along with ladies and hons galore.

Tuesday, 14th July

Two obituaries today. I was at Magdalen with Peter Greenham[§] and suppose knew him fairly well. He was a dim figure then, and remained

---

[*] Henry, 6th Marquess of Bath, had died on 30 June.

[†] Alexander Thynne, formerly Earl of Weymouth, now 7th Marquess of Bath (b. 1932). Brilliant and beautiful in youth, he became the country's most publicised eccentric, preaching free love and naturism, founding the Wessex Regional Party, becoming a rock musician, writing curious books, and filling the Elizabethan rooms of Longleat, Wiltshire with modern murals.

[‡] Lord Christopher Thynne had been managing the house and estate.

[§] Keeper of Royal Academy Schools, 1965–84 (1909–92).

dim in spite of his renown, for he became a very decent portrait painter. Pierrepoint* the hangman took a totally dispassionate view of his trade, for after all the decision to hang his victims was none of his doing. After his retirement, he pronounced himself against the death penalty.

Wednesday, 15th July

A party of Irish ladies came to see the garden. They were most appreciative. One of them said to me, 'This of course is the house where *Winnie the Pooh* was written.' I had to tell her that regretfully this was not the case, nor was I Christopher Robin.[†] I heard one lady ask another 'Who are they?', to get the reply, 'They made their money out of tassels.' Tassels is rather nice; but *what* money?

Sunday, 19th July

From Mr Carter's nice little bookshop closing down in Chipping Sodbury I bought a copy of my father-in-law's[‡] anthology for the troops, *Word from Home*. The epilogue is a poem by Newbolt called 'The Toy Band', incorrectly dated pre-1914 and celebrating the General's penny whistle escapade. Full of phrases like 'Fall in, fall in!', 'Follow the fife and drum!', 'Rubadub!', 'Wheedle-deedle-dee' and 'Come, boys, come!', which make one blush.

Monday, 20th July

These days, I find I can seldom discuss a subject with A. which is not concerned with our household affairs. She seems not to listen if I try to talk about anything else. Or rather, she is not interested in anything apart from the garden and her grandchildren, of which I can only admire the first and am bored and irritated by the second.

---

* Albert Pierrepoint (1905–92); most prolific British hangman of 20th century. A Yorkshireman, he came from a long line of executioners and hanged an estimated five hundred men and women between 1932 and 1956.

† They were presumably confusing J.L.-M. with the son of the children's writer A. A. Milne (1882–1956).

‡ Lieut.-Gen. Sir Tom Bridges (1871–1939); Governor of South Australia, 1922–7; m. 1907 (as her 2nd husband) Janet *née* Menzies. On the Western Front he once restored the morale of his exhausted troops with the aid of a penny whistle bought in a village shop.

I was appalled reading through a box of my articles and reviews recently. Pompous, jejune, middlebrow, stilted they are. I wish I could destroy every word I have written. As for my hated diaries, the BBC want my consent to a reading from them in August. I have asked Bruce Hunter to find out what extracts they want to use before agreeing.

Wednesday, 22nd July

I went to see Joan Cochemé in London this afternoon. Greeted by well-powdered, still pretty face. She is rising ninety, Eardley's contemporary, and seemed as pleased as I was to meet again. Said that E's painting was absolute rubbish, no good at all. Shamefully sad he never learned to improve. He never forgave her for withholding praise from his pictures. I said I went through same experience. Talked of Bloomsbury, of which she was a fringe member. Couldn't bear the squalid side of their life-style. Said Gerald Brenan* a dreadful pig of a man, lusting after young girls including his own children. Didn't care for Ralph Partridge,† who disliked his son Burgo.‡ Joan claimed to be as deaf as a post, yet missed not a word. And to be totally blind, though she noticed me glancing at my wristwatch.

Tuesday, 28th July

In London today I went to three exhibitions. First Edward Bawden,§ who disappointed a bit. He was a poster painter, which I had not realised; industrial designs for Shell and other firms, almost naïve and always clear-cut. A good influence on followers of this genre. Exhibition a tribute from his friends who thought the world of him. Then Marevna¶ at Wildenstein's, Russian contemporary of Picasso. Pointillist paintings of a faded nature. Dotty, like all Russians in exile.

---

* Bloomsbury Group writer of works on Spanish literature (1894–1987).

† Reginald 'Ralph' Partridge, MC (1894–1960); Bloomsbury personality, loved by Lytton Strachey; author of *A History of Criminal Lunacy and its Problems* (1953); m. 1st 1921 Dora Carrington, 2nd 1933 Frances Marshall.

‡ Burgo Partridge (1935–63); o. s. of Ralph and Frances Partridge; author of *A History of Orgies* (1958); m. 1962 Henrietta Garnett.

§ Edward Bawden (1903–89); English artist.

¶ Maria Vorobieva Marevna (1892–1984); Russian artist.

She led a louche life in Paris, tossed from lap to lap. Then in afternoon to Sisley at Burlington House. Admirable. Early paintings dark
and classical; gradually become impressionistic, almost of the calibre
of Monet. Very fascinating the group of nine paintings of the church
in his home town, in sun and rain, at dawn, midday and evening.

Wednesday, 29th July

M. telephoned to tell me about his new Norwegian actor friend,*
who is more beautiful than the dawn. The usual thing. I urged him
to visit the Sisley exhibition, but the name meant nothing to him. M.
is the only friend I have had who cannot share my artistic interests,
which causes a great lacuna in our relationship. In an arrogant sort of
way, I assume that every cultivated man has such interests. My rela-
tives, apart from Nick, do not, so I have little in common with them.

Friday, 31st July

Simon [Lees-Milne] motored to lunch with me in Bath. He brought
me a splendid cake for my birthday with our crest on top, done from
a butter-pat matrix of my grandfather's. He was extremely friendly as
always, sensible and nice. I admire his pertinacity. When he was made
redundant a few years ago, he suddenly remembered he had inherited
a number of ground rents in Lancashire and decided he must investigate them all. They turned out to include four acres of derelict land
near Oldham which were, as they say, 'ripe for development'. He had
a job to prove his entitlement, but did so after producing a deed dating
from James I's reign granting the land to our Lees ancestor. Even after
capital gains tax, it produced enough money for Simon's retirement.
He is blissfully happy and as busy as a bee caring for his house, garden,
wife and mother.

Tuesday, 4th August

An odd dream last night. I was at a huge conference and had no shoes.
So went to Harold Nicolson's room and took a pair of smart, shiny

---

* Morten Röhrt (b. 1954); actor with National Theatre, Oslo; first cousin twice removed
of Edvard Munch, Norwegian artist.

chestnut shoes (such as Harold never wore) and was arrested by a detective. I protested that I knew Harold well and he would not want to press charges. The detective was unmoved and began an investigation, as a result of which the opening of the conference was delayed. All the assembled speakers furious, and Harold nonplussed. Dream may relate to some trouble I have been having with middle toe of my right foot.

I have been reading Leonard Cheshire's[*] obituary. It is something to have been both VC and OM. I met him at Staunton Harold[†] when he was negotiating to take over the house from the old Ferrers.[‡] He was ascetic and unapproachable, and seemed aesthetically indifferent to my efforts to preserve the house. Totally humourless I would guess, like his wife whom I did not take to when we once met at Sally Westminster's.[§]

Thursday, 6th August

My birthday. A shock to see announced in *The Times* and *Telegraph* that I am eighty-four. A most beautiful day, with just a suspicion of crisp lawn, and slanting golden sunshine. I motored to Wickhamford with A. and Clarissa. While A. remained in the car I made C. climb the gate to the field facing the manor and we walked to the hedge between field and pond. She seemed to enjoy this, and when we went round to the church she claimed to be overwhelmed by the beauty of the nave and monuments. Door still kept unlocked. How much longer before the tombs are vandalised? The tranquillity of the graveyard. I think I would like my ashes scattered here.

At dinner, Clarissa announced to us both that she was considering marriage to Billy. What did we think? A. said she thought it a good idea. I said Billy was too unstable, with the full moon and all. A. later came round to my opinion and said that on reflection she opposed the marriage. C. will pay no heed of course. Why should she?

---

[*] Group Captain Leonard Cheshire (1917–92; VC 1944; OM 1981; Life Peer, 1991); wartime hero of RAF Bomber Command; founder (1948) of Cheshire Homes for the Disabled; m. 1959 Sue Ryder.
[†] Leicestershire seat of Shirley family. After a spell as a Cheshire Home, it is now (2004) being restored by the Blount family and opened to the public.
[‡] Robert Shirley, 12th Earl Ferrers (1894–1954); m. 1922 Hermione Morley.
[§] *Beneath a Waning Moon*, 29 June 1985.

Saturday, 8th August

David Westmorland has had a stroke, paralysing him down one side and depriving him of speech. We are distressed, they having been so kind to us during our trouble.

Friday, 14th August

Ian Dixon drives us to Chatsworth, where Debo presses him to stay to tea. This he does not do, I imagine from shyness. I accompany him to the door and give him a cheque for £80 to cover his kind service and the petrol. I am given the centre bedroom in which Dickens and Prince Charles have slept. Am fascinated by the bed canopy, with pink dome of either bees swarming or little roses. The sheets of the beds are starched at the top ends in the old-fashioned way. My hand towel dated 1907. A. is given the centre dressing room which I usually have, because the bed is low and nearer to the bathroom. Also staying for the weekend are Woman and her friend Margaret Budd,* E. Winn† and Peter Maitland.‡

Saturday, 15th August

Andrew tells that Lord Carrington says all the Balkan peoples with whom he has been in touch are ghastly, whether Serbs, Bosnians or Macedonians.

Monday, 17th August

Young Patrick James§ comes [to Chatsworth] for the night. He wishes to talk with me about the National Trust, for he is writing with Jennifer Jenkins yet another book, to appear in the centenary year of 1995.¶ A delightful boy, aged twenty-three or so and extremely bright. Beautiful manners and asks very pertinent questions. We sat after

---

* Friend (b. 1917) of Pamela Jackson, whose husband had been in same RAF squadron as Derek Jackson.
† Interior designer (b. 1925); social figure and renowned mimic.
‡ Group Chief Executive, Mallett plc, 1993–97 (b. 1937).
§ Patrick Esmond James (b. 1967); m. 1996 Natasha Davidson; landscape expert.
¶ *From Acorn to Oak Tree: The Growth of the National Trust, 1895–1994* (Macmillan 1994).

dinner in the yellow drawing room talking till late. He said he had seen a photograph of me staying at his great-grandmother's house in Yorkshire, as a friend of his grandmother, Helen Baring.* I only just remember, though don't recall the name of the house. Lady Ulrica was a sister of the beautiful Lady D'Abernon†; the daughter was dark and plain, but nice.

Tuesday, 18th August

Feeble comes to luncheon, bringing Frank Tait and a couple called Hubbard – she a Trustee of National Gallery, he a gardener and painter. We motor up the hill and walk round the lakes. Beautiful day, sun and cloud and long shadows. Hardy Amies comes for the night. He is very bent, but brain very much all right. Full of smart talk and amusing stories. At dinner he speaks fascinatingly about men's fashions since the eighteenth century.

Andrew eats little, and looks thin and drawn. Is inclined to be moody. Told A., only half in jest, that she was being disagreeable; and when I mentioned the Glorious Revolution, said sharply, 'If it hadn't been for it you wouldn't be sitting here now.' I don't feel altogether at ease, yet we get on. When we leave he protests that our visit has brought him joy and presses us to come for Christmas.

I have been reading a proof copy of M's *Ribbentrop*. A marvellous biography, absolutely first rate. Perhaps a bit too long towards the end. He tells me it is already shortlisted for the *Yorkshire Post* prize, though only estimated to sell 2,000 copies.

Friday, 21st August

Laden with gifts of food and purchases made by A. in the Chatsworth shops we are driven home by Alan. Without exception all the Chatsworth staff are charming. I had long chats with the clock winder (attending to sixty-four instruments inside the house on Wednesdays), and Henry the butler and Michael Pearman the librarian. A. much

---

* Helen Baring (b. 1906); er dau. of Brig.-Gen. Hon. Everard Baring, yr s. of 1st Baron Revelstoke and Lady Ulrica Duncombe, yst dau. of 1st Earl of Feversham; m. 1939 Major Gordon Foster; their daughter Rosanna (b. 1941) m. 1965 Professor Hon. Oliver James.
† Lady Helen Duncombe; m. 1890 Sir Edgar Vincent (1857–1941), banker, diplomatist and statesman, cr. Viscount D'Abernon.

benefited by our week's change and cosseting. For the last two days, Fergie's* behaviour provided the main topic of conversation.

Monday, 24th August

Francis Sitwell called at No. 19 this afternoon and took away some eight of Sachie's books. I said I would not part with them to anyone else. At the last moment I witheld *Southern Baroque Art*, which I could not bear to part with. Francis now a beefy middle-aged man. He venerates Sachie, and wants to build up a library of all his books. Told me he believed that his father's Alzheimer's was caused by the kitchen at Weston using aluminium saucepans. Apparently stewed fruit, which Sachie liked to eat most days, causes dangerous effects on the brain when cooked in this metal. Also believed S. was not awarded an honour until so late because Michael De-la-Noy† quoted in the press S's remark to him in private that Queen Victoria purposely employed homosexuals in her household as they were unlikely to interfere with the ladies-in-waiting and maids of honour.

Wednesday, 26th August

A most enjoyable day. Tony Mitchell motored me to Herefordshire, that nostalgic county. A relief to be away from the stone-wall country for a change. Tall, lush hedgerows engulf narrow lanes. We first visited Hope End. Much improvement since I was last there. It has been bought by a couple called Hegarty, she the daughter of a prosperous local farmer. They have constructed a small and exclusive hotel out of the back regions, where we had coffee and bought her cookery book. Few remains of the house known to Elizabeth Barrett, though the minaret still conspicuous. Such a charming setting, in a hollow with stream at east boundary. How Eardley would have loved it. Then back to Ledbury, still a beautiful small town surrounded by country. Visited huge church with detached tower and spire to inspect Biddulph monuments. One, a figure under a canopy of flowing drapery, is dated 1630 and must be about the first Baroque sculpture in England.

---

* Lurid photographs of the Duchess of York, who had separated from her husband in March 1992, had been published in the tabloid press, showing her having her toes sucked by John Bryan, her American 'financial adviser'.
† Writer (1934–2002), interested in royal and ecclesiastical subjects.

After lunch we drove to Eastnor where we lingered long. The castle an unromantic structure, which looks as if machine-made. Smirke was not an imaginative architect. Great hall frankly hideous and splits the house in twain. Family still resides, youngish couple [Hervey-Bathursts] who seem to be doing well. The best room is the fan-vaulted drawing room by Pugin. Splendid Pugin chandelier of mock brass; splendid views from windows of unspoilt country. Tony an admirable companion on such an expedition. How bored our wives would have been, we reflected. In Eastnor churchyard we saw terra-cotta figures by the infamous Lady Henry Somerset,[*] David Beaufort's great-grandmother. Rather beautiful, with a whiff of Pre-Raphaelitism. (Indeed, her family, the Somerses, had a connection with the Pre-Raphaelites through Mrs Cameron.[†])

I have decided that, as one of my recreations in *Who's Who*, I might include 'Visiting the haunts of illustrious writers and artists'.

Monday, 31st August

Caroline and the Morrisons called simultaneously this evening. C. extremely funny about her Outward Bound course in Lake District. Weather appalling. They lived on baked beans and slept in dormitory when not bivouacking. Activities included climbing sheer rock-faces and walking across ravines on single planks. She the oldest at sixty-four. Tried to conceal the fact that she went there in David's aeroplane for fear of appearing grand. Charlie and Rosalind came straight from Madresfield, where they move in before Xmas. They have much to do, for the taste of the departing tenant awful. Amazing that they want to move into that great barrack.

Listened to BBC documentary on Lennox [Berkeley]. Freda, voice more drawly than ever, spoke very well; so did the son Michael. Many composers and critics who knew Lennox contributed, including Desmond Shawe-Taylor, and we heard the voice of Lennox himself several times. Michael spoke frankly of how his father changed his sexual nature during his most creative period, which coincided with

---

[*] Lady Isabella Somers Cocks (1851–1921), dau. of 3rd and last Earl Somers; m. 1872 Lord Henry Somerset, yr son of 8th Duke of Beaufort (1849–1932; Comptroller of Royal Household, 1874–9; lived in Florentine exile following homosexual scandals); a notorious prude who espoused temperance and similar virtuous causes.
[†] Julia Margaret Cameron (1815–79); photographer and Pre-Raphaelite artist.

his marriage to Freda. And Freda spoke of his affair with Britten, which broke up because the gentle Lennox felt swamped by Britten's overpowering personality. Whereas I usually found Lennox's music rather dull, I greatly enjoyed the extracts played on this programme.

Wednesday, 2nd September

Whenever a radio announcer refers to the millions in East Africa dying of starvation, hoping to wring my heart strings and get me to send some money, a dreadful elation rises within me. Fewer people, I say to myself, no bad thing. Then I feel slightly ashamed of myself, though not as much as I should.

Friday, 4th September

Lunching with me in Bath, J.K.-B. talked about his lady friend. They are off to Rome together next week. He may sell his house and buy another with her, which would be cheaper for both.

Saturday, 5th September

Daphne [Fielding] tells us that Caroline has consented to abseil from the walls of Gloucester Hospital for charity. A foolhardy act, for the telly will be sure to film the stout duchess, probably upside-down with her skirt over her head. Daph came to tea with the Filers,* who asked if she was still writing. She replied, 'Well, I am preparing something; having difficulty in obtaining references, etc.' It is rather pitiful when the old are unable to admit they are on the shelf. For she will not write again; nor, I dare say, shall I. What I shall say to Grant [McIntyre] when he lunches with me on Monday I can't think.

Monday, 7th September

Went to dear Sheila Birkenhead's memorial service in Grosvenor Chapel. Full of folk, of whom I knew few. Frank Longford gave address, intimate but far too short; told us nothing except that Sheila

---

* James and Britté Filer, dendrologists; successors of Midi Gascoigne as owners of Mount House, Alderley.

was much loved, devoted to her family and causes, and ought to have written more books.

Grant lunched at Brooks's. He is very shy and terribly nice. Says it is absurd that I cannot write another book and pressed me to make an effort. Wants to me to do a volume of essays on departed friends. Then called on Geoffrey Houghton-Brown, looking emaciated and rather unkempt. Can't be bothered to go to the barber, or even to Mass at the Oratory a few yards away. Poor old G.

Jane Westmorland dined. A. in my absence had cooked a lovely dinner and laid the table. J. says her David may never speak again. The Princess of Wales visited him from Highgrove, teased him and made him smile. Smiling is as far as he gets.

Saturday, 12th September

We dine at the House. A. sits next to David and teases him which he likes. Derek Hill staying. He has done a sketch of Caroline; not a great success, mouth all wrong. Derek more enormous than ever, with belly like Falstaff's. Affectionate creature, his attention really all fixed on himself and his art.

Monday, 14th September

Went to see Clive Charlton at Bath Clinic. He said, 'At your age you can't expect to be wholly sane. Stop fussing, you have had a very good innings.'

Misha comes from London for picnic luncheon. I enjoy having him. He has developed the eccentric trick when making a profound statement of twisting his head to one side and lowering it towards the floor, then raising it, looking one straight in the eyes, and lowering it on the other side. He brings me the first copy of his *Ribbentrop*, handsomely produced. I say his illustrations are better than mine. Yes, he says, but then my book costs a penny more than yours.

Tuesday, 15th September

Went blackberrying. Most heavenly evening, still and golden with mist. Glowing ball of sun casting woolly shadows. The park never more beautiful. I stop at the circular wood I call Folly's Spinney, from which I fill my plastic pudding bowl full of foaming jet blackberries.

My thoughts are all of darling Folly, sensing her a little ahead of me, plucking the fruit and eating it in the way she alone of dogs used to do, and looking up with those beseeching golden eyes. It is a year and a half since she died and I still adore and miss her more than Anne Rosse, Johnny Churchill, Sheila Birkenhead or any of the friends lately gone.

Monday, 21st September

To London for the day. At Murray's I signed sixteen copies of *People & Places* for them to send. John spoke bitterly about the refusal of the National Trust to sell the book in their shops or even review it in their magazine. He is sending copies to the Chairman Lord Chorley* and Director-General Angus Stirling with letters of protest. He also talked of Jock's illness, hip trouble on top of prostate trouble. Poor Jock, always so jokey and debonair, has gone into deepest depression from which they fear he will not recover.

Went to Gooden & Fox for Gervase's exhibition of drawings and plans of National Trust houses, in aid of Stowe Gardens Appeal. Invited to luncheon upstairs, hosted by young Niall Hobhouse.† I was seated next to Lindy Dufferin‡ whom I enjoyed talking to. She has two large houses, Clandeboye and one in London, and lives in the whole of each. I said I thought of her living half in art circles, half in the jet. True, she said, but she is currently too busy with good works for the jet. Runs the Northern Ireland end of the Prince of Wales's youth employment scheme. We talked of Basil. I told her how brilliant he was as a boy, and that she ought to get hold of his school reports. I asked if there was a Lord Dufferin living. She said the marquessate was extinct, but she thought there might still be a baron living in Australia. Surely she must know? Said she was forming a trust for the preservation of Clandeboye, and asked me if I could find out about the Australian heir, not that she was sure she wanted to get into communication with him. 'You are interested in these sorts of things,' she said. 'Will you find out for me?' I didn't know whether to be pleased by this or not.

---

* Roger, 2nd Baron Chorley (b. 1930); accountant, member of government committees; Chairman of N.T., 1991–6.
† Of Hadspen House, Somerset (b. 1954); art dealer.
‡ Widow of Sheridan, 5th Marquess of Dufferin and Ava: see 29–30 May 1988.

Tuesday, 22nd September

I look up *Debrett* under Dufferin. The new Baron Dufferin and
Clandeboye and holder of three Blackwood baronetcies is an estab-
lished businessman with son who is an architect in private practice.*
Eminently suitable heirs, one would have thought, to Clandeboye and
Lindy's millions. They live in New South Wales, so I shall make
enquiries of Mary Downer.

Monday, 28th September

Dear M. rings me up to say he has read the Introduction to *People &
Places*, and it is vintage J.L.-M. I value his opinion when I sense he
isn't being kind. It is in his nature to be kind to all his friends no matter
how far they fall below his standards, so I have to scrutinise his tone
of voice to get at the truth.

Tuesday, 29th September

Nancy Dill,† with whom I spoke after church on Sunday, is wonderfully old-fashioned in speech. Always refers to her late husband as 'the
Field Marshal'. She asked us to lunch on Wednesday, saying 'the
Duchess' was coming. 'The Duchess of York?' I asked, as we had been
discussing her. No, just Caroline. She refers to Alvilde as 'your wife',
though she parted with, 'Goodbye Jim'.

Thursday, 1st October

I never liked Francis Watson much, though he was good company.
Always in good cheer, gossipy, mischievous, informative. Pleased with
himself, very. Always the society man, but scratch the surface and
there was a little bounder. One was pleased to see him, while dreading what he would say about one at the next party he attended.
Undoubtedly very clever, and an expert on French artefacts. Not
Keeper of the Wallace Collection for nothing. Jane a rather dreadful
woman, who revelled in the discomfiture of others. Why they

---

* Francis George Blackwood, 10th Baron Dufferin and Clandeboye (1916–91).
† Nancy Charrington (d. 1996); m. 1st Brigadier Dennis Furlong, 2nd Field Marshal Sir
John Dill (1881–1944).

married God alone knows; presumably both wished to keep up the pretence of being the marrying sort.

Friday 2nd–Friday 9th October

Venice for a week (almost), with Derry. Alexandra motors us to Heathrow, where we stand for ages in a motionless queue. Derry investigates, and discovers that all flights to Italy have been cancelled owing to wildcat strikes at Italian airports. So I stay at Brooks's, and have J.K.-B. to dine.

We leave the next day and stay with Anna-Maria for six nights. Derry so hates it that after two days he tells me he can't go on. Must get away somehow. We discuss situation. After all, we are self-invited guests, he previously unknown to her, living in self-contained guest flat and enjoying her hospitality; apart from meals (which are delicious, though served with such rapidity that I have no time to finish the smallest helping), we are free to do as we choose. He can't bear the formality, her teed up in the height of fashion, always in the same chair with maddening little dog on her lap. I urge him to make the best of the situation. Finally he relents, agreeing that A.-M. is an intelligent woman of undoubted generosity.

Weather at first atrocious. Buckets of rain, and we wake to the sound of sirens announcing *acqua alta*. D. buys gumboots for us both and we wade and splosh nearly up to our knees. Then rain stops, sun trickles through, and the tide quickly subsides.

I am getting very woolly and indecisive, and Derry's patience and goodness to me are beyond my deserts. A tiresome thing happened. I kept a diary in a little notebook, which I lost. Hope to goodness I did not leave it in the flat to be read by A.-M. If so, I am undone, though I don't believe I had the folly or bad taste to criticise her overtly. Still, I don't know that I can repeat this visit, my third.

Remembered highlights include sitting hatless in the sun on raft of *caffè* at bottom of A.-M's little *calle*, looking across at Giudecca and sipping cappuccino; looking from S. Giorgio across lagoon to Riva Schiavone, sunlight on level façades and purple storm clouds in background; roaming through Frari in early morning, few tourists because tickets now have to be bought; seeing S. Francesco della Vigna again after long neglect (wonderful interior with poetic, garlanded Negro-ponte of Madonna enthroned, birds and flowers at feet, briar roses behind). One night dining with A.-M. we met delightful heroic man called Roberto Frassetto. He was a frogman during war and blew up several warships (presumably ours, though I didn't like to ask). Now an oceanographer and leading expert on oceans, ozone layer, and Venetian tides and high water. He is blistering about the lies of politicians and their reluctance to accept the advice of the experts they employ, but remains an optimist.*

Wednesday, 14th October

Cannadine's† life of G. M. Trevelyan‡ interests me much. He was a big and splendid man, essentially a Roundhead, though he became something of a Cavalier as he aged. Apart from establishing history as a branch of literature, he was intensely honourable and virtuous and became a mentor of the élite. Did wonderful work for conservation, especially at the National Trust. A puritan in his private life, his habits spartan. No one loved the country of England's past greatness more than he, and he rightly despised the good-timer, wastrel aristocracy.

Caroline dined with us. Still shaken from her abseiling down Gloucester Hospital on Sunday. She made a mess of it and ended up dangling upside-down. It is gallant but absurd of her to undertake such tests of endurance at her age.

Tuesday, 20th October

Mrs Weideger, the woman writing about the National Trust who came to see me six months ago, interviewed me at Murray's for the *Independent*. She seemed determined to show the Country House Scheme of 1936 had been a failure. Young John received me warmly, showing me his letter to the *Daily Telegraph* expostulating with the N.T. for refusing to review my book in their journal. I told Grant frankly that I didn't feel up to writing the book he wanted, on old friends; he was sympathetic, and asked if I would like instead to show them some more diaries. I shall consider this.

---

* Frassetto (who led a daring wartime raid on the British Fleet in Malta) argued in 2001 that a system of floodgates costing \$2 billion was required to protect Venice; without these, the \$4 billion spent conserving the city would be wasted.

† Professor David Cannadine (b. 1950); Cambridge historian.

‡ George Macaulay Trevelyan (1876–1962); historian, Chairman of N.T. Estates Committee and Master (1940–51) of Trinity College, Cambridge; brother of Sir Charles Trevelyan, 3rd Bt, donor of Wallington, Northumberland to N.T.

At Brooks's, everyone seemed to have read *People & Places*. Gyles Eyre* came up to congratulate, and Raleigh Trevelyan,† nice man like retired bank manager, wanted to talk about the chapter on Wallington. Sat at luncheon with Graham Kinnaird,‡ rolled into a ball like an old hedgehog. Rues the times.

By taxi to Polish Embassy in Portland Place for Isabel Napier's award. The room we met in like third-world embassy, grim with hideous plush curtains and small coloured reproductions of Bellottos and Canalettos. Isabel looking charming in mauve dress, with shy and bewildered eyes. After a while Ambassador entered and read from a script in halting English, praising her wartime exploits with Polish forces. She replied charmingly, saying that there is nothing the old like more than to be remembered, and ending with a Polish proverb, 'Old loves never rust'.

Tea with Misha, suffering from hacking cough. He is quite pleased with reception so far of *Ribbentrop*, but having trouble with his biography of Jeremy Thorpe as most of the people he approaches are reluctant to speak to him. Then Nick [Robinson] dined at Brooks's, wearing tweed suit with scarlet pullover. He urged me to think again about the book I have refused to do for Murray's; advised me to read Ford Madox Ford's memoirs for inspiration.

Wednesday, 21st October

To John Wonnacott§ exhibition at Agnews. Powerful realist painter of naval dockyards, who makes of engineering something exciting and colourful. Then to Tibetan art at Burlington House. Too esoteric for me. Then to Christie's, where I enquire at information desk about James II's wedding garment. They tell me it is at South Kensington branch. When I ask if I can see it, a clergyman in black says Hello Jim. It is Father Derek Jennings,¶ who at once arranges with information lady for me to see it during afternoon.

---

* Dealer in water-colours and art critic (b. 1922).
† Publisher and writer (b. 1923); fourth cousin once removed of Sir Charles Trevelyan, 3rd Bt; author of guide book to Wallington.
‡ 13th and last Lord Kinnaird (1912–97).
§ British artist (b. 1940).
¶ Anglican convert to Roman Catholicism, formerly on staff of English Heritage (1946–95).

I lunch with Hugh Massingberd at Travellers'. He is flattering about
P.&P., which he is reviewing in *Sunday Telegraph*. Is enormous; eats
voraciously, ending with rice pudding. Recently had a cancerous
growth removed, almost disappointed not to be told he had six
months to live. So is writing an article on death.

The lady at Christie's South Kensington is the wife of Mordaunt
Crook.* Donning white kid gloves, she lovingly unfolds from tissue
paper the jacket and trousers of James II. I resist temptation to touch
for King's Evil. Long coat, and curious bottoms like plus-fours, coiffed
and pleated, more like Jacobean than Restoration wear. Gold and
silver thread on plum background. Stains about the crutch, and moth
holes. Otherwise marvellously preserved. It is the first known garment
to incorporate a Garter star. Tragic that the Guernsey seigneur has
to sell.

Saturday, 31st October

All this week I have been having a swimgloat over reception of *P.&P.*
Splendid notice on *Times* middle page; first-rate review by Peter Levi in
Spectator; *Country Life*. Much fan mail from friends and strangers. When
the girl called my name in the dentist's waiting room, a man came up to
me and asked to shake my hand. *House and Garden* has asked to interview me. *The Field* has begged me to write to the new head of English
Heritage protesting at their decision to shed half their historic monuments to local authorities. At moments euphoria has wafted me to such
heights of confidence that I feel I can still write almost anything.

Freda much upset by the proofs of Carpenter's life of Britten.† She
has asked for two references concerning Britten's affair with Lennox
to be removed. The usual over-emphasis on sex in this book.

Thursday, 5th November

Goddaughter Sally [Ashburton] lunches with me in London. Very
sweet she is, middle-aged, pretty blue eyes, welcoming nature. Talks
of her errant father Johnnie [Churchill] with deep affection, candidly

---

* J. Mordaunt Crook (b. 1937), Professor of Architectural History in University of
London, 1981–99; m. 2nd 1975 Susan Mayor.
† Humphrey Carpenter, *Benjamin Britten: A Biography* (Faber & Faber, 1992).

and non-censoriously. Laughs at his peccadilloes. Her surrogate
mother was Midge Tweeddale and Yester* was her home. I am surprised to learn she is married to a very rich man, a Baring, landowner
and banker, now Chairman of BP. She embraces me warmly on
parting. Doesn't care for her aunt Clarissa Avon, who had nothing
further to do with [her brother] Johnnie after a drunken incident
when her husband was Prime Minister.

Saturday, 7th November

We motor to luncheon with the Johnstons. Dear old house of every
date. We eat in the cosy kitchen, joined by Sylvia [Chancellor] and
Coote. Susanna is generous in spirit and deed, loads us with bottles of
lemonade. Sylvia talks about her son Alexander† who now has an edi-
torship in New York. I asked about his wife, whom she described as
'beautiful of the squirming sort'. At ninety-two, Sylvia has skin like
alabaster; and although her speech is a little slushy, she retains all her
old, sharp marbles.

Sunday, 8th November

Remembrance Sunday. A. comes to church for the first time since her
illness last March. Sits across the pew in discomfort. Cross with the
Somerset boys for not turning up, David being away. The old villagers
all attend. A moving ceremony, excellent trumpeter blowing from the
gallery. We lunch at the House with Caroline. I sit next to Jerry Hall,
difficult to converse with. Mick Jagger is furious with Chrissy Gibbs
for not forewarning him of the sale of Pitchford [Hall, Shropshire].‡ I
asked if he would have bought it, had he known. I might, he said.

---

* Marjorie Wagg (d. 1977); m. 1st Lieut.-Col. J. H. Nettlefold, 2nd 1945 (as his 2nd
wife) William Hay, 11th Marquess of Tweeddale (1884–1967) of Yester House, East
Lothian.
† Journalist (b. 1940); editor, *Spectator*, 1975–84; columnist on *New Yorker* and *The
Times*.
‡ Romantic half-timbered manor house which had passed by descent since 1473, and had
recently been sold with its contents by Mrs Oliver Colthurst to an Arab buyer, David
Mellor during his brief tenure as Secretary of State for the National Heritage having
decided that it was of insufficient interest to 'save for the nation'. J.L.-M. (as related in
his early diaries) had often stayed there during the war as the guest of General Sir Charles
Grant and the eccentric Lady Sybil.

Monday, 9th November

Guy Acloque called to dump some unwanted books for A's annual sale. Could not stop, but did so for an hour. Full of chat about the Queen's hopeless advisers, still living in the 1950s. And of course the Prince of Wales's equally hopeless friends. Spoke with great affection of Sally Westminster. Six months before her death she was treated in Oxford for an aneurism, but let on to no one. She had standards and style. Goodness radiated from her beautiful face. I said she was well-bred. Yes, he said, despite her banana-selling father* she was just that.

Derry and girl assistant came at eleven to photograph me for *Country Life*. I had resisted for weeks, but A. persuaded me. I made it a condition that I should not be taken at close range and not look into the eye of the camera. I wished to avoid that dazed-sheep look of the gaga old. I went out shopping while they set up their contraptions, and returned to find whole library disorganised – screens erected, furniture moved, books taken from shelves and strewn on floor. Derry complains that I blink when he snaps, and look bored as I did after dinner with Anna-Maria.

Thursday, 12th November

Papers today are full of Alan Clark,[†] and his role in the Arms for Iraq affair[‡] when he was a minister in the Tory Government. *The Times* contains a full-page article in which Alan states his views, which are totally cynical. He ends by saying that he is publishing his diaries next year, adding that he will make a contrast to the outstanding diarists of

---

* As Sally Westminster's sister Diana Petre had (to the Duchess's embarrassment) revealed in her book *The Secret Garden of Roger Ackerley* (1975), their father, beginning life as a guardsman and becoming head of the Fyffe banana company, had led a double life (the children of his 'official' family including the literary critic J. R. Ackerley [1896–1967]).

† Writer and politician (1931–99), er s. of Kenneth, Baron Clark, who had (temporarily, as it turned out) retired from parliament at 1992 general election. His diaries of his years as a minister in the Thatcher Government, also revealing much about his private life, were to cause a sensation on their publication in 1993.

‡ The affair concerned the prosecution of directors of the Matrix Churchill firm for the alleged illegal export to Iraq, prior to the Gulf crisis of 1990–91, of machine tools for munitions. The case collapsed after it emerged that the Conservative Government (in which Clark had been minister responsible for the arms trade) had been aware of, and possibly encouraged, the exports.

the mid-century – Chips Channon, Harold Nicolson, James Lees-Milne – all of whom were homosexuals. This does not please me, the only survivor. I spoke to M., who counselled against my remonstrating. But I thought I would write Alan a line on a postcard, just to remind him I am still alive.

Friday, 13th November

John Summerson was a splendid man, icily cerebral, cynical, contemptuous of sentimental conservationists. He once said he would rather lose an old building than ally himself with the wishy-washy preservers, whom he regarded as a lot of old women. He was handsome, resembling Pope Pius VII.* Wrote impeccable prose, and his books were readable as well as scholarly. He was original in his interpretation of great architects, and related architecture to the history of its time. He exploded the myth that John Thorpe built all the great houses of Elizabethan and Jacobean times, putting him in his place as a mere surveyor. He was always nice to me, though thought me a social butterfly and hopeless amateur. He was patrician in his disdain of the second rate and indifferent to the opinions of others. There has long been no one to touch him among architectural historians. I suppose Mark Girouard,† his able disciple, will now take his place.

Saturday, 14th November

Having taken the precaution of checking with Diana [Mosley], I lunched with Anne de Courcy‡ who is writing her biography. Mrs de C. and husband, distinguished retired man in his sixties, live at Barnsley [Gloucestershire] in large cottage adjoining the Verey§ garden. She is a delightful woman, sweet, shy, talking rather too much out of nervousness, and seems devoted to Diana. I disclosed to her my intimate feelings for Diana over many years, ever since I fell spell-

---

* Luigi Chiaramonti (1740–1823); the Pope (1800–23) who dealt with Napoleon.
† Writer and architectural historian (b. 1931).
‡ Anne Barratt; m. 1st Michael de Courcy (d. 1953), 2nd 1959 Robert Armitage; writer and journalist; her biography was published by Chatto & Windus soon after Diana Mosley's death in 2003.
§ David Verey (1913–84), architectural historian; m. 1939 Rosemary Sandilands (1918–2001), garden designer (who had compiled books on gardening with A.L.-M., though they had ultimately quarrelled).

bound by her beauty when she was sixteen. Otherwise don't believe I told her anything she didn't know already. He is a great friend of Anthony Wagner,* to whom he reads – my book at the moment.

Wednesday, 18th November

Two letters this morning which I have kept from A. First from Alan Clark in reply to the line I wrote him, charming of course but evading (as one would expect) the matter which led me to write to him. The second from Downing Street asking if I would agree to my name being submitted to the Palace for a CBE.† I deliberated about this on my way to Bath, and as soon as I arrived replied declining it. At my age, I can't face up to all the bother – the congratulations from all and sundry, the letters to be replied to, the investiture ceremony and cele-bratory dinner. It is too late. I am not interested, and quite content to be just plain me. I daren't tell A., for she might press me to accept. It might have been different had I been offered a knighthood in which she could have shared, or one of the honours in the personal gift of the Queen. The CH‡ is the only honour I really covet, but that would be beyond my deserts.§

Friday, 20th November

Tragic news of the burning of Windsor Castle. A chunk of English history wiped out in an afternoon. It seems most of the treasures saved, but George IV's rooms all gone. Poor Christopher Lloyd¶ has had a heart attack from the shock.

---

* Sir Anthony Wagner (1908–95); genealogist and writer on heraldry; Garter King of Arms, 1961–78, Clarenceux King of Arms, 1978–95; Eton contemporary of J.L.-M. He required readers, having gone blind.
† Commander of the Order of the British Empire.
‡ Companion of Honour (founded 1917 and restricted to 65 members); generally con-sidered the junior branch of the Order of Merit (founded 1902 and restricted to 24 members).
§ Another factor in J.L.-M's refusal (as he told the editor) was that he had been due to receive an honour on his retirement from the staff of the N.T. in 1966, but this had been withheld owing to complications in his private life at the time. J.L.-M's admirers had been lobbying for some years to have him 'honoured' – see entry for 18 November 1989.
¶ Christopher Hamilton Lloyd (b. 1945); Keeper of The Queen's Pictures from 1988.

Saturday, 21st November

I lunch with Peter and Deirdre Levi at Frampton-on-Severn, in a workman's cottage at the end of a pretty street with wide grass verges. Main object to meet Jeremy Lewis* who is writing Cyril Connolly's† biography. The son of Cyril and Deirdre‡ is a prettier version of Cyril (if not a contradiction in terms), but says little. I try to engage by asking him if he is still at school. He replies haughtily, 'I have retired from working in a bookshop.' Deirdre is a good cook, friendly, quick at repartee. He very clever and donnish. Does imitations – Maurice Bowra, the Queen Mother – demanding laughing rejoinders. Yet I like him immensely. No inhibitions here. For half an hour Jeremy and I talk 'dirt' about Cyril. I tell him he is brave to tackle such a deep and devious character, with no life outside friendship and letters. I leave him with two quotes from my diary when I learned of C's death in 1974.

I asked Peter how the old-fashioned Papists reacted when he left the Jesuits. He said he had been fearful of the reaction of Monsignor Gilbey,§ who expressed regret but said he would not allow it to interfere with their friendship. Deirdre said that, when she was living in sin with Cyril, she was cut dead by Evelyn Waugh, who told Cyril that adultery was all right for a man but not for a woman. When Cyril was in America, he visited the library which holds Evelyn's diaries and asked to look through them. He found such appalling entries about himself that he never got over it, and never felt the same about E. again.

Tuesday, 24th November

To London for the day. At Coutts [Bank], a jaunty young man tried to explain my tax affairs. I did not grasp much. He told me how much he admired A., a lady who knew her own mind and understood her own finances, unlike some people (this last remark with sidelong glance in my direction).

---

* Writer, publisher, journalist and literary editor (b. 1942).
† Writer and journalist (1903–74); editor of *Horizon*, 1939–50.
‡ Matthew Connolly (b. 1970); editor of *The Selected Works of Cyril Connolly* (2 vols, 2002).
§ The Rt Revd Monsignor Alfred Gilbey (1901–98); Roman Catholic Chaplain to Cambridge University, 1932–65; resident at Travellers' Club, Pall Mall.

Walking back to London Library I noted the plaque on 12 St James's Square, to 'Ada, Countess of Lovelace, 1815–1852, pioneer of the computing system'. A curious tribute to Byron's daughter. She must have taken after the awful mother, the mathematician Lady B.*

Bevis Hillier lunched with me at Brooks's. Told me he had lost his job editing the magazine at Sotheby's, who are getting rid of staff left and right, and is in some trouble financially. Has applied to be the Queen's public relations officer. He has a very nice quirky sense of humour.

The Queen's speech today at the Guildhall was very dignified and touching.† Delivered with quavery voice as she was suffering from laryngitis. Not pleading for sympathy, but regretting that the media have treated her with lack of understanding. Indeed, their treatment of her has been abominable. If they turn her out before I am dead, I shall shake the dust of England from my feet. But for where?

Saturday, 28th November

Julian Berkeley and Tony Scotland came to luncheon, bringing gift of precious orchid for A. Too much kissing for her liking, otherwise both enchanting. Tony told us how by devious means he tracked down pretender to the imperial throne in China, whom he found living in a sort of mud hut and doing lowliest jobs such as cleaning public urinals. He was nominated by the last reigning Emperor. Tony could only meet him accompanied by official interpreters, and was obliged not to say anything which might either embarrass him or annoy the Communist attendants.

We dined at the House, Tony Lambton staying. Very praising of *P.&P.*, but told A. that I should now concentrate on diaries, for I was

---

* Ada's passion for numbers was encouraged by her mother, who was determined that she should not become interested in poetry. Her claim to scientific fame rests on a description she wrote in 1843 of Charles Babbage's 'analytical engine', effectively the first computer. Her mathematical enthusiasms did her little good: she imagined she had discovered the perfect betting system, became an addicted gambler, and ended up losing the fortunes of herself, her husband (William King, cr. Earl of Lovelace, 1838), and several of their friends.

† She described as an '*annus horribilis*' a year which had witnessed the collapse of her two elder sons' marriages, the publication of Andrew Morton's book on Princess Diana, an increase in republican sentiment and the fire four days earlier at Windsor Castle.

above all a chronicler. When the women left the room, David recalled A's illness and how he, Caroline, Freda and I sat in gloom one evening in anticipation of her imminent demise. Merriment ensued in which I joined while feeling bitter sadness in the recesses of my heart.

Monday, 30th November

A letter from the Honours Secretary at 10 Downing Street saying the PM regrets my decision but respects my wishes. I am certain I have done the right thing. Another reason for refusing this absurd decoration is that many regard me as a snob. Yet I am not their sort of snob, and content to be an ordinary esquire, to which I am entitled by virtue of being armigerous. An ounce of heredity, as Olive Lloyd-Baker used to say, is worth a pound of merit.*

Tuesday, 1st December

To London for the night. Went to Janet Stone's eightieth birthday party at Kyle Gallery, conciding with viewing of paintings by her son Edward.† Here the whole world assembled. I stayed just ten minutes before going on to Richard Shone's Sickert‡ exhibition at Royal Academy. All lit from searchlights in the ceiling – a mistake, as it gives a shimmering impasto to the surfaces. The later paintings done from photographs, though fascinating, did indeed look like photographs – transient scenes captured for a second and immortalised. The early stuff I liked best, Whistlerish.

At 6.30 I went to a meeting of the Mount Athos Society in Holborn Viaduct. Presided over by charming Orthodox bishop to whom I was introduced afterwards by Derek [Hill].§ Steven Runciman¶ spoke of his two visits to Holy Mountain, the first in

---

* Owner of Hardwicke Hall, Gloucestershire (d. 1975); a 'tough, old-fashioned, dutiful spinster' (*Through Wood and Dale*, 2 June 1975); she had made her celebrated remark on the spur of the moment lunching with J.L.-M. and Betjeman on 19 March 1972 (*A Mingled Measure*).

† Artist (b. 1940).

‡ English artist (1860–1942).

§ With whom J.L.-M. had made several visits to the Holy Mountain in the 1970s and 80s.

¶ Hon. Sir Steven Runciman (1903–2000); Cambridge historian, leading expert on Byzantine Empire and Crusades.

1930s when gloom pervaded the almost empty monasteries, the second last year when this nonagenarian found much improvement and far more priests. His voice deep and rich, given to occasional soprano shrills; much gesticulation, and hands turned inwards over lap. John Julius [Norwich] gave me a lift back to Brooks's, where Stuart [Preston] and I dined together. Enjoyable reunion. He has become a sage, his knowledge of history and art immense, and his wisdom well-plumbed. I took a great shine to the dear old friend.

Wednesday, 2nd December

Lunched at White's with Freddie Stockdale. Absolutely charming early forties, healthy complexion and thick black hair, abounding in energy and enthusiasm. Tells me he is to remarry next week. Laughs off his success producing opera in clubs and country houses; says he is totally unmusical, though he turns the pages for the pianist at every performance. Said that, at Eton, he looked forward all week to Sunday evening chapel, just as I did; loved the frescoes, the Hone windows, the candle-light. His greatest friend was Charlie Lloyd. One day, C.L. ashamedly and wretchedly admitted to him that he had fallen hopelessly in love with a boy living on a Hebridean island. F.S. said, that's all right, let's discuss it next time. Two days later, Charlie committed suicide in the woods at Clouds Hill. F.S. has a roguish smile, rather like Francis Dashwood's. A remarkably attractive person whom I take to enormously.

Tuesday, 8th December

In train to London I read life of Kaiser. What a miserable, horrid and contemptible man. Totally unbalanced. His *battues* of wild birds and animals cruel and horrific. No wonder his enlightened parents loathed him. And he seems to have been largely responsible for the First World War.

Lunched with Bruce Hunter at Athenaeum. So gentle and sympathetic. Told me he had spent his summer holiday with a family in Munich, touching up his German. Mentioned he now lives with a lady, one Belinda; they have separate floors. A good idea, I tell him. He was full of advice regarding possible publication of further diaries by Murray's. Then to Strathearn Place, Misha very communicative and delightful. I left my diaries for 1953–4 and 1971–72 with him for his opinion.

Thursday, 10th December

David Freeman* comes from Tredegar to lunch. He resembles a frond of glistening seaweed, dreadfully thin and frail, and suffers from loneliness in that vast museum of a house on the edge of a philistine town in South Wales. But he has made a signal success of Tredegar, and recognises that at least he has a worthwhile job while most of his contemporaries are unemployed, if not destitute.

Tuesday, 15th December

As Chloë and her offspring have arrived to see A., I stay with Alex Moulton for the night. He has three friends to dine who are pheasant-shooting on his land tomorrow, all decent fellows. One of them, Derek Strauss,† is big in the City and knows everyone in the business world. Told me that Lord King‡ longs to be made a hereditary peer. Tiny Rowland is a rogue but not as bad as his arch-enemy, the shit Fayed;§ he exercises enormous influence, and could probably get Gaddafi to hand over the two assassins who brought down the airliner, if only the Government would ask him.¶ I recommended my Italian tailor in Bath to Alex, who said he would send for him to The Hall. 'I always send for my tailor. Wouldn't think of going to his shop.' I know my grandfather sent for his Jermyn Street tailor to Bewdley, but that was in 1908. When I asked Alex whether his CBE had stood him in good stead these past nineteen years, he replied, 'None at all. A perfectly useless honour. But it would have been churlish to refuse.' After dinner we sat in Alex's stiff upstairs drawing room while they drank port and smoked cigars. All rather a strain.

---

* Curator of Tredegar House, Monmouthshire, 1979–97 (b. 1956).

† Old Etonian City man (b. 1939), sometime Chairman of Strauss Turnbull.

‡ John King (b. 1918); Chairman, British Airways, 1981–93; cr. life peer as Baron King of Wartnaby, 1983.

§ Egyptian businessman, accused of 'dishonest misrepresentation' in a Department of Trade report.

¶ Western intelligence suspected named Libyan agents of being responsible for the explosion which destroyed Pan Am Flight 103 over the Scottish town of Lockerbie on 21 December 1988 – though the Gaddafi regime refused to hand over the suspects at this time.

Friday, 18th December

Driving along I hear Radio Four announcer say, 'And now we are on the subject of mortality, here is an extract from the diary of today's date for 1947 of James Lees-Milne.' I listen, without great interest, to an incident I had totally forgotten, in which I visit a sad, truculent old lady who wished to bequeath her worthless collection of bric-à-brac to the N.T. I am glad I was compassionate at the time.

I no longer have sexual twinges of any kind, only revulsion. And I far prefer the society of women to men. Does this mean that, were I still to have a propensity to sex, I would now be predominantly heterosexual? In fact I am now like any little prudish octogenarian spinster, turning away from the mere mention of the word sex.

Communication with A. is no longer easy because of her deafness. Also she is less on the uptake. Her mind, still so sharp on everyday affairs, has no interest in matters cerebral, or artistic or musical come to that. She never listens to music now unless I suggest it. Yet it was she who taught me to enjoy it.

Wednesday, 23rd December

At breakfast I told A. that I had been offered an honour by Downing Street, and turned it down. I had put off doing so fearing she might be upset and rebuke me. On the contrary, she received news with unconcern. I was surprised by her lack of surprise. When I gave my reasons, she agreed. There has been no further mention.

Sunday, 27th December

Coote who stayed the night [on 23rd] motored us to Chatsworth. Traffic awful and long delays.

For three successive days, Chatsworth was white with hoar frost. Only the gravel paths uncovered. Far whiter and more beautiful than snow. Grass sparkling like jewelry. Trees fairylike. Intense quiet. Not a breath of wind. Evenings misty of powdered blue, the lemon skyline reflected in the still river.

Clarissa [Luke] came from London, as did Woman's friend Margaret Budd. Woman herself of course, and Diana [Mosley] to my joy. We have long talks. She extremely thin, that soulful look, wonderful eyes and silhouette, sweetness of expression. Talks of the Duke of

Windsor* whom she loved, 'dear little man' with his wonderful manners. He so funny too, and she the best hostess imaginable, going out of her way to bring the shy into conversation, also funny at times, and always sharp.

We all attended Communion on Christmas morning, even Diana, a rare thing. She explained she was grateful to Edensor Church for the prayers for her recovery when she had her brain tumour years ago. To church again on Sunday. We walk up to front pews just after start of service, and are the first to leave. Debo and Woman go first to altar rails. This feudalism embarrasses me. Memorable sermon by old Mr Beddoes, who welcomes a robin in the church 'which some of you may notice'. A. noticed it was not a robin but a wren.

On Christmas Day, the Ds dispensed gifts to the staff by the enormous illuminated Christmas tree at the end of the south corridor. Suitable murmurs of gratitude and satisfaction. Andrew surreptitiously slipped envelopes into the hands of Henry and the footmen, all done with the greatest friendliness and affection. Absolutely no condescension, yet feudal – as was the reception of the carol singers on Christmas Eve, who came in by the wicket letting through sharp stabs of freezing air, and sang light-heartedly. We sat on the stairs and on benches round the central hall, the oldies wrapped in rugs, A., Woman and Coote having thrown their sticks on the floor.

Monday, 28th December

We leave for home. A. much enjoyed visit, which Coote thought far better than two years ago. Andrew and Debo seem totally content, in fact Darby and Joan. At breakfast she told us it was the eighth anniversary of his giving up the bottle. And what, she asked him, made you do it? He answered succinctly and fervently, God. Debo very sweetly said to me, 'Supposing Alvilde should die before you, you can always come up here to live. Just get rid of everything but your books. You can have a large room somewhere.' I told A., who was touched.

---

* The Windsors and the Mosleys had been country neighbours in France in the 1960s.

Wednesday, 30th December

Long talk with M. who spent Christmas reading the diaries I left with him.* He thinks them excellent and most readable, though wonders if they are too close in time to be published *in toto*. Says they contain much to indicate the diciness of our marriage at the time, and that if all that was omitted, what remained might be skimmed milk.

I read the obituary of Lord Massereene† whose father bought Knock from my Uncle Milne in 1930. This estate comprised 70,000 acres of Mull, including the forest of Ben Mhor. To think that, had Uncle Milne not been on the verge of death from throat cancer, I might ultimately have inherited this territory. Bare moorland certainly, windswept, cloudswept, rainswept, but how I loved it, the deer on those heights, the view of the outer islands – Staffa, Dutchman's Cap, not to mention Ulva where the Clerks of Ulva had an eighteenth-century house visited by Dr Johnson, and Inch Kenneth where Lady Redesdale went to live with Bobo during the war. The scowling peaks, the treacherous waters.

Thursday, 31st December

Lees Mayall has died. A friendly, boozy diplomat. He was always agreeable, and made a perfect chairman of the Bath Preservation Trust. A palliator, greatly liked.

Today we had our annual New Year's Eve luncheon [with Desmond Briggs and Ian Dixon] at Old Werrets. A. sat opposite me, so pretty, lively and amusing.

---

* Edited by J.L.-M. in 1993 and published by John Murray in 1994 as *A Mingled Measure*.
† John Clotworthy Talbot Foster Whyte-Melville Skeffington, 13th Viscount Massereene and 6th Viscount Ferrard (1914–92); Conservative Whip, House of Lords, 1958–65; President, Monday Club, 1981–92; m. 1939 Annabelle Lewis.

Index